Developing Thinking in Statistics

Books are to
the las

Developing Thinking in Statistics

Alan Graham

Los Angeles • London • New Delhi • Singapore

First Published 2006. Reprinted 2008

SAGE Publications Ltd
1 Oliver's Yard
55 City Road
London EC1Y 1SP

SAGE Publications Inc
2455 Teller Road
Thousand Oaks
California 91320

SAGE Publications India Pvt. Ltd
B 1/I 1 Mohan Cooperative Industrial Area
Mathura Road, New Delhi 110 044
India

SAGE Publications Asia-Pacific Pte Ltd
33 Pekin Street #02-01
Far East Square
Singapore 048763

British Library Cataloguing in Publication Data

A catalogue record for this book is available
from the British Library

ISBN 978-1-4129-1166-5 (hbk)
ISBN 978-0-1-4129-1167-2 (pbk)

Library of Congress Control Number: 2005934566

Typeset by Pantek Arts Ltd, Maidstone Kent
Printed in Great Britain by Cpod, Trowbridge, Wiltshire
Printed on paper from sustainable resources

Contents

Author

Alan Graham has written over 20 short plays for BBC Schools Radio under the series title *Calculated Tales*. Over the last 10 years, his work has concentrated on two main areas, Statistics and Graphics calculators. He has published numerous books in these and other areas, including *Teach Yourself Statistics*, *Teach Yourself Basic Maths* and the *Calculator Maths* series. Alan's main goal has been to help make the learning of mathematics both fun and accessible to all, taking in a variety of contexts including music and art.

Book Series

This is one of a series of three books on developing mathematical thinking written by members of the influential Centre for Mathematics Education at The Open University in response to demand. The series is written for primary mathematics specialists, secondary and FE mathematics teachers and their support staff and others interested in their own mathematical learning and that of others.

The three books address algebraic, geometric and statistical thinking. Each book forms the core text to a corresponding 26-week, 30-point Open University course.

The titles (and authors) are:

Developing Thinking in Algebra, John Mason with Alan Graham and Sue Johnston-Wilder, 2005

Developing Thinking in Geometry, edited by Sue Johnston-Wilder and John Mason, 2005

Developing Thinking in Statistics, Alan Graham, 2006

These books integrate mathematics and pedagogy. They are practical books to work through, full of tasks and pedagogic ideas, and also books to refer to when looking for something fresh to offer and engage learners. No teacher will want to be without these books, both for their own stimulation and that of their learners.

Anyone who wishes to develop an understanding and enthusiasm for mathematics, based upon firm research and effective practice, will enjoy this series and find it challenging and inspiring, both personally and professionally.

Developing Thinking in Statistics

> Statistical thinking will one day be as necessary a qualification for efficient citizenship as the ability to read and write. (H.G. Wells, 1865, quoted in Weaver, 1952)

Statistics is a key area of the school mathematics curriculum where mathematics and the real world meet. The term 'data handling' is sometimes used to refer to the same thing as 'statistics'. In this book, however, 'statistics' is given a wider meaning than 'data handling', covering the full range of ideas and concepts that inform one's thinking when posing and tackling real-world problems where data are used.

Although potentially a subject where teaching can be motivating and relevant to everyday concerns, statistics is nevertheless sometimes seen as boring, predominantly involving mechanical calculation. The aim in writing this book is to help teachers and others interested in statistical thinking to become excited about and inspired by the big ideas of statistics and, in turn, to teach them enthusiastically to learners.

INTRODUCTION

This book is for people with an interest in statistics/data handling, whether as a learner or a teacher, or perhaps as both. By working actively on the tasks rather than solely reading the text, you will gain in a number of ways.

For example, you will:

- be challenged to question your own understanding of statistical thinking;
- come into contact with a number of pedagogic strategies and principles that teachers will likely find useful in preparing for and conducting lessons;
- engage with a number of theoretical ideas about teaching and learning;
- learn more about working on and designing statistical tasks.

Throughout the book, tasks are offered for you to think about for yourself and, probably after some modification, to use with learners. It is vital to work on them yourself, in order to have immediate experience of what the text is highlighting. Should they seem too simple, or occasionally out of reach, then you can adapt the tasks so that you feel personally challenged by them. Should you wish to try out similar ideas with other learners, you will almost certainly need to adapt both the structure and the presentation of tasks so as to render them appropriate to their needs and experience.

Mention was made above to 'big ideas' – these include:

- measurement;
- sampling;
- modelling;
- variation;

- drawing practical inferences;
- randomness;
- uncertainty.

Such topics are presented here by means of a variety of approaches, including information and communication technology (ICT) based simulations and the medium of what is referred to as 'telling' stories and events. A 'telling' story is an important teaching strategy of the sort that has been used for several millennia (from biblical parables and Aesop's fables to problem pages found in modern magazines).

One of the problems with statistics is that it is a subject that comes with something of a reputation. Spend a few minutes now working at Task 0.1, which asks you to explore different negative attitudes to statistics. You are encouraged to spend several minutes thinking about this (and each subsequent) task and actually to write something down. As you will find in the later chapters, many of the key ideas of the book are presented in the context of such tasks. There is benefit to be gained from reading the comments to be found either at the end of the book (they start on p. 231) or, on occasion, as the text continues. The benefit will be considerably greater as a consequence of your having already worked and reflected on the questions posed and the issues raised. (Those tasks that have specific comments at the back of the book are marked with a 'C' in the task header.)

Task 0.1 Attitudes   **C**

Read the five statements below and try to express what attitudes may lie behind these observations.

(a) I'm a people person, not a numbers person.

(b) £1 000, £1 million, £1 billion, whatever. It doesn't matter, as long as you do something about the problem!

(c) I can't even balance my cheque book!

(d) Will I need to know that for the exam?

(e) Lies, damned lies and statistics!

Developing your ideas about what statistics is forms a large part of what this book is about. So a good place to start is with your current sense of the meaning and set of connotations of this term.

Task 0.2 What is 'Statistics'?

What does the word 'statistics' mean to you? Write a sentence or two that captures your present understanding.

There is obviously no 'right' answer to this question. You may have written something including 'working with tables of data' or 'calculations with real-world numbers'. Alternatively, you may have written something about the big ideas in statistics, such as 'variability' or 'uncertainty'.

As you will see in working through this book, emphasis is placed on the 'big ideas' of statistics. These are the unifying concepts around which the day-to-day routine tasks of data handling gather (statistical calculation, drawing graphs, and so on), without access to which learners would be able to make little sense of the subject.

STRUCTURE OF THE BOOK

The book consists of 15 chapters. These are divided into four blocks, the first three of which have four chapters each, whose contents run roughly parallel to one another, block by block. The first chapter of a block focuses on *describing*, the second on *comparing* and the third with *interrelating* (in the sense of connecting two variables), while the fourth is concerned with various aspects of *uncertainty* (particularly probability).

The underlying theme of Block 1 is 'words and numbers'. Block 2 focuses on pictures and graphs, while Block 3 is concerned with learning and teaching with ICT (specifically the graphics calculator, the spreadsheet and a computer statistical package). In these first three blocks, each chapter has five sections, whose numbering locates both the chapter and the section itself: Section 7.2 is the second section in Chapter 7. These sections vary both in page length and in the time that you may wish or need to spend on them. However, there is an expectation that each section is based on a notional average of two hours' work. The fifth section of each chapter addresses pedagogic issues concerned with the teaching and learning of statistics in school.

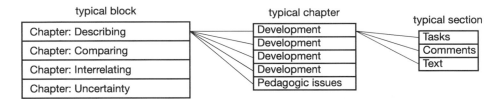

The final block has only three chapters in it, which first look at models and modelling, then at statistical investigations before, finally, providing an overview of issues relating to teaching and learning statistics.

SUMMARY

To use this book effectively, you will need to engage with the tasks yourself, make observations about what you notice, both in your activity and in reflection upon your own performance. Do not be distressed by getting stuck for a while on a task, as this provides an opportunity for you to experience the creative side of statistical thinking and to learn something about pedagogy from the point of view of a learner. If a task seems easy, then modify it so as to challenge yourself; if, after a reasonable period of struggle on your part, it seems too hard, find some way to simplify it. At the end of each chapter, you will be asked to reflect upon implications for teaching – in particular, for promoting statistical thinking with learners. Should you have the opportunity, it is strongly recommended that you try out suitably modified tasks with learners, so you can connect their experience with your own on similar tasks.

Acknowledgements

The writers and the publishers would like to thank the following for allowing their work to be reproduced in the book.

The Office for National Statistics for permission to use data from *Social Trends 34* (March 2005) in Figures 2.3 and Tables 5.1 and 5.2. Crown Copyright material is produced under Class Licence Number C01W0000065 with the permission of the Controller of HMSO and the Queen's Printer for Scotland.

The Daily Telegraph and Fischbacher, B (12th April 2005) for permission to reproduce the photographs taken from the article by Fleming, 'Smiles that destroy the myth of female intuition' in Chapter 2.

The American Statistician 35 (2) 1981, for permission to use Ehrenberg's Tables from the article 'The Problem of Numeracy', in Tables 3.3 and 3.4.

The *United Nations Millennium Indicators Database* for permission to use the data in Table 3.5

The Gallup Organisation Inc., Princeton, NJ for permission to use data from '*Teens' Supernatural Beliefs*' (1988) in Table 4.2.

Graphics Press USA, for permission to use John Snow's map of the patterns of cholera infection in Figure 5.3 and to reproduce the table in Table 6.1 from *the Visual Display of Quantitative Information*, Tufte E W (2001).

Michael Friendly, University of York, Canada (http://yorku.ca) for permission to use the diagram 'Causes of Mortality in the Army in the East' in Figure 5.9.

The New York Times Agency for permission to use the photograph in Figure 6.1.

Lucent Technologies Inc./Bell Labs for permission to reprint the photograph of John Tukey, Figure 6.4.

Graphics Press, USA for permission to use the 1985 timetable of the Tokaido Line at Yokohama Station, Sagami Tetsudo Complany, taken from Tufte, E W (1990) in Figure 6.8.

The Minerals Council of Australia for permission to use data from their information sheet 'Olympic men's 100m sprint results in athletics' in Table 7.2.

Nature Vol. 431, 30th September 2004, for permission to use the figure on the winning Olympic 100-metres sprint times for men and women in Figure 7.4.

The Daily Express (Express Newspapers), 14th June 2002, for the table of rainfall figures for June in Stratford-Upon-Avon, taken annually over a ten year period in Table 7.3.

Nick Sinclair for the National Portrait Gallery for permission to use the photograph of Sir Richard Doll in Figure 7.8.

David Tideswell for permission to use the photograph of robins in Figure 8.6.

The Guardian 4th December 2004 for permission to use the article by Hooper J 'Curse of 53, Italy's unlucky number' in Figure 8.13.

Introduction to Block 1

Statistical ideas can be expressed using alternative and complementary forms: words and numbers, pictures and ICT. Block 1 of this book looks at statistical ideas from the point of view of how they can be expressed using words and numbers, while pictures and ICT are the central themes of Blocks 2 and 3.

These first four chapters cover, in turn, the following ways of thinking: describing, comparing, interrelating and dealing with uncertainty. A variety of statistical 'big ideas' are explored – for example, relative and absolute differences, the notion of variability and the distinction between a statistical and a cause-and-effect relationship.

A number of useful and important teaching issues are offered; for example, the gambit of providing learners with 'telling tales' that are designed to illustrate an important statistical idea in an interesting and memorable context. Constructivism is an area of educational philosophy that describes how learners 'construct' meaning in their learning and you are asked to consider how this idea might relate to statistics learning. You will also be shown, and asked to use, a four-stage framework for tackling a statistical investigation.

1
Describing with Words and Numbers

In general, descriptions of things can be *verbal* or *numerical* in nature. This chapter explores some similarities and differences between these two forms of describing.

Task 1.0.1 Shapes

Spend about 20 seconds looking at the five shapes below. Then close the book and try to draw them as accurately as you can.

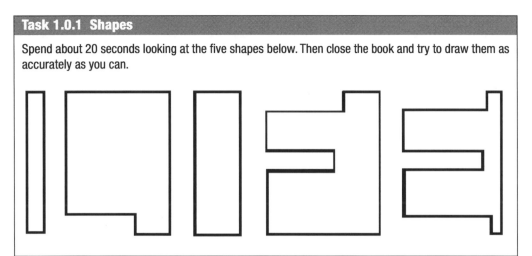

Some people have a good eye for shape and can do these sorts of tasks fairly easily. Others find it difficult to remember the details and perhaps tend to get mixed up, for example, when trying to remember shapes of similar type such as the last two. One problem is that there seems to be nothing that enables you to see these shapes as a whole – they appear to be just five unconnected things.

Task 1.0.2 The Bigger Picture

Place two straight edges horizontally across the top and bottom of the drawings above. Now look not at the shapes themselves but at the spaces in-between. Does a word jump out at you? Keep looking until it does. Eventually, you should find that that the individual shapes seem to have a 'life' of their own. Now have another go at drawing the five shapes. Is the task suddenly easier?

So, these five shapes are not unconnected after all. It is the experience of most people that, having grasped the 'bigger picture', the component parts are subsequently easier to discern. It is a facet of human nature that different people attend to different things and, indeed, the same person attends to different things at different times. This phenomenon is sometimes referred to as 'stressing and ignoring', a phrase that will be used more than once in this book. It describes an important aspect of learning, whereby, in order for a learner's attention to be directed to one aspect of a problem, it is helpful to shut out its other features.

It seems that information is hard to absorb when each fact stands in isolation from others, unconnected to a wider context or some overarching 'big idea'. Knowing about these big ideas will help provide learners with coherence and meaning to the many facts and techniques they are expected to acquire from a statistics course. An awareness of the big ideas enables a newly learned technique to be applied to other situations in the future, not just the one in hand. As novelist George Eliot observed:

> It has been well said that the highest aim in education is analogous to the highest aim in mathematics, namely, not to obtain *results* but *powers*, not particular solutions, but the means by which endless solutions may be wrought.

> (Quoted in Carlyle, 1855; italics in original)

Task 1.0.3 The Big Ideas of Statistics   C

Spend a few minutes looking at Table 1.1, which lists some of the know-how and techniques of statistics (row 1) and some big ideas (row 2). To help you to get a better feeling for the nature of a big idea, try to match up each item in row 1 with one or more corresponding terms in row 2. Are there any terms here you are unfamiliar with? How might you find out what they refer to?

TABLE 1.1 Matching Up

Know-how and techniques	Understanding and knowing how to calculate or draw: the range, the median, a bar chart, a scatter plot, the quartiles
Big ideas	Summarising, measures of location, spread and variation, interrelating

When you see a 'C' in the task header, remember to check 'Comments on Tasks' at the end of the book.

In common with many other disciplines, one big idea stands out from all others and that is *describing*. As you can see from the main title of this chapter, this is its central theme. Section 1.1 suggests that, in statistics, the central building block of thinking statistically is data. As Sherlock Holmes once remarked to Dr Watson, 'You were trying before you had sufficient data, my friend; one can't make bricks without straw' (quoted in Hanson, 2001, p. 628).

The two main themes in the first section are sampling and designing a questionnaire. Section 1.2 then explores questions of measurement, and you will be introduced to a number of different types of measuring scales. Data can involve both very large and very small numbers and how these are handled and represented is explored in Section 1.3. Summarising data often takes the form of calculating averages and spreads: these ideas are considered in Section 1.4. The final section looks at teaching and learning issues.

1.1 DESCRIBING WITH DATA

Depending on each individual's personality and training, everyone sees the world in a slightly different way. An artist's ways of seeing are predominantly tactile and visual, exploiting colour, texture and shape. A historian draws on and produces descriptions and analyses of past events, in order to gain insights about human behaviour. An author will describe her or his world with words, using metaphor, onomatopoeia and, on occasion, poetry. Each of these ways of seeing is valuable, and, when taken together, provide rich, diverse and complementary perspectives on human concerns.

What, then, is the particular *statistical* view of the world? It is essentially one based on quantitative descriptions, where the world is viewed on the basis of measures and counts, otherwise known as statistical information or data. Outside a narrow educational context, data are rarely collected without a clear reason or purpose. Typical questions that may inspire the need for data collection may be of the form, 'How big is A?' or 'Is A bigger than B (and by how much)?' or 'How is X related to Y?'. The nature of these questions is considered in more detail in, respectively, the first, second and third chapters of each of the first three blocks.

Once data have been collected, they need to be analysed in order for interesting or unexpected patterns to be identified. These patterns must then be interpreted in the context of the original question that started the investigation.

Four stages have now been identified that correspond to the following four important phases of a statistician's work. In summary, these are:

> *P* stage: pose a question;
> *C* stage: collect relevant data;
> *A* stage: analyse the data;
> *I* stage: interpret the results in the context of the question.

These four stages are referred to as the *PCAI* framework for conducting a statistical investigation: they are considered more fully later in the book, particularly in Chapters 2 and 14.

In this section, you will focus on the *C* stage of data collection, looking at two important aspects of how data are collected. The first concerns exploring how and why samples are taken in statistical work. In the second, you will look at how social data are collected, raising issues of polling and questionnaire design.

Sampling

A *census* refers to data collection where all the people or items of interest are measured or surveyed. However, when collecting information about a large population, it is often too inconvenient or expensive to measure every item: you must make do with taking a representative sample. This might take the form of choosing items randomly from a production line and measuring them to ensure that the values fall within acceptable tolerance limits. Alternatively, you may wish to survey the opinions of customers on how satisfied they are with the layout of a store or invite people to reveal their voting intentions just before a general election.

Task 1.1.1 Thinking it Through   **C**

Imagine that you wish your learners to carry out a poll of television viewing habits of young people. This will involve taking a sample from the learners at their school. Before carrying out the poll, there are certain questions that they will need to think through about choosing their sample. Write down two or three of these questions. How might you help learners to tackle these questions sensibly?

Inevitably, in any discussion with learners about choosing a sample, a key point to emerge will be the importance of choosing a *representative* sample. (Sampling is looked at again in Section 14.2.)

Questionnaire Design

Although many scientific and industrial data are collected by direct measurement, 'social' data (for example, people's opinions on social issues like crime and health) usually require the use of a well-designed questionnaire. Unfortunately, the wording of questions in newspaper questionnaires is sometimes blatantly loaded or biased. Look at this one published several years ago in the *Daily Star* under the headline 'We've had ENOUGH!'

> 1. I believe that capital punishment should be brought back for the following categories of murder:
>
> Children [ ] Police [ ] Terrorism [ ] All murders [ ].
>
> 2. Life sentences for serious crimes like murder and rape should carry a minimum term of:
>
> 20 years [ ] 25 years [ ].
>
> 3. The prosecution should have the right of appeal against sentences they consider to be too lenient [ ].
>
> Tick the boxes of those statements you agree with and post the coupon to: VIOLENT BRITAIN, Daily Star, 33 St. Bride St., London EC4A 4AY.

The fact that this article appeared alongside articles with headlines such as 'My mother's killer runs free' and 'Hang the gunmen' is likely to have biased the response to these questions. But it is the nature and limited range of choices offered that distorts the survey even more. For example, there are no tick boxes available for people who do not support the death penalty or who favour alternative forms of punishment to imposing longer jail sentences.

It may not be too surprising to learn that, of the 40 000 readers who responded (and just how representative were *they* of the readers of the *Daily Star* or the population as a whole?), 86% favoured restoring the death penalty for murder, 92% wanted a 25-year minimum sentence for serious crimes of violence and 96% supported the prosecution right of appeal against 'too lenient' sentences.

In this *Daily Star* example, the bias was obvious. However, bias can occur, even in a well-designed questionnaire where there is no intention to deceive. As Steven Barnett (former chairman of the Social Research Association) argued in an article in the *Guardian* newspaper in 1989:

> Ultimately, however reliable the sample, social surveys consist of an aggregation of very short dialogues between two complete strangers. When these dialogues attempt to address intimate questions of feelings and opinions on social issues, the scope for misinterpretation is considerable. (p. 5)

As can be seen from the *Daily Star* questionnaire, how the question is worded can have a crucial impact on the response given. (For example, many people are strongly in favour of the democratic right to withhold their labour in an industrial dispute, but would personally draw the line at striking.)

Task 1.1.2 Your Opinion about Seekers of Opinion

What are your attitudes to social research? Do you feel it provides worthwhile data or is largely a waste of time? If you do have negative feelings, try to note down precisely why you hold this view.

Some people think this sort of research is invalid on the grounds that, 'they didn't ask *my* opinion'. This is an unfair criticism – provided the sample has been sensibly chosen to represent, fairly, the overall population, its findings should provide a useful snapshot of opinion. Second, they may feel it to be deceitful, because sometimes surveys are used as a cheap device for pitching a sale about a related product. This is a valid point and a good reason for avoiding co-operation with certain 'surveys' conducted in the street or on the phone. Finally, people may think that surveys are a waste of time because the questionnaires they see are designed by school pupils carrying out a shopping survey or those in newspapers like the *Daily Star* example. This problem is compounded by the fact that many newspaper polls (for example, those soliciting voting intentions before an election) are carried out in a matter of days, with little time to check wordings or test accuracy.

Nevertheless, despite these obvious dangers and drawbacks, social research can fulfil an important and valuable function in identifying areas of need in society and trying to ensure that resources are used sensibly. This sort of justification for social research is rarely explained to the general public and is certainly an aspect of statistics that should be discussed with learners. As Steven Barnett (1989) remarked:

> Whatever the hazards, however, survey research has a critical role in the development of much social policy. Patterns of employment, of health care, of transport, or of criminal activity pose awkward social questions requiring urgent solutions which compete for scarce resources. Results of large-scale social research can therefore provide the basis for decisions which affect people's lives. For this reason, the responsible social scientist will take every conceivable measure to ensure that the scope for misunderstandings are reduced to an absolute minimum. (p. 5)

Task 1.1.3 Eliminating Questionnaire Bias   C

How do you think reputable polling agencies like MORI and Gallup try to ensure that the questions they ask are as clear and free from bias as possible?

1.2 DESCRIBING BY MEASUREMENT

The philosopher Aristotle (384–322 BCE) described a human being as 'a rational animal', believing in the power of reason as a natural human state. This view largely disappeared in the 'dark ages' (roughly 400–1300) in favour of the view that people should act on the basis of faith and emotion. René Descartes (1596–1650) was a key supporter of the re-emergence of rationality and argued that people should act according to the evidence of their senses and be informed by the power of reasoning rather than making decisions on the basis of divine inspiration.

However, rational decision-making is still treated with suspicion in certain quarters – based on a fear, perhaps, that individualism is being suppressed by the imposition of conformity, with no room to express one's individual personality. This is an attitude of mind raised in some of the quotations listed in Task 0.1. People are correct to be sceptical when attempts to achieve rationality are conducted in a crass or inappropriate manner. People fear that decisions based on quantification and measurement may miss the point – perhaps this runs the risk of including only the easy-to-identify factors and under-representing more subtle human characteristics. As French philosopher and mathematician Blaise Pascal (1623–62) expressed it:

The heart has its reasons, which reason does not know. (1670, IV: 277)

Perhaps the moral here is that there are many ways of seeing the world, of which a useful and sometimes illuminating means involves quantification and statistical analysis.

Measuring Scales

The purpose of measuring is to describe things and the two most basic forms of description are words and numbers. In the next task, you are asked to think about these two ways of describing.

Task 1.2.1   Words or Numbers   **C**

What are some strengths and weaknesses of using 'words' and 'numbers' to describe things? List some examples of things that are better described by words and others that are better described by numbers.

When different but related words are used as descriptors, it is often helpful to be aware how they relate to each other. Sometimes it is possible to elicit a natural ordering for these words that may not have been obvious initially.

Task 1.2.2   Only Words?   **C**

Look at the three lists of words below. Can you think of any sensible way of ordering them?

(a) sit, walk, roll, crawl, run;

(b) gold, wood, silver, ruby, paper;

(c) rayon, cotton, linen, silk, wool.

Task 1.2.2 shows that, depending on context, certain sets of words do *sometimes* have a natural order. Clearly, there are other sets of words that *always* possess a natural ordering (for example, small/medium/large, months of the year, days of the week, and so on). However, care must be taken when the words are used in a cyclic arrangement – to take the example of days of the week, does Monday come before or after Thursday? The answer is that it depends which Monday and which Thursday you are referring to.

Turn your attention now to *numbers* and their properties for describing things. As you will see from the next task, numbers also operate in different ways, depending on context.

Task 1.2.3 Twice   **C**

Read the statements below. If you feel that any are incorrect, write down why.

(a) Manchester United scored six – twice as many as their rivals Charlton Athletic.

(b) She turned up at 6 p.m. – twice as late as the advertised starting time of 3 p.m.

(c) He turned up six hours late – twice as late as his sister who came only three hours after the advertised starting time.

(d) The temperature was 15 °C, but the next day it was twice as hot, at 30 °C.

(e) The first tremor measured 2.0 on the Richter scale. That was followed by one twice as strong – it measured just over 4 on the Richter scale.

The next two sub-sections look at two key ideas in the area of measurement – the Stevens taxonomy for sorting out measures and their properties, and the distinction between discrete and continuous scales of measure.

The Stevens Taxonomy

There has long been confusion and debate about measurement and the nature of measurement scales. This became a major issue in the field of psychophysics in the 1930s. (Psychophysics is concerned with describing how an organism uses its sensory systems to detect events in its environment.) In 1932, a British committee investigated questions such as: 'By how much must the frequency of a sound be raised or lowered before a person can *just* detect a difference in pitch?' (Such a difference is referred to as a *limen*.) The committee concluded that subjective judgements of this sort could not be a basis of measurement.

S.S. Stevens (1906–73)

This is where Stanley Smith Stevens, a professor of psychophysics at Harvard University, joined the debate. He argued that the fault lay not with the particular measures, such as the limen, but with the fact that there existed no clear schema for understanding the nature of measurement. In a seminal paper (Stevens, 1946), he described a taxonomy of measurement based on four classes of scales. He named these 'nominal', 'ordinal', 'interval' and 'ratio' scales and they are discussed below.

A *nominal* (or *naming*) *scale* of measurement is used for named categories such as race, national origin, gender, surname, and so on. For the purposes of counting such data, it is common to code the names with numbers: for example, 0 = male and 1 = female. Sometimes numbered data are actually nominal, in the sense that the number is no more than a label, with no conventional quantitative significance: for example, the numbers on the shirts of footballers or marathon runners, telephone numbers and university learner numbers are all nominal. All that can be done with nominal measures is to count how many fall into each category (and maybe compute the corresponding percentages).

An *ordinal* (or *ordered*) *scale* of measurement involves data which can be ranked in order (first, second, third, and so on), but for which the numbers cannot be used for further calculation. For example, a questionnaire on attitudes to university fees may ask respondents to indicate their attitude on a five-point scale, ranging from 1 = very strongly opposed to 5 = very strongly in favour. As with nominal data, the number of responses falling into each category can be counted and percentages calculated, but now the values can be ordered by size. (Ideas of ordering were raised in Task 1.2.2.)

An *interval scale* of measurement is a rather subtle concept – numbers are used for measurement of the amount of something, but the scale is such that the zero is arbitrary. This idea occurred in Task 1.2.3, with the questions about time of day and temperature. Zero degrees (0 °C) does not mean 'no temperature'. It is an arbitrary point on the temperature scale associated with the temperature at which water freezes at sea level (under normal atmospheric pressure). Contrast this with measures such as mass or length: a length of 0 cm does mean 'no length' and something that is 20 cm is twice as long as something that is 10 cm. Most psychological tests, such as measures of personality and academic 'ability', are interval measures. (If a learner receives zero on an exam, it does not mean that he or she knows nothing about the course.)

Interval data have all the properties of nominal and ordinal data but, additionally, the intervals between adjacent values are equal. This means that they can be added and subtracted (so, 40 °C is 10 °C warmer than 30 °C or a person may increase their IQ score by 5 points). However, the operations of multiplication and division do not apply appropriately to interval scales. For example, as you saw in Task 1.2.3, a temperature of 30 °C is not twice as warm as a temperature of 15 °C.

A *ratio scale* of measurement has all the properties of an interval scale but, additionally, the operations of multiplication and division can be used meaningfully. Thus, it is fair to say that an age of 16 years is twice as much as an age of 8 years, or that someone weighing 66 kg is twice as heavy as someone weighing 33 kg. Change the years to days or the kilos to pounds and the relationship of 'twice as much' is unaffected. Examples of ratio measurements include mass, length, speed or acceleration and, unlike with interval scales, zero really does mean 'none' of whatever quantity is being measured.

You can consolidate your understanding of Stevens's taxonomy of measuring scales by tackling Task 1.2.4.

Task 1.2.4 Testing Your Take on the Taxonomy   C

(a) Classify the following measures according to Stevens's taxonomy:

  (i) A questionnaire asking: 'How would you rate the service of our catering staff?'

   Excellent ( ) Good ( ) Fair ( ) Poor ( )

  (ii) Windspeed, measured in knots.

  (iii) Bathroom scales, measuring in kg.

  (iv) The UK is made up of four separate countries: England, Scotland, Wales and Northern Ireland.

  (v) Wind force, measured on the Beaufort scale (0 = calm, 1 = light air, 2 = light breeze, …, 12 = hurricane).

(b) Is it possible for temperature to be measured on a ratio scale?

(c) How can time of day and time elapsed be distinguished using the Stevens taxonomy?

The Discrete/Continuous Distinction

There is another means of distinguishing types of measurement scale, namely, the difference between discrete and continuous scales.

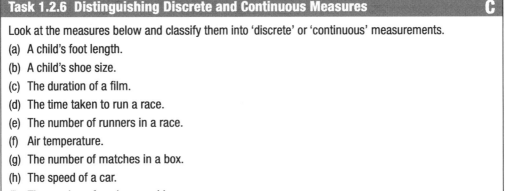

Task 1.2.5 Grammar, Timothy!   **C**

(a) Overheard: Timothy, aged 9, was in a bookshop with his mum. Holding up the new Harry Potter book, he said, 'Mum, guess how much pages are in this book'.

    Why is Timothy's grammar incorrect?

(b) Distinguish the meanings of the words 'fewer' and 'less'.

(c) What 'big idea' connects your answers to parts (a) and (b) and how does it relate to statistics?

The distinctions in parts (a) and (b) above are essentially the same. Words like 'how many' and 'fewer' refer to measures of discrete, separate, countable items, whereas 'how much' and 'less' refer to something that cannot be counted out, such as amount of water, size of slice of a pie, and so on. The terms used in statistics to make this distinction are 'discrete' and 'continuous', respectively.

The key feature of a continuous variable is that, as the name implies, one value flows continuously into the next with no gaps or steps. Between any two values of a continuous variable there is an infinite number of other possible values. Examples of continuous variables include height of plants in a nursery, air temperature and waiting time in a dental surgery.

Contrast this with a discrete variable, where the possible values that it can take are restricted, with gaps between adjacent values. Examples include size of household, marks scored in a test and outcome when rolling a die. It is not possible to have a household size or die score of, say, 3.17. (It is, of course, possible to have an *average* household size of 2.4 or an *average* die score of 3.17, but these numbers arise as a result of calculating an average and such averages are not usually an actual item of the data from which they were calculated.)

Task 1.2.6 Distinguishing Discrete and Continuous Measures   **C**

Look at the measures below and classify them into 'discrete' or 'continuous' measurements.

(a) A child's foot length.

(b) A child's shoe size.

(c) The duration of a film.

(d) The time taken to run a race.

(e) The number of runners in a race.

(f) Air temperature.

(g) The number of matches in a box.

(h) The speed of a car.

(i) The number of goals scored in a season.

(j) Time displayed on a dial watch.

(k) Time displayed on a digital watch.

(l) Annual salaries of teachers.

Now look at the two sentences below and then tackle Task 1.2.7.

> The UK is made up of four separate countries: England, Scotland, Wales and Northern Ireland.

> The UK is made up of four separate countries: Wales, England, Scotland and Northern Ireland.

Task 1.2.7 Wales Has Been Moved!   C

The two sentences are identical except that, in the second, the word 'Wales' has been moved to a different position in the sentence. Clearly, these sentences have exactly the same number of characters, yet they do not occupy the same number of lines of text – a matter of great importance to, say, a newspaper editor.

Try to explain this phenomenon, using the ideas of this section.

One difficulty with making the discrete/continuous distinction is that, in the real world, measurement of a continuous variable can never be carried out with perfect accuracy. Inevitably, rounding reduces the number of possible values that the variable can take from a theoretical infinity of possibilities to something finite. This means that, in practice, *all* measurement can be thought of as being discrete. However, the distinction is still a useful one to make, particularly when it comes to displaying data graphically.

1.3 LARGE AND SMALL NUMBERS

There is no doubt that most measurement involves numbers; sometimes these can be huge numbers and at other times extremely tiny. It is often hard to know how to react to being told certain numerical information without knowing whether it is a lot or a little. A 'mental muscle' that needs regular exercise is the ability to make sensible, 'ball-park' estimates, particularly with large and small numbers. Estimation tasks are a useful and entertaining way of developing your number feel – finding out how big things are to some order of magnitude.

Rough Calculations

Some facts you either tend to know or not, as the case may be. (How far is it from John o'Groats to Land's End or what is the approximate population of the world?) Other 'facts' may not be known precisely, but with a bit of intelligent guesswork and a few 'back-of-an-envelope' calculations, a rough estimate can be made. Sometimes, for certain purposes, a rough estimate is all that is required. For example, in 2004, a van driver drove through Dover with 1 million cigarettes in the back. When questioned, he claimed these were for his 'personal use'. On the basis of a rough calculation, Customs officials estimated that even a heavy smoker would have enough smoking material for 'personal use' to last for 50 years!

Task 1.3.1 Rough Estimates   **C**

Make a rough guess and then an estimate of the following. As you do so, think about the estimates and calculations that you carried out along the way and what 'facts' and assumptions they were based on.

(a) How long will it take for 1 million seconds to tick by? (Make a guess before getting out your envelope.)

(b) How long would it take for 1 billion seconds to tick by? Note that modern usage of the word 'billion' refers to 1 000 million. (Make a guess before making your estimate.)

(c) The population of the world is roughly 6.5 billion people. How many people in the world die each day?

(d) The population of the UK is roughly 57 million. How many cigarettes are smoked annually in the UK?

(e) How fast does human hair grow, in km per hour?

Having an understanding of the orders of magnitude of numbers is an important life skill that is best developed by letting learners explore a wide range of real-world contexts, which is something for which statistics lessons provide many opportunities. In the next task, you are asked to think further about how this skill can be developed.

Task 1.3.2 Adapting Tasks   **C**

Take one of the five statements listed in Task 1.3.1 and adapt or extend it for use with another learner.

If you used a calculator with Tasks 1.3.1 and 1.3.2, you will, no doubt, have come into contact with numbers expressed in scientific notation (also sometimes referred to as 'standard form'). This notation is inescapable when calculators and spreadsheets are used and is a topic that learners from age 14 on need to be able to handle with confidence. It is considered further in Task 1.3.4.

Visualising

In 1999, the eyes of the sporting world were focused on Wales with the opening of the Millennium Stadium, which was built on the historic Cardiff Arms Park site. Designed for all-year, all-weather use, the stadium was the first in the UK with a retractable roof and the first of its type in the world with 75 000 seats. If you have never attended a major public event, it is hard to imagine what 75 000 people gathered together in one place looks like, let alone what it sounds like when they all start shouting or singing at the same time. What would help you or a learner to get a feel for a number as large as this?

Writer Bill Bryson (2004) has a knack of making statistical information both meaningful and palatable to his readers, by providing a helpful mental picture of the magnitudes involved. Here are a few examples taken from his book, *A Short History of Nearly Everything*.

- A typical atom has a diameter of 0.00000008 cm. … Half a million of them lined up shoulder to shoulder could hide behind a human hair. (p. 176)
- An atom is to a millimetre as the thickness of a sheet of paper is to the height of the Empire State Building. (p. 177)
- Avogadro's number, the number of molecules found in 2.016 grams of hydrogen gas (or an equal volume of any other gas at the same temperature and pressure), is equal to 6.0221367×10^{23}, which is equivalent to the number of popcorn kernels needed to cover the US to a depth of 9 miles, or cupfuls of water in the Pacific Ocean, or soft-drinks cans that would, evenly stacked, cover the Earth to a depth of two hundred miles. (p. 139)
- Astronomers today believe that there are perhaps 140 billion galaxies in the visible universe. … If galaxies were frozen peas, it would be enough to fill a large auditorium – … say … the Royal Albert Hall. (p. 169)
- The most striking thing about our atmosphere is that there isn't very much of it. It extends upwards for about 190 kilometres … if you shrank the Earth to the size of a standard desktop globe, it would only be about the thickness of a couple of coats of varnish. (p. 313)
- [On how far back the Cambrian era is.] If you could fly backwards into the past at a rate of one year per second, it would take you about half an hour to reach the time of Christ, and a little over three weeks to get back to the beginnings of human life. But it would take you twenty years to reach the dawn of the Cambrian period. (p. 395)

Task 1.3.3 Visualising Facts   **C**

Here are some facts. How would you try to visualise these numbers?

The capacity of the Millennium stadium, Cardiff: 75 000 people.

The capacity of the Centre Court at Wimbledon: 15 000 people.

The capacity of the London Palladium theatre: about 2 200 people.

The length of time humans have been around (4 million years), compared with the length of time the earth has been around (4.6 billion years).

Here are some of the examples given in this section of very large and very small numbers.

- The number of seconds that have elapsed since the creation of the earth is about 15 000 000 000 000 000 000.
- There are perhaps 140 billion galaxies in the visible universe.
- Human hair grows at roughly 0.000000014 km per hour.
- A typical atom has a diameter of 0.00000008 cm.

These are very extreme numbers and it is almost impossible to understand how large or how small they are. The problem lies with the sea of zeros that such numbers contain when expressed in conventional notation. Scientific notation (sometimes called standard form) provides an alternative way of representing numbers that overcomes this problem.

The number 37 200 can be written in standard form as 3.72×10^4 or sometimes as 3.72E4.

The number 0.00000437 can be written in standard form as 4.37×10^{-6} or sometimes as 4.37E‾6.

Task 1.3.4 Converting Numbers into Standard Form   C

(a) Using the two examples above as a guide, convert the following numbers into standard form.

15 000 000 000 000 000 000

140 billion

0.000000014

0.00000008

(b) Type these four numbers into a scientific or graphics calculator and press '=' (or ENTER) to check that your answers to part (a) are correct.

(c) What are the advantages of displaying these numbers in scientific notation?

Handling numbers in standard form needs a fair degree of practice, as you will see from Task 1.3.5.

Task 1.3.5 Calculating with Standard Form   C

Predict what answer would be displayed on a calculator or spreadsheet to the following calculation: 2.4E36 – 2.4E12. Then perform the calculation and explain why this answer has resulted. What issues are there here that you might wish to share with learners?

1.4 SUMMARISING – AVERAGES AND SPREADS

So far in this chapter, descriptions have come in the form of individual words or numbers. An important feature of statistics is that, usually, *many* measures are made in order to describe things. This may take the form of an experiment or a survey in which a batch of data items together represents the description in question. (A *batch* is another name for a data set.) This move from single numbers to many numbers is a very big idea in statistics, one that is not always obvious to learners when they first study the subject.

Once data have been collected, whether from a survey or scientific experiment or something else, it is often hard to 'see the wood for the trees'. Some sort of organisation or simplification is necessary in order to gain a sense of what the data seem to be 'saying'. Where possible, data can usefully be organised into a table (table layout is discussed in Section 3.2) or summarised into a single figure (sometimes called 'a statistic').

If that single figure is a summary of where the data are *centred* (often called a measure of *location*), then the numerical summary is known as an *average*. If the aim of the summary is to understand how widely *dispersed* the data are, then a measure of *spread* is needed. Whatever the purpose of the summary (to describe the location or the dispersion of the data), they have one thing in common – summarising enables a large number of figures to be reduced to a single representative figure. This has obvious benefits in terms of providing a useful overview. However, summaries inevitably bring corresponding costs in terms of the loss of data and an investigator needs to steer a sensible path between these two aspects, namely, too much and not enough information.

The three best-known measures of location are the three averages, the mean, the mode and the median.

Task 1.4.1 Learner Definitions   **C**

Here are plausible definitions of these three averages provided by a learner. Try to decide which is which and then, if required, improve the learner's definitions.

Definition 1: If there are 20 values, it's 10.

Definition 2: Add them together and divide by how many there are.

Definition 3: It's the biggest frequency.

At a more advanced level, two other useful 'averages' in some circumstances are the *geometric mean* and the *harmonic mean*.

The geometric mean: just as the arithmetic mean of two numbers is found by adding them and dividing by two, the geometric mean is found by multiplying them together and then taking the square root. The geometric mean of n numbers is found by multiplying them all together and then taking the nth root. (Finally, note that the geometric mean cannot be used when any of the values are ≤ 0.)

An example of where the geometric mean is useful is in calculations of vibrating frequencies in the tuning of musical instruments. The vibrating frequency of middle C on a piano is 256 Hz. The vibrating frequency of the C above middle C (one octave above) is twice this value, at 512 Hz. There are 12 semitone intervals between these two notes and in order to ensure that the intervals are equal, the geometric mean must be calculated. One way of explaining this is that, as the 12 semitone steps of the octave together multiply to 2 (in order to double the frequency from 256 to 512), each step is the twelfth root of 2, or roughly 1.059. So the semitone above middle C (named C sharp, written C#) has a vibrating frequency of 256 × 1.059, or roughly 271 Hz; the next semitone in the sequence (named D) has a vibrating frequency of 256 × $(1.059)^2$, or roughly 287 Hz; and so on all the way up to C above middle C, with a frequency of 512 Hz.

The harmonic mean: a common problem for learners is in the calculation of average speeds. If the average speed for the outward journey is, say, 40 kph and the average speed of the return journey is 60 kph, it is not the case that the average speed of the round trip is 50 kph. The arithmetic mean simply does not apply to this situation and what is required is the harmonic mean. This involves taking the following steps:

* take the reciprocals of the values 40 and 60: 1/40 and 1/60;
* find the arithmetic mean of the reciprocals: (1/40 + 1/60)/2 = 5/240;
* take the reciprocal of the result: the reciprocal of 5/240 = 240/5 = 48.

So, the overall average speed of the round trip is 48 kph.

So, why does it work? In this particular example, further investigation by learners may reveal that the key to understanding calculations involving speeds is to concentrate on the time elapsed for each part of the journey. Since speed is equal to distance divided by time, there is an inverse relationship between speed and time. It follows that in order to average the times of the two parts of the journey, you need to find the average of the reciprocals of the two speeds.

A message here for learners is that it is always useful to consider problems from basic principles rather than mindlessly applying a formula.

Task 1.4.2 Create Your Own Task   **C**

Now create a task of your own for helping learners to think about a measure of spread – the range. What might another measure of spread be?

In Section 1.2, you read about the Stevens taxonomy for classifying scales of measurement. This way of thinking is very helpful when checking which numerical summaries can and cannot be applied to certain measures. For example, since calculation of the mean involves adding numbers together, this choice of summary would not be suitable for nominal or ordinal data, where there is no uniform interval between values. This is easiest understood with specific examples, as the next task will reveal.

Task 1.4.3 When Averaging is Appropriate   **C**

Note down four data sets, one each based on nominal, ordinal, interval and ratio measuring scales, respectively. Decide whether each can be summarised using the mean, the mode and the median. Try to make a general conclusion (in the form of a table) about which forms of average operate correctly with each of the four Stevens scales of measure.

1.5 PEDAGOGY: PREPARING TO TEACH A TOPIC

This section highlights some thoughts about teaching and learning statistics in relation to the topics of this chapter.

Task 1.5.1 Preparing to Teach

Choose a particular statistical topic that you may be required to teach a learner or group of learners (for example, types of average, ways of plotting statistical data or a topic in probability).

How would you prepare the lesson? Write down up to six key teaching issues that you would need to consider in the course of your preparation. Note that this is not an invitation to divide up the statistical topic into six sub-topics. Rather, you are asked to consider what aspects of learner learning you will need to bear in mind.

There is clearly no single correct answer to these questions of preparation of a topic – people prepare in various ways, depending on their own subject knowledge, particular interests and their perceptions of the needs of the learner(s) that they have in mind.

In this chapter, and indeed in all the chapters of the book as far as Chapter 12, the final section looks at pedagogic (that is, teaching) issues in terms of the following six themes. They will be referred to as the 'Preparing to Teach' framework (or PTT for short).

- *Language patterns* – learners may be using some of the technical terms and expressions already but perhaps without the standard mathematical meaning.

- *Imagery* that will help learners to create a richer inner sense of the topic, from which further connections can be made.
- *Different contexts* that can be used to enhance understanding and motivate learners by demonstrating that the topic has useful currency outside the classroom.
- *Root questions* – the sort of questions that prompted people to develop general techniques, thus giving rise to the topic.
- *Standard misconceptions* or different or incomplete conceptions.
- *Techniques and methods* that learners need to be able to master and recognise when to use them appropriately.

Task 1.5.2 Using PTT   **C**

How do the six pedagogic themes relate to the topic that you chose in Task 1.5.1? Write notes under each of the six PTT headings.

2

Comparing with Words and Numbers

In an attempt to make sense of the world, it seems to be a characteristic of the human mind to want to search for patterns and make comparisons. This applies to learning associated with the development of all the human senses. The young child is constantly engaging with questions such as:

- is this light brighter than that one?
- is this surface rougher than that one?
- is this voice higher in pitch than that one?

So fundamental to the human mind is the desire to seek out patterns that sometimes people see patterns, even when they are not there. For example, Sutherland (1992, pp. 267-8) reported that during the 'blitz' in the Second World War, Londoners developed elaborate theories about patterns of targets in the German bombing – largely based on explanations that could not possibly be true, given the high degree of variability and inaccuracy. For example, following a particularly intensive period of bombing suffered by the (poorer) East End of the city, one popular theory emerged that the Germans were trying to drive a psychological wedge between rich and poor – a theory that was firmly debunked after the war, when a calmer analysis revealed the patterns to be random. So, an issue of concern to Londoners was based on making comparisons (about the intensity of the bombing) between one area of London and another. The point of relevance to this chapter is that making comparisons seems to be a basic and natural human instinct that can be observed in a wide variety of situations.

Research suggests that pattern seeking seems to be hard-wired into our brain functioning. A report was published in *Scientific American* (Treffert and Wallace, 2002, p. 21) of a group of volunteers who were shown random sequences of circles and squares, while measurements were made of the blood flow to their prefrontal cortex (the part of the brain used in memorisation during moment-to-moment activity). Even though these subjects knew that the patterns were random, this brain layer seemed to 'notice' apparent short-term patterns and then show a reaction whenever they were violated.

Chapter 1 addressed the important human need to describe or summarise information, in order to understand its main features. Verbal descriptions are sometimes required in order to capture descriptions of certain subtle human qualities, but, particularly when comparisons are needed, describing with numbers is a useful alternative. In this chapter, some of these ideas will be extended, although the emphasis now is on using measurement in order to make *comparisons*.

Section 2.1 looks at how the process of making numerical comparisons needs to be considered in the light of how much variation is exhibited by the data. A similar theme is explored in Section 2.2, although the emphasis there is on comparing *spreads* rather than *locations*. An important distinction when making comparisons is between relative and absolute differences and this is the theme of Section 2.3. Section 2.4 sets out a useful four-stage framework for carrying out a statistical investigation (*PCAI*, mentioned in Section 1.1), one that is used repeatedly throughout the rest of the book. The final pedagogy section explores teaching and learning issues based on the PTT framework, which was introduced at the end of Chapter 1.

2.1 COMPARING SIZES

People take decisions every day of the type 'Is A bigger than B?' This may be based simply on visual inspection ('Does the bookcase look smaller than the gap I want to fit it into?'), but when the differences are close or hard to do by eye, formal measuring may be needed.

Often, verbal descriptions of size (large, small, medium, …) are good enough for everyday purposes, but again there are situations where greater precision is required. For example, a heavy goods vehicle (HGV) is clearly a large truck, but how large is 'large' here? For the purpose of licensing and insuring such vehicles, an HGV is formally designated as a road vehicle intended to carry goods, with a maximum laden weight in excess of 7.5 tonnes. On certain stretches of motorways in the UK, there are road signs advising drivers of large vehicles to stop at the next emergency phone and contact the police. But, as a driver of 'large' truck, how would you know this meant you?

The question of how large is large clearly needs some attention here and indeed the definition of 'large' is spelled out in the road sign (see right). When words alone are not sufficiently explicit, sizes often need to be spelt out numerically.

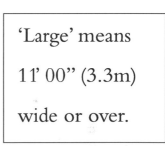

'Large' means

11' 00" (3.3m)

wide or over.

Here is an example whereby the outcome was informed by a numerical comparison.

My cousin in Ireland had been increasingly worried about his Aunt Betty. After a bad fall and an extended stay in hospital, she had become immobile and seemed to have lost all confidence in trying to walk again. Betty was 93 and it looked as if she could no longer look after herself, even in her own 'sheltered' accommodation. It was suggested to her that she would have to go into a care home. Her response, as we knew it would be, was to put her head in her hands.

My cousin, being Betty's next of kin, did not want to take responsibility for this action. Talking it over with a friend, his attention was drawn to a research finding quoted in Sutherland (1992: 116). He got hold of the article, which described a study of 55 elderly women who had entered nursing homes. Of these, 17 felt that they had not entered the home of their own free choice, while the remaining 38 did feel that they had freely chosen to go there. A follow-up study was carried out on how these 55 women fared in the first 10 weeks in their care home. Of the first group, all but one of the women had died. Of the second group, all but one survived the first 10 weeks. There were no health differences between the two groups at the time of entry to the nursing homes.

Reading these statistics gave my cousin quite a jolt. He asked a health professional from the local hospital whether these facts confirmed her experiences. They did. Rather than trying to decide what was in Aunt Betty's best interests, he spent time involving Betty in making the decision for herself: 'You must say what *you* want, auntie.' The good news was that Betty's choice to return to her own sheltered home was respected. Within weeks, her mobility had improved and she returned to a life not very different from what it was before the fall – something that would have been thought impossible a few months before.

Now tackle Task 2.1.1, which asks you to think about some investigations that involve making comparisons.

Task 2.1.1 Taller, Better, Lighter   C

Imagine that you were trying to answer the three questions below. Note down what form of measuring you would have to carry out and what related issues you would need to investigate, in order to answer the following questions.

(a) Are men taller than women?

(b) Are women better drivers than men?

(c) Your friend has been on an expensive, controversial diet and believes that it helped her to lose 3 kg. Does the diet work?

Variation

While it is true that some women are taller than some men, it is *generally* the case that men are taller. A problem with this previous sentence lies in the use of the word 'generally'. In mathematics, a generality is something that is true 'for all cases': for example, *in general* the sum of two odd numbers is even. However, as the term is used in everyday situations (and that is how it has been used here), it is taken to mean 'mostly but not necessarily always'. Thus, a patient might say to a doctor, 'In general, my health has been good, but I still have my bad days'.

What sets statistics apart from the rest of mathematics is that in statistics events occur under conditions of uncertainty. Whereas in pure mathematics *all* even numbers possess the property of evenness, a *statistical* variable may take a range of different values that are usually unpredictable in advance. To take the case of the heights of men and women, both vary considerably and there is overlap in the ranges over which the variation take place. This means that, if a woman and a man were chosen randomly from the population, there is a better than even chance of the man being taller, but still a reasonable chance that the woman would be taller.

On the other hand, comparisons are sometimes made between two different variables where there is very little variation. For example, when comparing the lengths of batches of 50 mm and 55 mm screws, it is very unlikely that the longest screw from the 50 mm batch would ever turn out to be as long as the shortest screw from the 55 mm batch.

The whole point of making comparisons is to decide whether the items under consideration are different. The difficulty is distinguishing the nature of any observed differences, as these could be due to two quite different explanations. The first is that the items are from different populations. The second is that they are taken from the same population, but the differences between them are due to natural variation. Where variation is wide (as with people's heights), observed differences between two measures are more likely to be explained by natural variation. But if variation is small, given the same degree of observed difference, it is more likely that the two measures really do come from different populations. Measurement of variation is looked at more closely in Section 2.2 and finding helpful ways of picturing variation will be a theme of Chapter 6.

Comparing Like with Like

Question (b) of Task 2.1.1 ('Are women better drivers than men?') raises a number of interesting measurement issues to do with making comparisons. First, the term 'better driver' is not well defined: it could mean 'safer' or 'more proficient' (that is, better technically).

To answer the question of whether women are *safer* drivers than men, it is clear from available statistical data that women drivers are involved in fewer accidents than men. It would be easy to conclude that they are therefore safer drivers. Many explanations are offered to justify this conclusion (men are more aggressive, men try to show off in a car, women are more aware of the consequences, women are more timid, and so on). Even if these psychological differences between the sexes are true, there is no guarantee that they translate into differentiated driving behaviour. However, one key factor that needs to be taken into account is the fact that, on average, men drive more miles annually. This means that men are more exposed to the risk of accidents. Only when men's and women's driving accident records are examined on the basis of equal road mileage can a fairer comparison be made, *by comparing like with like*.

Task 2.1.2 Four Times as Dangerous	C

A newspaper article claims that if you were out driving at 7 p.m., you are four times as likely to be killed as at 7 a.m., because there are roughly four times as many fatal road accidents at that time. Do you agree with this conclusion?

Looking for Other Explanations

The third question posed in Task 2.1.1 asked whether there was evidence that your friend's diet was successful. A key question here is, 'successful, compared with what?' She certainly lost (a little) weight, but maybe she would have lost that weight anyway for other reasons. For example, there may have been changes in her level of stress or of exercise. Also, most people experience a small degree of variation in their weight over time, so some of this weight change may be simply due to natural variation. So, there is no guarantee that the treatment was what caused the weight loss. Psychological factors can affect results in these sorts of treatments.

In a study reported in Sutherland (1992, p. 98), two groups of overweight women were given bogus treatments to encourage weight loss. This involved them reading aloud while listening to their voices being played back through headphones with a short delay – a slightly stressful experience that tends to cause stuttering. Group A was subjected to this treatment for long periods while Group B was only required to endure it for minutes at a time. One year later, all the women were re-weighed. The average weight loss for Group A was roughly 3 kg, while the average weight loss for Group B was roughly 150 g (about one twentieth of the first group).

This might seem to suggest that the 'bogus' treatment actually worked. However, there are other explanations. Even though the treatment was dubious, it is likely that those women who had made greater effort and sacrifice felt the need to justify their efforts and so lost more weight than the other group. This is one reason that quack medicines or treatments (for hair loss, cigarette smoking, and so on) tend to be expensive – if it costs you a lot in terms of time, money, effort or public 'face', you have a stronger vested interest in making it work (or at least in convincing others that it was successful)!

2.2 COMPARING SPREADS

One point raised in the previous section is that it is often misleading to attempt to answer questions of the form, 'Is group A bigger than group B?' by a simple comparison of averages. How A and B vary will have considerable bearing on how any differences should be interpreted. In this section, you are asked to look at some of the common measures of variation and how they are calculated. These are the *range*, the *interquartile range* (IQR) and the *standard deviation*. The section ends with a useful way of summarising the spread and location summary values of a set of data, which is known as a five-figure summary. As you will see in Chapter 6, the numbers contained in a five-figure summary are closely connected to a box plot (also known as a box-and-whisker diagram).

Range

The range is the simplest of all measures of spread: it is simply the minimum value in the set subtracted from the maximum value.

For example, the heights of eight people were taken, giving the following results:

1.62 m, 1.74 m, 1.81 m, 1.66 m, 1.77 m, 1.45 m, 1.60 m, 1.69 m.

To find the range, you need to identify the smallest and the largest values and then subtract smallest from largest. With a small data set, this may be easy to do, but with a larger data set it may be necessary first to sort the numbers in order from smallest to largest before subtracting, thus:

1.45 m, 1.60 m, 1.62 m, 1.66 m, 1.69 m, 1.74 m, 1.77 m, **1.81 m**.

Range = 1.81 m – 1.45 m = 0.36 m.

Note that when the range is stated, its unit of measure needs to be included (if these same heights had been recorded in centimetres, the answer would have been 36 cm rather than 0.36 m).

The main advantages of the range are that it is easy to understand and involves no complicated calculation. The main disadvantage is that having just one unrepresentative member of the data set can greatly affect the value of the range and so distort the impression of the degree of spread in the rest of the set. For example, if a ninth extremely tall person, measuring 2.18 m, were included in the set, the value of the range would go up from 0.36 m to just over double this value (0.73 m).

Task 2.2.1 The Range as a Measure of Spread   **C**

Imagine that you are planning to demonstrate to learners this disadvantage of using the range as a measure of spread. Choose a context in which you think your learners will be interested. Make up two data sets for comparison, one of which contains an extreme outlier. Write notes about some of the issues that you would hope to draw from a discussion of these data sets.

Interquartile Range

The range is the interval between the maximum and minimum values in the data set. In Task 2.2.1, a weakness with the range was identified, namely, that it is too easily affected by a single, unrepresentative value at either extreme. As was suggested in the comments to this task, learner attention can be drawn to this drawback of the range in order to help them see the need for a measure of spread that is not so easily affected by extreme outliers. (Note: outliers are looked at again in Section 7.1.) This problem can be overcome by excluding some of the values at either end of the distribution and choosing a different interval, such as that between the upper and lower quartiles – the *difference* between the quartiles – giving rise to the interquartile range (IQR). In effect, the IQR measures the range of the middle 50% of the data.

The two quartiles involved in calculating this measure of spread, the IQR, are often referred to as Q1 (the lower quartile) and Q3 (the upper quartile). To find the values of the quartiles, sort the data in order of size and then identify, respectively, the values one quarter and three quarters of the way through the sorted set. As you may have already guessed, Q2 is the symbol often used to stand for the median – the value that is two quarters of the way (that is, halfway) through the data set.

Calculating the Quartiles

Although the lower and upper quartiles sound simple to define (the values that lie one quarter and three quarters of the way through the data set when the values are placed in order), in fact the exact calculation of the values of the quartiles is something of a minefield. It is tempting to introduce learners to the calculation of the quartiles starting with a simple and very small data set. However, it is with these small data sets that the problems in calculating the quartiles arise. Task 2.2.2 provides a simple example to illustrate the point.

Task 2.2.2 Calculating Quartiles in Small Data Sets

In the comments to Task 2.2.1, the ordered estimates (in seconds) for the nine 11-year-olds were: 40, 42, 43, 47, 49, 50, 58, 60 and 65, while for the eight 16-year-olds their estimates were: 21, 55, 57, 57, 58, 61, 65, 65. What are the values of Q1, Q2 and Q3 for these two data sets? What problems do you anticipate when teaching these calculations to learners?

The median value of the 11-year-olds' data set of nine values is the fifth one, namely 49 seconds. With even-numbered data sets, like that for the 16-year-olds, there is no unique value that lies at the halfway point. To calculate the median for this sort of set, the usual convention is to take the mean of the two middle values, which in this case is the mean of 57 and 58 (the fourth and fifth values), namely 57.5 seconds. (In the case of an even number of data points, the median is not an item of the original data set.)

Unfortunately, however, there is no single agreed convention for calculating the lower and upper quartiles: whichever method you choose may seem a little messy and confusing to most learners. In Chapter 6, you will read about the 'exploratory data analysis' (EDA) approach to data handling, pioneered by statistician John Tukey. Tukey's method for calculating Q1 is to choose the lower half of the data *including the median of the batch* and then find the median of this (smaller) set of values. Similarly, to find Q3 (the upper quartile of the batch), Tukey includes the median value of the set. However, in both cases, he only does so if the median is a member of the original data set. Where the median is not a member of the original batch, Tukey excludes it from the determination of both Q1 and Q3.

In this example, then, finding Q1 of the 11-year-olds' data involves finding the median of the five values 40, 42, 43, 47 and 49, which is 43 seconds. By a similar calculation, the corresponding value of Q3 is calculated to be the median of the five values 49, 50, 58, 60 and 65, which is 58 seconds.

However, where there is an even number of values in the initial data set, the median will not itself be a member of the data set, in which case, according to Tukey's method, it is to be excluded from both halves of the data set in calculating the quartiles. This is the case with the 16-year-olds' data: as you saw above, the median is 57.5 seconds. So, for Tukey, Q1 is found as the median of 21, 55, 57, 57, which is 56 seconds, and Q3 is the median of 58, 61, 65 and 65, which is 63 seconds. (In this case, notice that none of Q1, Q2 or Q3 is a data point from the original data set.)

If you were to key these numbers into a graphics calculator, such as one from Texas Instruments's TI-83 or TI-84 families, you will find that the values of Q1 and Q3 for the 11-year-olds are given as 42.5 and 59 seconds, respectively, as opposed to the values of 43 and 58 we found above, following Tukey's method.

Task 2.2.3 Calculating Quartiles with a Calculator   C

What algorithm do you think these calculators use for calculating the quartiles?

Using Large Data Sets

Clearly, introducing quartiles by means of simple data sets is not that simple. An alternative would be to start with a very large data set (say with 200 values) and ask learners to look for the value of the 'middle' data point and those a quarter and three quarters of the way through. These give the values of Q1, Q2 and Q3 as, respectively the 50th, 100th and 150th items, when placed in order of size. This definition may have to be adjusted later, but the error will be small for data sets of this sort of size, because the two adjacent values in even-numbered sets are likely to be very close in size. Learners could apply both methods listed above (Tukey's method and the calculator approach) and confirm that there is little difference between them for large data sets.

Overall, it is important for learners to establish the following two big ideas when learning about these summary statistics:

- they are only really useful for large data sets, in which case all the rules for calculating them will give more or less the same values (except in pathological cases);
- these summaries are only used as general description measures, so the exact values are not that important.

Five-figure Summary

If you wished to summarise a set of data with just five numbers, a useful selection, covering the full range of the data would be:

Minimum value (Min), Lower quartile (Q1), Median (Med), Upper quartile (Q3) and Maximum value (Max).

Imagine these placed below a line, as in Figure 2.1.

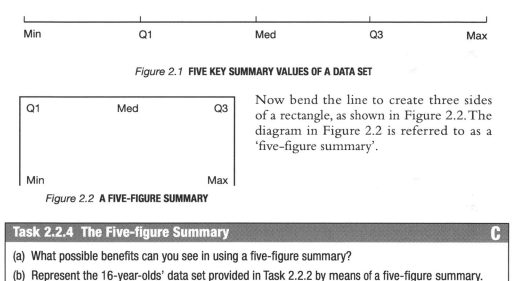

Figure 2.1 **FIVE KEY SUMMARY VALUES OF A DATA SET**

Now bend the line to create three sides of a rectangle, as shown in Figure 2.2. The diagram in Figure 2.2 is referred to as a 'five-figure summary'.

Figure 2.2 **A FIVE-FIGURE SUMMARY**

Task 2.2.4 The Five-figure Summary   C

(a) What possible benefits can you see in using a five-figure summary?

(b) Represent the 16-year-olds' data set provided in Task 2.2.2 by means of a five-figure summary.

Standard Deviation

At higher levels of statistical work (for learners aged over 16), the best-known and least-loved measure of spread is the *standard deviation*. An alternative name for the standard deviation is the 'root mean squared' (RMS) deviation. In other words, it is the (square) *root* of the *mean* of the *squared* deviations. This is a bit of a mouthful for most people, but it is actually a useful mnemonic for remembering how it is calculated. When you reach Block 3 of this book (Chapters 9–12), you will be offered the chance to use a graphics calculator and a spreadsheet to lay out the calculation of the standard deviation and make sense of it with a minimum of pain.

A common way of calculating the standard deviation of a data set is:

- first, to calculate the mean;
- then, to find the deviation of each value from the mean;

- then, to square the deviations and find the mean of these values (this value is called the *variance*);
- finally, to find the square root of the variance to get the standard deviation.

Before the days of calculating machines, learners spent many unhappy hours calculating standard deviations: it is not proposed that you do that here. However, you do need to have an idea of what it is and why it was devised in the first place.

A feature shared by both the range and the interquartile range is that they are each calculated on the basis of just two values – the range uses the maximum and the minimum values, while the IQR uses the two quartiles. The standard deviation, on the other hand, has the distinction of using, directly, every value in the set as part of its calculation. In terms of representativeness, this is a great strength. But the chief drawback of the standard deviation is that, conceptually, it is harder to grasp than other more intuitive measures of spread. As you will see from the next task, these features crop up in other statistical measures.

Task 2.2.5 Turning to Location   C

Which measure of central location uses all the values in the data set in its calculation? Which one uses a single value?

There are other issues about the standard deviation that are worth exploring, some of which are picked up on in Chapter 10, where you will have the support of technology.

2.3 RELATIVE AND ABSOLUTE DIFFERENCES

Did you know that rich people give more to charitable causes than poor people? Of course, the rich have more to give, so this is not too surprising. However, when calculated as a percentage of earnings, the rich give, on average, 1% while the poor give, on average 3% of their earnings (quoted on 19 November 2004, BBC Radio 4, *You and Yours*). So maybe the rich are not so generous after all.

Differences can take two possible forms, usually called 'relative' and 'absolute' differences. The next two tasks introduce the distinction and illustrate why it is a useful one to make.

Task 2.3.1 First Impressions   C

What first impression does the table of data below suggest? If you wished to gain a more informed second impression, what additional information would you like to be given?

TABLE 2.1 'Most Sporty Nation' Table (Athens Olympic Games, 2004)

1. USA	35 gold medals
2. China	32 gold medals
3. Russia	27 gold medals
4. Australia	17 gold medals

Source: www.athens2004.com/en/OlympicMedals/medals.

Task 2.3.2 Second Impressions   **C**

Below are the populations of the four countries concerned. Use these figures, together with the gold medal table, to reach a more informed conclusion about which is the most sporty nation.

Populations (millions):

USA 289, China 1308, Russia 143, Australia 20.

Source: www.mnsu.edu/emuseum/information/population/.

'Dotheboys Comprehensive School' boasts that compared with all the secondary schools in the city, they have the largest number of learners each year gaining five GCSEs at Grade C or better. This may not be surprising, since Dotheboys is by far the largest school in the area. In order to make comparisons between institutions or countries of different size, *absolute* figures such as these are fairly useless by themselves. A *relative* measure such as a proportion or a percentage will ensure that the comparison is fairer. Note that relative comparisons depend crucially on the introduction of a divisor and it is not always obvious to novices which divisor to choose. For example, in Task 2.3.2, the divisor was population size, but another possibility might have been the number of athletes from each country attending the games. Similarly, with the Dotheboys Comprehensive School example, the divisor could have been the total school population or the number of learners taking the examinations or the number of learners eligible to take the examinations. Basically, the choice of divisor must be made with care, bearing in mind the precise comparison you want to make.

Task 2.3.3 Big Dipper   **C**

Which do you think is riskier, riding on a white-knuckle fairground machine such as 'Nemesis' or 'Oblivion' at Alton Towers or cycling on a main road in the UK?

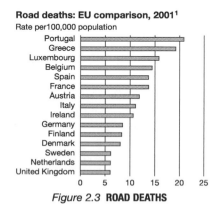

Road deaths: EU comparison, 2001[1]
Rate per 100,000 population

Figure 2.3 **ROAD DEATHS**

In the comments to Task 2.3.3, it was suggested that 'roughly 10 people die on our roads every day'. Do you believe this figure? How might you check it? One useful source of interesting data, available in a book and freely available on the web, is the UK government publication *Social Trends*. The 2004 edition provides relevant data in the form of the horizontal bar chart in Figure 2.3.

Study the bar chart and then answer the questions in Task 2.3.4.

Task 2.3.4   Relative and Absolute, Revisited   C

(a) Is the statement, that 'roughly 10 people die on our roads every day', a relative or an absolute figure?

(b) By reading off the horizontal bar chart in Figure 2.3, estimate the scale of road deaths for the UK. Is this a relative or an absolute figure?

(c) By means of a suitable calculation, check if these two figures are mutually consistent.

2.4 STATISTICAL INVESTIGATIONS

As you will see from later chapters, a major theme of this book is the importance of placing statistical work in meaningful and purposeful contexts. Although it is not suggested that all statistical work be conducted as part of a statistical investigation, nevertheless an investigation is an excellent vehicle for teaching statistics that will develop useful skills in a motivating way. The defining characteristic of an investigation is that it is based on a *question* that learners want to answer. Practising statistical computations without relating them to a question is like practising scales on a piano but never playing a tune, or learning how to trap, head and pass a soccer ball but never getting to play a game. Certainly there is a place for practice, but putting practised routines to work is essential if learners are to turn a useful skill into a usable one.

As you saw in Chapter 1, the four stages of a statistical investigation used throughout the book can be summarised by the acronym *PCAI*, which refer to:

- *P* : pose the question;
- *C* : collect relevant data;
- *A* : analyse the data;
- *I* : interpret the results.

These four stages are explored in greater depth later, particularly in Chapter 13. In this section, you are asked to use them as a framework for planning how you might think through an investigation on the theme of human intuition.

Stage *P*: Pose the Question

Many classroom statistical projects such as traffic surveys or ways of getting to school start with the *C* stage of collecting data. The problem that learners then face is that, without a clear question, there are no criteria for deciding what to do next. This vagueness of purpose tends to ripple through the rest of the investigation, making it hard for learners to choose an appropriate calculation or graphical representation, or to come to any conclusion about what the data reveal.

Task 2.4.1   Thinking Up a Question   C

Imagine that you wish to carry out statistical work with students that involves them doing a traffic survey or listing ways of getting to school. For each of these projects, think up two questions that might make them more purposeful. One should be a 'describing' and the other a 'comparing' question.

Now turn your thoughts to carrying out an investigation on something much more vague and subtle – human intuition.

Task 2.4.2 Defining Intuition

Spend a few minutes thinking about the following aspects of human intuition and then note down your thoughts before reading on.

- How would you define human intuition?

- Pose a 'comparing' question about intuition that you might want to investigate.

- How could you measure intuition and what sort of data would your investigation yield?

Cognitive psychologists define intuition as the fast processing of information, so that the person is able to make a judgement before knowing the reasons for their choice. There are many possible questions and ways of investigating intuition. One that was carried out by Professor Richard Wiseman of the University of Hertfordshire is whether women's powers of intuition exceed those of men. An account of this investigation can be found in the 12 April 2005 issue of the *Daily Telegraph* (Fleming, 2005). Wiseman measured one aspect of intuition, namely, people's ability to identify the sincerity or otherwise of different smiles.

Stage *C*: Collect Relevant Data

Look at the two photographs. One purports to show a genuine smile and the other a false smile. Can you tell the difference?

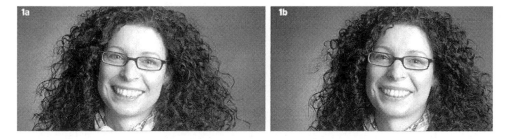

In his investigation on intuition, Wiseman invited more than 15 000 men and women to look at 10 pairs of photographs of smiling faces – one real and the other false – to see if they could tell which was the phoney smile. If you want to try out the investigation for yourself, visit the following website where five pairs of the photographs can be found: www.telegraph.co.uk/news/main.jhtml?xml=/news/2005/04/12/nsmile12.xml

---

Task 2.4.3 Matching the Data to the Question

Do you think the data from this experiment will provide a good measure of people's intuition? Explain your answer.

The match between the data and the question posed in the investigation is only, at best, partial. Intuition covers a very wide range of aspects and a person's ability to distinguish real from false smiles only taps in to one small part of one. So, you may already be alerted that care will need to be exercised when making any conclusions at the *I* stage of the investigation. Interestingly, before doing the experiment, Wiseman asked the participants to rate their intuitive abilities. Of the women, 77% rated themselves as highly intuitive, compared with 58% of the men.

Stage *A* : Analyse the Data

The data that resulted from this experiment took the form of over 15 000 scores, ranging from a minimum of 0 (no correct guesses) to a maximum of 10 (all guesses correct).

Task 2.4.4 Doing a Calculation	C

Bearing in mind that the aim of this investigation was to see whether women or men were better able to distinguish real from false smiles, what calculations do you think would be appropriate?

Stage *I* : Interpret the Results

In the *Daily Telegraph* article that featured this piece of research (Fleming, 2005), much was made of the fact that men proved to be better at reading women's faces than women were at reading men's. The views of three 'experts' were sought to explain these differences. Here is what they had to say.

> Richard Wiseman: 'This could be because women experience emotions more fully and are more expressive. If men have a more limited emotional system, this may make it easier for them to fake it.'

> Susan Quilliam (a relationship psychologist): 'Women are not good at spotting insincerity because they are programmed to look on the bright side. Women will be less likely to notice and to want to see fakeness in any situation.'

> Gladeana McMahon (a cognitive psychologist): 'It may be that women have been labelled as intuitive because they tend to talk more about their feelings.'

Task 2.4.5 What Are They Really Saying?	C

(a) Read these three comments carefully and make an evaluation about what they seem to be saying.

(b) What are your own interpretations of these findings?

One point worth making about the statistical summaries of men's and women's intuition is that there was very little difference between men's and women's performances overall, but only in their performances when reading the faces of the opposite sex (for which the men did somewhat better). There is, however, a corollary to this result, namely, that it must follow that the women were *better* than the men in reading the faces of *their own* sex. If you are unsure about the validity of this conclusion, consider the following simple, made-up example based on a sample of three men and three women.

In Table 2.2, when the three men viewed pictures of men, they were poor at reading their expressions, leading to an average of 50% success (column 1). However, these three men were very good at reading the opposite sex, gaining an average of 90% success in column 2. The men's overall average score was therefore 70%. Assume that the women scored the same overall average scores of 70%, but their reading of the opposite sex was less good than the men (80% as compared with 90%). The data below illustrate this situation.

TABLE 2.2 Men's and women's success rates

Men (same sex)	Men (opposite sex)	Women (same sex)	Women (opposite sex)
5	9		8
5	9		8
5	9		8

Task 2.4.6 Deducing the Missing Data   **C**

Look at the column of missing data in Table 2.2 (showing women's scores on reading sincerity of the faces of their own sex from a photograph). If the three women all have the same scores in this column, work out what this value must be in order to maintain the same overall average as the men of 70%. How does this result compare with the men's scores in reading their own sex?

2.5 PEDAGOGY

'Telling' Tales

For thousands of years, stories, legends, parables and fables have been used to good effect in teaching. Such an approach has many advantages – a 'ripping yarn' engages the learner's interest in the first place, it provides a memorable context on which a better understanding of new ideas can be hung and, if sufficiently powerful, merits retelling over and over. A 'telling' tale is one that not only entertains the listener, but also is one that contains some wider issue, moral or 'big idea'. Put another way, it enables the movement 'from the particular to the general'. Whereas abstract ideas on their own can sometimes be difficult to grasp, this is often easier when the ideas are placed within a human (or otherwise interesting) context.

As you may already be aware, an attempt has been made to incorporate 'telling' tales into the writing of this book. This is an approach that you may want to try out with learners. Throughout the rest of this book, you will be encouraged to apply this teaching strategy to your own learning and teaching. As you work with learners, you will be asked to use telling tales with them and invite them to think up some of their own. One example in this chapter was the (true) story of Aunt Betty.

Task 2.5.1 Aunt Betty   **C**

Without looking back to the text, try to remember the story of Aunt Betty, so that you have a picture of her and her circumstances. Then make a note of the statistical point that this story helped to make.

In Chapter 1, the six themes referred to as 'Preparing to Teach a Topic' (PTT) were listed. In this section, these themes are used to direct your thinking towards teaching and learning issues that relate to comparing.

Language Patterns

Task 2.5.2 Statistical Words and Phrases   **C**

Make a note of about 10 of the key statistical words and phrases that were used in this chapter. With a particular learner or group of learners in mind, choose two of these terms and plan how you might help your chosen learner(s) gain a better understanding of them.

Imagery

Task 2.5.3 Visualising   **C**

Think back to an example from earlier in this chapter that you might like to use when working with another learner or learners, such as the distinction between relative and absolute differences. How might you use 'visualising' to clarify the key ideas? What other concepts mentioned in this chapter might be clarified by the use of imagery?

Different Contexts

In Section 2.4, you looked at an investigation on measuring and comparing intuition between men and women. This is an interesting context for learners to look at, not least because it draws attention to a variety of important issues about ambiguity of measurement and the difficulties of interpreting the results in such situations. You could consider accessing the website and using these photographs with your learners to see how they compared with the respondents in the survey. Alternatively, they could select 10 volunteers to create photographs of real and fake smiles and carry out a parallel investigation of their own.

This chapter focused on investigations involving comparing. The next task asks you to think in more detail about how you might prepare a lesson on helping learners make statistical comparisons.

Task 2.5.4 Contexts   **C**

Two of the big ideas of statistical thinking discussed in this chapter were 'investigating differences' and 'relative comparison'. With a particular learner or group of learners in mind, note down several examples of everyday contexts that would illustrate or further enrich these topics for your learner(s).

Root Questions

Task 2.5.5 Root Questions C

Below are a number of statistical terms. Make a note of the sorts of root questions that might create a need to use these measures and representations:

standard deviation, five-figure summary, standard form.

Standard Misconceptions

A common misunderstanding about the median is that learners sometimes think it is the *positional number* of the middle value rather than its numerical *value*. For example, to take the estimation data for the eight 16-year-olds given in Task 2.2.2, learners may say that there are 8 values, so the median = 4.5, rather than the value lying halfway between the fourth and fifth value, when placed in order of size. One way of remedying this problem is to ask them to estimate the summary values *before* calculating them; this gives them a better sense of what these values refer to, rather than simply calculating with numbers unthinkingly. It also gives them a 'ball-park' figure against which they can check the reasonableness of their answer.

Task 2.5.6 Misconceptions C

What other misunderstanding or partial understanding do you think some students may have about the median and how might you try to remedy it?

Techniques and Methods

Task 2.5.7 Techniques C

Think back to the discussion in Section 2.2 about introducing the calculation of the quartiles. Try to find an imaginative way of presenting this topic that you might not have used or thought of before, so that the focus is on the big ideas rather than the detailed algorithm of the calculation.

3 Interrelating with Words and Numbers

There are many ways of 'seeing' the subject of statistics and clearly no one way is correct by itself. In this book, a particular structure and development have been chosen, in order to set out one version of the subject. At this point, it would be worthwhile trying to get a clear picture of the story that underpins the opening chapters.

- 'Describing' is how humans make sense of their world; words and numbers are both useful tools for creating descriptions that others can share. Describing was the theme of Chapter 1.
- Sometimes it is useful to describe things not just singly but in groups or batches, which requires the collection of 'data' and the subsequent summarising of such data sets. Data are the building bricks of statistics.
- When a comparison between two things is required, a statistical approach is to collect data from a set of each and compare the results. Comparing was the theme of Chapter 2.

Now, in Chapter 3, you are asked to look at what happens when you start to explore relationships between two things. This involves asking questions such as the following:

- 'Is there a connection between speed of reaction and acuity of eyesight?'
- 'Is salary linked to level of education?'
- 'Are ice cream sales linked to air temperature?'

In Section 3.1, you will be introduced to the basic idea of a bi-variate relationship. Section 3.2 looks at how a relationship can be depicted using two-way tables of data, with a particular look at how these can be set out in a clear and helpful way. Section 3.3 draws an important distinction between a statistical relationship and one of cause and effect. Section 3.4 looks at two important features of a statistical relationship, *regression* and *correlation*, while, as usual, the final section is about pedagogic issues (including a sub-section on constructivism).

3.1 RELATIONSHIPS

It was a few days after her third birthday that Caitlin sadly viewed her diminishing balloon and said, 'The more the long time, the littler my balloon grows!'

Despite her slender years, Caitlin seems to have got to grips with the essence of what is sometimes referred to as a bi-variate (that is, two-variable) relationship. In this example, the variables are 'time' and 'size of balloon'.

Bi-variate relationships can often be expressed in the form of a 'double comparative', which is the form that Caitlin used with her balloon relationship. This is 'the *more* of X, the *more* of Y' or sometimes, as in Caitlin's case, 'the *more* of X, the *less* of Y'. In the first case (the more, the more), the relationship is an increasing one and the two variables have a direct (or positive) connection. In the second case (the more, the less), there is an inverse (or negative) relationship.

Task 3.1.1 Direct and Inverse Relationships   C

(a) Write down two examples of direct relationships of the form, 'the more, the more'.

(b) Write down two examples of inverse relationships of the form, 'the more, the less'.

(c) Here are some proverbs expressed in the form of a 'double comparative'. See if you can identify them.

  (i) The greater the number of chefs, the less appetising becomes their soup.

  (ii) It is not the case that the more money you have, the happier you become.

  (iii) The less similar two people are, the greater the attraction.

  (iv) The better your fortune in games of chance, the worse your fortune in affairs of the heart.

  (v) The more workers there are, the less each one has to do.

  (vi) The less time the feline predator is around, the greater the opportunity for the rodents to frolic.

  (vii) The shorter the time interval before repairs are undertaken, the fewer repairs will be required.

Explanatory and Response Variables

An important feature of bi-variate relationships is that the data come in pairs. The pairs may take many possible forms; for example: 'before' and 'after', 'left eye' and 'right eye', and so on. Table 3.1 shows the heights and weights of six individuals. The attribute that creates the pairings are the names of the individuals – two data items were collected from each individual.

TABLE 3.1 Height and weight data

Name	Height (m)	Weight (kg)
Ahmed	1.67	74
Barrie	1.69	78
Carrie	1.53	53
Deena	1.60	58
Evelyn	1.63	51
Faruk	1.70	63

An attribute of paired data is that the number of items in both lists *must* be the same. The most helpful way of getting an instant handle on paired data like these is to plot them as a scatter plot, and this is something that you will look at closely in Chapter 7. In order to be able to plot these data, the first decision that needs to be made is which variable to place on the horizontal and which on the vertical scale (or axis). There is a convention attached to this choice, which is that the *explanatory* variable (sometimes referred to as the *independent* variable) goes on the horizontal scale and the *response* variable (sometimes referred to as the *dependent* variable) goes on the vertical scale.

Note that there is a difference between the sort of paired data given in Table 3.1 (where each of the 12 values in the six data pairs can vary randomly) and the sort of paired data generated in a scientific investigation, such as an experiment on Hooke's Law (which relates the extension of a spring to the mass attached to it). In this sort of experiment, the 'x'-values (in this case, the various masses) are chosen and fixed in advance and only one of the 'variables' (the length of the spring) is genuinely free to vary. The terms 'independent' and 'dependent' variables are more commonly used in this sort of situation.

Task 3.1.2 Independent and Dependent Variables   **C**

In the Hooke's Law experiment, which variable is the independent and which the dependent variable?

A dictionary definition of an *explanatory variable* might be something like: 'a variable in an experiment or study whose presence or degree determines the change in the response variable'.

To take the example of too many cooks spoiling the broth, the explanatory variable is the 'number of cooks', as their number determines the quality of the broth, rather than the other way around.

Task 3.1.3 Choosing the Explanatory Variable   **C**

Look at the following relationships and try to pick out the explanatory variable.

(a) Heights and weights of a group of people.

(b) An individual's pulse rate and number of minutes spent jogging.

(c) Child's age and shoe size.

(d) Distance from home to school and journey time.

(e) The height of the sun in the sky and the time of day.

(f) The weight of the heart and the weight of the liver in mice.

When considering a particular relationship, it is not always clear which is the explanatory variable. In order to make this judgement, you need to make certain assumptions about the 'cause-and-effect' nature of each relationship. As you will see in Section 3.4, this choice is not always easy.

3.2 LAYING OUT TABLES

Tables of bi-variate data are often referred to as two-way tables, for the very good reason that they are two-dimensional. Two variables or attributes will be represented in the table; one horizontally and the other vertically. The size of a table is normally defined in terms of the numbers of its rows and columns (not including the row and column headings) – in that order: for example, a 2 × 3 table has data contained in two rows and three columns.

The table of heights and weights shown in the last section consisted of six rows and three columns, so would be referred to as a 6 × 3 table. Look at the 2 × 2 table (Table 3.2), which summarises the mobile phone ownership by boys and girls in a particular class. Then tackle Task 3.2.1, which will give you the opportunity to think more carefully about the ideas in Section 3.1 and how they relate to data presented in a table.

TABLE 3.2 Mobile phone ownership

	Owns a mobile phone	Does not own a mobile phone
Girls	13	4
Boys	9	6

Task 3.2.1 Clarifying the Measures   **C**

Look at the two row headings ('Girls' and 'Boys'). These are two categories from a broader general measure; a person's sex.

(a) Now look at the two column headings. What is the general measure of which these are the two categories?

(b) Using the Stevens taxonomy discussed in Chapter 1, which type of scale of measure are these – nominal, ordinal, interval or ratio?

(c) Would you say these measures could be described as 'variables' or 'attributes'?

Many people find looking at a table containing a mass of numbers rather off-putting. In fact, where a page of textbook prose contains a table, the human eye seems to want to leap straight over it, as if it were not there. This may be for the very good reason that many tables of data are poorly presented and not designed for ease of understanding.

A.S.C. Ehrenberg

An influential pioneer in improving the presentation of data has been A.S.C. Ehrenberg, former professor at the London Business School. Ehrenberg could see that in order to read a table of figures successfully, there was a heavy loading on short-term memory – one needs to remember some or all of the numbers contained in the table, at least momentarily, and this is what causes overload.

During the late 1970s and 1980s, Ehrenberg revolutionised people's thinking about how tables could be reorganised to make them easier to read and analyse. To illustrate the point, Ehrenberg (1981), in one of his seminal papers on the subject, provided two tables (see Tables 3.3 and 3.4), referred to below as 'before' and 'after'. The first is typical of the sort of hard-to-read table that is still too common in textbooks, while the second is Ehrenberg's improved version.

TABLE 3.3 Quarterly sales of product X in eight cities (Ehrenberg's 'before' table)

£000	Quarter 1	Quarter 2	Quarter 3	Quarter 4
Bolton	31.3	29.1	25.2	29.3
Edinburgh	135.2	126.9	132.1	208.3
Hull	70.3	81.3	70.9	84.0
Leeds	276.8	258.6	223.0	336.2
Luton	23.5	27.5	22.7	27.1
Plymouth	41.4	44.0	33.2	50.2
Sheffield	233.4	220.1	193.6	220.9
Swansea	62.3	66.4	61.8	76.7

TABLE 3.4 The cities ordered by population size (Ehrenberg's 'after' table)

Sales in £000	Q1	Q2	Q3	Q4	Av.
Sheffield	230	220	190	220	220
Leeds	280	260	220	340	270
Edinburgh	140	130	130	210	150
Hull	70	81	71	84	76
Swansea	62	66	62	77	67
Plymouth	41	44	33	50	42
Luton	24	28	23	27	25
Bolton	31	29	25	29	29
Average	110	107	94	130	110

Ehrenberg set out six guiding principles, which are:

1. Give marginal averages to provide a visual focus.
2. Order the rows or columns of the table by the averages or by some other measure of size.
3. Put figures to be compared in columns instead of rows (with the larger number on top if possible).
4. Round to two figures.
5. Use clear layout to guide the eye.
6. Include a brief verbal summary.

Task 3.2.2 Good Table Layout   C

Look carefully at both Table 3.3 and 3.4 and note how they differ. Which of Ehrenberg's principles can you see exemplified in Table 3.4?

Ehrenberg suggested that his six guiding principles should be known and acted upon by both the users and producers of data. His advice to users who were unhappy with having to deal with badly designed tables was to 'send incomprehensible data back to its maker with constructive comments, since it is easier for the analyst to rearrange the figures than for every potential user to try to make sense of them' (p. 70).

Look at Table 3.5 and then try Task 3.2.3.

TABLE 3.5 Literacy rate of 15–24-year-olds

	Algeria	Egypt	Libya	Morocco	Tunisia
Women in 1990	68.1%	51.0%	82.7%	42.0%	75.2%
Men in 1990	86.1%	70.9%	98.9%	68.0%	92.8%
All in 1990	77.3%	61.3%	91.0%	55.3%	84.1%
Women in 2004	85.6%	66.9%	94.0%	61.3%	90.6%
Men in 2004	94.0%	79.0%	99.8%	77.4%	97.9%
All in 2004	89.9%	73.2%	97.0%	69.5%	94.3%

Source: United Nations millennium indicators data base:
millenniumindicators.un.org/unsd/mi/mi_indicator_xrxx.asp?ind_code=8

Task 3.2.3 Re-laying the Table

The data on which Ehrenberg demonstrated his principles were fictitious. Table 3.5 is a table of real-world contemporary data, the layout of which leaves something to be desired. Apply as many of Ehrenberg's principles as seem appropriate (or any other ideas of your own) to improve the table's presentation.

Table 3.6 shows one possible alternative layout.

- Ehrenberg's principle 3 suggests putting figures to be compared in columns rather than rows. The arrangement below allows you to compare the yearly figures easily and hence the improvement in literacy rates. However, the original layout allows for easier comparison of countries.
- In the original layout, the countries were in alphabetical order: in Table 3.6 they have been arranged in decreasing order of overall literacy (Ehrenberg's principle 2). Note that Ehrenberg suggested using decreasing rather than increasing values as you go down the columns, on the grounds that people would find it easier to subtract a smaller number from a bigger number just above it.
- A row has been added showing the mean literacy rates of the five countries (Ehrenberg's principle 1). Notice that it would be quite meaningless to calculate the mean of the six rates for each country, so there is no extra column.
- Numbers have been rounded to two figures (Ehrenberg's principle 4) and also the % sign has been omitted from each cell but included in the title.
- A mixture of bold and non-bold borders for the cells has been used to guide the eye (Ehrenberg's principle 5).
- A brief verbal summary has been included (Ehrenberg's principle 6).

TABLE 3.6 Literacy rate (%) of 15–24 year-olds in five North African countries

	All		Women		Men	
	1990	2004	1990	2004	1990	2004
Libya	91	97	83	94	99	100
Tunisia	84	94	75	91	93	98
Algeria	77	90	68	86	86	94
Egypt	61	73	51	67	71	79
Morocco	55	70	42	61	68	77
Mean	74	85	64	80	83	90

Between 1990 and 2004, all five countries improved their literacy rate, particularly among women. However, the literacy rate among women is still considerably less than that among men in all five countries.

One final thought about reading data in tables: are all the figures in this table to be believed (for example, the remarkably high rates of literacy in Libya)? Learners should be encouraged not simply to accept statistical information because it is printed 'in black and white' on the page. Reading any table of data requires a reality check against common sense and common knowledge.

3.3 CAUSE AND EFFECT

In statistics, it is one thing to demonstrate that there is a statistical relationship between two things. However, this is not at all the same as demonstrating that the change in one was brought about by the change in the other. Cause-and-effect relationships are notoriously difficult to prove and if you can help learners to become more careful in making unwarranted assumptions in this area, then your work as a teacher of the big ideas of statistics will not have gone to waste.

In this section, you will read a number of stories or situations and be asked to tackle some puzzles or problems. As you think about each of the examples provided, devote some of your thoughts to asking how it relates to ideas of cause and effect.

Task 3.3.1 Fire the Firefighters?   C

Suppose you were to collect annual data on the number of fires and the number of fire engines in Birmingham over the past 50 years.

(a) What statistical connection would you expect to find?

(b) How would you explain the connection?

Task 3.3.2 The Four-card Problem   C

Here is a problem attributed to psychologist Peter Wason (1966). Imagine that the following four cards are visible on the table.

You are told that each card has two faces, with a letter on one face and a number on the opposite face. Which cards would you need to turn over in order to test whether or not the following rule is true?

Rule: Any card with an 'A' on one face has a '3' on the other.

Health

In the UK, in 2005, roughly £93 billion was spent on health care, including private health care sector spending of £10 500 million (see the Kings Fund website: www.kingsfund.org.uk/electionbriefings/funding.html).

That works out at roughly £1 500 per head of population. Is this expenditure making people better?

Task 3.3.3 On the Mend   C

Every day, thousands of people start a course of medical treatment for some ailment. Many (though not all) get better. Maybe the treatment worked – or perhaps there was some other reason that they got better. What alternative explanations can you think of?

Task 3.3.4 Down with Milk   C

It was noted in the 1930s that cancer levels were much higher in England than in Japan. Medical experts also observed that, at that time, much more milk was drunk in England than Japan. They concluded that that milk was a likely cause of cancer.

Note down any alternative explanations.

Task 3.3.5 Blaming the Parents   C

In studies of the profile of drug addicts, certain psychoanalysts have argued that the parents of such people appear to be emotionally removed from their children. This has led to the conclusion that, where there is a poor emotional relationship between a child and its parents, the child is more likely to become a drug abuser.

What alternative explanations can you think of?

Task 3.3.6 Israeli Pilots   **C**

Israeli Air Force officers conducted an analysis of the effect of praise on their trainee pilots. They found that when they praised their performance after a mission, the trainees tended to perform worse on the subsequent mission. It was therefore recommended to the officers that they should criticise the trainees when they flew badly, but not praise them if they flew well.

What alternative explanations can you think of for the findings of this study?

Establishing Cause and Effect

This section has looked at the dangers of inferring a cause-and-effect relationship where none exists. The key point is that just because a statistical relationship can be observed between two variables, this does not prove that one has *caused* the other. There is always the possibility that some other factors – often referred to as *confounding variables* – have affected the outcomes without your being aware of it. However, it would be poor teaching to suggest to learners that no relationships are based on cause and effect just because causality is hard to prove conclusively.

Statisticians have traditionally taken one of two approaches to this issue. The first is to show that there is (or is not) a statistical relationship and then leave it to others to explain the exact mechanism. However, this is rather a unsatisfactory approach, as it leaves too many questions unresolved. The other, as was the case with research about smoking and health, is to conduct studies that would rule out different possible confounding factors. This can be done by ensuring that samples are chosen so that all other factors are kept fixed.

However, there is still the possibility that there are yet other confounding factors that have not been thought of, leading to the view that the link between smoking and ill-health has not been conclusively proved. This was a smokescreen behind which the influential tobacco lobby sheltered for many decades while, one by one, the possible confounding variables were researched and accounted for. Today, most sensible people take the view that there are no further factors that are worth considering and that the link between smoking and ill-health has been proved beyond all reasonable doubt.

Further discussion of this issue and the landmark study on smoking and health by Doll and Hill (1954) are provided in Section 7.3.

3.4 REGRESSION AND CORRELATION

Regression

Unlike in mathematics, where relationships tend to be clearly defined and unambiguous, statistical relationships tend to reflect the general messiness of the real world from which the data were drawn. To take a simple example, the height and weight data given in Section 3.1 could be plotted in the form of a scatter plot to give the pattern opposite (see Figure 3.1).

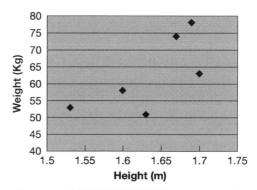

Figure 3.1 **A SCATTER PLOT OF HEIGHT AND WEIGHT**

A common practice in statistics is to use paired data in the form of a scatter plot to help visualise the nature of the relationship in general between, say, height and weight. There is not a very clear pattern here but, in general, weight increases as height increases. Regression, as the term is used in statistics, is the procedure of fitting a trend line or curve to a scatter of points in such a way that it best describes the general nature of the relationship − in this case, between height and weight.

The choice of whether the best function to choose is linear, quadratic or something else is often referred to in this context as modelling or choosing a suitable regression model. The best regression model to choose to describe the relationship between height and weight may well be linear (a straight line). Having made the choice of which model to use (linear), the technical side of regression is to work out where the best-fit line is, either visually by drawing it in by eye or algebraically by finding its equation.

Suppose, on the other hand, you were carrying out a scientific experiment to establish the nature of the relationship between the time of a pendulum's swing (T) and the pendulum length (L). The experimental data will show a non-linear pattern. Due to the inaccuracies of measurement, it will not be immediately obvious to learners what the underlying model is and they may need help to see that the underlying model is of the form $T = kL^{0.5}$.

Making Predictions

The regression line is useful because it allows predictions to be made about the response variable corresponding to particular values of the explanatory variable of your own choosing. *Interpolation* is the term given to predictions made within the known range of data. *Extrapolation* requires extending the regression line beyond this range in order to make the predictions. Clearly, there are dangers in extrapolation, as it cannot be certain that the regression trend will continue in the same manner for values beyond the known range.

These are ideas that you will look at more closely in later chapters, particularly Chapters 7, 11 and 14.

Task 3.4.1 Meanings of Regression   C

Outside the world of statistics lessons, the term 'regression' is generally taken to mean 'returning to some more primitive state'. For example, a child may be said to have regressed, if she returns to eating with her fingers after having successfully been taught to use a knife and fork.

Can you relate this use of the term 'regression' to the idea of statistical regression?

Regression to the Mean

'Regression to the mean' describes a natural phenomenon whereby, after a short period of success, things tend to return to normal immediately afterwards. This notion applies particularly to random events. For example, suppose that you were to roll an ordinary die, and it came up 5. If you were to roll the die again, its outcome would be independent of the outcome on the first roll. However, the chances are that the next roll will be lower than 5. This does not mean that you have lost your magic touch, but merely that the '5' was a hard act to follow.

To take another example, imagine that two extremely tall parents had a son, Brian. By virtue of his genetic inheritance, you might expect Brian to be taller than the average person. However, because his father was exceptionally tall and there is an element of chance in people's stature, Brian's height will tend to regress to the mean and he is likely to end up shorter than his father, but still be well above average height.

Now apply this principle to the Israeli trainee pilots in Task 3.3.6. Suppose that their performance from one mission to the next contained a large random component. When a trainee performed exceptionally well on a particular mission (and gained praise from his officers), it is in the nature of random variation that his performance next time may be less good. His poorer performance was not as a result of the praise, but merely due to a natural regression to the mean.

Here is another example of regression to the mean in a sporting context. Justin Rose is a successful British golfer who turned professional in 1999, after an exceptionally successful year as an amateur. His first year as a professional was a disappointment and the source of much media speculation (he was spoiled by success, he had lost his 'bottle', there were problems in his private life, and so on). In fact, no such explanation was necessary. Given that chance always plays a part in a golfer's performances, he had probably enjoyed a particularly favourable run of luck during his last year as an amateur player and his luck simply 'regressed to the mean' during the following year.

The same phenomenon can be applied to all sporting events, particularly where there is a strong element of chance such as golf or soccer. In sports such as tennis or snooker, where there are many more scoring opportunities, there is not such a dependency on chance – in these sports, sudden boosts or dips in form are less common, leaving newshounds with less scope for filling their column inches with speculative explanations for what is mostly just natural variation.

Of course, it is sometimes the case that a player or team really does start playing poorly. How, then, can you distinguish a result that shows regression to the mean from a genuine change for the worse? One answer to this is to take a longer-term view. In other words, do not just compare recent poor performance with the good run that immediately preceded it, but choose a larger sample of past experience against which to make comparisons.

Correlation

Whereas regression is about attempting to specify the underlying relationship that summarises a set of paired data, correlation is about assessing the strength of that relationship. Where there is a very close match between the scatter of points and the regression line, correlation is said to be 'strong' or 'high'. Where the points are widely scattered, the correlation is said to be 'weak ' or 'low'.

Spurious Correlation

Where correlation exists, it is tempting to assume that one of the factors has *caused* the changes in the other (that is, that there is a cause-and-effect relationship between them). Although this may be true, often it is not. When an unwarranted or incorrect assumption is made about cause and effect, this is referred to as *spurious correlation* and many examples were provided in Section 3.3.

Task 3.4.2 Reasons for Claiming Spurious Correlation   **C**

When a cause-and-effect relationship is assumed, attempts should always be made to seek out other explanations for why such a pattern might exist. Look through the examples in Section 3.3 and try to list several possible generic types of alternative explanation.

3.5 PEDAGOGY

As in the final section of previous chapters, this section looks at teaching and learning issues, based on many of the PTT themes. The section ends with a brief discussion of an important educational philosophy, constructivism.

Language Patterns

Task 3.5.1 Words   **C**

Make a note of the key statistical words and phrases that were used in this chapter. With a particular learner or group of learners in mind, choose two of these terms and plan how you might help your chosen learner(s) to gain a better understanding of them.

Imagery

A helpful picture can often get an idea across more quickly and effectively than a detailed verbal explanation. For example, the following series of diagrams might help clarify for learners the different possibilities in terms of deciding which is the cause and which the effect in the fire-engine example (Task 3.3.1).

(The arrow represents 'cause(s)'.)
(a) Fire engines $\longrightarrow$ Fires
(b) Fires $\longrightarrow$ Fire engines
(c) Population increases $\longrightarrow$ Fires
$\searrow$
Fire engines

Task 3.5.2 Visualising

Think back to another example from earlier in this chapter that you might like to use when working with a learner or learners. How might you use 'visualising' to clarify the key ideas?

Different Contexts

Task 3.5.3 Contexts   **C**

With a particular learner or group of learners in mind, make a note of a big idea of statistical thinking contained in this chapter, such as the notion of spurious correlation, and write down examples of everyday contexts that would illustrate or further enrich the topic for your learner(s).

Standard Misconceptions

Task 3.5.4 Misconceptions	C
Bearing in mind the content of this chapter and the particular learner(s) you have in mind, choose a topic that you think may be the basis of a learner misconception (or perhaps a 'partial conception'). Try to explain the misconception, why it may occur and how you might try to remedy it.	

Techniques and Methods

Task 3.5.5 Techniques	C
Bearing in mind the content of this chapter and the particular learner(s) you have in mind, choose a technique or method that you would like your learner(s) to master. Try to find an imaginative way of presenting it that you might not have used or thought of before.	

Constructivism

To end this section on pedagogic issues, attention turns to one of the most influential areas of educational philosophy in the past 20 years, constructivism, in order to consider what implications it has for teaching and learning statistics.

The roots of constructivism can be traced back to Jean Piaget's (1970) notion of genetic epistemology. Since then, it has taken different forms: Ernst von Glasersfeld (1984) introduced radical constructivism, which had its roots in psychology with its focus on the individual. Social constructivism, as the name suggests, is rooted in sociology, with an emphasis on social factors that affect learning.

The central idea underpinning constructivism concerns how learners learn. They are not, argue the constructivists, empty vessels into which the teacher pours knowledge. On the contrary, they suggest that learners construct their own knowledge and understanding, based on information that they already have and on new information that comes from various sources, including the teacher's input.

According to von Glasersfeld, learners adapt and adjust their understanding of the world as the world around them changes. The 'urge to know' therefore becomes the 'urge to fit' (in the sense of adapting to the environment), where learning and adaptation are seen as complementary. Based on this philosophical position, he argues that knowledge cannot be transferred directly from one person to another but, rather, must be built up by each individual learner.

So what are the implications of this idea for learning and teaching? As von Glasersfeld (1996) argues:

> Learners' answers and their solutions of problems should always be taken seriously. At the moment they are produced, they mostly make sense to the learner even if they are wrong from the teacher's point of view. Ask learners how they arrived at their answer. This helps to separate answers given to please the teacher from those that are the results of understandings or misunderstandings. (p. 25)

The statistics educator David Moore (1990) propounds what he and others refer to as 'naïve constructivism'. By this, he suggests that you tend to get a better understanding if you work at things yourself and integrate them into your existing knowledge. This sensible and down-to-earth view resonates with a phrase associated with the 1970s Nuffield Primary Mathematics Project, 'I do and I understand'. Such a view is linked to personal motivation and increased interest and enthusiasm due to 'ownership' of the learning by the learner.

For a useful summary of some of the key ideas of constructivism, read the short article by Nyaradzo Mvududu (2005) 'Constructivism in the statistics classroom: from theory to practice'. The author closes this readable article with the following comments:

> A constructivist-oriented teacher must be skilled in structuring the social climate of the classroom such that learners discuss, reflect on and make sense of statistics tasks. Statistics instructors need to (a) study how learners think about the particular statistical topics they teach and (b) work to understand their learners' thinking at a level deeper than everyday communication. (p. 52)

There is not space in this book to explore in detail the various forms of constructivism that have emerged in recent years. To keep things simple, you are asked to focus mainly on the core ideas suggested by David Moore. The challenges for you in statistics education are first to consider whether you subscribe to his views of learning and, if so, how they can be manifested in your teaching of statistics.

Task 3.5.6 Ownership   C

How can you organise your teaching in ways that give learners a stronger sense of personal motivation through ownership of their learning?

4 Uncertainty

> In the world nothing can be said to be certain except death and taxes.
> (Benjamin Franklin, 13 November 1789, letter to Jean-Baptiste Leroy)

A key feature of real-life decisions is that they involve uncertainty. Whether you are choosing your job, house, car or partner, you do not really know how things are going to turn out. Life's events tend to have not just one but two or more possible outcomes. One particular outcome may, in your judgement, be more likely than others, but you simply do not know which one will happen until 'after the event'. Of course, it is easy to have 20:20 hindsight, but before the event, as Descartes (1637, p. 2) advised, 'when it is not in our power to follow what is true, we ought to follow what is most probable'.

Section 4.1 looks at three ways of thinking about and measuring uncertainty – chance, odds and probability – as well as some theoretical perspectives on how probability can be understood. In Section 4.2, you are asked to test your intuition about a number of classic probability problems and paradoxes. Section 4.3 explores some common beliefs and superstitions about probability, while Section 4.4 considers several areas of misconception. As usual, the final section looks at issues of pedagogy.

4.1 CHANCE, ODDS AND PROBABILITY

Chance

Task 4.1.1 Words of Chance   **C**

(a) Here are four words or phrases used to describe degrees of uncertainty: 'fifty-fifty', 'likely', 'improbable', 'certain'. Sort them in order from least to most likely.

(b) Write down 10 or 12 different words or phrases used to describe degrees of uncertainty. Include them with the four above and sort them again in order from least to most likely.

(c) Make a note of terms that were difficult to separate. If this exercise were done by a number of people, which terms do you think they would agree on and which would cause some disagreement?

(d) Thinking back to the Stevens taxonomy introduced in Chapter 1, to which of the four measuring scales (nominal, ordinal, interval and ratio) would you classify words or phrases used to describe degrees of uncertainty?

(e) If you have time, use the internet to explore the derivation of some of these terms and phrases.

For the needs of most everyday situations that involve talking about chance events, words like 'likely' and 'improbable' are sufficient. However, sometimes greater precision is needed. It is when people are asked to map their understandings of these terms onto a number line that differences of opinion are revealed. This movement, from the language of uncertainty to some numerical measure, represents the shift from 'chance' to 'probability'.

Probabilities are conventionally measured on a number scale from 0 to 1, where 0 means impossible and 1 means certain.

Task 4.1.2 From Words to Numbers   C

(a) Take your list of chance terms that you sorted in Task 4.1.1 and allocate to each a numerical value in the range 0 to 1. You may find that this exercise causes you to rethink some of your original orderings.

(b) Draw a probability line as shown in Figure 4.1.

| 0 | 0.5 | 1 |

Figure 4.1 **A PROBABILITY LINE**

Label the terms from part (a) using the letters A, B, C, ... and then place them in their appropriate positions on your probability line.

(c) Did you find that the letters were evenly spaced across the probability line or were there clusters? How do you account for this pattern?

(d) Were there any other patterns in the placement of these terms?

Odds

Betting odds are a well-known but not well-understood way of quantifying chance. The odds attached to a particular runner or player (horse, dog, tennis player, and so on) are, roughly speaking, a measure of how likely punters think they are to win a particular race or contest. (It is, of course, more complicated than that, because bookmakers also build in some margin of profit into these numbers.)

The men's Tennis Masters Cup is an end-of-year event played by the top eight players on the Association of Tennis Professionals (ATP) tour.

Table 4.1 shows the odds that were offered in November 2004.

If you were to bet, say, £1 on Carlos Moya, then, were he to win, you would receive £101 (that is, your winnings of £100 plus your 'stake' of £1). Roger Federer is what is referred to as an 'odds-on' favourite. This term refers to odds that are so low (or 'short') that, if successful, your winnings will be less than the amount of your stake. Odds of 8/11 (often referred to as '11 to 8 on') mean that you must bet, say, £11 to win £8. 'Short odds' are offered on Roger Federer because he is the outstanding favourite. Gaudio and Coria are 'long odds' bets, otherwise known as 'long shots'. (As a footnote, Federer did win this competition. It was his twenty-third consecutive win against a top 10 opponent. He collected $1.52 million for a season total of $6.35 million – just short of Pete Sampras's all-time record of $6.5 million in 1997.)

TABLE 4.1 Tennis Masters Cup odds

Player	Odds
Federer, Roger	8/11
Safin, Marat	5
Roddick, Andy	5
Hewitt, Lleyton	10
Henman, Tim	50
Moya, Carlos	100
Gaudio, Gaston	250
Coria, Guillermo	250

Task 4.1.3 An 'Odds' Way of Thinking   C

(a) To convert odds to a probability, divide the amount bet by the total amount of the return if the bet is successful. Convert the eight odds listed in Table 4.1 into probabilities and add them together. How could this figure be used to compute an estimate of the probabilities of each player winning the competition?

(b) What are the implications of the use of odds for teaching? Do you think they should be introduced and, if so, how can they be linked to probabilities?

Task 4.1.4 Odds and Probability   C

Do the terms 'short odds' and 'low probability' refer to roughly the same degree of likelihood?

Subjective Probability

Bruno de Finetti (1906–85) was an Italian mathematician with interests in both psychology and economics. One of his many concerns was measuring subjective probability (the intuitive sense that people often have about the likelihoods of certain events occurring, when there are no clear objective measures available). In order to quantify people's intuitions, he devised what is known as de Finetti's game, in which the individual is asked to rate their intuitions against an imaginary lottery. For example, suppose that you wish to assess a friend's strength of belief that a particular soccer team (Team A) will win the World Cup. Ask her to choose one of two actions.

> *Either*
> (a) wait for the final to take place and you will give her £1 million if Team A wins;
> *or*
> (b) offer to draw, at random, a ball from a bag containing 50 red and 50 black counters. If you draw a black counter, you will give her £1 million.

Once your friend has made a choice between these two options, repeat the game with different odds in option (b) – depending on their first choice, reduce (or increase) the proportion of black counters to, say, 20% (or 80%). Continue adjusting option (b) until your friend feels indifferent between options (a) and (b), at which point you have a quantitative measure of her subjective probability. According to Amir Aczel (2005), it seems that most people do have well-defined, measurable intuitions about subjective probabilities, but they are not consciously aware of this. The benefit of playing de Finetti's game is to force people into being more aware of the factors that contribute to their judgements and to come up with a more precise quantification of their opinions.

Bayes's Theorem

While still on the theme of subjective probability, consider the contribution of the Reverend Thomas Bayes (1703–61). Bayes is known particularly for his work on subjective probability and Bayes's theorem is still very much discussed – and its significance challenged – by statisticians today. His theorem provides a way of applying quantitative reasoning when you are trying to choose among several alternative hypotheses. These are evaluated by deducing the consequences of each one, then conducting experimental tests to observe whether or not those consequences actually occur. If a hypothesis makes a prediction that does occur, it strengthens your belief in the truthfulness of the hypothesis. Conversely, an observation that contradicts the prediction would reduce your confidence in the hypothesis.

For example, Hypothesis A might predict that a certain outcome has a 20% chance of occurring, while Hypothesis B might predict a 50% chance of the same outcome. In these situations, the occurrence or non-occurrence of the outcome would shift your relative degree of belief from one hypothesis towards another. Bayes's theorem provides a way of calculating these 'degree of belief' adjustments.

In other words, Bayes's theorem enables you to calculate the probability of a particular hypothesis being true, given the actual outcome that occurs. This is the reverse of conventional ways of thinking about probability, where you start with a hypothesis and use it to calculate the probability of various outcomes occurring.

A practical area where Bayes's theorem has considerable application is in the justice system, where juries sometimes make judgements on the basis of faulty probabilistic reasoning. Robert Matthews (1994) provides an example of the case of Andrew Deen who, in 1990, was sentenced to jail for 16 years for raping three women. Based on DNA and blood-sample evidence, the jury was told that the probability of the samples having come from someone other than Deen was 1 in 3 million. However, this is not the same thing as saying that this was the (tiny) probability of Deen being innocent and Bayesian theory demonstrates the distinction between these statements.

As Matthews points out:

> In essence the theory as it relates to legal proceedings has two stages. The first stage involves calculating the value of the so-called likelihood ratio, a measure of the probabilities of getting specific evidence if the accused is innocent and if the accused is guilty. In the case of DNA evidence, this ratio is usually large and could run into millions. The next stage is to multiply the probability of the suspect being guilty before the discovery of the new evidence by the likelihood ratio. The result is the new probability of guilt, given this evidence.

> Therefore to assess the evidence properly, the jury would have needed to know the probability of Deen's guilt before the forensic evidence was given. If that prior probability of guilt was small – that is, if there is little other evidence to corroborate the forensic evidence – then even the impressive probabilities of genetic finger-printing can be dramatically diminished. (p. 12)

Bayes's theory can also help jurors to assess the weight to put on a confession by the accused. If they come to the conclusion that an innocent person is just as likely to 'crack' under police interrogation as a guilty one, then they would be wrong to take the confession as increasing the probability of guilt.

Theoretical and Empirical Probability

There are two additional views of probability, referred to as 'theoretical' and 'empirical' probability. Calculations of the likelihoods of various outcomes from rolling dice or tossing coins are often based on an understanding of the symmetries of the objects and therefore on knowing that 'in theory' all separate outcomes are equally likely. Such calculations are based on taking a 'theoretical' view of probability (Figure 4.2(a)).

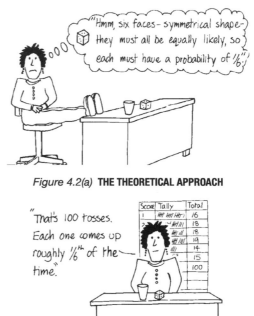

Figure 4.2(a) **THE THEORETICAL APPROACH**

The empirical approach (Figure 4.2(b)), as the name suggests, means actually rolling up your sleeves and rolling dice, tossing coins and spinning spinners. If you find that, for example, 100 tosses of a coin produced 54 heads, then the empirical probability of 'getting heads' would be 54/100, or 0.54.

4.2 INTUITION ABOUT PROBABILITY

Figure 4.2(b) **THE EMPIRICAL APPROACH**

> Intuition: that strange instinct that tells a woman she is right, whether she is or not.
>
> (Attributed to Oscar Wilde)

How well do you trust your intuition about situations involving probability? If you are like most people, the sensible answer might be, 'not much'. In this section, you are asked to tackle some questions and puzzles and see where your intuition leads you. Later, in Chapter 12, you will be guided through a number of computer and calculator simulations, in order to understand the solutions.

Jannie and Peter

Read the two accounts below about Jannie and Peter and then answer the questions in Task 4.2.1.

My next-door neighbour Jannie is a secondary school teacher. She is very interested in history and her idea of a perfect evening is to watch a television programme about archaeology.

Peter is 28, has always been keen on sport and is particularly fond of ball games. He also loves music and for the past seven years has worked hard developing his skills on the guitar.

Task 4.2.1 Jannie and Peter   C

(a) Is it more likely that Jannie teaches Classical Studies or English?

(b) Read the following statements about Peter and rank them in order of likelihood from least likely to most likely.

- Peter plays in a successful rock band.
- Peter is a member of a tennis club.
- Peter plays in a successful rock band and is a member of a tennis club.

(c) Are there more English words ending in '-ing' or words with 'n' as the penultimate letter?

Hospital Births

Task 4.2.2 Red Star Births   C

Imagine two hospitals, one large with an average of 45 births per day and a smaller one that averages only 15 births daily. Over a year, there are roughly equal numbers of boys and girls born in each hospital. In each hospital, a 'red star' day is when more than 60% of births that day are girls. Each hospital counts its number of red star days over a year.

Which of the following do you think is true:

- each hospital has roughly the same number of red star days;
- the larger hospital has more red star days than the small one;
- the smaller hospital has more red star days than the large one?

The Birthday Problem

Task 4.2.3 Shared Birthdays   C

(a) Imagine that you are in a room with lots of people. What is the smallest number of people in the room to be certain that at least two people share a birthday?

(b) Now imagine that there are 30 people in the room. Estimate the probability that at least two people in the group share a birthday.

The Monty Hall Dilemma

The so-called 'Monty Hall' dilemma was discussed in the popular 'Ask Marylin' question-and-answer column of the US magazine *Parade*, on 9 September 1990. The 'Marylin' in question calls herself Marylin vos Savant. It all started when a seemingly simple question from Craig. F. Whitaker of Columbia, MD, was published in her column.

Marylin's 'solution' to the problem caused an avalanche of correspondence, mostly from people who disagreed with her solution. In fact, many mathematicians, statisticians and others who should have known better got a lot of public egg on their faces as they rushed to print during 1991–92. Even the *New York Times* ran a front-page article about it (Tierney, 1991).

Some readers with access to computers ran computer simulations (www.cut-the-knot.org/hall.shtml) and finally the truth for this version of the problem was established and accepted. There are many Java applets freely available on the web running such simulations, such as: www.open.ac.uk/applets/Goingup.html and www.shodor.org/interactivate/activities/monty3/

In Chapter 12, you will be guided through such simulations, but for now, tackle the question as set out in Task 4.2.4.

Task 4.2.4 The Monty Hall Dilemma C

Here is the original problem as sent in by Craig. F. Whitaker. Try it now.

Suppose you are on a game show, and you are given the choice of three doors. Behind one door is a car, behind the others, goats. You pick a door, say number 1, and the host, who knows what is behind each door, opens another door, say number 3, which has a goat behind it. He says to you, 'Do you want to pick door number 2?' Is it to your advantage to switch your choice of doors?

4.3 LUCK OR JUDGEMENT?

Here is another telling story.

> The children were to be driven, as a special treat, to the sands at Jagborough. Nicholas was not to be of the party; he was in disgrace. Only that morning, he had refused to eat his wholesome bread-and-milk on the seemingly frivolous grounds that there was a frog in it. Older and wiser and better people had told him that there could not possibly be a frog in his bread-and-milk and that he was not to talk nonsense; he continued, nevertheless, to talk what seemed the veriest nonsense, and described with much detail the colouration and markings of the alleged frog. The dramatic part of the incident was that there really was a frog in Nicholas' basin of bread-and-milk; he had put it there himself, so he felt entitled to know something about it. (Munro, 1993, p. 325)

Probability is about making decisions under uncertainty − indeed, where there is no uncertainty, no decision is required, as you would simply choose the outcome that you know will occur. A 'good' or 'rational' decision favours the Cartesian principle that 'when it is not in our power to follow what is true, we ought to follow what is most probable'. Of course, rational decisions sometimes turn out to be wrong. That does not mean that the decisions were bad − they may have been the best choices, *given the information available at the time*. In the Munro extract above, the 'older and wiser and better people' made the best decision they could in the circumstances, but they were not in possession of the full facts.

In the long run, the vagaries of chance tend to even out, but in particular cases it can happen that the long shot comes in first. This is the corollary of a 'good' decision that has bad consequences − a 'bad' or 'irrational' decision that turns out to be right. People tend to take credit when their choices turn out to be successful ('I just felt lucky today' or 'I had a very good feeling about these numbers'), but remain silent or blame the situation when they are unsuccessful. As a novelist (as well as playwright, director, poet, essayist, painter, set designer and actor) Jean Cocteau is credited with saying, 'I believe in luck: how else can you explain the success of those you dislike?'

Task 4.3.1 Give Me Credit!   C

People sometimes refer to being guided by the stars or magnetic force fields or to having hunches. (As an aside, a 'hunch' is said to derive from the gambler's superstition that it is lucky to touch the curve of a hunchback.)

Make a note of some other ways that people (a) take credit for lucky successes and (b) make excuses for failures.

The phenomenon of giving significance to chance events is nicely captured by Garrison Keillor (1985) in the following extract:

> The stone plaque on the façade fell off one hot July afternoon, the plaque that reads CENTRAL BLDG. 1913, and crashed on the sidewalk, almost hitting Bud Mueller, who had just stopped and turned to walk the other way. If he hadn't, he would have been killed. He didn't know why he had turned. 'It was like something spoke to me right then,' he said. Others realized then that *they* had been on the verge of walking by the Central Building moments before and something had spoken to them. 'You know, I was thinking, "Maybe I will go to Skoglund's and purchase a pencil," but then something said, "No, you wait on that," so I didn't go. If I had gone, it would have killed me,' Mr. Berge said. He was one of many whose lives had been spared by a narrow margin. (p. 4)

Task 4.3.2 Your Turn

These sorts of anecdotes are useful resources for livening up a lesson. Find an example from your own experience, or from someone that you know, where credit was taken for a lucky success or excuses were made for a bad decision.

Superstitions

> Shallow men believe in luck. Strong men believe in cause and effect.
>
> (Attributed to Ralph Waldo Emerson, 1803–82)

The term 'superstition' tends to be used to describe a practice that is not believed in by the person referring to it. In their influential book about children's beliefs, the authors Iona and Peter Opie (1959) chose not to use the term 'superstition' with the children they interviewed, on the grounds that it would likely result in them mentioning only those practices that they did not believe in. They also feared that this would result in a devaluing of folklore and traditional customs. Instead, they used phrases such as 'magic practices' and 'ways of obtaining luck or avoiding bad luck'. They also coined the term 'half-belief', which helped allow the children some degree of ownership of a belief that they may have been shy about revealing to others. Alternatively, perhaps a better term than 'superstition' to use with adults or older children might be 'supernatural belief'.

Some superstitions fulfil a useful social purpose by instilling in children certain virtuous qualities such as tidiness, thrift, cleanliness and hard work.

Task 4.3.3 Virtuous Superstitions C

Find examples of two or three superstitions that seem to promote virtuous qualities.

Table 4.2 shows the extent to which, in 1988, American teenagers claimed to believe in supernatural phenomena.

TABLE 4.2 US teens' supernatural beliefs (in 1988)

	Male %	Female %	Ages 13–15	Ages 16–17
Angels	73	74	74	73
Astrology	53	64	60	56
ESP	54	46	47	54
Witchcraft	30	28	26	34
Bigfoot	33	11	22	24
Ghosts	28	16	19	25
Clairvoyance	24	19	15	30
Loch Ness Monster	22	10	16	16

Source: The Gallup Organisation, Inc., Princeton, NJ.

Task 4.3.4 Patterns of Belief C

Look at Table 4.2. What are the main features that stand out for you? How would you account for them?

Availability Error

People tend to give greater weight to the data that they have just been exposed to than other relevant data. This human characteristic is exploited by casinos where all heads turn to observe a win, as a result of the noisy clatter of coins in the metal tray of a fruit machine. At other times, when punters are losing, the machines maintain a steadfast silence. The same strategy is used in lotteries, where the organisers make great play of publicising the winners. Thus, evidence of 'being a winner' is more available to punters than 'being a loser', which hardly makes front-page news, as the (spoof) cutting opposite illustrates.

This phenomenon, where people give greater attention to recent or easily available data, is often referred to as an *availability error*.

Birmingham woman fails to win lottery

Mrs Denise O'Reilly, 41, of Acocks Green said yesterday, 'I've been playing the lottery on and off for about four years and I haven't won yet.' Her husband, Brian, 44, has had two premium bonds since 1990 and is still waiting! 'They've never been lucky at things like that', said friend and neighbour Anita Kelley (54).

4.4 (MIS-)CONCEPTIONS IN PROBABILITY

Why do coloured balls in urns, dice, coins and spinners feature so heavily in many statistics courses? The short answer is that these are *simple* random number generators with unambiguous equally likely outcomes. They permit the exploration of basic ideas of probability without the complications of context to confuse the learner. There may be 'better' contexts in which to introduce ideas of probability that provide stronger motivation for learners, but often they are difficult to model. For example the event, 'will it rain tomorrow?' has two outcomes, yes and no. But problems arise when it comes to assigning probabilities to these outcomes, as these will vary from situation to situation and from one person's opinion to another. Also, the mathematics of 'rain tomorrow?' is complicated by the fact that the two outcomes ('rain' and 'not rain') are not of equal likelihood. Contrast this with a symmetrical, two-faced coin or six-faced die, where the outcomes are unambiguous and equally likely.

This mismatch between the neat world of probability models and the messiness of chance events in the everyday world may have contributed to a common misconception that where there are, say, two outcomes, they are *always* equally likely. ('I've got a fifty-fifty chance of passing my driving test, because there are only two possibilities, "pass" and "fail".')

Dice

There are many misconceptions in probability held by both children and adults. Here are just four claims in the mathematics of rolling a die:

- a six is hardest to get;
- if you roll the die gently, you will get a low score and if you roll hard, you will get a high score;
- blowing on the die makes the desired outcome more likely;
- if you get a six on the first throw, you are less likely to get a six on the next throw.

Task 4.4.1 Is it True?   C

(a) Choose one of the four claims above and devise a way of testing whether or not it is true.

(b) Can you account for why someone should subscribe to some of these beliefs?

The Gambler's Fallacy

At the time of writing, according to the UK lottery website (lottery.co.uk), the lottery number that has come up most often is 38 (with 142 occurrences), while the least commonly occurring number is 20 (with only 90 occurrences). How might this information affect your choice of lottery number next time you buy a ticket? One response might be to say that 38 is clearly a 'good bet', so it is worth including in your choice of six numbers. Alternatively, you could take the opposite view and argue that 20 is overdue and so it is a good bet. As it happens, both views are bunkum, as in each case you are committing the gambler's fallacy.

For each of the 49 numbers available, the odds are always the same, no matter which numbers have been selected in the past. This fallacy is commonly committed by gamblers who, for example, bet on black at roulette when red has come up three times in a row. The chances of black or red coming up next are the same regardless of which of the two colours have come up in previous turns. The underlying idea here is *independence* of events. Unless the random number generator is biased, or someone is being dishonest, all outcomes are independent of what has gone on before.

Task 4.4.2 The Lottery *is* Biased   **C**

Suppose a learner remarks, 'You say that the odds for each of the 49 numbers coming up are the same but you can't prove that. The fact that number 38 has come up much more often than number 20 proves the exact opposite.' How would you respond to this learner?

People sometimes appeal to the 'law of averages' to justify their faith in the gambler's fallacy. They may reason that, since all outcomes are equally likely, in the long run they will come out roughly equal in frequency. However, the next throw is very much in the short run and the coin, die or roulette wheel has no memory of what went before.

Clever Hans

Often people are faced with events that appear to challenge the basic laws of science and the rules of normal human experience. While wishing to allow for the possibilities of new ideas, a healthy scepticism is an initial sensible response to such claims. Two useful questions to pose in this context are:

- What is the causal mechanism? For example, how might an astrologer explain how the gravitational attraction of the planets at the time of one's birth affects one's personality (bearing in mind that the gravitational pull of the delivering mid-wife far outweighs that of distant planets).
- What alternative explanations are there?

The following story of Clever Hans is an account of how such questions were used in investigating the case of an equine genius.

> Wilhelm Von-Osten was a Russian Aristocrat who, during the late 19th century, owned a stallion that became famous for its mathematical prowess. Using an abacus and a blackboard, he schooled the horse in basic arithmetic, rewarding it with a bite of carrot when it gave the correct answers to his questions. The horse (Clever Hans) emerged as an equine genius, eagerly tapping out with his hoof the correct solutions to problems. Some people looked upon it as a hoax, but Von-Osten remained unshaken in his belief that Hans was an equine genius.

> On 6th September 1904, a commission of thirteen people from a variety of backgrounds visited Von-Osten's stable yard. The dignitaries were both amazed and unable to detect the slightest sign of fraud, or even involuntary cueing on the part of Von-Osten.

> Later, a scientist called Oskar Pfungst devised a series of tests designed to explore the limits of Clever Hans's understanding of arithmetic and language. His experiment confirmed that Hans was indeed clever, but not in the way his master had believed. Pfungst discovered that the horse could not give correct

answers if Von-Osten did not know the solution. He concluded that Von-Osten was unwittingly supplying the answers to Clever Hans. The question was, how?

Further research revealed that Von-Osten was 'controlling' the horse's counting behaviour by almost imperceptible alterations in his own body posture. During the training period, the horse had learned to paw the ground when Von-Osten's head inclined slightly forward to get a better view of the hoof. In anticipation of the correct 'answer', he unconsciously tended to straighten himself and that was the cue the horse took to stop. Pfungst found that even a slight elevation of Von-Osten's eye-brows or a subtle flaring of his nostrils were sufficient to halt the counting. Von-Osten died in 1909, bitter and disillusioned.

(Adapted from www.dogtraining.co.uk/hans.htm)

4.5 PEDAGOGY

As usual, this final section looks at teaching and learning issues based on five of the six PTT themes.

Language Patterns

Because life is uncertain, the language of chance is securely placed within most cultures. Most people are interested in these matters, and chance events in their real world can be a good starting point for learners to learn about probability. Gambling and games of chance are also useful but, as has been mentioned earlier in this chapter, for religious or moral reasons, not all teachers or parents wish to appear to endorse gambling by including these ideas in classroom tasks.

Nevertheless, the vocabulary of uncertainty can be a rich starting point for teaching this topic.

Task 4.5.1 Words	C
Section 4.1 looked at some of the words used to describe chance. Carry out a survey with several learners, where you ask them to attach numerical probabilities to various terms used to describe chance. Then look at the location and spread of the numerical measures of each word – which terms are used precisely and which more loosely?	

Imagery

Task 4.5.2 Visualising	C
Think back to an example from earlier in this chapter that you might like to use when working with another learner or learners. How might you use 'visualising' to clarify the key ideas?	

Different Contexts

Now read this tall tale about Uncle Jim.

Uncle Jim hated flying. No matter how safe people told him it was, he was always worried that someone would have a bomb on the plane. His family doctor was little help so, in desperation, he visited a statistician.

'Tell me,' he asked, 'what are the chances that someone will have a bomb on a plane?'

The statistician looked through her tables and said, 'A very small chance. Maybe one in a hundred thousand.'

'So what are the odds of two people having a bomb on the same plane?'

'Extremely remote,' she replied. 'About one in ten billion.'

Uncle Jim nodded and left her office.

And from that day on, every time he flew, he took a bomb with him.

Task 4.5.3 Telling Tall Tales

Above is a 'tall tale' on the theme of 'Independence and the Gambler's Error'. Rewrite the story to make the same point, using a context that would be attractive to your learners.

Standard Misconceptions

One learner was asked to imagine tossing a drawing pin in the air 20 times, recording how often it came up on its side and how often on its back, pointing up. Note that, typically, around 60% of drawing pins land on their backs. The learner predicted that, since there were only two ways it could land, he would expect them to be about fifty-fifty.

Random number generators do not always need to be symmetrical. This misconception of assuming equal likelihood for each outcome is fostered in a restricted learning environment, where learners see only such situations (that is, dice, coins and spinners). It is therefore very important for learners to be aware of situations where the different outcomes are not equally likely (as with the drawing-pins example).

Task 4.5.4 Misconceptions

Bearing in mind the content of this chapter and the particular learner(s) you have in mind, choose a topic that you think may be the basis of a learner misconception (or perhaps a 'partial conception'). Try to explain the misconception, why it may occur and how you might try to remedy it.

Techniques and Methods

Task 4.5.5 Techniques   C

In addition to drawing pins, think up some other simple examples where learners would find it easy to carry out experiments, but where the outcomes were not equally likely or predictable in advance.

Introduction to Block 2

Just as Block 1 looked at how statistical ideas can be expressed using words and numbers, attention turns in Block 2 to doing the same job with pictures. As was the case for the previous block, the four block chapters deal in turn with describing, comparing, interrelating and uncertainty.

The statistical 'big ideas' addressed include the contribution of John Tukey to the development of an intuitive and pictorial way of interpreting data known as Exploratory Data Analysis (EDA). This approach encourages the picturing of data as a way of helping learners to make statistical decisions. You will see how probability models can inform these sorts of questions. You will also look at some 'real-world' statistical investigations such as the question of whether female athletes will ever out-sprint men and a classic study from the 1950s which investigated the link between smoking and health.

Teaching ideas include the use of 'people graphs', where learners create data pictures based on where they choose to stand, an investigation on distinguishing authorship and a suggestion for a class project on constructing cheating charts. Once again, throughout the block, use is made of the four-stage framework for tackling statistical investigations.

5 Describing with Pictures

In Block 2 of this book (Chapters 5 to 8), you will see some of the ways in which pictures (graphs and charts) can provide insights not easily discernible from the data alone. Section 5.1 looks at some of the historical examples of charts contained in books by Edward Tufte. Section 5.2 considers when and why bar charts and pie charts can be used to portray information, while histograms are discussed in Section 5.3. Section 5.4 looks at the statistical contribution of Florence Nightingale, and in particular her invention of a chart that she called a *coxcomb*. As usual, the chapter ends by considering teaching and learning issues.

5.1 EDWARD R. TUFTE

Edward Tufte is an author and former Professor at Yale University, where he taught courses in statistical evidence and information design. His website is: www.edwardtufte.com

He is best known for two beautiful books, entitled *The Visual Display of Quantitative Information* (2001) and *Envisioning Information* (1990). Not only have Tufte's ideas on visual design influenced the choices that people make when creating maps, diagrams or graphs, but his publications comprise a fascinating historical record of the development of maps and pictures. In this section, you will explore some of these historical examples.

Time Series Plots

A key contributor to the early development of graphs and diagrams was William Playfair (1759–1823), not to be confused with the Scottish architect, William Henry Playfair (1789–1857). Our Playfair was a Scottish political economist who is considered one of the great inventors of statistical graphics. Playfair's book *Commerical and Political Atlas*, published in 1786, contained 44 charts, all but one of which were time series plots. These are graphs depicting how a particular variable (perhaps sales, population or, in the example in Figure 5.1, the balance of trade) changes over time. The term 'time series' means, literally, 'a graphic showing how a series of values are changing over time'.

Prior to Playfair's charts and graphs, statistical information was normally displayed in tables. Of tables, Playfair (1786) wrote:

> a man who has carefully investigated a printed table, finds, when done, that he has only a very faint and partial idea of what he has read; and that like a figure imprinted on the sand, is soon totally erased and defaced. (Quoted in Tufte, 2001 p. 32)

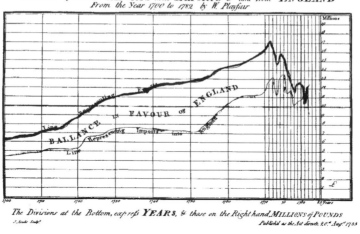

Figure 5.1 **ENGLAND'S BALANCE OF TRADE**

Source: Tufte (2001, p. 32)

Even in the eighteenth century, he acknowledged that people were suspicious of the potential of graphs for distorting the truth:

> As to the propriety and justness of representing sums of money, and time, by parts of space, tho' very readily agreed to by most men, yet a few seem to apprehend that there may possibly be some deception to it, of which they are not aware. (Quoted in Tufte, 2001 p. 52)

There is not space here to do justice to Playfair's contribution to statistical graphs. The issue of the potential of graphs and charts to distort information, whether deliberately or unintentionally, will be taken up in Chapter 7.

A Multi-Variable Chart

In *The Visual Display of Quantitative Information*, Tufte shows a classic chart by Charles Joseph Minard (1781–1870), which he refers to as 'probably the best statistical graphic ever drawn' (Figure 5.2). It is a combined map, graph and chart that documents the losses suffered by Napoleon's army in the disastrous Russian campaign of 1812.

Beginning in June 1812 at the Polish–Russian border (on the left side of Figure 5.2) with 422 000 men, the paler band shows the army's outward journey east. The thickness of the band shows the size of the army at each stage. The path of Napoleon's retreat from Moscow (which began in October 1812) in the bitterly cold winter is depicted by the dark lower band, which is linked to temperature and time scales (shown at the bottom of Figure 5.2). In the disastrous crossing of the River Berezina during the retreat, nearly half (22 000) of the remaining 50 000 men perished. The army finally returned to Poland with only 10 000 men, just over 2% of the number who set out.

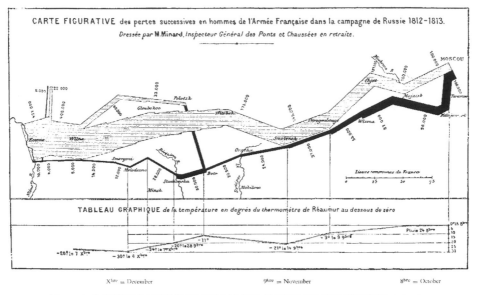

Figure 5.2 **MINARD'S FIGURATIVE CHART OF NAPOLEON'S RUSSIAN CAMPAIGN 1812–13**
Source: Tufte (2001, p. 41).

Task 5.1.1 Interrogating the Map   **C**

(a) There are six variables depicted here. How many can you spot?

(b) What, for you, is the main impact of this chart?

(c) Minard's chart has been used to suggest that Napoleon's army froze to death during the fierce Russian winter. What evidence is there for this here?

Dot Map

Figure 5.3 is another chart given by Tufte that is of great historical significance. It is the 'dot map' created by Dr John Snow to investigate patterns of infection during the cholera epidemic in London of 1854.

Using only written accounts of the locations of the deaths, no clear patterns were discernible about where they were taking place and, consequently, there was no information about what might be the possible cause. Snow's moment of insight was to mark dots to show the locations of the deaths on a map of the worst affected area and crosses to indicate the locations of the water pumps.

Task 5.1.2 Cholera Patterns   **C**

The fact that Snow marked the location of the pumps on the map indicates that he suspected these to be a major part of the problem. Study the map and try to decide which of the pumps looks most likely to be implicated in spreading the epidemic.

In researching ideas for this book, a number of members of the public were asked to record anecdotes that involved the use of statistical ideas. Here is an example from a manager of a Health and Fitness Club in the English Midlands.

Figure 5.3 **A DOT MAP OF CHOLERA INFECTION**

Source: Tufte (2001, p. 24).

Whenever an accident occurs in the gym or pool, it is logged into the incident book. Over a period of some weeks, there seemed to be a larger than expected number of falls around the pool. I decided to log not only the fact of the incident, but also where the fall occurred. When the locations of the falls were marked on a map, they clearly clustered around one particular section of the poolside. Further enquiries revealed why – the cleaners' equipment did not stretch all around the pool. They cleaned as far as they could in both directions, but this left a short section that remained greasy. The problem was solved by providing the cleaners with a longer extension lead.

Task 5.1.3 Your Own Picture

Make a note of any situation where you had direct experience of a map or picture providing an insight that would not otherwise have been possible.

To end this section, here is a selection of some of the key features of a well-designed statistical graphic as set out by Tufte. It should:

- use position to represent numbers;
- show the data fairly;
- encourage the eye to compare different pieces of data;
- be able to reveal both the broad overview and the fine detail.

Particularly within the school context, this final feature is worth considering further. Clearly there is a degree of conflict between the desire to see the big and the small picture. In most situations involving graphs, the broad detail is the more important aspect, particularly where it is possible to return to the original data should you need to check something in the fine detail.

5.2 PIE CHARTS AND BAR CHARTS

Used imaginatively and sensibly, a graph can really bring data to life. For example, here are some dry, dusty facts about Australian aboriginals and later settlers to Australia.

- It is estimated that aboriginals have lived in Australia for at least 60 000 years.
- European settlers have been there since Captain Cook first visited it in 1770.
- Some 2.2% of the Australian population identified themselves as being of aboriginal origin in the 2001 census.

Representing the first two facts on a time line produces the graphic in Figure 5.4.

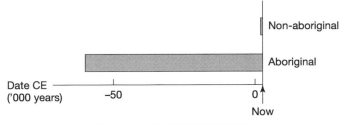

Figure 5.4 **AUSTRALIAN TIME LINE**

This graphic is like a horizontal bar chart, except for the fact that the bars are right-aligned rather than having the usual left-alignment. The graph really gets across the point that the aboriginals lived in Australia undisturbed by Europeans for 99.5% of their time there. In fact, the non-aboriginal bar is barely visible when placed alongside the era of the aboriginal people alone. It is worth emphasising that this chart does not show the relative sizes of the two populations, but only their existence along a time line.

Comparison by size could be represented using a pie chart as shown in Figure 5.5. This shows vividly the tiny proportion of the Australian population that are, today, of aboriginal origin. A bar chart, with either vertical or horizontal bars indicating the aboriginal and non-aboriginal percentages, could also be used to depict this information.

Note, however, that a pie chart would be quite inappropriate as a way of representing the comparative lengths of time that the two groups have lived on the continent. A pie chart can only be meaningfully used to represent distinct parts of a whole. If a

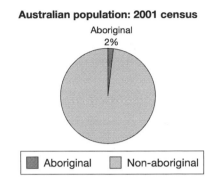

Figure 5.5 **A PIE CHART OF THE AUSTRALIAN POPULATION**

pie chart were drawn with an aboriginal sector representing 60 000 years and a non-aboriginal sector representing (2 000 − 1700) = 300 years, it would imply that they were somehow sharing a total of 60 300 years, as well as having no overlap, which is clearly nonsense!

A good rule of thumb for checking the validity of a pie chart is to ask what the whole pie represents. The one in Figure 5.5 is valid, because the whole pie represents the whole Australian population and the sectors show the slices of the pie (percentages of the population) corresponding to the aboriginals and the non-aboriginals.

Pie Charts

Look at the data in Table 5.1 and focus on the first and third columns ('Year' and 'Mean female age of first marriage'). Think about how to represent this information as a pie chart. Then undertake Task 5.2.2.

TABLE 5.1 Marriage and divorce data in England and Wales (mean age, years)

| | First marriage | | Divorce | |
	Males	Females	Males	Females
1971	24.6	22.6	39.4	36.8
1981	25.4	23.1	37.7	35.2
1991	27.5	25.5	38.6	36.0
2001	30.6	28.4	41.5	39.1

Source: Social Trends, 34 (2004 edition), table 2.12.

This pie chart is quite pretty (and could look even prettier in colour), but is actually totally useless as a way of presenting these figures. Lumping these four sectors together has produced a complete pie that means nothing − the whole point of using a pie chart is to show how the 'whole' subdivides into its component parts.

Pie charts are rarely useful for depicting numerical data. They should be reserved for categorical data (or 'nominal' measures, using the Stevens terminology that was introduced in Chapter 1). Also, arranging 'Year' in a circular manner around the circumference of the pie is not helpful, as it makes comparisons difficult − time in years is linear and should be arranged on a straight line.

Task 5.2.2 Crusty Pie   **C**

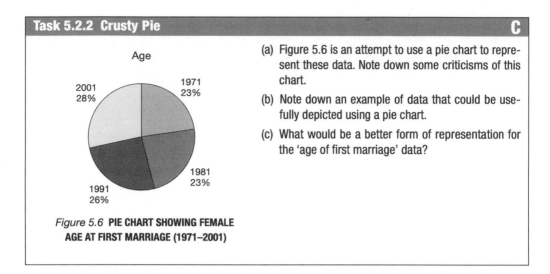

(a) Figure 5.6 is an attempt to use a pie chart to represent these data. Note down some criticisms of this chart.

(b) Note down an example of data that could be usefully depicted using a pie chart.

(c) What would be a better form of representation for the 'age of first marriage' data?

Figure 5.6 **PIE CHART SHOWING FEMALE AGE AT FIRST MARRIAGE (1971–2001)**

Pie charts would be suitable for depicting categorical data such as hair or eye colour, ethnic group, favourite school subject, marital status, and so on. As a general rule, it is conventional to draw the first slice of the pie from 12 o'clock and the slices are then arranged clockwise. Where data are ordinal, the slices should retain their natural order on the pie. For nominal data, where order does not matter, the pie chart is easier to read if the slices are ordered by size, from largest to smallest. You will get a chance to look at some of these issues again in Block 3 (Chapters 9–12), when you will be asked to use ICT to experiment with graphs and charts.

Bar Charts

Task 5.2.3 Bar Chart to the Rescue   **C**

Make a sketch of the 'female age at first marriage' data as a bar chart.

For these data, the bar chart solves both of the problems identified with the pie chart. First, there is no implication that the four bars taken together form any coherent whole. Second, presenting them in a linear manner on the horizontal scale makes comparison (based on the relative heights of the bars) easy.

Another example where it would be appropriate to use a bar chart to depict discrete numerical data would be to show the frequencies of getting 1, 2, 3, 4, 5 and 6 on, say, 30 rolls of a die.

5.3 HISTOGRAMS

Use of a histogram should be strictly reserved for continuous numerical data or for data that can be effectively modelled as continuous, such as wages in £. Unlike bar charts, therefore, the bars of a histogram corresponding to adjacent intervals should not have gaps between them, for obvious reasons. Figure 5.7 comprises two examples of well-constructed histograms.

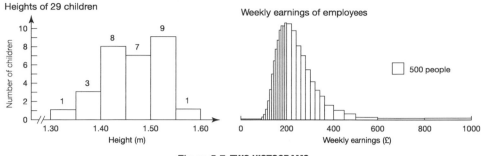

Figure 5.7 **TWO HISTOGRAMS**

Task 5.3.1 Say What You See

Look closely at the two examples in Figure 5.7 and note any differences in the way they have been presented.

There is a vertical scale on the first histogram, but not on the second. Also, in the first example, the frequencies of each interval are marked above the corresponding bars. These features are appropriate with the first histogram, because the interval widths are all equal and therefore the frequencies are directly comparable by means of the heights of the bars. Contrast this with the earnings example, where there is a great deal of variation in the interval widths used. In this latter case, the heights of each bar are not directly comparable. Instead, a key is provided to show what *area* of the histogram corresponds to 500 people.

When it comes to drawing a picture of continuous data, you need to think through carefully where one interval ends and the next one begins. Failing to do this can result in overlaps or gaps between adjacent intervals, which can cause confusion. However, this is a situation where common sense should prevail. For example, to take the earnings histogram in Figure 5.7, if salaries are typically given in thousands of pounds, the exact positions of the boundaries can be rounded to the nearest £1, £10 or £100. The main thing is that the drawing should convey the correct *impression* without being too fussy.

Look at the population data in Table 5.2 and then tackle Task 5.3.2.

TABLE 5.2 Population by age and sex (UK, percentages)

	Under 16	16–24	25–34	35–44	45–54	55–64	65–74	75 and over	All ages (=100%) (millions)
Males									
1971	27	14	13	12	12	11	7	3	27.2
1981	23	15	15	12	11	11	8	4	27.4
1991	21	14	16	14	12	10	8	5	27.9
2001	21	11	15	15	13	11	8	6	28.8
2002	21	12	14	15	13	11	8	6	28.9
2011	19	12	13	14	14	12	9	7	29.5
2021	19	11	13	12	13	13	10	8	30.3

TABLE 5.2 Continued

Females									
1971	24	13	12	11	12	12	10	6	28.8
1981	21	14	14	12	11	11	10	8	28.9
1991	19	13	15	13	11	10	9	9	29.5
2001	19	11	14	15	13	11	9	9	30.2
2002	19	11	14	15	13	11	9	9	30.3
2011	17	11	13	14	14	12	9	9	31.0
2021	17	10	13	12	13	13	11	10	32.1

Source: *Social Trends*, 34 (2004 edition), Table 1.2.

Task 5.3.2 Making Sense of the Data

Spend a few minutes looking at these data and try to make sense of them – knowing what the data represent is an essential first step to graphing them.

Key points to notice are:

- the first column shows the dates at which the populations are measured or predicted;
- columns 2 to 9 show the percentage of the male or female population that fall into the various age intervals (under 16, 16–24, and so on);
- the final column shows the actual or predicted size of the male and female populations for each year – this is the base from which all the percentages in the columns to the left have been calculated. To take the first row as an example, there were 27.2 million males in the UK, 27% of whom were under 16 years of age.

Task 5.3.3 Marking the intervals   C

Focus on just a single line of Table 5.2 – corresponding to males in 1971. Using the continuous age line below, mark on it the eight intervals: 'under 16', 16–24', and so on.

Write above each mark the numerical value of its exact location.

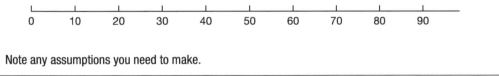

Note any assumptions you need to make.

Having sorted out details of where the intervals fall, the next stage is actually to draw the 1971 male data as a histogram. A first attempt has been made in Figure 5.8. (There is a strong hint from the caption that there is room for improvement with this first attempt.) Look at it carefully and then carry out Task 5.3.4.

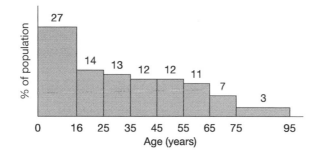

Figure 5.8 **DODGY HISTOGRAM BASED ON THE POPULATION DATA**

Task 5.3.4 Dodgy Histogram

Can you spot the 'deliberate mistake' in the drawing of this histogram? How could it be corrected?

The main problem is that columns have been drawn so that the percentages corresponding to each interval are proportional to the *heights* of the columns, rather than to the areas. When people look at graphs like these, it is to the height of each column that their eyes are naturally drawn. As you already know from Task 5.3.3, the interval widths are not all equal. In order to ensure a fair comparison based on area of the columns, rather than height, the wider columns should be scaled down in height and the narrower columns scaled up. This can be done using the following two steps:

- identify a convenient basic interval for each column (say, 10 years) as a basis of comparison for all the intervals;
- for each interval in turn, calculate the percentage of the population falling into a 10-year portion of this interval – this calculation gives the required height of each column. To take an example, the first column (containing 27% of the population) has an interval of 16 years. You would expect the percentage of the population falling into a 10-year portion of this interval to be (10/16) × 27 or roughly 17. So, this is a measure of the correct height to which the first interval should be drawn.

Task 5.3.5 Corrected Histogram   C

Based on the suggestions above, recalculate the correct heights of each column of the histogram and redraw it correctly.

5.4 FLORENCE NIGHTINGALE (1820–1910)

Florence Nightingale's story is usually portrayed as one woman's crusade to improve the quality of life of ordinary soldiers who were dying, needlessly, in their thousands in Scutari during the Crimean War. But she also needed to convince the authorities of the full extent of the scandal of military medical care and encourage them to be prepared to make fundamental changes in the supply of essential medical facilities and to improve the basic hygiene and diet of soldiers in hospital.

She had some useful weapons at her disposal. First, she came from a wealthy upper-class family that moved in the highest echelons of Victorian society. So, when she was denied the basic supplies and food that were needed, she could turn for support to influential friends like the then Secretary at War, Sidney Herbert. And she also had private means of her own, sometimes having to resort to bypassing the military bureaucracy by purchasing the supplies she needed out of her own pocket.

But Florence Nightingale's other weapon was that she was knowledgeable about statistics, and keen to exploit that knowledge. Indeed, she became a formidable and respected statistician, pioneering a number of original and imaginative measures and forms of graphical representation. She unleashed on a sceptical male military world an array of well-researched and clearly presented statistics which changed attitudes and allowed fundamental reforms to take place.

She kept and published a careful record of the causes of mortality in British military hospitals during the Crimean War (1854–56). For example, she showed that, in the single month of January 1855, 3168 soldiers died in British hospitals. Of these, 2889, or just over 90%, died of non-battle causes (mostly cholera and typhus). But she was not content simply with presenting these data as dry, impersonal numbers. She wanted them to make a real impact, particularly if they were to be understood by the statistically unsophisticated, that is, by just about everyone in the mid-nineteenth century. Table 5.3 shows the data (based on estimates) that she found so shocking.

TABLE 5.3 Florence Nightingale's data

Date	April 1854	May	June	July	Aug.	Sept.	Oct.	Nov.	Dec.	Jan. 1855	Feb.	Mar.
Battle	3	14	19	46	55	86	185	322	138	279	322	169
Non-Battle	28	24	12	396	863	795	367	597	1631	2889	1830	1118
Total	31	38	31	442	918	881	552	919	1769	3168	2152	1287

Task 5.4.1 Representing Mortality Levels

As you can see, the number of deaths from non-battle causes each month greatly outweighed the corresponding battle-related deaths. Find a way of representing these figures pictorially so that these differences are very clear, even to a statistical novice (a rough sketch will be sufficient).

Just as Minard's classic chart powerfully captured the loss of Napoleon's army, Nightingale's invention of a diagram that she called a 'coxcomb' (a kind of lace with an edging like a cock's comb) did likewise (Figure 5.9). Indeed, she published her coxcomb diagram along with the phrase, 'the loss of an army'. Today, this form of representation is known as a 'polar-area diagram'.

The area of each wedge of the diagram in Figure 5.9 is a measure of the extent of hospital deaths. Again, to increase the impact of the figures on her audience, largely composed of public figures who were untrained in statistical understanding, she devised a novel way of working it out as a mortality rate.

The number of deaths was given monthly and each month's figure was expressed as a percentage of the monthly average number of deaths, calculated over the 12 months of that year. For example, the monthly average number of non-battle deaths during 1854 was roughly 879. In January 1855, the actual number of non-battle deaths was 2889, which is 329%, as a percentage of the monthly average.

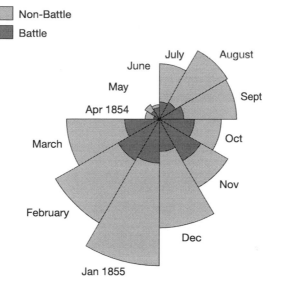

**Causes of Mortality in the Army in the East
April, 1854 to March 1855**

Non-Battle

Battle

From: F. Nightingale, 'Notes on Matters Affecting the Health, Efficiency and Hospital Adminstration of the British Army', 1855

Figure 5.9 **COXCOMB OR POLAR-AREA DIAGRAM**

Source: www.math.yorku.ca/SCS/Gallery/noframes.html

Task 5.4.2 Summarising the Coxcomb   **C**

(a) Spend a few minutes studying Figure 5.9 to gain an understanding of the patterns of death levels over this 12-month period.

(b) Bearing in mind some of the issues raised in Section 5.2, how successfully do you think Nightingale's diagram depicts these data to make the point that she wished to get across? In particular, do you feel that the circular arrangement is helpful?

The main success of this diagram is the (correct) use of area to depict numerical size. Also, the use of two concentric circles is a neat way of seeing two distributions at once.

There are some difficulties with the chart, however. First, it is not clear that the circular arrangement is helpful – although the months of the year are cyclic, that is not an important issue here and clearly there is nowhere to go after all 12 sectors are in place. Second, her choice to start in the 9 o'clock seems arbitrary and the modern convention of starting at 12 o'clock seems (at least to modern eyes) to be more natural. Finally, if her graph is designed to show the benefits of her hygiene reforms, it fails to do so because it stops before the results of these reforms took effect.

For comparison, Figure 5.10 shows the same data represented as a component bar chart.

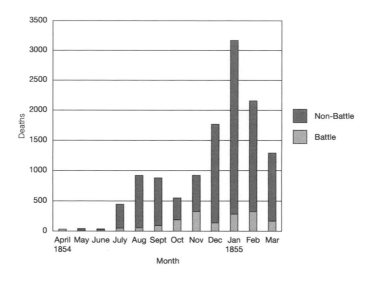

Figure 5.10 **NIGHTINGALE'S DATA REPRESENTED AS A COMPONENT BAR CHART**

Between October 1854 and January 1855, just three months later, the levels of mortality had increased by a factor of six. Her sanitary reforms went into operation in March 1855. By the late spring, mortality levels had dropped to something like one twentieth of the level a few months earlier.

In defiance of the military authorities, Florence Nightingale published data and analyses such as these. The statistical sections of her reports, normally relegated to dusty shelves, she printed off separately and circulated them to every Member of Parliament. It was the power of her data, combined with the intuitive simplicity of the calculations and graphical representations that she herself devised – as well, of course, as her political shrewdness – that brought these sorts of data, and the needless deaths they described, to life in the public consciousness.

Task 5.4.3 Investigating the Coxcomb   **C**

It is not a good idea to assume that a particular graph always provides a fair representation of the data. To test out the coxcomb, measure as accurately as you can with a ruler the radii of the October 1854 and January 1855 wedges of the coxcomb. Using a suitable calculation, check the claim above that these wedges show an increase in mortality by a factor of about six over this three-month period.

In fact, the coxcomb was Nightingale's second attempt at comparing areas in this way. The first, which she referred to as a 'bat's wing', was drawn such that the *length* of each radial line was proportional to the mortality levels. This was misleading, since the eye is naturally drawn to comparing areas. Nightingale recognised her error (after publication) and felt obliged to include an erratum note.

Florence Nightingale took the view that the ruling classes of Victorian England (both those in the military hierarchy and in government) were either unwilling or unable to see the truth about conditions in Scutari and elsewhere unless presented with irrefutable evidence. Her life's work as a statistician, therefore, centred around two key themes. First, she needed data that she could trust. The data had to be accurate, comprehensive and comparable between hospitals and between regions. This resulted in her long-running campaign to standardise hospital record-keeping. Second, she was aware that most of the decision-makers around her were statistically illiterate and tables of figures, however accurate, were simply not winning over their hearts and minds. This led her to devise creative and innovative forms of diagrammatic and graphical representations of her data, which demonstrated the underlying patterns in a way that no one could ignore. For a readable account of these issues, see Cohen (1984).

5.5 PEDAGOGY

As usual, this section on teaching and learning issues asks you to carry out tasks based on the six PTT themes.

Language Patterns

Task 5.5.1 Words   **C**

(a) Make a list of the key statistical words and phrases that were used in this chapter.

(b) With a particular learner or group of learners in mind, decide which of these words and phrases it would be appropriate for them to know.

(c) How might you help them gain a better understanding of these ideas?

Imagery

Task 5.5.2 People Graphs   **C**

A simple but effective way of illustrating the nature of a bar chart is to create a *people graph*, as follows. Ask a group of children to sort themselves, say, by hair colour (dark, brown, fair, red). A bar chart can be formed if they stand, equally spaced in four parallel rows. How might this idea be extended to form a pie chart?

Decide for what age of learners creating people graphs could be an effective teaching strategy. How would you bridge the gap between a people chart and one drawn on paper?

Choose one of the other graphics covered in this chapter. How might you use 'visualising' to clarify the key ideas to learners?

Different Contexts

Learners only need to flick through a newspaper or magazine or to watch a current affairs programme on television to see a range of statistical graphs and charts. Clearly, there is scope for incorporating some of these into statistical lessons, in the context of trying to make sense of someone else's statistical picture. The other side of this coin is for learners to use statistical pictures in order to represent their own data.

For example, Rosie's passion is music and, in particular, using her *iPod* MP3 player. With her music stored on a computer, she can instantly identify the various genres of music in her collection and the number of artists within each genre. Figure 5.11 is a pie chart representing Rosie's music collection, by musical genre. At a glance, she can use the chart to gain an insight into her musical tastes.

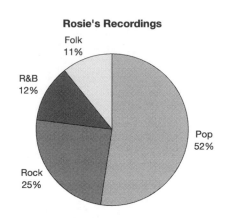

Figure 5.11 **A PIE CHART OF ROSIE'S RECORD COLLECTION**

Task 5.5.3 A passion for Pie Charts   C

(a) Rosie's pie chart depicts the number of *separate tracks* in her collection that fall into each category. How else might the pie chart categories be organised?

(b) Make a short list of other contexts that your particular groups of learners might find motivating.

(c) Choose two of the graphics described in this chapter and sketch possible graphics that might arise within the contexts you have identified.

Root Questions

Task 5.5.4 Words Versus Pictures

Section 5.1 ended with four key features that characterise a well-designed graphic. Here are one person's notes for an activity designed to convey this in an interesting manner:

- set up a competition called 'words versus pictures';
- one learner is asked to convey certain information in words using, say, less than 100 words;
- a second learner must depict the same information using a graphic representation plus a maximum of five words for titles and labelling;
- the two representations are compared and other learners decide which is 'better' and why;
- follow up with a discussion of the strengths and weaknesses of each approach.

For what age of learner is this task appropriate? Bullet point 2 talks of 'certain information'. Decide on two different pieces of information that would be appropriate to use and decide how this information could be presented.

Standard Misconceptions

Task 5.5.5 Getting it Wrong C

Bearing in mind the content of this chapter and the particular learner(s) you have in mind, choose a topic that you think may be the basis of a learner misconception (or perhaps a 'partial conception'). Try to explain the misconception, why it may occur and how you might try to remedy it.

Techniques and Methods

Task 5.5.6 Made by Hand C

A feature of data presentation with a computer is that it is achieved with just a few clicks of the mouse. Drawing a graphic by hand demands some technical skill and may take a long time. A key pedagogic issue is how long to spend on the various methods of creating graphics.

(a) List the technical skills that your learners would need if they were to be able to create a pie chart without a computer. What are the gains and losses if they were only to use a computer instead?

(b) Choose another graphic from this chapter and repeat (a).

---

6 Comparing with Pictures

This chapter offers a second opportunity for you to think about questions of comparison in statistics. In Chapter 2, you considered this idea based on using words and numbers – now it is applied to pictures. One of the 'big ideas' of statistics, highlighted in Chapter 2, was the following root question that underpins many statistical investigations: 'Is A bigger than B?' Here are some examples:

- 'Are pupils faster than teachers at texting with mobile phones?'
- 'Is traffic heavier on a Saturday than a Sunday?'
- 'Are people's speed of reaction faster using their dominant hand than their non-dominant hand?'
- 'Are girls better able to distinguish colours than boys?'

At an advanced level of statistical work, there are certain formal tests that are used to make comparisons between two data sets – for example, the z-test, the t-test, the chi-squared test, and so on. However, these are beyond the scope of this book and another way must be found to answer questions of comparison. An acceptable alternative is to depict the two data sets graphically and then make visual comparisons. Two graphics that are particularly good for comparing sets of data are the box plot and the stem plot and these are examined in Sections 6.2 and 6.3. Section 6.4 asks you to work through a statistical investigation based on comparing writing styles. The chapter ends, as usual, with a section on pedagogy.

The first section looks at some examples of how a well-chosen graphic can create a particular impression.

6.1 GETTING THE MESSAGE ACROSS

In a Brooklyn courthouse in 1987, alleged Mafia godfather John Gotti (known as the 'dapper don'; Figure 6.1), along with his six co-defendants, was tried on and acquitted of racketeering and conspiracy charges. The failure to convict after a widely reported, seven-month trial was a serious blow to the US government's campaign against organised crime.

A key factor in securing Gotti's release was the final exhibit (Table 6.1) prepared by Gotti's defence team and handed to the jury just before they retired to make their decision. It was a chart listing the names of the seven key witnesses who had testified against Gotti and the various crimes of which these witnesses had themselves been convicted. Study Table 6.1 for a few minutes and then try Task 6.1.1.

Figure 6.1 **JOHN GOTTI (1940–2002)**
Source: The New York Times Agency

TABLE 6.1 The criminal activity of seven witnesses

Criminal activity of government informants

Crime	Cardinale	Lofaro	Maloney	Polisi	Senatore	Foronjy	Curro
Murder	X	X					
Attempted murder		X	X				
Heroin possession and sale	X	X		X			X
Cocaine possession and sale	X		X	X			
Marijuana possession and sale							X
Gambling business		X		X		X	
Armed robberies	X		X	X	X		X
Loansharking		X		X			
Kidnapping			X	X			
Extortion			X	X			
Assault	X		X	X			X
Possession of dangerous weapons	X	X	X	X	X		X
Perjury		X				X	
Counterfeiting					X	X	
Bank robbery			X	X			
Armed Hijacking			X	X			
Stolen financial documents			X	X	X		
Tax evasion				X		X	
Burglaries	X	X		X	X		
Bribery		X		X			
Theft: auto, money, other			X	X	X	X	X
Bail jumping and escape			X	X			
Insurance frauds					X	X	
Forgeries				X	X		
Pistol whipping a priest	X						
Sexual assault on minor							X
Reckless endangerment							X

Task 6.1.1 Creating a Bad Impression   C

(a) Without thinking about it for more than a few seconds, estimate, roughly, the percentage of boxes that are marked with an X.

(b) Look at the order of the criminal activities shown down the left of the table. How do you think these have been ordered?

(c) What overall impression does this table convey?

Now You See It

Task 6.1.2 Don't Blame the Drink!   C

Look at the glass of wine below in Figure 6.2. Make a rough estimate of what percentage of the glass is filled.

To check your estimate, a calculation can be made to find the ratio of the volume of wine in the glass to the maximum capacity of the glass. Both of these are roughly conical in shape, so you need to know that the formula for the volume of a cone is $(4/3)\pi r^2 h$, where r is the radius of the circular 'base' of the cone and h is its height.

If you measure the level of the wine as a percentage of the total depth of the glass, it is roughly 80% of the way up the glass. Correspondingly, the radius of the circular wine surface is also 80% of the radius of

Figure 6.2 **A GLASS OF RED WINE**

the circular top of the glass. So, applying the formula for the volume of a cone, the ratios of the volume of wine to maximum capacity of the glass is determined by squaring the ratio of the radii and multiplying by the ratio of the heights. (Note that, when computing these ratios, the constants 4/3 and π cancel out.) In other words, the volume ratio is found by calculating $(0.8)^3 = 0.512$, which is roughly one half.

A fundamental way in which pictures change reality is that when any image (such as this photograph of the wine glass) is printed on a page, the three-dimensional world that it represents collapses into two dimensions. Inevitably, therefore, comparisons such as the one presented in Task 6.1.2 will be misleading. Since only two dimensions are available on a printed page, the eye tends to compare areas, not volumes.

To illustrate this point, the shaded triangle in Figure 6.3 represents half the area of the total triangle. If you measure the heights of the triangles, you will find that the shaded triangle is roughly 70% of

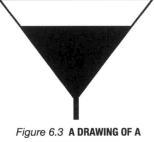

Figure 6.3 **A DRAWING OF A GLASS OF RED WINE**

the height of the larger one, not 80% as it was in the three-dimensional (3-D) case. So, that is why this particular 'glass' does look roughly half-full, even though, as a picture of a 3-D glass, it would be only $(0.7)^3$, or roughly 35% full.

Cleverly drawn pictures can sometimes disguise or render invisible what is there. At other times, they can make you see things that are not really there. It is helpful to be aware of how these illusions are achieved, as some of the illusionist's 'tricks of the trade' can also be found in distortions used in graphs and diagrams.

6.2 EXPLORATORY DATA ANALYSIS (EDA)

John Wilder Tukey (Figure 6.4) was born in New Bedford, Massachusetts, in 1915. He gained degrees in chemistry, followed by a doctorate in mathematics and, from 1939 on, taught mathematics at Princeton University. He directed Princeton's Statistical Techniques Research Group from its founding in 1956.

Although internationally known for his studies in mathematical and theoretical statistics and their applications, Tukey led

Figure 6.4 **JOHN TUKEY (1915–2000)**
Source: stat.bell-labs.com/who/tukey/

the way in the field of Exploratory Data Analysis (EDA). The seminal work in EDA is Tukey (1977). Exploratory Data Analysis is more than just a collection of data-analysis techniques; it provides a philosophy of how to dissect a data set. It stresses the power of *visualisation* and aspects such as what to look for, how to look for it and how to interpret the information it contains. Most EDA techniques are graphical in nature, because the main aim of EDA is to explore data in an open-minded way. Using graphics, rather than calculations, keeps open possibilities of spotting interesting patterns or anomalies that would not be apparent with a calculation (where assumptions and decisions about the nature of the data tend to be made in advance).

Although bar charts, pie charts and histograms have been around for a long time, the EDA movement brought with it a number of exciting new ways of visualising data that are gradually becoming established in school and college statistics syllabuses around the world. Whereas traditional approaches to data analysis emphasised the mean as the key measure of location and the standard deviation as the fundamental measure of spread, EDA stresses the median and the interquartile range respectively. Note that these summary measures are not the result of performing an abstract calculation, but are based on picking out particular values from the set, when sorted in order of size. A key feature of visualisation, in EDA terms, is imagining the data items laid out on a number line (or in a series of rows) and matching this to a helpful graphic.

You have already seen in Chapter 2 an example of a visualising technique that is normally attributed to EDA – the five-figure summary. In this chapter, you will look at two further examples: the *box plot* (also known as the *box-and-whisker diagram*) and the *stem plot* (also known as the *stem-and-leaf diagram*). They have been included in this chapter because they not only provide excellent ways of summarising single sets of data, but also offer particularly powerful ways of *comparing* two or more data sets.

Box Plots

A *box plot* is a simple but powerful means of gaining an overview of a set of data by marking, on a number line, the five key summary statistics: Min, Q1, Med, Q3 and Max. For example, here are the examination scores (in order) of 14 students.

23, 35, 41, 45, 55, 55, 58, 60, 62, 66, 69, 72, 73, 73.

The summaries (as calculated both by the calculator and by Tukey's method) are:

Min = 23, Q1 = 45, Q2 = 59, Q3 = 69, Max = 73.

In Task 6.2.1, you are asked to go through the main steps of translating these summaries into a box plot.

Task 6.2.1 Creating a Box with Whiskers	C
Imagine that you are working with students who require detailed instructions on how to draw a box plot. Using the example of the data set of 14 marks above, write down the main steps, suitable for an audience of your choosing.	

The box plot shows the locations of the quarter points of the data. The left and right whiskers correspond, respectively, to the values of the bottom and top quarters of the values, the central box corresponds to the values of the middle 50% of the values and the median line separates these into the second and third quarters of the data. The strength of this diagram is that you can see at a glance where these five key summaries fall in relation to each other and thereby gain a useful visualisation of the overall distribution of values. For instance, in this example, the right whisker is shorter than the left one, and the right portion of the box is shorter than the left.

Task 6.2.2 The Long and the Short of a Box Plot   C

Think about the implications of a lack of symmetry in a box plot in terms of where the data values are concentrated.

For cases where the left whisker is longer than the right whisker, are either of the following statements true?

- Values are more densely packed into the bottom 25% than the top 25% of the batch.
- Values are more densely packed into the top 25% than the bottom 25% of the batch.

It is when two or more data sets are to be compared that box plots really come into their own. Consider the data sets below, which were collected from a class project on texting speeds. A group of Key Stage 3 (KS3) students challenged their teachers to a speed-texting competition. The 21 participants (12 students and 9 teachers) were each required to send a short text message on a mobile phone. Their times and the summaries for each group (Table 6.2) are given below. For convenience, the data have been sorted in order of size.

Teacher times (secs):   18, 27, 28, 31, 33, 33, 36, 47, 51.
Student times (secs):   19, 19, 21, 24, 24, 25, 27, 29, 30, 30, 33, 41.

TABLE 6.2 Student and teacher summaries

	Min	Q1	Med	Q3	Max
Teachers	18	27.5	33	41.5	51
Students	19	22.5	26	30	41

Task 6.2.3 Box Plots Compared   C

(a) What inaccuracies do you think might have cropped up in this experiment and how might they have been dealt with?

(b) Sketch two box plots, one above the other, for the teacher and student times. Make sure that both plots relate to the same horizontal scale.

(c) Comparing the two box plots, what can you conclude about the relative performances of the teachers and the students?

It is clear from the completed box plots that the students' times are generally faster than those of the teachers. The only redeeming feature of the teachers' performance was their one exceptionally fast time of 18 seconds, but for all the other four summary values, the students outperformed them. In fact, the median student time (26 seconds) was actually faster than the lower quartile teacher time (27.5 seconds). Put another way, half of the students were faster than the best quarter of the teachers. Also, the worst performing student (timed at 41 seconds) performed better than the slowest quarter of the teachers (the fastest of these apparently being shown at 41.5 seconds, but recall that this Q3 figure is actually a computed average of 36 and 47 seconds).

Deciding on Differences

In Task 6.2.3, you were asked to compare, visually, the student and teacher box plots. Clearly, student times are, overall, faster than those of their teachers, but there was quite wide variation in the two sets of times and therefore considerable overlap between the two box plots. When comparing two sets of data in order to decide whether or not there is a difference, two key factors need to be considered – whether there is a difference in the *location* of the two data sets and how widely the two sets of values are *spread*.

Imagine two schools, A and B, where a similar experiment on measuring texting speeds was carried out. In both schools, the difference in location between student and teacher times was very similar to the data above (with medians of 26 and 33, respectively), but the spreads were very different.

These are represented by the two pairs of box plots (Figure 6.5).

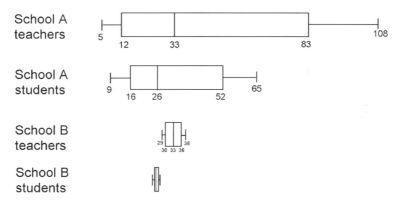

Figure 6.5 **TEACHER AND STUDENT BOX PLOTS FROM TWO SCHOOLS**

Task 6.2.4 Location and Spread

(a) For which of these schools, A or B, would you feel able to claim with greater confidence that the students have outperformed the teachers?

(b) In general, when comparing two sets of data, how do their locations and spreads affect your judgement when deciding on differences?

(c) Can you think about a third factor (as well as location and spread) that might affect the process of deciding on differences?

The differences are more convincing in school B, where the spreads are small. In general, differences are more convincing when the locations differ widely and the spreads are narrow.

A relevant third factor is the batch size. The larger the batch size, the more confident you can be that the shape and position of the box plot has settled down. Where, say, just five or six values are plotted, these may be fairly unrepresentative of the whole batch and the shape and position of the box plot may change considerably as more data are collected.

In summary, then, when deciding on differences between two data batches, you need to look for:

- a *large* difference in location;
- *small* spreads in the batches;
- *large* batch sizes.

As was mentioned at the beginning of this chapter, students under the age of 16 are not expected to make use of formal tests of significance. When deciding on differences, therefore, these students must look elsewhere to inform their decision-making. One alternative is to perform relevant calculations (for example, averages) and make *numerical* comparisons. The alternative explored here is to make *visual* comparisons based on helpful graphics such as box plots. However, where students are making visual comparisons, they should be aware of the relevance of location, spread and batch sizes to inform their interpretation. Another option to consider is the creation of several samples. This is easier to achieve by means of simulations using a computer or graphics calculator, something that is explored in Block 3.

6.3 STEM PLOTS (OR STEM-AND-LEAF DIAGRAMS)

Another visual representation attributed to John Tukey and the EDA movement is the *stem plot* (also known as the *stem-and-leaf diagram*). Task 6.3.1 asks you to think through the procedure of drawing a stem plot based on the data you used in the previous section. For convenience, the data are repeated below.

Student times (secs):   19, 19, 21, 24, 24, 25, 27, 29, 30, 30, 33, 41.
Teacher times (secs):   18, 27, 28, 31, 33, 33, 36, 47, 51.

Task 6.3.1 Creating a Stem-and-leaf Diagram	**C**
Imagine that you are working with students who require detailed instructions on how to draw a stem plot. Using the example of the student and teacher times above, write down the main steps, suitable for an audience of your choosing.	

The students' completed stem plot should look like this.

```
0|
1| 99
2| 144579
3| 003
4| 1
5|
```

1|9 means 19

Note that, in this example, as shown in the 'key' at the bottom, the tens correspond to the stem, while the unit parts of the numbers are the leaves. Conventionally, the leaves are placed in increasing order of size along each branch corresponding to the 'tens' branch to which they are linked. When teaching stem plots to older students, a number of deeper questions may arise and you are asked to think about some of these in Task 6.3.2.

Task 6.3.2 Deeper Questions about a Stem Plot   **C**

(a) Unlike the box plot or histogram, a stem plot incorporates and displays each separate data value. What are the advantages and disadvantages of this feature?

(b) What other features does a stem plot share with a box plot and a histogram?

(c) Is it important that the values on each branch are ordered?

(d) What are some advantages and disadvantages of the convention of drawing a stem plot so that the values on the stem increase downwards?

A useful feature of a stem plot is that the values maintain their natural order, while at the same time they are laid out in a way that emphasises the overall distribution of where the values are concentrated (that is, where the longer branches are). This enables you easily to pick out key values such as the median and quartiles.

Task 6.3.3 Interpreting the Stem Plot   **C**

From the stem plot based on student times, pick out the Min, Max and Med values.

Comparing Stem Plots

Just as box plots are a good way of comparing two data sets, so too are stem plots. However, this is not done with one placed above the other (as is the case when comparing two box plots), but rather with them placed back-to-back. This is illustrated in Figure 6.6.

Teacher times (secs)   *Student times* (secs)

Teacher	stem	Student
	0	
8	1	99
87	2	144579
6331	3	003
7	4	1
1	5	

4 l 1 means 41

Figure 6.6 **A BACK-TO-BACK STEM PLOT**

Task 6.3.4 Interpreting the Back-to-back Stem Plot

(a) What features can be compared using a back-to-back stem plot?

(b) What similarities can you observe between this representation and others, such as a histogram?

With a back-to-back stem plot, you can compare, at a glance, the extreme values of the two data sets. Also, as has already been observed, the length of each branch is a good indication of where the values are concentrated. So, this allows you to see immediately that the modal interval for the students is 20–29 seconds, whereas for the teachers it is 30–39 seconds.

As was mentioned in the comments to Task 6.3.2, a stem plot is very similar to a histogram with equal class intervals, except that the picture has been turned through 90°. Thus, all the interpretations afforded by a histogram are also available with a stem plot, with the added advantage that two sets of data can now be compared directly.

The particular data sets used here were easy to display as a stem plot – each number consisted of two digits, so naturally the 'tens' digit formed the stem and the 'units' digit filled the leaves. Data are not always so co-operative and sometimes you will need to be a little creative when displaying the numbers in a stem plot, as you will see in the next task.

Task 6.3.5 Making the Data Fit the Stem Plot

Making whatever adjustments you feel necessary, display the two data sets below as separate stem plots.

2, 4, 4, 5, 5, 5, 6, 6, 7, 7, 7, 8, 8, 9.

431, 506, 544, 582, 610, 627, 674, 711, 729.

Can you come up with a sensible general rule for creating a stem on a stem plot?

Ideally, the optimum number of branches on a stem plot should be somewhere between four and eight. With small data sets, anything more or less than that makes it hard to perceive any underlying shape to the distribution. With this first data set, something unconventional may be required, such as grouping the data in twos. This time, the stem value marked 4 refers to the range 4–5, not 40–49.

The final stem plot will look something like this.

```
2|2
4|44555
6|66777
8|889
```

8|9 means 9

Note that the key is particularly important here as 8|9 is more conventionally taken to mean something like 89 or 0.89. You may take the view that this particular form of stem plot is so unconventional as to be confusing for students. An alternative approach might be to use a dot plot, with dots corresponding to 8, 9, and so on, as shown in Figure 6.7.

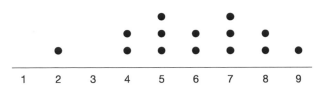

Figure 6.7 **DOT PLOT SHOWING THE FIRST DATA SET FROM TASK 6.3.5**

Whereas with the first data set, each item had too few digits to make a conventional stem plot, the second set had the opposite problem. The simplest solution is to round each value to two figures, thus:

430, 510, 540, 580, 610, 630, 670, 710, 730.

You can then make the plot using the hundreds digits as the stems and the tens digits as the leaves, as follows.

4 | 3
5 | 148
6 | 137
7 | 13

7 | 1 means 710

To end this section, Figure 6.8 contains a timetable that has been used by Japanese rail passengers for many years (and probably all were quite unaware of the term 'back-to-back stem plot').

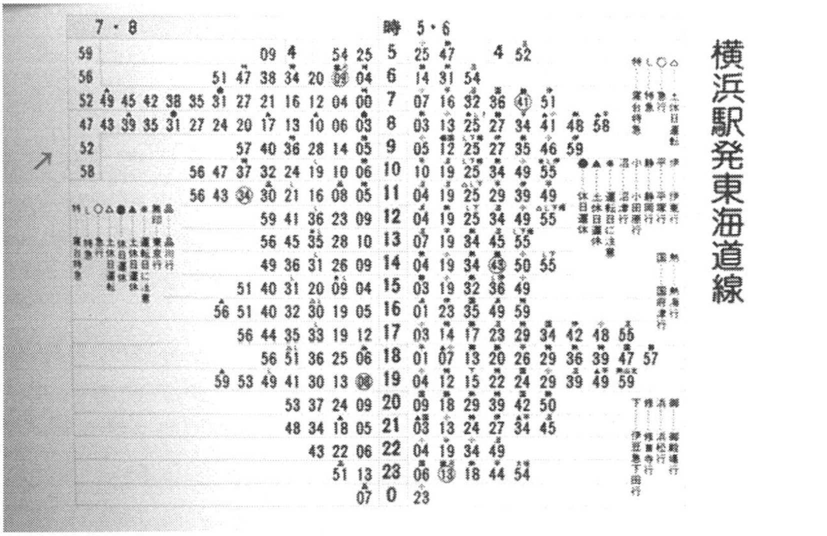

Figure 6.8 **TOKAIDO LINE AT YOKOHAMA STATION (SAGAMI TETSUDO COMPANY, 1985 TIMETABLE, P. 72)**
Source: Tufte (1990, p. 47).

The central stem corresponds to hours, while the leaves are arranged as pairs of digits, corresponding to minutes. The left half of the schedules refers to platforms 7 and 8, while the right half refers to platforms 5 and 6. Note also that time increases *downwards* on the vertical stem.

6.4 A STATISTICAL INVESTIGATION ON COMPARING

In this section, you are asked to carry out a statistical investigation, comparing the writing of three authors, Jane Austin, J.K. Rowling and J.R.R. Tolkien. Clearly, there are many subtle features that characterise particular authors' styles – for example, their use of metaphor, description, imagery, and so on – but here you are simply asked to concentrate on writing characteristics that are easily defined and measured. As you tackle this investigation, notice that it has been organised into the four key stages introduced in Block 1 that mark out the thinking required in order to conduct a statistical investigation. (These are also described in the Key Stages 3 and 4 Programmes of Study in England.) The stages are *Pose* the question, *Collect* relevant data, *Analyse* the data and *Interpret* the results (summarised as *PCAI*). Throughout this book, other investigations are offered for you to try and these are also organised using these four headings. A more general discussion on issues relating to conducting a statistical investigation appears in Chapter 14.

The *P* Stage – Pose the Question

Posing a suitable or sensible question is a crucial part of the *PCAI* data-handling cycle, since it is the key to everything that follows in the investigation. Students will not find this initial step easy, particularly if they have not had much previous experience of working investigatively. Ensuring that each student has a sense of individual choice and personal ownership of the investigation will be important. But, at the same time, the teacher will not want them to embark on an extended piece of work that is likely to fail. Consequently, considerable teaching skill and tact will be required to help them move from a vague, general idea to formulating a realistic question that can be investigated.

Here are five considerations that might help students to come up with a good question for investigation. Choose a question that is:

- actually a question, rather than simply an area for investigation – an investigation based on a *question* is more likely to draw on statistical and mathematical skills and provide greater focus and clearer direction;
- personally interesting to you – not only will this bring greater motivation, but also your common-sense knowledge about the context should help ensure that the investigation proceeds along sensible lines;
- likely to draw on data that will be available within the time frame of the investigation – for example, do not investigate the growth of flowers or plants during the winter months;
- specific, so that it is answerable from data – questions that are too vague and general are harder to answer;
- measurable – think through in advance what you will measure and whether it will help to answer the question.

In general, it is useful for students to be familiar with the *PCAI* cycle when they are at the question-posing stage. A useful exercise when first selecting a question is for them to go through in their minds how the investigation might develop at the subsequent *C*, *A* and *I* stages. If they can foresee a stumbling block, this might be because of some problem in the wording of the investigation, in which case they can try to come up with a rewording that gets around the problem.

Task 6.4.1 Choosing the Right Question   C

Think about the general area of this investigation (comparing authorship) and write down as precisely as you can two or three questions that you feel would be both interesting and also answerable by students below the age of 16. Bear in mind the *C*, *A* and *I* stages that are likely to follow, and adjust the wording of your questions accordingly.

In this section, you are asked to follow through a short investigation based on the question: 'Which of the authors writes the simplest sentences?' Before thinking about collecting relevant data, note down your instinctive response to this question. This will make it more interesting when you reach the final stage of your investigation and you can compare what you found with what you expected.

The *C* Stage – Collect the Data

How can you measure the complexity of the sentences written by different authors? One simple approach would be to take a sample of, say, 30 sentences from each author and count the number of words in each sentence. A possible weakness of this approach is that it does not take word length into account. Both of these factors, the number of words and word length, can be compounded by counting, say, the number of letters per sentence or even the number of syllables. The latter approach is the one you are asked to take here.

The books selected were:

Pride and Prejudice (by Jane Austen)
Harry Potter and the Goblet of Fire (by J.K. Rowling)
Lord of the Rings: The Two Towers (by J.R.R. Tolkien)

The next choice is how to select the sentences from these books.

Task 6.4.2 Selecting the Sentences   C

Consider several ways of selecting the sentences and weigh up their advantages and disadvantages in terms of collecting the data fairly.

There are other measuring choices to be made when measuring sentence length, whether you are counting words, syllables or letters. For example, the ambiguities of pronunciation sometimes make it difficult to know precisely how many syllables are in each word. Where letters are being counted, rather than syllables, you need to decide whether or not to include punctuation marks and spaces between words.

Table 6.3 shows the syllable lengths of 30 randomly chosen sentences from these three books. In the next sub-section, you are asked to analyse these data visually.

The *A* Stage – Analyse the Data

As you may have already guessed from the way the data have been presented, they were entered into a spreadsheet. The eight relevant summary statistics (Mean, Range, IQR, Min, Q1, Median, Q3 and Max) for the Austen and Tolkien data were calculated and are displayed in Table 6.4.

TABLE 6.3 Syllable lengths from sentences of three authors

	Austen	Rowling	Tolkien
1	50	26	33
2	63	12	33
3	9	42	4
4	10	26	2
5	37	23	6
6	8	62	7
7	33	27	14
8	46	80	15
9	30	44	10
10	34	42	18
11	38	67	14
12	50	73	28
13	39	35	13
14	10	64	6
15	60	30	16
16	68	10	62
17	50	13	17
18	54	34	40
19	30	20	4
20	16	17	11
21	78	54	5
22	136	31	10
23	57	42	44
24	12	29	45
25	10	26	9
26	59	40	29
27	8	37	14
28	30	28	10
29	49	13	8
30	79	52	7

TABLE 6.4 Eight summary statistics for Austen and Tolkien

	Austen	Tolkien
Mean	41.8	17.8
Range	128	60
IQR	36.8	18.3
Min	8	2
Q1	19.5	7.3
Median	38.5	13.5
Q3	56.3	25.5
Max	136	62

Producing these summaries is an important step at the *A* stage of an investigation and one that is greatly supported by ICT. Information and communication technology can also support creating helpful visual representations of the data, something you will look at again more closely in Block 3.

Task 6.4.3 Visualising the Data   C

Represent, visually, the Jane Austen and J.R.R. Tolkien data, in order to compare their levels of difficulty (to save time, a rough sketch will be sufficient here). How fairly does your choice of representation describe the data sets overall?

The *I* Stage – Interpret the Results

The final stage of the investigation is to interpret the results produced in the *A* stage.

Task 6.4.4 Interpreting the Box Plots   C

(a) Based on the summaries and box plots, what can you conclude about these two authors, Jane Austen and J.R.R. Tolkien?

(b) You have now completed one complete pass around the *PCAI* cycle. This does not necessarily mean that you have completed the investigation. What further thoughts or ideas do you have?

(c) If you have time, you could carry out a similar investigation based on the Rowling data, starting with your intuitive guess as to how her sentence lengths would compare with these other two authors.

6.5 PEDAGOGY

As usual, in this section on teaching and learning issues, you are asked to carry out tasks based on the six PTT themes.

Language Patterns

Task 6.5.1 The Long and the Short of it   C

The terms 'box plot' and 'box-and-whisker diagram' were used to describe the same representation. This is also true of the terms 'stem plot' and 'stem-and-leaf diagram'. What are some advantages and disadvantages of using these different terms with learners?

Imagery

Task 6.5.2 People Plots   C

Recall how, in Task 5.5.2, people graphs were suggested as means of visualising vividly both bar charts and pie charts. Can you think of similar activities to illustrate box-and-whisker and stem-and-leaf diagrams? Consider, for example, an investigation where each student has recorded the number of seconds it took them to send a (standard) text message.

Different Contexts

Task 6.5.3 Sporty Plots   C

Many people are interested in sport. With a particular learner or group of learners in mind, think of examples from sporting contexts where box-and-whisker and/or stem-and-leaf diagrams would be useful to make comparisons between sets of data.

Root Questions

Task 6.5.4 Root Question   **C**

Consider the term 'difference' as it might be used in statistics.

Make a note of a possible root question that connects it to ideas of natural variation.

Standard Misconceptions

Task 6.5.5 Symmetrical Box Plots?

a) Recall the box plot produced in Task 6.2.1. Imagine that one of your students produced the box plot in Figure 6.9 from the same data. In fact, all the box plots they produce show the same perfect symmetry. What fundamental misconception do you think they might have? How you might try to remedy it?

b) Bearing in mind the content of this chapter and the particular learner(s) you have in mind, write down some possible misconceptions. For each misconception you can think of, describe how you, the teacher, would become aware of it and how you might remedy it.

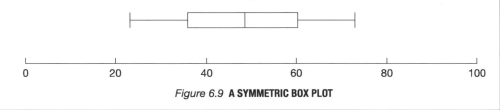

Figure 6.9 **A SYMMETRIC BOX PLOT**

Techniques and Methods

In this chapter, box plots and stem plots have been suggested as means of comparing data sets. In Chapter 5, bar charts, histograms and pie charts were discussed and, of course, these diagrams too can be used to make visual comparisons of sets of data. For example, two pie charts can be placed side by side or compound or component bar charts (these are explained in Block 3) can be used to compare more than one attribute at a time.

With such a variety of types of charts available, it is not easy to decide which to use in any particular instance. A list of the factors that influence your choice could include the following:

- some are much easier than others to draw by hand;
- a stem plot is good for numerical data in the range 0–99, where the stem and leaves correspond, respectively, to tens and units. It is less satisfactory for more awkward decimals, where the meaning of the stem and the leaves is not so obvious. Also, stem plots are not useful for large data sets.

Task 6.5.6 Comparing Charts of Comparison   **C**

(a) Make as full a list as you can of other factors that might affect your choice when you want to make a visual comparison of data sets.

(b) Is this task a good one for your students to carry out?

7 Interrelating with Pictures

Chapter 6 was about looking for differences between attributes (for example, 'men versus women', 'children versus adults', and so on). The information required to answer such questions were two sets of numerical data, one for each attribute. Now consider the following question that might be the subject of a class investigation: 'Can people with longer legs run faster?'

There are two possible approaches to tackling a question like this. One is to adapt it to match the approach taken in Chapter 6, by creating two groups of people ('the long-legged' and 'the short-legged') and then measuring their respective running speeds. (Note that the two batches do not need to be of equal size.) The data for these two data sets could then be compared numerically using averages or visually using box plots or stem plots.

However, this classification of people into two leg lengths creates rather an artificial distinction. Leg length is not an attribute like 'gender' or 'hand dominance', but a full-blown variable with all the features of a ratio scale. The second approach, the one featured in this chapter, is to acknowledge that leg length and running speed are both variables. This will mean using paired (that is, bi-variate) data in order to explore the relationship between them. In Chapter 3, you looked at such relationships in terms of words and pictures. Here you will look at the power of pictures (particularly scatter plots and line graphs) to explore such relationships.

A particularly common example of interrelating can be seen in *time series* plots – that is, tables or graphs showing how some quantity (say, height, weight, earnings, sales, and so on) changes over time. A feature of time series graphs is that the variable 'time' is always placed on the horizontal axis, for the simple reason that time is always the 'explanatory' variable in such situations.

Section 7.1 looks at some of the data that can be found on the CensusAtSchool website and examines how such data can be made the basis of an 'interrelating' investigation. Sections 7.2 and 7.3 consider ideas of regression and correlation. Section 7.4 provides examples of ways in which pictures can *mis*represent data, while the final section looks at pedagogic issues.

7.1 THE CENSUSATSCHOOL DATA SOURCE

In this section, you are asked to look at some possible school-level investigations based on data found at the CensusAtSchool website: www.censusatschool.ntu.ac.uk The CensusAtSchool project is run by the Royal Statistical Society Centre for Statistical Education, based at Nottingham Trent University. It is an international children's census set up to collect and disseminate real data for use by teachers and pupils in data handling, ICT and projects across the curriculum. Countries currently represented are UK, South Africa, Australia, New Zealand and Canada. You will have the opportunity to look at this site more closely in Block 3 and use it as it has been designed to be used, namely, supported by ICT.

Table 7.1 contains a small selection of the many thousands of data items available at this site. These 20 boys and girls were aged 11 to 14 years and all measurements provided are in centimetres.

TABLE 7.1 Some 'typical' data from the CensusAtSchool website

Gender	Height	Foot length	Head circumference	Vertical reach
M	172	28	56	221
M	161	28	57	225
F	153	24	52	199
M	168	28	55	222
M	161	23	56	202
M	166	26	59	215
M	149	24	52	204
F	153	24	56	198
M	162	26	57	202
M	170	25	45	189
F	150	22	53	195
M	161	24	54	201
F	166	25	56	220
M	155	24.5	60	218
M	155	25	48	215
F	155	18	47	190
F	162	24	58	212
M	155	15	60	188
F	155	22	52	203
M	161	22	50	217

The graphs in Figure 7.1 were drawn from Table 7.1. Note that they have been deliberately left unlabelled in order to provide you with a challenge for Task 7.1.1.

Task 7.1.1 Which Variables?   **C**

Look at the four unlabelled graphical representations in Figure 7.1.

(a) Using your judgement, decide which graph corresponds to which pairs of data columns.

(b) In the case of the three scatter plots, which variable is plotted on the horizontal axis?

(c) What patterns do you observe in the data?

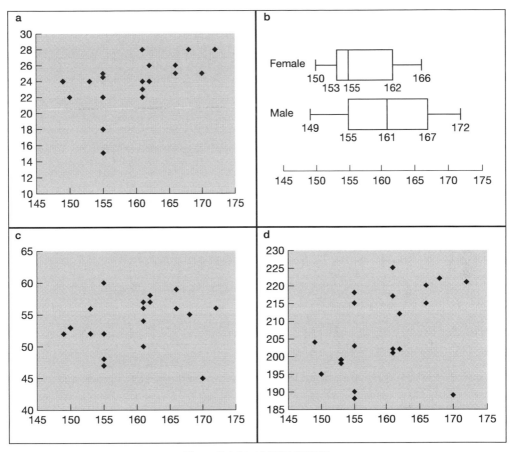

Figure 7.1 **(a)–(d) FOUR GRAPHS**

All four of the graphical representations show something about these learners' heights. The box plots depict the female and male heights, so this is an example of comparing, not interrelating. The three scatter plots show the relationships among foot length, head circumference and vertical reach, plotted against height. In each case, the variable 'height' is plotted on the horizontal scale, for the reason that it can be considered the 'explanatory' variable. (A person's foot length, vertical reach, and so on, can be more reasonably thought to be 'explained' by their height, rather than the other way around.)

In the three scatter plots, there is a clear pattern of certain points sharing the same vertical (and horizontal) lines. Points that share the same vertical line on the plot are values with the same height (in fact, five of these 30 learners are all 155 cm and four are 161 cm). It should not be assumed, however, that any two of these learners are *exactly* the same height. It is possible that learners numbered 15, 16, 18 and 19 all believed themselves to be roughly the same height as learner 14, so they were all 'put down' as 155 cm without much in the way of formal measurement taking place. Another possibility is that these particular learners simply rounded their heights to the nearest 5 cm.

Outliers

As was mentioned in the comments to Task 6.4.3, an outlier is an observation that lies an 'abnormal' distance from other values in a batch of data. There are two possible explanations for the occurrence of an outlier. One is that this happens to be a rare but valid data item that is either extremely large or extremely small. The other is that it is a mistake – maybe due to a measuring or recording error.

The question of just how abnormal a value needs to be in order to be classed as an outlier is often based upon a subjective judgement. Sometimes, the particular context can lead you to suspect that an error has occurred. For example, in the context of these data, there is the added dimension that for each data item there are linked data items measuring different variables for the same person. This provides some sort of cross-check as to the reasonableness of a particular data item. (Would you expect a boy of this height to have a foot of that length, and so on?) One strength of using visual representations is that when certain values fail to fit in with the rest, their positions tend to stand out clearly as outliers.

Task 7.1.2 Outliers   C

Look again at the three scatter plots in Figure 7.1.

Identify any apparent outliers and indicate your reasoning.

7.2 REGRESSION

As you read in Chapter 3, regression is the process of fitting a line or curve to a set of points representing paired data. The whole procedure makes more sense when the data are viewed pictorially in the form of a scatter plot, where the overall 'shape' of the data and the underlying trend can be appreciated.

Linear Regression

Most elementary examples of regression involve fitting a *straight* line to the data. This is known as linear regression, for obvious reasons. However, if learners only ever see linear regression, this can encourage them in the mistaken belief that regression always involves fitting a 'straight line of best fit' to data. As you will see in Chapter 11, linear regression is not always the most appropriate model to use.

It is important for learners to be aware of why anyone might want to carry out regression at all. As you will see from the next task, the main reason is to be able to make *predictions*. Note that the example of prediction explored in Task 7.2.1 is based on time series data, where the prediction applies to some future *time*. Statistical prediction is not restricted just to time series data, but can apply to any situation where paired data are modelled by a regression line or curve. For example, a regression line connecting, say, height with foot length can be used to predict a particular person's foot length based on knowing their height.

Pose the question: a plausible investigation might be, 'When, if ever, will women outperform men at sprinting?'

Task 7.2.1 Women Sprinting

Read the cutting from *The Times* newspaper (Figure 7.2). It is based on an article that appeared in *Nature* magazine (Tatem et al., 2004), entitled, 'Momentous sprint at the 2156 Olympics?'

How could you test a claim such as this? Try to frame your responses using the *PCAI* stages of a statistical investigation stated in Chapter 6.

Collect relevant data: in order to make predictions such as these, some historical data are required about how men's and women's 100-metre sprint times have improved. Table 7.2 shows the men's and women's 100-metre winning sprint times at the Olympic Games from 1928 until 2004. (Note that the data for 1940 and 1944 are absent because the Olympic Games were not held during the war years.) It should be pointed out that these data allow comparisons to be made between the *best* female and male sprinters, rather than any comparison between all women and all men.

Analyse the data: the scatter plots of the two data sets look like Figure 7.3. The next logical step would be to fit a regression line or curve to each set of points and then extend the lines to predict times in the future. A key question to consider is whether a linear model is appropriate to fit the data. These data were analysed using *linear* regression in the article in *Nature*, producing the graphs shown in Figure 7.4.

Athens might have produced a memorable Olympics, but its place in history will be nothing compared with the games of 2156. Scientists predict that this is the year in which women will overtake men as the fastest sprinters in the world.

The women's 100 metres champion in 150 years will breast the tape in a time of 8.079 seconds, fractionally quicker than the winning men's mark of 8.098 seconds, British researchers have calculated. (*The Times*, 30 September 2004, p. 5)

Figure 7.2 ***THE TIMES* NEWSPAPER ARTICLE**

TABLE 7.2 Winning Olympic 100 m sprint times (1928–2004)

Year	Female	Male	Year	Female	Male
1928	12.2	10.8	1972	11.1	10.2
1932	11.9	10.3	1976	11.1	10.1
1936	11.6	10.3	1980	11.1	10.3
1948	11.9	10.3	1984	11.0	10.0
1952	11.6	10.4	1988	10.6	9.9
1956	11.6	10.5	1992	10.8	10.0
1960	11.2	10.2	1996	10.9	9.8
1964	11.5	10.0	2000	10.7	9.9
1968	11.1	9.9	2004	10.9	9.8

Source: www.minerals.org.au/olympics/

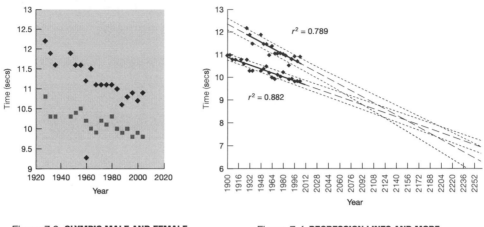

Figure 7.3 **OLYMPIC MALE AND FEMALE 100 M SPRINT TIMES (1928–2004)**

Figure 7.4 **REGRESSION LINES AND MORE**

These graphs show the winning Olympic 100-metre times for men (lower points) and women (higher points), with superimposed best-fit regression lines (solid black lines) and coefficients of determination (r^2). The regression lines are extrapolated (broken heavy lines) and 95% confidence intervals (light dotted lines), based on the available points, are superimposed. The projections intersect just before the 2156 Olympics, when the winning women's 100-metre sprint time of 8.079 seconds will be faster than the men's at 8.098 seconds.

Note: a 95% confidence interval is the range of values within which you can be 95% confident that the 'true' population value lies. So, the more widely scattered the points on the graph are, the wider would be the confidence interval and, in this example, the further apart these two light dotted lines would be. The fact that the confidence interval is narrow, in this example, is a measure of how strong the *correlation* is here. Ideas of correlation and how it is measured (including the coefficient of determination) are discussed in Section 7.3.

Task 7.2.2 Is a Linear Model Appropriate?

Look carefully at the data points for both men and women. Do you think that a linear model is appropriate?

Visually, both sets of points do look reasonably linear. However, based on just 20 values each (for both men and women), it is dangerous to place too much faith in a particular model. For example, place a finger over the women's data point corresponding to the particularly fast 1988 time of 10.6 seconds and then consider the pattern of the remaining points. Is it your impression now that the women's data appear to be levelling off over the 40-year period from 1964 to 2004? If removing a single value from the data set has the effect of leading you to rethink the model, then you might conclude that the model itself is not a very robust one.

A term often used to describe the model chosen to fit a set of points on a scatter plot is the *fit*. The vertical interval between any point (the *data* point) and the corresponding point on the regression line is referred to as a *residual*. It follows, therefore that the relationship between data, fit and residual can be expressed as:

DATA = FIT + RESIDUALS.

For a particular choice of regression model, investigating the residuals can be a useful way of testing how good the fit is. If there is a discernible pattern in the residuals, this would suggest that the model (that is, the fit) could be improved. A fit can be considered 'good' if there are no discernible patterns in the residuals.

The fourth stage of an investigation is '*Interpret the results*' and some issues of interpretation are picked up in the next two tasks. The explanation of the graphs from *Nature* (mentioned above) talks of *extrapolation* – a process of extending the model *outside* the known range of values in order to make predictions. *Interpolation* is when predictions are made from the underlying regression model *within* the range of known values.

Task 7.2.3 Is the Extrapolation a Step too Far?

How confident would you be in the time predicted in *The Times* article (Figure 7.2), that, 'the women's 100-metres champion in 150 years will breast the tape in a time of 8.079 seconds'?

There are several issues raised by this prediction. The main concern is that it rests on certain assumptions about the regression model – namely, that it is both highly accurate and that this same accuracy holds when extrapolated 150 years into the future. To be fair to the *Nature* article authors, they acknowledge these concerns by using phrases such as 'should these trends continue …', thereby displaying a degree of caution about the predictions that is lacking in the opening remarks of *The Times* report. Another objection is the questionable three decimal place accuracy contained in the stated time of 8.079 seconds, which is considerably more accurate than can be warranted on the basis of extrapolating this regression model 150 years into the future. Tatem et al. also acknowledged that there might be other possible 'confounding influences' that would affect the validity of the conclusions.

Task 7.2.4 Other Factors

What other factors might affect these predictions?

One historical reason that men have outperformed women in sport has been to do with social factors – in the past, women were not expected to achieve sporting excellence and, correspondingly, they were given little encouragement or financial backing. Gradually, as these social inequalities have narrowed, explanations for differences in performance must increasingly look to physical differences between the sexes, as future gains in women's levels of achievement may not be so readily brought about by social changes. So, aside from these social factors, there are certain inescapable biological differences between men and women that are always likely to affect their capabilities as sprinters. For example, testosterone in men tends to create more muscle and oxygen-carrying haemoglobin than women possess. Also, female reproductive hormones mean that women, even including super-lean athletes, tend to carry around more fat for their body weight than men, which slows them down.

There are a number of other factors that bring into question the data on which these regression models are built – for example, the historical accuracy of timings, variations due to differences in environment (for example, enhanced performances at altitude) and the use of illegal stimulants.

Nevertheless, however well researched the data or sophisticated the model, one thing is certain – improvements in performance cannot continue for ever, since neither men nor women will ever run the 100-metres race in zero time: therefore, a linear pattern must eventually fail to provide a satisfactory model.

Non-linear Regression

For most learners studying up to Key Stage 4 (KS4), linear regression means simply fitting a straight line to a set of points by eye and then using the line as a prediction tool, either for interpolation or extrapolation. At a more advanced level, regression means finding the *equation* of the line (or curve) of best fit. Consider a relationship between two variables x and y, where x is the explanatory variable. The general form of the linear regression equation used to model the relationship between x and y can be written as $y = ax + b$.

Essentially, the task of deriving the linear regression line boils down to determining the values of these coefficients a and b (which are referred to as the *regression coefficients*, for obvious reasons). Once a and b are known, the equation may be used to predict values of y for particular values of x. It should be remembered, however, that these predictions will not be perfect, since the regression model will almost certainly not be a perfect fit for the data and a careful examination of the errors (in the form of the residuals) may reveal further ways of improving the model.

In the case of quadratic regression, there are three regression coefficients, a, b and c, corresponding to the general quadratic regression equation $y = ax^2 + bx + c$. Exponential regression consists of determining two regression coefficients, a and b corresponding to the general exponential regression equation $y = ab^x$, and so on.

Task 7.2.5 Finding the Regression Coefficients

Focusing just on linear regression and learners up to KS4, how might you help them to work out these regression coefficients?

There are two main options here. One is to fit the line by eye and then deduce the slope and intercept, which are, respectively, the values of a and b. However, for learners with limited algebra, this may prove quite a demanding procedure. A second alternative could make even greater demands on the learner's algebraic understanding, as well as their arithmetic skill. This is to work out the regression coefficients by applying the method of 'least squares' to the data values. Fortunately, ICT can come to the rescue here to calculate these coefficients directly from the data. However, this ease of calculation has a flip side – most learners will have little idea what has happened inside the magic technological box to produce these values. This is an important dilemma for the teacher and one that is explored in Chapter 11.

Variability in One Dimension

As you saw in Chapter 6, a dot plot can prove a simple but effective means of illustrating variation in a single variable.

Look at Table 7.3, which will be used to illustrate variation.

TABLE 7.3 June rainfall and sunshine data in Stratford-upon-Avon

Year	Rainfall (mm)	Sunshine (hrs)
1992	46.4	192.9
1993	58.3	186.8
1994	9.9	104.5
1995	6.5	180.4
1996	14.6	235.1
1997	111.9	117.9
1998	100.7	119.3
1999	53.8	174.3
2000	22.5	149.4
2001	21.1	190.7
Mean	44.57	165.13

Source: *Daily Express*, 14 June 2002, p. 17
Note: The figures are for the month of June in Stratford-upon-Avon, Warwickshire, taken annually over a 10-year period.

A dot plot can be drawn either horizontally or vertically (see Figures 7.5(a) and 7.5(b)).

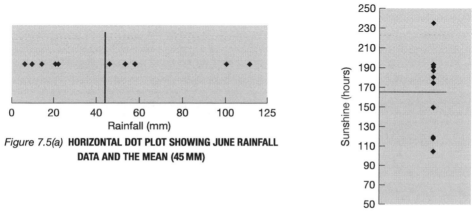

Figure 7.5(a) **HORIZONTAL DOT PLOT SHOWING JUNE RAINFALL DATA AND THE MEAN (45 MM)**

Figure 7.5(b) **VERTICAL DOT PLOT SHOWING THE JUNE SUNSHINE DATA AND THE MEAN (165 HOURS)**

Look at the rainfall plot (Figure 7.5(a)). As you can see, the mean has been marked in at 45 mm. (Here, the mean is chosen rather than the median, because it is deviations from the mean that are of interest.) Consider the position of each point in comparison with the mean. The deviation of each point to the left of the mean will be negative, while the deviations of all points to the right of the mean will be positive.

Task 7.2.6 Deviations from the Mean   C

Write down an important property of the mean in relation to these deviations.

The extent of the variability of rainfall or amount of sunshine can also be calculated numerically using some measure of spread, such as the IQR or the standard deviation. In the case of standard deviation, the calculation is based on computing a form of average deviation of all the points from the batch mean. As you will see in the next sub-section, these ideas are closely paralleled when you move from one dimension to two.

Variability in Two Dimensions

Now, examine the scatter plot in Figure 7.6, which captures, in two dimensions, the relationship between sunshine and rainfall over this 10-year period. This plot was created in the spreadsheet application Excel and, in this case, the linear regression line has been added in order to emphasise the underlying trend. (As an aside, Excel uses the 'least squares' method to calculate and draw the regression line. Also, one of the properties of the least-squares regression is that it passes through the (meanX, meanY) point. You could confirm this by calculating the means for rainfall and sunshine and check that the point corresponding to these two means really does lie on the line.)

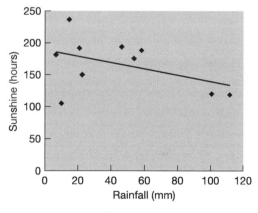

Figure 7.6 **REGRESSION LINE ON SCATTER PLOT**

Task 7.2.7 From 2D Back to 1   C

How could you use the scatter plot above to re-create the separate dot plots of the two variables?

Just as a mean drawn onto a dot plot provides a representative summary of the data values in one dimension, so a linear regression line represents a summary of the relationship between the data pairs in two dimensions.

7.3 CORRELATION

In Section 7.2, you read about an investigation by Tatem et al. on predicting future men's and women's sprint times. One of the figures included on the *Nature* graph was a coefficient of determination, r^2, which was given as 0.789 for the analysis of women's times and 0.882 for the men's times. In order to understand this notion, it is helpful to think of the regression line as being your best guess at explaining how the y-values (sprint times) vary, subject to changes in the x-values (year).

So, for any chosen year, the regression line 'predicts' the corresponding sprint time. The value, r^2, explains how much of the variability in the y-values can be predicted by the regression line. The part that cannot be explained is due to the fact that there is a degree of variation of the points around the line. If the regression line passed through every point on the scatter plot exactly, the line would be able to explain all of the variation in y and so r^2 would be 100%, or 1.0. In general, the wider spread the data points are from the line (or curve) of fit, the weaker the correlation and the lower the value of r^2.

The coefficient of determination, r^2, takes values from 0 (a situation of zero correlation) to 1 (where there is perfect correlation). A more commonly used measure of correlation is the correlation coefficient, r, which is the square root of the coefficient of determination. Possible values for r fall within the range $^-1$ to 1, where $^-1$ means perfect negative correlation, 0 is zero correlation and 1 is perfect positive correlation. Negative correlation refers to situations where the trend line slopes downwards to the right.

Figure 7.7 provides a few examples to help you match different levels of correlation to the corresponding pictures.

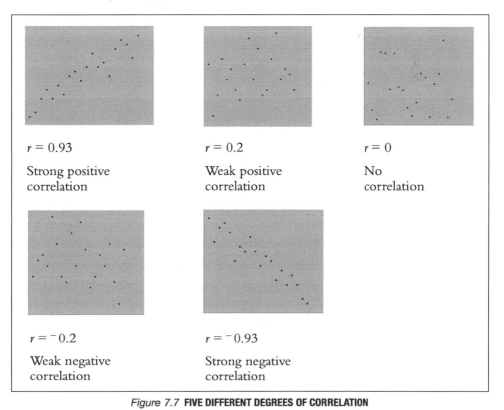

$r = 0.93$

Strong positive correlation

$r = 0.2$

Weak positive correlation

$r = 0$

No correlation

$r = ^-0.2$

Weak negative correlation

$r = ^-0.93$

Strong negative correlation

Figure 7.7 **FIVE DIFFERENT DEGREES OF CORRELATION**

Proving Causality

In Chapter 3, several examples were given of the dangers of inferring causality where correlation existed between two variables. It was pointed out that there may be many other 'confounding variables' that are actually part of the causal chain. It may be the case that the correlation is merely a 'statistical association', rather than one that is genuinely cause and effect. To take another example, there is a strong statistical association between global warming (as measured, say, by the rising temperature of the seas) and GCSE maths grades in the UK over the past 20 years. You may come up with many possible confounding factors to challenge the 'obvious' conclusion that such warming expands the minds of the learners.

Task 7.3.1 Coping with the Confounding Variables

Imagine that you were researching a health issue, such as the relationship between smoking and health. How might you move towards a causal explanation, given the complicating effects of possible confounding variables?

Figure 7.8 RICHARD DOLL
(1912–2005)
Source: Nick Sinclair for
The National Portrait Gallery:
ref.PNG P564(7)

In June 1954, the *British Medical Journal* published a 'preliminary report' by Richard Doll (Figure 7.8) and Bradford Hill that was to have a far-reaching impact on people's attitudes to smoking for decades to come. The article, entitled 'The mortality of doctors in relation to their smoking habits', described a study of some 40 000 male UK doctors which had taken place over 29 months between 1951 and 1954. Here is an extract from the opening page of the article.

While, therefore the various [previous] authors have all shown that there is an 'association' between lung cancer and the amount of tobacco smoked, they have differed in their interpretation. Some have considered that the only reasonable explanation is that smoking is a factor in the production of the disease; others have not been prepared to deduce causation and have left the association unexplained.

(Doll and Hill, 1954, p. 1451)

Doll and Hill went on to explain that retrospective studies were unsatisfactory, because they were unlikely to throw light on the nature of the association. Their 'prospective' study involved contacting 60 000 male doctors, asking them to provide data about their age and smoking habits, and then monitoring their health over two and a half years. Of the 40 000 doctors who participated, 789 died during that period and, of these, 36 died of lung cancer. All of these 36 doctors were smokers. Four smoking categories were identified: non-smokers, smokers of 1–14 cigarettes per day, smokers of 15–24 cigarettes per day and smokers of 25+ cigarettes per day. The authors compared the 'observed' number of deaths in each category with the 'expected' number of deaths in each smoking category 'if smoking were quite unrelated to the chance of dying of lung cancer' (p. 1452).

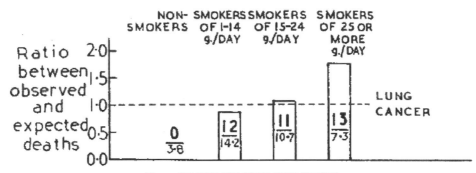

Figure 7.9 **DOLL AND HILL'S (1954) GRAPHIC**

This information was presented in a table, as well as pictorially (see Figure 7.9). The diagram shows that the heavier smokers tended to have a greater ratio between observed and expected deaths. This sharp gradient suggested a strong relationship between death by lung cancer and amount smoked.

Doll and Hill considered (and satisfactorily accounted for) a number of possible alternative explanations to these findings. For example, it was possible that doctors, knowing that they had contracted a fatal disease might be disinclined to complete the study. However, records of all deceased respondents were obtained from the Registrar-General's records along with the cause of death. They also considered the possibility that, where someone was known to be a heavy smoker, the diagnosis of cause of death might be biased in favour of lung cancer. However, if this did occur, one might expect a disproportionate reduction in the diagnoses of other causes of death and this did not occur.

This preliminary publication was just the beginning of an important prospective study. In the follow-up reports, published every 10 years, more information became available – leading to results, for example, that smoking decreases expected life span by up to 10 years, and that more than 50% of all smokers die of a disease known to be smoking related.

7.4 CHEATING CHARTS

An important aim in statistics teaching is to help raise learners' awareness of situations where they are being duped or misled. Nowhere is this more of an issue than in the presentation and misrepresentation of graphs and charts. There are a number of standard ways of distorting and misrepresenting graphical information that learners should be aware of and these are explored in this section.

A class of KS4 learners were given the following project. Each of five groups was given, in a sealed envelope, a different form of graphical misrepresentation. (For example, Group A was given the task of depicting a bar graph for which the lower portions of the bars had been truncated.) They were then asked to find or collect suitable data and use that particular type of misrepresentation deliberately to distort the data and thereby draw an incorrect conclusion. Each group then presented their data, graph and conclusion to the rest of the class, whose job it was to work out how they had cheated. The project ended with a round-up of all five 'cheats' and, over the following weeks, the learners were on the look-out to spot these in newspapers, magazines and on television. Because of the way in which the project was set up, there is a range of different types of graph here, not just those to do with interrelating, which is the theme of this chapter.

The five learner presentations are summarised below.

Group A

Data

Here are the viewing figures for a particular Monday in November 2004 for two of the most popular television 'soaps'.

Eastenders 11.0m
Coronation Street 13.8m

Conclusion

The graph (Figure 7.10) shows that '*Corrie*' is outstandingly the nation's favourite soap – in fact, over three times as popular as *Eastenders*.

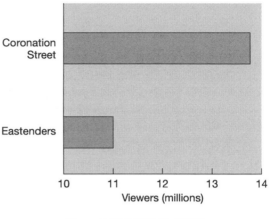

Figure 7.10 **GROUP A's GRAPH**

Group B

Data

The unemployment numbers shown in Table 7.4 were estimated from Figure 4.19 in *Social Trends*, 34.

Conclusion

The graph (Figure 7.11), based on the data below, shows how unemployment is rising steadily, year on year.

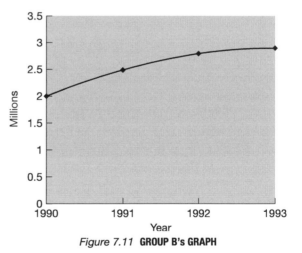

Figure 7.11 **GROUP B's GRAPH**

TABLE 7.4 UK Unemployment (millions)

1984	3.3	1991	2.5	1998	1.8
1985	3.2	1992	2.8	1999	1.8
1986	3.2	1993	2.9	2000	1.7
1987	3.0	1994	2.7	2001	1.5
1988	2.5	1995	2.5	2002	1.6
1989	2.1	1996	2.4	2003	1.5
1990	2.0	1997	2.1		

Group C

Data

As found from Figure 13.13 of *Social Trends*, 34, the percentage of UK households with home computers rose from 28% in 1997 to 48% in 2003.

Conclusion

Figure 7.12 shows the huge increase in owner-ship of home computers.

28%

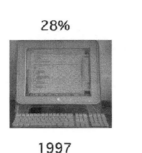

48%

1997   **2003**

Figure 7.12 **GROUP C's CHART**

Group D

Data

The bar chart in Figure 7.13 shows how our class gets to school.

Conclusion

This graph shows that most pupils walk to school, closely followed by car, then bus and finally train.

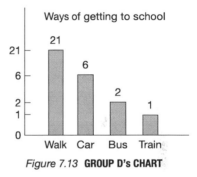

Figure 7.13 **GROUP D's CHART**

Group E

Data

These data show the number of crimes in the UK involving the use of firearms from 1997 to 2002.

'97/98	'98/99	'99/00	'00/01	'01/02
4903	5209	6843	7362	9974

Source: *Social Trends*, 35, Table 9.5.

Conclusion

Figure 7.14 shows a gentle increase in crimes involving the use of firearms over this period.

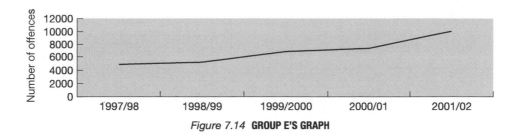

Figure 7.14 **GROUP E'S GRAPH**

Task 7.4.1 Spot the Cheat   **C**

(a) Look at each of the representations in turn and try to identify the form of misrepresentation used. Make a sketch of how the data might be represented more fairly.

(b) Make a note of any other possible form of distortion that you can identify.

7.5 PEDAGOGY

As usual, this section looks at teaching and learning issues, based on the six PTT themes.

Language Patterns

Task 7.5.1 Simplifying   **C**

A number of fairly sophisticated statistical ideas were discussed in this chapter. List five or six of the more difficult ideas and try to explain them for yourself in your own words. Then choose two of them and note down how you might present these ideas for a less sophisticated learner.

Imagery

Task 7.5.2 People Plots   **C**

How might the idea of 'people plots', introduced in the previous two chapters, help to support a learner's understanding of some of the ideas in this chapter?

Different Contexts

Task 7.5.3 Across the Curriculum   **C**

Try to find one or more other area of the curriculum where questions of *interrelating* might reasonably involve using and depicting data. Research several examples within that curriculum area. Use these examples to prepare an illustration of how visual comparisons might be used in other parts of the school curriculum.

Root Questions

Task 7.5.4 Correlation for a Younger Audience · C

Clearly, ideas involving the calculation and exact meaning of the correlation coefficient are too advanced for most learners at KS4 or below. Yet there are some important ideas about correlation of which even young learners should be aware. With a particular learner age in mind, note down some thoughts for how you might introduce to them some key aspects of the principles of correlation.

Standard Misconceptions

Learners will sometimes join adjacent points on a scatter plot, regardless of whether this is an appropriate or helpful thing to do.

Task 7.5.5 Dot-to-dot · C

(a) When is it appropriate and when inappropriate to join adjacent dots on a scatter plot?

(b) How can learners be helped to understand this subtle idea?

Techniques and Methods

Task 7.5.6 Preparation for Scatter Plots · C

What preparatory mathematical skills will learners require if they are to be able, successfully, to explore the idea of investigating relationships in paired data?

8
Picturing Probability

Like the rest of Block 2, this chapter looks at the learning and teaching implications of using pictures to investigate and communicate statistical ideas. But, being the final chapter in the block, it is also concerned with probability. As you might expect, therefore, you will be asked to revisit some of the problems and questions posed in Chapter 4, but this time representing them using helpful pictures.

Section 8.1 sets out some of the main ideas and terms of basic probability. Section 8.2 then looks at the notion of probability distributions and their importance when making decisions with data. In Section 8.3, you will read about an investigation into children's understanding of probability carried out by Michael Shaughnessy and Matthew Ciancetta. Section 8.4 introduces Jerome Bruner's three modes of thinking (*enactive*, *iconic* and *symbolic*) and applies them to probability ideas. As usual, the final section looks at teaching and learning issues.

8.1 SOME BASICS IN PROBABILITY

In this section, you are offered a quick run through some of the basic ideas in probability. If any of these are new to you, you will need to look elsewhere for more detailed explanations of these concepts. The tasks in this section are designed to help you think more deeply about some of the ideas and to consider how they might be introduced to learners.

Trials and Events

There are a variety of terms and concepts in probability that confuse both learners and teachers. A key term is the word used to describe a trial or experiment in probability, such as rolling a die, tossing a coin or spinning a spinner. These are often mistakenly and confusingly referred to as 'events' and until this terminological difficulty is dealt with, all that follows will be baffling to learners.

Task 8.1.1 Trials and Events	C
How would you distinguish the terms 'trial' and 'event'?	

Sample Space

A sample space is a set of all possible outcomes for a trial or experiment. For example, the sample space for rolling a die is normally written as {1, 2, 3, 4, 5, 6}.

The sample space for rolling a pair of dice has 36 outcomes, as follows: $\{(1, 1), (1, 2) (1, 3), \ldots, (6, 6)\}$.

Conditional Probability

One feature of probability is that the likelihood of a particular event can sometimes change as a result of some earlier event having taken place. For example, if you are drawing one ball at a time, *without replacement*, from a bag containing, say, three white balls and two red balls, then the probabilities of the various outcomes at each stage will vary, depending on which balls have already been removed. Contrast this with sampling *with replacement*, where the probabilities remain fixed.

Breathalyser tests provide a useful context for this idea. Table 8.1 contains an example taken from a Schools Council (1981, p. 5) publication, *Statistics in Your World*, in the unit 'Testing testing'.

TABLE 8.1 Results of 100 tests with a breathalyser

	Positive	Negative	Total
Drunk	23	6	29
Sober	8	63	71
Total	31	69	100

(In this example, the positive/negative categories are the result of taking a breathalyser test, while the drunk/sober judgements are a matter of legal definition from subsequent tests, tests which are accepted as authoritative.)

Task 8.1.2 Conditional Probability   **C**

(a) From the table above, calculate the proportion of:
   (i)   people who gave a positive reaction to the test;
   (ii) drunk people who gave a positive reaction to the test;
   (iii) people who gave a negative reaction to the test;
   (iv) sober people who gave a negative reaction to the test.
(b) What are the two types of error that can occur in a breathalyser test? On the basis of these data, estimate their probabilities.
(c) How might you use a table like this to introduce to learners the basic idea of conditional probability?

The questions posed in part (a) of Task 8.1.2 are based on proportions. A conceptual leap is required to translate these numbers into probabilities. This may require the learners to imagine choosing, at random, a person from the group of drunk drivers and asking, 'What is the probability that this person will test positive?', and so on.

Having established the link with probability, learners also need to grasp the notion of conditionality. One reason that they find ideas of conditional probability confusing may be a failure to think through the various probabilities contained in the question. For example, a clear distinction needs to be made between the proportion of all drivers who give a positive reaction to the test and the proportion of drunk drivers who give a positive reaction to the test. It is also important to find a shorthand way of expressing these ideas, so that they are clear, yet easily manipulable. The usual notation is of the form, p(N|S), where N refers to 'negative' and S refers to 'sober'. This expression p(N|S) means, 'the probability of an individual being tested negative, given that he or she was sober'.

Tree Diagrams

A tree diagram is a useful visual tool in teaching basic probability ideas. For example, the breathalyser data above can be presented in the form of a tree diagram to demonstrate the component proportions as follows.

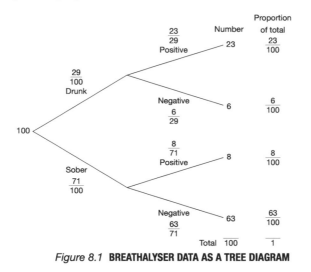

Figure 8.1 **BREATHALYSER DATA AS A TREE DIAGRAM**

As an aside, the tree diagram in Figure 8.1 has been drawn so that the drunk/sober distinction precedes the positive/negative judgement. In practice, these stages are the other way around – the roadside breathalyser test takes place *before* the formal tests that determine whether the driver is declared drunk or sober.

Look at the learner task below and then tackle Task 8.1.3.

Typical learner task

A family has three children.

(a) Show all the possible combinations of the sex of the children.
(b) Assume that the probability of any child being male (M) and being female (F) are each 1/2. Calculate the probability that all three children are not of the same sex.

Task 8.1.3 Tree Diagrams   **C**

Draw a tree diagram and complete this learner task.

In what ways is the tree diagram helpful in tackling questions like these? What are the limitations of using a tree diagram?

Venn Diagrams

Venn diagrams are traditionally used as a way of visualising sets. The notation used to define the various regions of the Venn diagram is set out in Figure 8.2 (in the simple two-circle case).

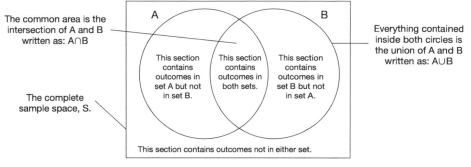

Figure 8.2 **A TWO-CIRCLE VENN DIAGRAM**

Task 8.1.4 Venn Diagrams   **C**

A Venn diagram is certainly useful for handling sets and subsets, but what has this got to do with probability?

Tables

Tables are also a useful way of illustrating probabilities and the various rules. Suppose that Tables 8.2(a) and 8.2(b) show a random sample of 764 learners sorted according to sex and whether they are in Further or Higher Education.

TABLES 8.2(a) and (b)

TABLE 8.2(a) Random sample of students by sex and education (fictitious)

Sample	Male	Female	Total
Further ed.	223	312	535
Higher ed.	101	128	229
Total	324	440	764

TABLE 8.2(b) Proportions based on Table 8.2(a)

Proportions	Male	Female	Total
Further ed.	0.29	0.41	0.70
Higher ed.	0.13	0.17	0.30
Total	0.42	0.58	1.00

A common misunderstanding is to confuse $p(A|B)$ and $p(B|A)$. This can be tackled from tables such Tables 8.2(a) and 8.2(b), by asking learners to calculate their respective conditional probabilities. For example, the calculations below distinguish the following two probabilities:

- that a learner is male, given that they are in Further Education;
- that a learner is in Further Education, given that they are male.

The point here is that calculating these values gives clearly different results.

$p(M|FE) = 223/535.$
$p(FE|M) = 223/324.$

Mutually Exclusive Events

Two or more events are mutually exclusive when the occurrence of one excludes the possibility that the other(s) can occur (that is, literally, they exclude each other). For example, when rolling a die, the events 'getting a 1' and 'getting an even score' are mutually exclusive, because they cannot both occur at the same time. (When drawn as a tree diagram, the branches from any particular node show the mutually exclusive outcomes at that stage.) Learners often find this difficult, partly for the reason that they do not clearly distinguish the trial from its outcomes. A key idea is that the concept of mutual exclusivity applies only to the events that result from a single trial (say, spinning a spinner or tossing a coin). Independence, on the other hand, is a concept that relates to performing two or more trials (for example, tossing a coin *and* rolling a die).

The Multiplication Rule

The probabilities of two separate events, A and B, are written as $p(A)$ and $p(B)$, respectively. In general, the probability of *both* of these events occurring is the product of the two probabilities. However, once A has already occurred, this may (or may not) affect the likelihood of B's occurrence. So, to be on the safe side, this rule is usually written as:

$p(A \text{ and } B) = p(A) \times p(B|A)$

Or, in words:

The probability of both A and B occurring equals the probability of A multiplied by the *probability of B given that A has already occurred.*

A key area of confusion for learners when using the multiplication rule is that they tend to believe that multiplication always makes numbers bigger. However, since probabilities are always in the range 0 to 1, multiplying two probabilities always makes these numbers smaller. It would be convenient to tackle this potential confusion by appealing to common sense: the phrase 'The likelihood of A *and* B occurring'. However, learners also tend to believe that 'A *and* B' has a greater probability than either 'A' or 'B' separately, so there are no easy insights here. Learners may need to spend considerable time with several practical and numerical examples before they are convinced that 'the probability of A and B' is usually less likely than either 'the probability of A' or 'the probability of B'. The probability with the greatest likelihood is 'the probability of A *or* B' (because it means A or B or both occurring).

Independence

Two events, A and B, are independent if the fact that A occurs does not affect the probability of B occurring. A possible source of confusion is a failure to realise, when considering independence, that these events A and B result from *different trials*.

Some examples of independent events are:

- a coin landing on tails and rolling a 1 on a die (the trial being tossing a coin and rolling a die);
- choosing a 10 from a deck of cards, replacing it and then choosing an ace as the second card;
- getting a 4 on a roll of a die and then getting a 1 on a second roll of that die.

An example of events that are not independent would be choosing an ace from a deck of cards, *not replacing it*, and then choosing a heart from the same deck.

When two events, A and B, are independent, it follows that $p(B|A) = p(B)$, so the probability of both occurring is:

$$p(A \text{ and } B) = p(A) \times p(B).$$

Task 8.1.5 Picturing Mutual Exclusivity and Independence   **C**

In this section, two representations were introduced that are used in probability – a Venn diagram and a tree diagram. Which would you prefer to use to teach about mutual exclusivity and which to teach about independence? Give your reasons.

8.2 PROBABILITY DISTRIBUTIONS

Something that lies at the very heart of probability and uncertainty is the fact that, in the events of the real world, things vary. Ronald Fisher, often referred to as the founder of modern statistics, had this to say about the nature of variation (written in 1925).

> The populations which are the object of statistical study always display variation in one or more respects. To speak of statistics as the study of variation also serves to emphasise the contrast between the aims of modern statisticians and those of their predecessors. For until comparatively recent times, the vast majority of workers in this field appear to have had no other aim than to ascertain aggregate, or average, values. The variation itself was not an object of study, but was viewed instead as a troublesome circumstance which detracted from the value of the average. (p. 3)

There are many ways in which one can describe variation. One is to measure it quantitatively using statistics such as the range, the interquartile range or the standard deviation. However, it can also be described visually. In this section, you will look at how suitable pictures can reveal insights into the exact nature of variation in different circumstances.

Golf and Dice Scores – Discrete Data

One of the great annual golf tournaments is the US Masters tournament, which was won in 2005 by Tiger Woods (Figure 8.3). As with most sports, golf is a statistical junkie's paradise and among the many obscure facts posted on golfing websites is the number of shots taken by each player on each round of the 18-hole course.

For example, Table 8.3 shows the scores taken by the 50 players at the eighteenth hole on their first round.

Figure 8.3 **TIGER WOODS WINNING THE GREEN JACKET (US MASTERS, 2005)**

*Source:*www.masters.org/images/pics/large/b_10_green jacket.jpg

TABLE 8.3 Masters score, hole 18

Score	3	4	5	6
Frequency	3	34	12	1

Source: www.masters.org/en_US/scores/hbyh/hbyh1_2.html

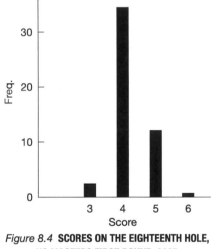

Figure 8.4 **SCORES ON THE EIGHTEENTH HOLE, US MASTERS FIRST ROUND, 2005**

These figures can be represented in a bar chart, as in Figure 8.4.

The scores range from a minimum of 3 to a maximum of 6. The most common scores lie in the middle of the range (4 and 5), while the least common scores are at the extremes (3 and 6). The overall shape of the distribution is that it peaks in the middle and tails off at the extremes.

Questions such as the following could be posed.

- What was the most common/least common score?
- How many scores of less than 5 were recorded?

These sorts of questions can be answered by looking at the heights of the bars or, in the latter case, to add two or more bars together.

Task 8.2.1 Varying Golf Scores

(a) How would you describe the pattern of these golf scores?

(b) What sorts of questions might this information allow you to pose and how might you use the bar chart to answer them?

(c) How is this connected to probability?

(d) Find two other sporting contexts where one could gain access to discrete frequency data like these and use them to illustrate variation.

The move from questions of fact based on the data in Table 8.3 to questions of probability is a subtle but important one. It is a shift from what has already happened to what might happen in the future under similar circumstances. For example, 3 out of the 50 scores were less than 4. A corresponding probability question might be: 'If *a randomly chosen player* from the tournament were asked to play this hole again, *under similar playing conditions*, what is the probability that his first round score would be less than 4?' A reasonable answer to this question might be about 3/50 or 0.06. Note, however, the two caveats marked above in italics.

A related question would be to ask: 'If a player were chosen at random from this tournament, what is the probability that his score was less than 4?' However, with this wording, the answer is *exactly* 3/50.

Other contexts could include:

- soccer – the number of matches containing 0, 1, 2, (and so on) goals;
- cricket – the number of wickets taken by a bowler in each match over a season.

Task 8.2.2 provides another example of discrete data – the scores on the roll of a die.

Task 8.2.2   Dice Distribution

Imagine that you were able to roll a fair die hundreds of times and then plot the outcome frequencies using a bar chart. How might the overall shape of the distribution of dice scores compare with that of the golf scores?

The range of dice scores will run from 1 to 6, rather than 3 to 6 and, in both cases, the bars will be separated by spaces, emphasising the fact that the data are discrete. However, unlike with the golf scores, you would not expect the dice distribution to peak in the middle. On the contrary, given the large batch size, you might expect the frequencies of these six outcomes to be almost exactly equal. This shape, where the heights of each bar are uniformly equal, is referred to as a *uniform distribution*, for obvious reasons.

Make the 'probability shift' now into the future and consider how likely it is that the next roll of a fair die will produce a 1, 2, 3, and so on. Based on an assumption of equal likelihood, it is now reasonable to assume that each outcome is exactly equally likely, with a probability of 1/6. This affects how you will draw the corresponding bar chart, as you can see from Figures 8.5(a) and 8.5(b).

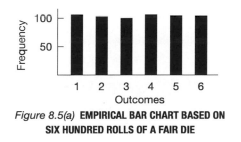

Figure 8.5(a) **EMPIRICAL BAR CHART BASED ON SIX HUNDRED ROLLS OF A FAIR DIE**

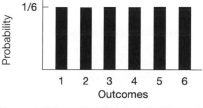

Figure 8.5(b) **THEORETICAL BAR CHART FOR THE NEXT ROLL OF A FAIR DIE**

Task 8.2.3   Comparing the Bar Charts

Note down two important differences between these two bar charts.

The bars on the empirical bar chart are not all exactly the same height, because you might expect some small differences due to natural variation, even though the six outcomes are equally likely. On the theoretical bar chart, all the bars are equal, because it describes a model or idealised form of a perfect die with equally likely outcomes.

The empirical bar chart describes the results of an actual experiment so the vertical scale reads 'Frequency'. The theoretical bar chart describes your best estimate of the likelihood of getting 1, 2, 3, and so on, *on the next roll of a perfect die* and so it reads 'Probability' on the vertical scale.

Robin Egg Weights – Continuous Data

As has already been mentioned, a feature of discrete data such as golf or dice scores is that they can be represented using a bar chart, one where each bar is of the same width and there are gaps between the bars. For a bar chart, then, the height of each bar is a measure of its frequency. This contrasts with graphing a continuous variable like weight or height, where a histogram should be used rather than a bar chart, and frequencies are represented by area rather than height. This is considered below, by means of an examination of the weights of robins' eggs.

Figure 8.6 **ROBINS FEEDING**
Source: www.bbc.co.uk/stoke/
features/2003/05/robin_mating.shtml
Courtesy of David Tideswell

The eggs of common birds are difficult to distinguish by colour alone. Typically, a robin's egg weighs around 2.7 g. An average clutch contains five or six eggs and their combined weight represents a remarkable 80 per cent of the adult robin's total body weight (Figure 8.6).

Task 8.2.4 Whose Egg?   C

Suppose that you are shown a whiteish egg weighing 3.1 g. Do you think this could be a robin's egg? What additional statistical information would you need to know about the weight of robin eggs, in order to help answer this question?

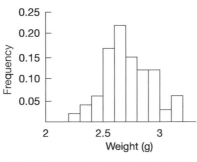

Figure 8.7 **EMPIRICAL DISTRIBUTION OF ROBIN EGG WEIGHTS**

The histogram in Figure 8.7 shows the distribution of weights of 100 robin eggs.

The egg-weight histogram is based on empirical data. Any decision that you might make about any future egg will be based on a similar-looking theoretical probability distribution, which you might expect to look like that in Figure 8.8.

Task 8.2.5 Whose Egg Revisited?

Draw a vertical line on the histogram corresponding to the weight of the unmarked egg.

Based just on this weight information, how likely is a robin to have laid this weight of egg?

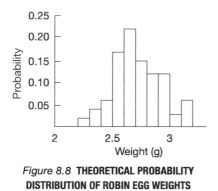

Figure 8.8 **THEORETICAL PROBABILITY DISTRIBUTION OF ROBIN EGG WEIGHTS**

The height of each column now corresponds to the probability of a randomly chosen robin's egg falling into this weight interval and this is calculated by dividing the corresponding frequency by 100 (the number of eggs in the batch). Whereas, with discrete data, probabilities of particular outcomes were represented by *lengths* of the corresponding bars, with continuous data such as weight or height, the probability that the next value falls within a given range is represented by the *area* contained within the probability distribution above that range of values.

In the case of the unusually large egg weighing 3.1 g, the probability of the next robin's egg you weigh being 3.1 g or more corresponds to the shaded area in Figure 8.9. This principle of relating probabilities to areas under probability distributions lies at the heart of statistical decision-making and is one that many learners at a higher level fail to grasp fully.

In this example, the shaded area corresponds to about 7% of the entire probability distribution, so, based on this particular probability model, there would be roughly a 7% chance of getting an egg at least as large as this *by chance alone*. On the basis of this information, you can then form a judgement of whether you really believe that this is a robin's egg.

Note that this is just one possible model of the distribution of robin egg weights, based upon data from a particular batch of 100 eggs. If another batch were selected, the picture might look slightly different. However, it is likely that all such models would follow the pattern common to most measurements in nature – that it peaks in the middle and tails off to both extremes.

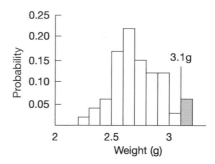

Figure 8.9 **BIRD EGG-WEIGHT PROBABILITIES**

Task 8.2.6 A Perfect Model

Now imagine creating the perfect probability model of robin egg weights.

How might you adjust your batch selection, measurement and choice of display of the data to create a more perfect picture of the underlying probability model?

What shape would you expect the 'perfect' model to take?

In order to achieve the perfect model, you will need to increase the batch size to infinity, measure each egg to the accuracy of an infinite number of decimal places and, when drawing the data as a histogram, reduce the widths of each bar to zero.

These adjustments are, of course, impossible to achieve in practice. However, it is possible, mathematically, to create a model of the perfect distribution that appears to match the picture of variation common to many growing things in nature very closely.

It is called the *normal* curve – sometimes referred to as the bell-shaped curve or the Gaussian curve, after its inventor, Carl Friedrich Gauss (1777–1855) – and is shown in Figure 8.10. The mathematical formula defining a normal curve is also shown in Figure 8.10.

The 'perfect' theoretical probability distribution – the 'normal' curve

Look at the right-hand side of the equation, for which X is the random variable. Ignoring constants like 2 and π, notice that the probability function, $p(X)$ is determined by just two parameters, the mean, μ, and the standard deviation, σ (pronounced, respectively 'mew'

$$p(X) = \frac{1}{\sqrt{2\pi\sigma^2}} \, e^{\frac{-(X-\mu)^2}{2\sigma^2}}$$

Figure 8.10 **THE NORMAL DISTRIBUTION**

and 'sigma'). As you will see when you study Block 3 (Chapters 9–12), this is a useful property of the normal distribution, as it will allow you, easily, to create artificial but realistic data for a particular variable, using just these two numbers, the mean and standard deviation.

8.3 TESTING CHILDREN'S UNDERSTANDING OF PROBABILITY

In 2002, Michael Shaughnessy and Matthew Ciancetta presented a paper to the Sixth International Conference on Teaching Statistics (ICOTS 6) entitled, 'Students' understanding of variability in a probability environment' (www.stat.auckland.ac.nz/~iase/publications.php?show=1).

In it, they investigated how important it was for learners to clarify the sample space when investigating a probability task. Here is the problem that their learners were asked to tackle.

These two fair spinners are part of a carnival game. A player wins a prize only when both arrows land on black after each spinner has been spun once. Jeff thinks he has a 50–50 chance of winning.

Do you agree?

A Yes   B No

Justify your answer.

B = black, W = white

Task 8.3.1 Two Spinners	**C**

(a) Complete your own answer to this question.

(b) Note down several reasons why you think learners might fail to get the correct answer.

A possible reason that some might fail to get the correct answer of B is a failure to understand, fully, the question. In particular, they may not have grasped that *two* conditions must be satisfied in order to win the prize.

As reported in Shaughnessy and Ciancetta's paper, only about 20% of the learners in grades 6 to 8 (aged 12–14 years) chose option B, and of these, some gave incorrect or quirky reasons for their answers. Here are three of the quirkier responses.

No, Jeff does not have a 50–50 chance of winning this game because:

- you can never tell with spinners;
- carnival games are rigged;
- anything that you believe can happen.

Where learners gave the correct answer with correct reasoning, they tended to list the sample space or use the multiplication principle. The reasoning of learners who thought there *was* a 50–50 chance of winning the game was largely based on the half-black, half-white areas in the spinners. ('They're half of a circle, so 1/2 is 50% and the other half is 50%'; 'Both spinners have an equal amount of B and W so it's 50–50'; 'The circles are exactly in half', and so on.)

Interviews with these learners showed that they did not have much practical experience with probability tasks in terms of actually trying them out for themselves. Shaughnessy and Ciancetta conducted a follow-up investigation of 28 learners aged 14–16, where each learner played the game 10 times with actual spinners and recorded their results. They were then given the 'carnival' question again to see if these practical experiences affected their judgement. The results of this experiment are set out in Table 8.4.

TABLE 8.4 Summary frequencies for learners interviewed on the spinner game

n = 28	'Before' data	'After' data
Yes, game 50–50	15	5
No, game not 50–50	13	23
Correct reasons	5	12
Incorrect reasons	23	16

Task 8.3.2 Consequences

What conclusion can you draw from these data?

What conclusions might you expect these learners to come to on the basis of carrying out these 10 trials as described above?

The percentage of learners giving the correct response went up from 46% (13/28) to 82% (23/28), which is a very significant increase.

It is likely that almost all of the learners who actually play the game 10 times will find that they win the game less than five times. At this point, they can choose to believe that they were simply unlucky or take the view that their original 50–50 theory was flawed. An interesting consequence of this experiment was that many of these learners 'discovered' empirically that the game had to be less than 50–50 for wins. It is likely that this really did change their intuition about how the game was structured, thereby enabling them to consider why it was not 50–50 – something that many of them had resisted considering before.

Interestingly, one might imagine that the five learners who maintained their belief that the game was 50–50 did so as a result of getting particularly high scores (such as 4 or 5) in their experiment. In fact, this was not the case; the results of these learners ranged from 0 wins, 10 losses up to 3 wins, 7 losses. For these learners, the departure from 50–50 was perhaps not sufficiently large to warrant a change of view.

It is possible that increasing the number of trials from 10 up to, say, 30 may have helped these learners. However, the authors questioned whether these learners were able to relate their intuitions to the experimental results at all. They may have had a poor intuition about how extreme a result must be in order to question their initial model. This is something that you will look at again in Chapter 12, when you are asked to explore how calculator and computer simulations can help to develop this sort of intuition.

Another interesting consequence was that seeing the actual data and seeing the variation in repeated samples of 10 trials led a number of the learners, without prompting, to construct the sample space for themselves. This encouraged the authors to believe that 'there is a connection between the concept of sample space in probability and the concept of expected variation of the value of a random variable in statistics' (Shaughnessy and Ciancetta, 2002, p. 5). Expressed more simply, they suggested that the act of spelling out clearly all the possible outcomes of a particular trial makes learners more aware of how things vary and can thereby become better equipped to understand the underlying probabilities.

Task 8.3.3 Wrong Justification

What is wrong with the following learner justification for why Jeff had a less than 50–50 chance of winning this game?

'The chance is 1/3 as there are three outcomes, BB, WW, BW.'

This is a very common error. The problem lies with the BW outcomes which learners may classify, misleadingly, as 'one of each'. This masks the fact that there are two ways of achieving this result (BW and WB). A sensible approach is for the teacher to encourage learners to be explicit about setting out the sample space, perhaps by using a tree diagram.

8.4 PICTURING PROBABILITY PROBLEMS

Jerome Bruner

Jerome Bruner (Figure 8.11) was born in New York in 1915. He had a difficult start in life, undergoing, at the age of 2, several cataract operations. His father died when he was 12, after which the family moved frequently and Jerome's education was greatly interrupted by frequent changes of school. However, despite these early setbacks, he excelled at school and university. Among other jobs, he held the post of Professor of Psychology at Harvard for 20 years (1952–1972) and then Watts Professor at Oxford University (1972–1980).

Figure 8.11
JEROME BRUNER (1915–)

Bruner's major contribution to education theory has been in the development of cognitive psychology as an alternative to the behaviourist theories that dominated psychology in the first half of the twentieth century. He demonstrated how thought processes could be classified into the following three distinct 'worlds of experience':

- enactive mode (manipulating objects, spatial awareness);
- iconic mode (visual recognition, the ability to compare and contrast);
- symbolic mode (abstract reasoning).

These three modes are often referred to as 'EIS': expressed simply, they correspond to 'action', 'pictures' and 'symbols'. In contrast to Piaget, who related each of his (four) modes to a specific period of childhood development, Bruner believed that, for a particular learner, while one mode was dominant during a given developmental phase, all modes were present and accessible throughout.

Bruner argued that information or knowledge is most effectively gained by personal discovery and advocated that learners should be allowed to pursue learning independently. Through discussion, a teacher would help learners to select and process information, construct hypotheses and make decisions, based on their own thinking capabilities.

EIS and Probability

In Chapter 4, you were introduced to a number of classic problems in probability. These were: Jannie and Peter, '-ing' words, hospital births, the birthday problem and the Monty Hall dilemma.

These are all problems that most learners have some difficulty in grasping. Thinking particularly of Bruner's 'E' and 'I' modes of thinking, it may be possible to find alternative ways of presenting or re-presenting these problems, so as to make them more tractable for learners.

Task 8.4.1   Jannie – Classical Studies or English Teacher?

Reread the problem describing 'Jannie' in Task 4.2.1. Given these background facts about her, you were asked whether it is more likely that Jannie teaches Classical Studies or English. Try to find an iconic mode of representation that might make the solution easier for learners to grasp.

What lies at the heart of this problem is that the base of English teachers is very much larger than that of Classical Studies. It is possible to adapt a Venn diagram to gain insights into this situation. With Venn diagrams, there is usually no meaning attached to the actual size of the regions. However, in Figure 8.12, it has been drawn so that the areas are in proportion to the relative frequencies of each region.

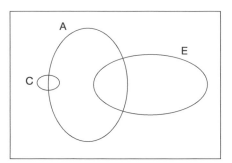

Figure 8.12 **A THREE-CIRCLE VENN DIAGRAM**

The three groups of people are the Classical Studies teachers (C), English teachers (E) and people who like watching television programmes on archaeology (A). Notice that, as drawn here, roughly half of the Classical Studies teachers enjoy watching television programmes on archaeology, whereas only about a quarter of English teachers do.

However, because the base of English teachers is so much larger than that of Classical Studies teachers, this has a much greater effect on the overall result. In probability terms, the question can be restated as follows. Given that you are presented with a person who enjoys watching television programmes on archaeology, you are considering only ellipse A. Considering only the regions within ellipse A, then, are you more likely to also be within ellipse E or ellipse C? The answer is the former, because the area of intersection A∩E is much larger than A∩C.

Task 8.4.2 Applying Bruner's Modes to Other Problems	C

Consider the problems below from Chapter 4 and explore how Bruner's modes of thinking might be used to help learners gain deeper insights into these problems:

Peter – Rock band or tennis; '-ing' words; hospital births; the Monty Hall dilemma.

For each example, indicate which mode, E, I or S, you used.

8.5 PEDAGOGY

This section looks at teaching and learning issues about probability, based on the six PTT themes.

Language Patterns

Task 8.5.1 Simplifying

A number of important ideas on probability were introduced in this chapter. List as many as you can and try to explain them for yourself in your own words. Then choose two of them and note down how you might present these ideas for a less sophisticated learner.

The following terms were introduced in this chapter: sample space, trial, event, outcome, tree diagram, Venn diagram, union, intersection, conditional probability, independence, mutually exclusive events, probability distributions, normal (Gaussian or bell-shaped) curve/distribution, Bruner's EIS modes.

Although probability ideas are often dealt with symbolically in textbooks, this sort of abstract treatment may mask the meaning and significance of the underlying ideas for learners. For example, the idea of 'independence' has applications in a wide variety of everyday situations with which learners can strongly identify. The notion of the 'gambler's fallacy' rests on a misconception of statistical independence and this was discussed in Section 4.4. Many learners believe that, because their turn has not come up for a long time, it is more likely to come up soon.

This may be true of certain situations (your turn to do the washing up, for example), but is not true of random situations, where the die or coin have no memory of previous 'successes' and 'failures'. A useful exercise for learners is to distinguish between these two types of situation and so gain a greater insight into the meaning of the term 'random'. They might also be interested in the article in Figure 8.13 about the 'Curse of 53' in Italy and try to see how it relates to the idea of statistical independence.

Imagery

Curse of 53
Italy's unlucky number

John Hooper in Rome

Millions of Italians will today nervously wait to see if the most costly losing streak in their country's gambling history comes to an end.

Already, an estimated €2bn (£1.38bn) has been lost by punters convinced that a "missing number" in Italy's biggest lottery is more likely than any other to come up.

The latest victim of what has become known as Venice 53 is a pensioner from Frosinone, south of Rome. He was reported yesterday to have fallen into the hands of loan sharks after losing €80,000. Elsewhere, there have been stories of entire families ruined by repeated losing bets on Italy's state-run draw, the Lotto.

Fifty numbers between 1 and 90 are drawn every week – five in each of ten cities around the country. Punters place bets on which numbers, or combinations, will come up – and where.

So far, the number 53 has 163 times failed to be plucked from the basket in Venice. More money has now been staked on this *ritardatario*, or delayed number, than on any in the history of the draw.

This has brought Italy's state lottery monopoly an unlikely bonanza at a time when the economy is barely growing. Officials predicted the take this year would be up by almost 40%.

Source: Hooper (2004, p. 18).

Figure 8.13 ***GUARDIAN* NEWSPAPER ARTICLE**

Task 8.5.2 Sample Space

The term 'sample space' conjures up an image of outcomes of some trial or experiment existing in space. Is this a useful image to develop and, if so, how might it be developed in learners?

The notion of outcomes covering a space is a very useful mental image, as it ties in strongly with the use of Venn diagrams and tables for clarifying the nature of possible events resulting from a trial. There are two important aspects to this. First, when enumerating the various outcomes that comprise an event, the number of (equally likely) outcomes should correspond, visually, with the area of that part of the diagram represented by the event in question – the greater the probability, the larger the area. Secondly, where events overlap (for example, when rolling a die, consider the two events 'getting an even score' and 'getting a score greater than 2'), the various regions in the Venn diagram help to clarify the various combinations of events that might occur.

Different Contexts

Task 8.5.3 Tossing Spinners and Urns?

A commonly heard objection to using dice, coins, spinners and urns in teaching probability is that they are abstract and irrelevant to learners' lives and would be much better replaced with more everyday scenarios. What are some of the arguments for and against this view?

Dice, coins and spinners are indeed abstract and fairly irrelevant to learners' lives. They have the additional disadvantage that they often connect to tasks involving prediction and gambling, and there may be religious and cultural difficulties here for the teacher. However, their very abstraction brings certain benefits, such as the elimination of contextual ambiguity. For example, when a 'perfectly symmetrical' die is rolled, learners can quickly accept the equally likely nature of the six outcomes and recognise that, for each roll, the probabilities of the outcomes are all equal to 1/6. This is a useful shared starting point for any subsequent investigation about the nature and properties of equal likelihood. Contrast this with more 'interesting' or everyday contexts for conducting probability investigations, such as the chance of being chosen to represent the class on the school council or the probability of getting your favourite meal in the school canteen.

In many cases, these situations are either not based on chance alone or are already predetermined (personal preferences come into play when choosing people for teams or committees and the cook knows in advance what meals will be on offer). These contexts may make for interesting discussion points, but they offer poor models on which to base an investigation of equal likelihood, not least because they are unlikely to be based on equally likely outcomes.

If you wish to avoid dice and coins, an alternative approach to investigating the settling down of relative frequencies is to use real-world statistical data. For example, suppose learners wanted to estimate the probability of a home win in a Football Association premiership match chosen at random. They could look at the proportion of home wins in the first week of a season, the first month, the season to Christmas, the whole season and over a number of seasons.

Root Questions

Task 8.5.4 Sample Space

Identify a root question about probability that connects with ideas of sample space. How might you present this idea to learners?

One of the conclusions drawn by Shaughnessy and Ciancetta (Section 8.3) was that encouraging learners to take an empirical approach to probability (that is, them actually carrying out the experiment) led them to list the elements of the sample space and this helped provide them with clarification of the problem and insights into the solution. It is also possible that the listing of the sample space helped to distinguish for learners the trial or experiment from its outcomes. There is evidence that many learners and some teachers have difficulties with probability because they confuse these two aspects – that is, distinguishing 'what you do' from 'what you get'. A possible related exercise for learners, therefore, might be to provide them with a list of trials and events and their task is to match them up.

Trials: rolling a die, tossing a coin, tossing a drawing pin, spinning a spinner, ...
Events: landing on its back, getting a 6, getting an even number, getting heads, ...

Standard Misconceptions

Task 8.5.5 You Can Never Tell with Spinners

The research report by Shaughnessy and Ciancetta outlined in Section 8.3 indicated several potential areas of learner misconception. Identify one of these and briefly outline a short research project that you might carry out with one or more learners in order to investigate this further.

One of the learner's justifications was that there were three possible outcomes of the carnival game exercise, BB, WW and BW, and that therefore these outcomes were equally likely, with a probability of 1/3 each. There are two issues here linked to learner misconceptions. First, this threefold identification of the sample space is correct only if the order of the spinners is ignored. If this learner had identified the sample space using a tree diagram, he or she would have discovered that there are two ways of achieving 'one of each colour' (that is, BW and WB). It may not be obvious initially to learners that the 'number of ways' is important in determining the relative probabilities of each outcome.

Secondly, some learners believe that, in general, all outcomes are equally likely, even when they are not. ('I'll either pass my driving test or fail it, so I've got a 50-50 chance!') One way of unpicking these two interconnected areas of confusion is to provide learners with challenges similar to the carnival game, where the outcomes are not equally likely – for example, predicting the most/least likely scores on the sum of two dice. Such an experiment may involve the following steps.

- Set up the task description and ask the learners for their intuitive response – what would you expect?
- Ask the learners to provide a justification for their response.
- Invite them to carry out the task empirically to see whether their hypothesis is justified.
- For those learners whose intuitions have been challenged, ask them to think of alternative explanations.

Techniques and Methods

Task 8.5.6 Empirical Approaches to Probability

An issue that emerged from Section 8.3 was the importance of practical approaches to probability in supporting learners' intuitions. What are some of the issues that this raises for the teacher?

One of the apparent paradoxes in probability is that, while the outcome of the next roll of a die or toss of a coin may be unpredictable, there *are* nevertheless underlying patterns in the outcomes overall. Specifically, when a fair die is rolled many times, there is a 'settling down' effect as the proportion of each outcome (1, 2, 3, ..., 6) gradually approaches 1/6. In the limiting case, as the number of rolls reaches infinity, the shape of the probability distribution becomes uniform.

Practical approaches involving learners actually rolling dice and tossing coins are good for revealing the unpredictable nature of randomness. But, within the time constraints of a lesson, they are less good for showing these underlying patterns – achieving the 'settling down' effect may require a larger number of rolls or tosses than realistically there is time for in a class lesson. For example, in the carnival game task described in Section 8.3, each learner was asked to carry out 10 plays in order to test their intuitions about whether the game was 50–50. With a sample size as small as 10, a learner might reasonably feel (even if they could not clearly articulate it) that the settling-down effect had not yet occurred and therefore there was insufficient empirical evidence to support or challenge either hypothesis.

Another possible way of speeding up practical approaches is to take advantage of ICT simulations. However, this brings with it other dangers, such as learners losing a clear sense of what the experiment is actually about and, indeed, whether the machine simulation really is a fair substitute for the actual experiment.

Introduction to Block 3

In Blocks 1 and 2, you looked at four statistical themes (describing, comparing, interrelating and uncertainty) through the media of words, numbers and pictures. Block 3 considers the same four themes, but in the context of ICT, using mainly spreadsheets and graphics calculators but to a lesser extent statistics packages and Java applets.

The statistical 'big ideas' include the role of terminology and notation in statistics, and the idea of a *parameter* and how it differs from a *statistic*. Spreadsheets and calculators permit the calculation of two different standard deviations and you will look at why they differ. You are asked to reconsider many of the problems posed in earlier chapters with the aid of ICT tools. Having tackled these tasks, you will be able to consider which tool is best to use for which occasion and how students can be supported in making such choices.

Teaching ideas are largely based on ICT-based investigations. These include the generation of data as well as helping students to deepen their understanding of the calculations performed automatically by technological tools (for example, finding the standard deviation).

9

Describing with ICT

Chapters 9 to 12 look at issues to do with using ICT in the teaching of statistics. As with Blocks 1 and 2, the four chapters deal, respectively with the themes of describing, comparing, interrelating and uncertainty.

The opening section of this chapter looks at a wide range of general issues to do with the use of ICT in statistics teaching and includes brief descriptions of some of the better-known software applications. Section 9.2 looks more specifically at teaching statistics with ICT, while Sections 9.3 and 9.4 look at some particular ways in which a spreadsheet package such as Excel can support statistics learning. The final section explores some of the pedagogic implications of using ICT. This closing section ends with an explanation of why, when you use ICT to calculate the standard deviation of a set of data, you are offered two possible answers.

9.1 THE PLACE OF ICT IN STATISTICS EDUCATION

The question, 'Why integrate ICT into mathematics teaching?' is the title of the fourth chapter of Adrian Oldknow and Ron Taylor's (2000) book on teaching mathematics with ICT. In their attempt to answer this question, they suggest the following three possible reasons:

- desirability (basically, ICT is a 'good thing');
- inevitability (the technology is here and its traditional alternatives are increasingly disappearing);
- public policy (ICT use in education is endorsed and indeed prescribed by government).

Technology can bring many benefits to learners' statistical learning, not least by the way in which it encourages interaction with data. As Peter Johnston-Wilder (2005) argues:

> the possibility of interacting with different representations of data can enable the user to receive feedback from the visual display and build a sense of how to set up such displays to communicate most effectively. Such interactivity can help to enable users to see statistical displays as dynamic and general, rather than static and particular. (p. 102)

A general question to be explored involves 'which technology to use for which occasion' and, indeed, whether to use it at all.

Task 9.1.1 Pros and Cons   C

List at least three potential benefits and at least three potential drawbacks of using ICT in the teaching of statistics.

Throughout Chapters 9–12, you are asked to consider the implications of using ICT in the teaching and learning of statistics. There are many interesting technologies in this category, such as:

- computer applications (statistical packages, spreadsheets, web browsers);
- computer demonstration software (for example, Java applets);
- graphics calculators.

You will also consider a variety of possible tasks for which these technologies can be used by learners – for example:

- data handling (displaying, summarising and graphing data);
- accessing data from other sources as part of an investigation;
- using data simulations in order to investigate and interact with certain statistical patterns or principles.

You may have thought of further benefits of using ICT in statistics, including the use of word processors by learners to support their initial thinking and planning, and to be able to type up a report of what they have done. In an article by Neville Hunt (2005), you can read how a teacher can use the mail-merge facility of a word processor to generate different exercises for each learner. There are many other articles by Neville Hunt published in *Teaching Statistics* and elsewhere on the use of ICT (particularly Microsoft Excel) to teach statistics. These are referenced on his website: www.mis.coventry.ac.uk/~nhunt/pubs.htm

Task 9.1.2 Tools and Goals · C

Clearly these different technological tools serve different purposes in the broad goal of teaching statistics.

Spend a few minutes thinking about which tools serve which goal. The table below should help you to organise your thinking about this. One cell has already been completed. The placing of 'handling data' (HD) in this first cell suggests that the role of statistical packages in the carrying out of a statistical investigation is well served by *handling* the *data* that forms part of the investigation. Try to complete as many other cells as you feel appropriate. For simplicity, restrict your entries to the following categories: 'handling data' (HD), 'accessing data' (AD) and 'data simulations' (DS).

	Goal	
Tool	Carrying out a statistical investigation	Learning statistical concepts
Statistical packages	HD	
Spreadsheets		
Web browsers		
Java applets		
Graphics calculators		

Educational Software

Some technologies (for example, the statistical package *Tinkerplots*) have been specifically designed for educational use, while others, such as the powerful spreadsheet
package *Excel*, have not. Indeed, most statistical software has been designed primarily for
use in business or higher-education contexts. This raises the question of how suitable
they are for younger school-age learners. As Biehler (1995) argues: '[Young learners]
need a tool that is designed from the bottom-up perspective of statistical novices and
can develop in various ways into a full professional tool (not vice versa)' (p. 3).

Task 9.1.3 Educational or Professional Tools?   **C**

How do you feel about your learners using professional rather than educational software and hardware? Do you agree with Biehler that statistical novices should start off using proprietary tools
designed specifically for their needs?

Statistical Packages for Schools

There are a number of excellent statistics packages aimed at the school market. Three
that are now well established in the USA are *Fathom*, *TI-Interactive!* and, aimed at a
younger age group, *Tinkerplots*. From the UK, also look out for *Autograph*.

Well-designed statistical packages do more than simply summarise and graph data.
Here are some additional features to look for:

- linked data formats – data are simultaneously displayed in a variety of formats,
  including raw data, dot plot, box plot, histogram, and so on;
- dynamic adjustment – if a data item is altered in one format, it is automatically
  altered in all other formats;
- simulation – it is easy to generate (and display) simulated data using a variety of the
  random models provided.

Tinkerplots

Details of *Tinkerplots* can be found at: www.umass.edu/srri/serg/projects/tp/
tpmain.html

Tinkerplots is a highly imaginative and accessible package that is suitable for young
learners. The website provides helpful movie clips that will give teachers and learners
a quick and informed overview of what the package does and how it operates. When
a data batch is first opened, the values appear as a confused mass of small circles (sig-
nalling the disorder inherent in raw data). The user can quickly sort or group the data
by a variety of features, simply by dragging points around the screen. Good use is
made of colour and the emphasis is very much on exploiting how data look graphically as an aid to analysing them and then interpreting any conclusions that might be
drawn from them.

Fathom

Details of *Fathom* can be found at: www.keypress.com/fathom/

Fathom is a powerful statistics package (available in both PC and Mac versions) and is suitable for use with learners aged 14 and upwards. It provides the following features:

- dynamic selection of data and linking between different formats – for example, when you add or drag a point, everything that depends upon it (such as any calculated statistics) automatically updates;
- exploration tools that encourage learners to ask 'what if?' questions;
- over 200 real-life data sets, which are provided with the package;
- sampling and simulation tools that enable learners to set up populations and sample from them repeatedly, thereby helping them to get a feel for the sampling process and the creation of sampling distributions;
- 'sliders' that can stand for a parameter in any mathematical model and which then can be referred to by name in a formula;
- a comprehensive resource book, which offers a range of mathematical and statistical activities;
- drag-and-drop data, which enables users to import their own data from other resources, such as *Excel* documents or the Internet (simply click on a URL and drag it into *Fathom*);
- linked highlighting, whereby if you highlight a selection of points in the table, they are also highlighted in any graphic representation, and vice versa – this can be very useful in interpreting the data.

Autograph

Autograph is a mathematics package designed to support the teaching of graphs and statistics, devised by Douglas Butler of Oundle School. The graphs section can be used with elementary topics such as co-ordinates through to quadratic equations and far beyond. The statistics component allows the user to handle both raw data and probability distributions. The package can be used to create dynamic models that will enable you to set up and test hypotheses. Used in conjunction with a word processor, such as *Word* from *Microsoft Office*, the program is a useful tool for preparing and presenting project work and reports. A wide range of support material and supplementary activities can also be found at the publisher's website (www.autograph-math.com).

As with other software applications, there tends to be a fairly steep learning curve for the first-time user. While some experienced computer users can often make intelligent guesses at how particular features work, by means of transferring certain principles from other software packages, many features of a new package nevertheless need careful handling at the start. Increasingly, professionally designed applications are supported by demonstrations available on a website or disc, which can prove an excellent starting point. *Autograph* is well supported with a variety of resources, including 'demos' and classroom resources: you are recommended to watch one of the *Autograph* demonstrations now.

Task 9.1.4 Running the Demo

Access the Autograph home page using the URL: www.autograph-math.com

Click 'Autograph in Action' on the left of the screen.

Double click on the first 'Statistics' demo file, named Rawdata.

Click the green arrow on the Player button bar to play the demonstration of how to display a histogram describing a data set of 200 marks. It moves fairly quickly and takes just 53 seconds. If you are watching the demo via the Lotus ScreenCam application, you can pause at any point, replay or fast-forward using the icons in the Player button bar. Watch the demonstration carefully (several times, if necessary) and write down the stages that you see demonstrated.

If you have access to the application *Autograph*, carry out for yourself the procedure shown on the demonstration. You may like to watch the demonstration again more than once, until you are fairly confident that you will be able to do this.

9.2 TEACHING STATISTICS WITH ICT

Now that ICT has become more firmly established in mathematics and statistics teaching at school level, teachers have many more choices to make when planning their statistics lessons. This section looks at some of the software and learner issues that might arise.

Software Issues

The question for teachers here is not simply whether or not to use ICT but also, presuming the answer is in the affirmative, which hardware/software to use for which purposes. These decisions will vary, depending on the topic, the age, ability and experience of the learners and the type of course being taught (specialist or general).

Task 9.2.1 Which Software?   **C**

(a) Write down the names of several computer applications (as well as the graphics calculator) that you might use with learners as part of their statistical education. Try to classify each application into *one or more* of the following headings:

(i) specialist;

(ii) generalist;

(iii) specifically geared to education.

(b) What are some advantages and disadvantages of each of these three categories of application?

(c) What problems could you foresee when using these applications across the curriculum in school?

It is one thing to be aware of the range of applications available to learners in their learning of statistics, but it is quite another to know what ICT tools (if any) are most suitable in the various teaching situations that a teacher faces.

Task 9.2.2 What to Choose?

(a) What criteria might you use to decide whether or not to make use of ICT when teaching a particular topic in statistics?

(b) If you should decide to use ICT for teaching a particular topic, how might you make the decision of which tool to use?

To answer the first question, Oldknow and Taylor (2000) refer to three criteria offered by the UK Teacher Training Agency (www.teach.gov.uk) when making decisions about ICT use.

- Decisions about when, when not, and how to use ICT in lessons should be based on whether ICT supports good practice in teaching the subject. If it does not, it should not be used.

- In planning and in teaching, decisions about when, when not, and how to use ICT in a particular lesson or sequence of lessons must be directly related to the teaching and learning objectives in hand.

- The use of ICT should either allow the teacher or the pupil to achieve something that could not be achieved without it; or allow the teacher to teach or the pupils to learn something more effectively and efficiently than they could otherwise; or both. (p. 50)

You may feel that these criteria are rather stringent, making it difficult for a teacher to justify the use of ICT in all but a few situations. Also, the second criterion does not allow for the possibility that the teaching and learning objectives might include providing the opportunity to use and develop skill with ICT in the context of, say, a statistical investigation.

There are no easy answers to the second question, concerning which tool to offer to learners for which situations. There are many practical factors to take into account here, including where and how the ICT tools are made available to them. For example, possible scenarios are that:

- calculators, computers and software are available to all learners at all times and home access can be assumed;
- a computer suite at school is available to learners at all times;
- a single computer and electronic whiteboard is always available in the classroom;
- the use of computers in school only takes place in a timetabled room.

In Task 9.1.2, you considered the following three potential roles for ICT in statistics teaching: handling data, accessing data and data simulations. There may be other possibilities that you have thought of yourself. Your choice of which tool(s) to use will be based on the following two general considerations: the availability of ICT tools and the roles or purposes to be achieved. Task 9.2.3 asks you to reflect on these considerations by linking the various tools to the *PCAI* framework for tackling a statistical investigation.

Task 9.2.3 ICT Tools and the *PCAI* Framework   C

Note down four or five key ICT tools that you might wish learners to use in statistics learning and try to link the nature of their use to each of the four *PCAI* stages of a statistical investigation.

Learner Issues

Another factor for a teacher to consider is how decisions on the use of ICT in teaching are influenced by the availability of hardware and software to learners in their homes. The General Household Survey showed that, in April 2003, 69% of households consisting of a couple with children and 52% of households consisting of one adult with children had internet access at home (in *Social Trends*, 34, table 13.15). Well over half of all households at that time had a computer and, with each year that has passed since 2003, these figures have risen steadily. This raises the question of whether learners can be expected to gain access to data and have use of the computer to explore statistical ideas as part of homework. While this has the advantage of exploiting available resources and encouraging learner independence, some learners may have better computing facilities at home than in the classroom, but some will not, raising difficult questions of equity.

A second learner-related issue is the extent to which they can be expected to tackle the more sophisticated, generic ICT tasks themselves. For example, at what age would you expect learners, independently, to use or master the following: programming a graphics calculator, devising and using formulas in a spreadsheet, setting up and generating simulations, and so on? Also, how much understanding would you expect learners to have about what is going on inside the electronic box? At the one extreme, there is a danger of them simply pressing buttons with no real understanding. At the other, they may be so wrapped up in the technology that they lose sight of the statistical task or concept in hand. Many of these and related issues are explored in Oldknow and Taylor (2000) and in Johnston-Wilder and Pimm (2005).

The Formatting Power of Technology

The Danish professor of mathematics education Ole Skovsmose has written about a range of socio-political issues to do with mathematics education. One account (Skovsmose, webref) refers to what he calls the 'formatting power of mathematics'.

Skovsmose suggests that mathematical ideas and ways of thinking have formatted society/technology in the sense that the organised, structured way of thinking that is mathematics has informed technological developments in the world and indeed affects the ways in which humans think about their world. For example, it could be argued that many of the things that people take for granted – measurements of space and mass, clocks and calendars, building plans, machine design, and so on – are all strongly influenced by mathematics, without people being aware of it. Skovsmose goes on to question whether mathematics education is organised in a way that encourages learners to accept and adjust to mathematical formatting or to become more critically aware of it.

Now reverse the argument. Rather than considering Skovsmose's proposition that mathematics formats technology (and, through it, society at large), consider how technology can be exploited to format learner thinking about mathematics and statistics. To be specific, is it possible that by looking carefully at the way that calculator/spreadsheet menus and commands are organised, learners can gain insights into some big statistical ideas? This is an open question and one that you are asked to consider as you read the next four chapters. It is raised again in Sections 9.5 and 10.5.

9.3 FIRST STEPS WITH A SPREADSHEET

In this section, you are asked to try out some investigations on a spreadsheet for yourself. Note that if you are using a spreadsheet package other than *Excel*, you may have to make a few small adjustments to the instructions provided. It is not assumed that your ability to use a spreadsheet is very advanced, but you are *expected* to be able to:

- enter numbers or text into cells;
- enter a formula and fill down or across;
- select cells containing data and use the Graph Wizard to graph the data.

Two powerful spreadsheet features that tend to characterise the 'describing' type of investigation are considered in this section: *summarising* and *graphing* of data. They are presented through the following three contexts.

First-class post? is a very simple postal data investigation to start you off.
Teaching standard deviation provides an example of how the spreadsheet can be used to lay bare the structure of calculations that many learners find hard to follow.
Reanalysing the Florence Nightingale data revisits data you looked at in Chapter 5.

First-class Post?

In May 2004, as part of an investigation into the state of the Royal Mail's services, 20 BBC correspondents and producers were asked by the BBC *Breakfast* TV programme to send 100 letters by first-class post across the country.

The testers were paired and each person posted five letters, first class, to their opposite number. All the letters were posted by 3 p.m. on Wednesday, 5 May. Table 9.1 shows how many had reached their destination by late afternoon of Thursday, 6 May.

TABLE 9. 1 First-class arrivals

Glasgow to Plymouth: 3	Cambridge to Southampton: 5
Plymouth to Glasgow: 5	Southampton to Cambridge: 3
Cardiff to London: 0	Tunbridge Wells to Orkney: 5
London to Cardiff: 4	Orkney to Tunbridge Wells: 0
Belfast to Manchester: 0	Jersey to Dumfries: 0
Manchester to Belfast: 0	Dumfries to Jersey: 0
County Durham to Warwickshire: 5	Stoke to Bristol: 1
Warwickshire to County Durham: 1	Bristol to Stoke: 5
London to Buckinghamshire: 4	Cheltenham to Carlisle: 5
Buckinghamshire to London: 5	Carlisle to Cheltenham: 5

Source: news.bbc.co.uk/1/hi/programmes/breakfast/3689417.stm

Task 9.3.1 Next-day Mail   C

The Royal Mail's licence target is for 92.5% of first-class mail to arrive by the following day.

(a) Use a spreadsheet to investigate whether they have met this claim.

(b) What further investigations do these data invite you to explore?

(c) In fact, during 2004, just over 92% of first-class letters did arrive on time (although during the wildcat strikes in the autumn, this figure dropped to about 80%). How do you square these figures with the results of the BBC survey?

Teaching Standard Deviation

Many learners struggle to make sense of the standard deviation formula. In the following task, learners had been investigating leaves in a biology lesson and needed to calculate the standard deviation of the 20 leaf lengths that they had collected. However, they were unable to understand the formula. Imagine that you have been called in to help them.

Task 9.3.2 Laying Bare the Standard Deviation Calculation   **C**

One way of explaining the standard deviation is through the phrase 'root, mean, squared deviation'; in other words, it is the square *root* of the *mean* of the *squared* deviations. Devise a way of exploiting the spreadsheet in order to spell out to learners how this statistic is calculated.

How might you conduct this lesson?

Reanalysing the Florence Nightingale Data

Chapter 5 provided data based on that which Florence Nightingale used to bring to the attention of the authorities the tragic events in the Crimea, where many more soldiers were dying of non-battle causes than on the battlefield. It is interesting to speculate just how she would have presented her data had she had access to a computer package such as the spreadsheet Excel. In this sub-section, you are asked to examine this hypothetical question yourself. (For convenience, the data from Chapter 5 are repeated in Table 9.2.)

TABLE 9.2 Florence Nightingale's data

Date	April 1854	May	June	July	Aug.	Sept.	Oct.	Nov.	Dec.	Jan. 1855	Feb.	Mar.
Battle	3	14	19	46	55	86	185	322	138	279	322	169
Non-battle	28	24	12	396	863	795	367	597	1631	2889	1830	1118
Total	31	38	31	442	918	881	552	919	1769	3168	2152	1287

Task 9.3.3 Entering the Data   **C**

Into a blank spreadsheet screen, enter the column headings into row 1 and the row headings into column A.

Enter into the other cells data from the rows 2 and 3 of Table 9.2.

Using a suitable formula, create the final row of data.

Task 9.3.4 Graphing the Data   **C**

(a) Select cells A1:M3 and use the Graph Wizard to choose and create two suitable column graphs of the data (avoid 3-D displays at this stage).

(b) Of the two options that you have chosen to display, which one makes Nightingale's point more clearly? Give your reasons.

Task 9.3.5 Other Formats **C**

What other options does Excel offer for graphing these data?

Use the 'Radar' option in the Chart Wizard. Investigate how this graph form works and how it compares with the coxcomb.

9.4 MORE STEPS WITH A SPREADSHEET

In this section, two further examples are provided for you to consider how the spreadsheet application Excel can be used in the teaching of statistics.

Delivery Times

The 'First-class post?' investigation from Section 9.3 demonstrated a very simple use of the spreadsheet, namely, to sum a column of simple numerical data. Staying within a postal context, you are now asked to look at something slightly more complicated, this time involving handling 'time of day' data.

A group of 12–13-year-old learners were comparing notes on when the post arrived at their homes. As they were usually in school at delivery times, they could only take the word of stay-at-home parents on weekday delivery times. The general consensus was that the post was fairly erratic during weekdays and they really could not predict when it might arrive.

In order to investigate this question, they enlisted the help of a co-operative mum who agreed to note the times of postal delivery at her home over roughly a two-month period in the summer. Her data are shown in Table 9.3.

TABLE 9.3 July and August postal delivery times

Sunday	Monday	Tuesday	Wednesday	Thursday	Friday	Saturday
	9.37	9.19	9.59			8.51
	9.13		15.40		9.52	8.48
	10.28	9.06	9.18	8.18	10.01	8.23
	9.47	9.09	9.50			8.38
		9.28	9.37			
	9.41	10.06	9.44	9.46	9.49	8.21
	9.35	8.47	10.07	10.21		8.35
			8.52	9.54	10.50	

These data raise an important issue about the use of the decimal point. If the first time, 9.37am, were entered as the decimal 9.37 a.m., it would be interpreted by the computer (or any calculator) as 9 hours and 0.37 of an hour – in other words, 9 hours and, roughly, $0.37 \times 60 \approx 22$ minutes (that is, 22 minutes past 9 in the morning). Fortunately, Excel has a work-around that avoids this problem – simply enter the times using colons rather than decimal points to separate the hours from the minutes and Excel will handle these data correctly as times in hours and minutes in subsequent calculations. (This is not entirely true, but more of that later.)

Task 9.4.1 Understanding the Data   **C**

(a) Before entering the data, spend a few moments looking at the figures, trying to spot special features and possible anomalies.

(b) What questions arise from these figures that you might investigate more fully with Excel?

Task 9.4.2 Exploring the Data in Excel   **C**

(a) Enter the times data into a blank spreadsheet, remembering to separate the hours and minutes using colons and omitting the exceptional value (the second Wednesday time of 15:40).

(b) Investigate whether Saturday deliveries are earlier than weekday deliveries and also if they are less or more widely spread.

Task 9.4.3 Interpreting the Results   **C**

Based on the summaries displayed in the spreadsheet, what can you conclude about delivery times on weekdays and on Saturdays?

Conflating Scores

Teachers commonly add (or average) scores that learners get in different tests or examinations. Provided the marks are based on the same total score, and are therefore equally weighted, this is a valid procedure. However, how averaging scores affects overall learner position is not always well understood. Consider the made-up example in Table 9.4, where the same 10 learners (named A to J) sat examinations in Mathematics and English.

TABLE 9.4 Maths and English scores

Learner	Maths	English
A	21	85
B	29	83
C	35	82
D	42	81
E	55	80
F	61	79
G	70	78
H	82	77
I	88	76
J	91	75

Task 9.4.4 Entering and Summarising the Data   C

As you can see, all 10 learners did consistently well on the English paper, but the Mathematics marks are widely spread. Also, notice that these data have been artificially created so that the learner order from best to worst in Mathematics is the exact reverse of their corresponding order for English.

(a) When each learner's English and Mathematics marks are averaged, which of the two subjects do you think will have a greater effect on the overall average?

(b) Enter the data above into columns A, B and C of the spreadsheet and find the mean and range of each set of scores.

(c) In column D, calculate, for each learner, her or his mean score for both Mathematics and English.

(d) Test your guess to the question posed in part (a).

This exercise was carried out with a group of 15-year-old learners. As one learner observed, after this particular light had dawned:

> Oh yes – if we take an extreme case and give every learner full marks in the English paper, they may as well not have bothered taking it for all the effect it has on the overall position – it's entirely down to their Maths scores.

Two Features of Excel

To end this section on spreadsheets, here are two features of Excel that you may not have been aware of.

1. *Strange pies in* Excel: when a learner is tackling a simple task such as selecting a list of data and choosing the pie chart option, strange things that can occur, such as that it can deliver a pie with equal slices, each with the name of one of the points. Neville Hunt has documented several of these anomalies – see a range of publications in *Teaching Statistics* and several articles available on-line from his website (www.mis.coventry.ac.uk/~nhunt/publicat.html).

2. *Updating calculations in statistical packages*: in general, spreadsheets automatically update calculations should you change the value of a data point. This is not usually true with specialist statistical packages, where you will normally have to 'recalculate' if you change any data values. This is a major difference from spreadsheets.

9.5 PEDAGOGY

This section looks at teaching and learning issues in relation to ICT, based on some of the PTT themes. The final sub-section looks at the existence of two versions of the standard deviation that can be displayed on most ICT screens and explains the difference between them in the context of an important idea in statistics known as statistical estimation.

Language Patterns

An influential idea is learning theorist Lev Vygotsky's concept of the *zone of proximal development* (ZPD). He defined the ZPD as the gap between what children can do by themselves and what they can be helped to learn with competent assistance. The ZPD gap can be bridged by support from, say, the teacher or from appropriate ICT, and this assistance Vygotsky referred to as *scaffolding*. The tasks provided through scaffolding are just beyond the level of what the learner can do alone. At a certain level of learner mastery, the teacher will decide that scaffolding is no longer necessary, at which point he or she starts to provide less and less support, a process known as *fading*.

Task 9.5.1 Scaffolding and Fading   C

How might these ideas of scaffolding and fading apply to learners' use of ICT tools?

Imagery

A big idea in statistics, and indeed in mathematics, is that ideas can be represented and interpreted in different forms – for example, in words, numbers, letters, tables and pictures. This idea is often referred to as using *multiple representations*. A strength of ICT is that it enables learners to develop their understanding of multiple representations in statistics by representing a data set in several different linked forms (for example, as raw data, as a dot plot and as a box plot).

Task 9.5.2 Teaching Spread

(a) Imagine that you are planning to teach a lesson on *spread*. Choose a suitable data set and plan how learners might use ICT to explore the different ways that the data might be presented to help gain insight into the notion of spread.

(b) List some of the possible benefits of such an exercise, as well as any ways in which the use of ICT may limit pupil understanding of spread.

Standard Misconceptions

In Chapter 5, reference was made to a common misconception about the calculation of the median. It can be illustrated by the following pupil transcript.

> To find the median of the eleven scores below, I add one and divide by 2. So the median equals 6.
>
> 36, 72, 51, 50, 62, 66, 49, 82, 68, 63, 45.

This learner is confusing the calculation required to identify the median *item* with finding the *value* of the median item. (S)he is applying a mechanical procedure, but has lost sight of an important feature of any summary statistics – its representativeness of the data set from which it was calculated. Clearly, the answer 6 is not in any sense typical of these 11 scores.

It will help if learners are able to use real data in such calculations, as this will make it easier for them to 'stay with the data' and thereby appreciate what sort of value might be representative. Where calculations are practised using made-up numbers, learners are denied this feedback of context to reinforce the meaning and usefulness of the summary value. Ideally, in a class setting, such calculations can be practised using an item of data from each learner (for example, height, pulse rate, and so on). This enables the distinction to be drawn between the median learner and the median value (that is, the height or pulse rate of the median learner).

The spreadsheet in Figure 9.1 was created using the following steps, which basically mirror the stages required to calculate the median using pencil and paper. The data are the number of heartbeats per minute measured for each learner in a class of 25 learners during a biology lesson.

- enter the raw data into cells A1:A25;
- select cells A1:A25, copy and paste into cell B1;
- with cells B1:B25 still selected, use the Sort… command to sort these values into ascending order;
- identify the middle value in cells B1:B25 (this is cell B13) and highlight it. This is the median. Note: the word 'MED' has been typed into cell C13 to draw attention to this value;
- into cell B27, enter the command **=median(A1:A25)** to confirm the value of the median (69).

	A	B	C
1	68	54	
2	79	57	
3	85	59	
4	57	60	
5	82	62	
6	68	62	
7	77	63	
8	81	65	
9	62	65	
10	65	67	
11	76	68	
12	81	68	
13	76	**69**	MED
14	65	71	
15	63	71	
16	59	72	
17	67	75	
18	69	76	
19	62	76	
20	60	77	
21	54	79	
22	72	81	
23	71	81	
24	75	82	
25	71	85	
26			
27	Median	69	
28			

Figure 9.1 **HEARTBEAT DATA**

Note that the **=median()** command has performed the calculation when applied to the unsorted data in column A. The same value would have resulted if the same command had been applied to the sorted data in column B.

Techniques and methods

> ### Task 9.5.3 Laying Bare a Calculation   C
>
> (a) In Task 9.3.2, you saw how the spreadsheet could be used to lay bare the standard deviation calculation. Choose another statistics topic at a level of difficulty suited to your learner(s) and plan a spreadsheet lesson based on this 'laying bare' principle.
>
> (b) How would you link your lesson plan for part (a) to the fact that the spreadsheet can (probably) perform the same calculation directly using a single function?

Why Two Standard Deviations?

If you enter a set of data into a graphics calculator or spreadsheet and then try to find its standard deviation, you will be presented with two possible versions of this statistic, usually referred to as the sample standard deviation (S_x) and the population standard deviation (σ_x). What distinguishes these two measures would normally be considered beyond the scope of learners up to 16 years of age. However, since the learners' calculators or computer displays are likely to show both versions, their teacher needs to offer some sort of story as to what distinguishes them. What follows is a brief explanation of the theoretical background to these two formulations of the standard deviation.

The story starts with an important idea in statistical work – the notion of *statistical estimation*. This involves selecting a *random sample* from some population and finding certain summary values from the sample (for example, the mean and standard deviation) in order to make estimates of the mean and standard deviation of the population from which the data were sampled. Using the sample mean as an estimator of the population is straightforward – provided the sample was chosen randomly, the sample mean is a perfectly good estimator of the population mean. But unfortunately, for reasons not explored here, the standard deviation of the sample consistently underestimates the population standard deviation. It is therefore said to be a biased *estimator*. As a way of correcting the bias, the standard deviation formula requires a tweak that will make the result slightly bigger. This is (partially) achieved by changing the denominator in the standard deviation formula from n to $n-1$ (where n is the sample size), thereby increasing the overall value of the result. (Note that the divisor $n-1$ creates an unbiased estimate for the *variance* but when applied to the standard deviation it is not totally unbiased.)

If you choose to treat this random sample as a free-standing data set, then its standard deviation is calculated in the conventional way with a denominator of n. In such a situation, the data set is being treated as a population in its own right and calculation of its standard deviation is described as finding the *population standard deviation*, σ_x. However, it is when this random sample is used to estimate the standard deviation of the wider population that the 'tweaked' formula is used – that is, you need to use the *sample standard deviation*, S_x. Calculators do not all use the same notation when referring to these two forms of the standard deviation, so you may need to check the manual.

At this point, you may need to reread the last two paragraphs in order to grasp what the terms sample standard deviation and population standard deviation refer to. Then tackle Task 9.5.4, which should help you to sort out the distinction between them.

Task 9.5.4 Sample Standard Deviation and Population Standard Deviation   **C**

(a) Which formula for standard deviation gives the bigger answer, σ_x or S_x?

(b) Under which circumstances would you choose to use the S_x version of the standard deviation, rather than σ_x?

(c) What potential confusions might learners experience in terms of distinguishing these two measures of spread?

10 Comparing with ICT

This chapter picks up the 'comparing' theme of Chapters 2 and 6, but this time in the context of using ICT tools. Whereas Chapter 9 asked you to explore the spreadsheet, this chapter includes both the spreadsheet and the graphics calculator.

The chapter starts with some issues of terminology and notation that need to be addressed, by virtue of the fact that certain key words and symbols appear naturally on calculator and computer screens. Sections 10.2 and 10.3 provide some specific examples of statistical work that can be done using a graphics calculator. Even if you have never used one before, do try to work through these sections with a suitable calculator − detailed keying instructions are provided for the uninitiated. Section 10.4 turns to making comparisons on a spreadsheet, while the final section, as usual, deals with pedagogic issues. Important matters that are raised in this closing section are some of the choices, concerns and forms of preparation required by the teacher, in order to make best use of the graphics calculator in the classroom.

10.1 TERMINOLOGY AND NOTATION IN STATISTICS

An essential feature of mathematics and statistics, particularly at a higher level, is the use of shorthand notation for a variety of concepts and measures. While this can be a strength in terms of providing conciseness and precision, statistical notation often proves to be an obstacle for learners in the early stages of learning. With learners under 16, the problem can be minimised by avoiding the use of abstract notation where possible. However, where ICT is used, certain on-screen notations are hard to avoid, but fortunately, well-designed ICT applications tend to use notation in a fairly standard way. Just as explorations of subtraction with a four-function calculator have introduced young children to the world of negative numbers following subtraction of bigger from smaller ('What's this little dash before the answer, Miss?'), so certain ICT tools can be an extremely fruitful 'way in' to bringing some key statistical notation to the attention of learners.

This first section looks at a number of important terms, many of which underlie the notation that you will later consider on the graphics calculator and within computer applications. Although some of these terms may refer to ideas that are more advanced than those at the statistical level you are currently teaching, there are three important reasons why it is useful to get to grips with their meaning:

- discussions of elementary statistical ideas with learners should be based on a clear and correct choice of language, so that they build on a solid foundation when they move on to more advanced work;
- in preparation for teaching at a more basic level, the teacher often needs to consult a more advanced textbook or website, for which a good grasp of statistical terminology and notation may be required;

- as has been indicated, many of these terms will inform your understanding of the statistical notation used in calculator and computer application displays.

Data Sets, Populations and Samples

Another term for *data set* is *batch*. Throughout this book, the term *data set* has been used to describe a collection of data. In many textbooks, however, data sets are often termed *samples*. Are data sets and samples the same thing? And how do these terms relate to a *population*?

Task 10.1.1 Data Set, Population and Sample
Write down your understanding of the terms 'data set', 'sample' and 'population'.

A *data set* is a collection of data. There is no hidden agenda in the use of this term – it is simply a collection of numbers and use of the term 'data set' provides no hint as to why the data have been collected or how they are likely to be used.

 Sample, on the other hand, is a loaded term. Where there is a sample, there must be a wider *population* from which the data in the sample have been 'sampled'. So, a sample is a subset of a population. There will also be some reason why the sample was taken in the first place. Mostly, samples are collected in the context of *sampling* – that is, deriving information from a sample in order to come to certain conclusions about the population from which the sample was taken. For example, in market research, people's opinions are sampled in order to gauge the views of the population as a whole. (Where the entire population's views are sought, this is termed a *census*.)

 Everyday use of the word *population* is often restricted to human populations (the population of the UK, the world, ...). The word derives from the Latin verb *populare*, meaning 'to inhabit'. In biology, the term *population* is not restricted to humans, but includes other animal and plant species. The widest of all possible contexts is used in statistics, where one can talk about *populations* of light bulbs, screws or bags of crisps. So, in statistics, a population refers to all of the objects in the context under consideration, whether animal, vegetable or mineral. What all populations share is that they comprise the entirety of those things under consideration.

Statistics and Parameters

In this sub-section, two important terms are explored and defined: *statistics* and *parameters*.

Task 10.1.2 Statistics
Write down your understanding of the term *statistics*.

Confusingly, the word 'statistics' has (at least) three commonly used meanings. These are:

- a subject – a branch of applied mathematics concerned with collecting, analysing and interpreting quantitative data;

- numerical information, or data – for example, the information collected in a market survey;
- summary values calculated from a data set (such as the mean and standard deviation).

Clearly, aspects of these definitions can be disputed: for example, with regard to the first definition, some would argue that statistics is not restricted to quantitative data. Indeed, many would claim that statistical thinking begins *before* data are collected (in other words, the data collection is usually in response to some question).

Task 10.1.3 Parameter

Write down your understanding of the term *parameter*. How do *parameters* relate to *statistics?*

A parameter refers to the characteristics of something. For example, file names, page lengths and font specifications could all be considered parameters of a piece of text, while wattage and type (screw or bayonet) are the key parameters of a light bulb.

When juxtaposed with the word *parameter*, the singular term *statistic* is normally used in the sense of the third meaning listed below Task 10.1.2, namely, 'summary values calculated from a data set'. Linking the terms *parameter* and *statistic* has particular relevance in the context of sampling. In general, the summary values of a sample are referred to as (sample) statistics, whereas the corresponding key values of the population are referred to as its parametric values or parameters. (Note: it is actually slightly more subtle than this. In practice, the exact values of the population summary values are unknown and the terms 'population mean' and population standard deviation' are derived from a distribution used to model the population. The parameters are the values in this (mathematical) distribution.)

Statistics are normally attributed standard English letters (for example, sample mean is often written as m), whereas population parameters are denoted using Greek letters (for example, population mean $= \mu$). As you will see in Task 10.2.6, this distinction has implications for the notation used in calculator (and computer application) menus.

Subscripts

Here is an example of subscripts as they might be used in a statistics textbook.

The sample mean m of a set $\{x_1, x_2, x_3, \ldots, x_i, \ldots, x_n\}$ of n observations from a given data set is calculated as $\frac{1}{n}\Sigma x_i$.

Task 10.1.4 Why subscripts?

(a) When are subscripts used in statistics and what is their purpose?

(b) Why do you think learners find them confusing?

In word processing, a subscript is a number or letter that appears slightly below the character to which it is linked (as opposed to a superscript, which appears slightly above the linked character). Subscripts and superscripts are both usually smaller than the juxtaposed character as well. In statistics, subscripts are used as a way of labelling particular values of a variable, say, x. For example, the first x-value will be denoted by

x_1, the second by x_2, and so on. When the subscript is a letter (as in x_i for example), the i refers to the general position of the x-value. Note that subscripts imply an ordering of the data – the value of each subscript tells you the position of the value in a list, but not its actual value – x_1 is first, x_2 is second, and so on.

Learners may be confused by subscripts because they are a secondary layer on top of a basic algebraic notation, which they may already be unsure about. Also, unlike superscripts (which they may understand as referring to indices), the exact meaning of subscripts in a formula is less obvious and not operationalised in the same way.

Formatting Learner Thinking

In Section 9.2, it was suggested that a possible benefit of using ICT in the teaching of statistics is that the structure and organisation of the software and the notation used to provide various statistical tools all combine to format learner thinking about the nature of statistical ideas and how they interrelate. As you work through the remainder of this chapter, be on the lookout for examples of this phenomenon. Another item for you to keep in mind as you look at examples of graphics calculator and spreadsheet use is why or when a teacher or learner might choose one rather than the other in statistical work.

10.2 SUMMARISING WITH A GRAPHICS CALCULATOR

In this section, you will be introduced to the statistical features of the graphics calculator. Throughout this book, the graphics calculator facilities used are based on the Texas Instruments TI-83 and TI-84 families of calculator. If you are using a different model, you will need to adapt some of the instructions.

Two of the main ways in which ICT can be used to support data handling for learners up to age 16 are:

- entering data in one or more of the lists and summarising the data lists;
- drawing statistical plots.

These two themes are taken up in this and the next section.

It is worth noting that these themes fall within the A stage of the $PCAI$ cycle that has been used throughout this book to describe the four main stages of data handling – posing a question, collecting data, analysing data and interpreting the results.

Entering Data into Lists

The data used here are taken from the CensusatSchool website and show the heights (in cm) of a data set of girls and boys aged 11–12 (Table 10.1). As the theme of this chapter is 'comparing', this is an opportunity to compare their heights.

Task 10.2.1 Making a Fresh Start   C

(a) Note that these two data sets are of unequal size. Does this matter?

(b) Before entering the data into lists, it is sensible to reset your calculator. There are two choices here; either reset all RAM or use the **ClrAllLists** commands from the MEM menu. Note that choosing to reset all RAM will also remove all stored programs, which you may not want to do. The instructions for resetting the calculator are given below.

TABLE 10.1 Heights

Female (cm)	Female (cm)	Male (cm)	Male (cm)
153	160	146	162
142	153	150	173
151	147	156	142
149	156	142	155
155	162	152	164
152	146	149	
151	153	137	
158	141	138	
157	147	155	

- Press **2nd** **[MEM]** and choose the Reset option.
- Choose whether you want to reset the entire memory (all RAM) or just the defaults; press **1** or **2** as appropriate.
- You are given a final chance to rethink your choice. Press **2** to confirm.
- If you have reset only the defaults, you should also clear the lists by pressing: **2nd** **[MEM] 4** **ENTER**

```
RAM  ARCHIVE  ALL
1:All  RAM...
2:Defaults...
```

```
ClrAllLists
              Done
```

Task 10.2.2 Entering the Data into Lists

Follow the instructions below to enter the female and male heights into two lists.

- Move to the list editor by pressing **STAT** **1**.

- With the cursor in list L1, enter each female height in turn, pressing **ENTER** after each data entry.

- When list L1 is completed, press ▷ to move the cursor to list L2 and enter the male heights. Note: L2 is shorter than L1.

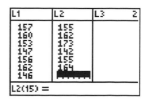

Task 10.2.3   Notation in the List Editor   C

You may have noticed that information showing the location of the current cursor position is displayed at the bottom left of the list editor screen. How do you interpret this information and how does this choice of notation compare with that used in other software applications and in mathematics generally?

Summarising and Comparing

Task 10.2.4   Summarising the Data in Lists   C

Follow the instructions below to summarise the data in the two lists, L1 and L2.

- Press [STAT] ▷ to enter the Stat Calc menu.
- To summarise the data in L1, choose the **1-Var Stats** command by pressing 1. Then press [2nd] [L1] [ENTER] to complete the command.
- Scroll down to see eleven summary statistics and try to work out what each one represents. Make a note of the values of the following summaries for the female heights: mean, minimum, Q1, median, Q3 and maximum.
- Use a similar method to summarise the data in list L2 and again note down the same six summary statistics.

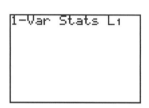

Note: this calculator uses $\bar{x}$ rather than m to represent the mean.

Task 10.2.5   Interpreting the Summaries   C

What conclusions can you draw from these two sets of summary statistics about the heights of boys and girls? Do you have any suggestions about why the heights of girls and boys might differ in this way?

Task 10.2.6   Notation in the 1-Var Summary

(a) Why is this summary referred to as '1-Var'? What do you think a '2-Var' summary would be used for?

(b) In Section 10.1, a distinction was made between the use of Greek and standard English lettering in statistical notation. To what extent have these summaries followed this notation?

(c) Distinguish between the two standard deviations, Sx and σx.

As the name implies, a one-variable (1-Var) summary deals with summaries applied to a single variable. Usually this means that the command applies to a single list containing the data to be summarised. Contrast this with the command **2-Var Stats L2,L3** which refers to a situation where there are paired (that is, 2-variable) data stored in lists L2 and L3. In this case, the command provides summaries for interrelationships between the two lists as well as for each list separately. However, the command **1-Var Stats L1,L2** could also be valid for frequency data where the x-values are stored in L1 and the corresponding frequencies are in L2.

There are three examples of the use of Greek letters in the 1-Var Stats display – two uses of the capital letter Σ (sigma) and one of the lower case letter sigma, σ. The letter (capital) sigma can be dismissed straight away; it means 'the sum of', so Σx means the sum of the x-values and Σx^2 means the sum of the x^2-values. However, it is the lower case σ that indicates an example of a parametric value among these 11 summaries. As you can see, there are two standard deviation values here and learners will want to know which one to use. The one written σx is the population standard deviation, whereas sx is the sample standard deviation.

This distinction was discussed in Section 9.5 under the sub-heading 'Why two standard deviations?' and provides an example where ICT provides choices that require the teacher to confront topics that might otherwise be left alone. This may be a good or a bad thing, depending on circumstances.

You will be asked to use the girls' and boys' height data again in Section 10.3, so please retain these two lists in your calculator.

Practising Calculator Skills

To end this section, consider some further ideas for investigations that you and your learners can use to consolidate ICT skill, based on the theme of comparing. As a teacher, there are times when you might wish to make the processes involved in data gathering the main focus of the lesson. But at other times, you may wish to make a different point, such as to achieve rapid and easy data collection with a minimum of fuss. A good context for this is to choose one group of people and invite them to make an estimate of something – perhaps to guess the cost of a first-class postage stamp, the age of a person or building, the date of an invention, and so on. Ideally, the question should be as unambiguous as possible (for example, the 'cost of a washing machine' raises too many questions about which make and model, whether or not it is 'whisper silent', and so on). The data at the end of this chapter, were collected from 23 adults (age range 21–69 years) given in Table 10.4 (p. 159).

Task 10.2.7 More Comparing

Choose two suitable data columns from Table 10.4 at the end of the chapter, enter them into two empty lists of the graphics calculator, and use the 1-Var summaries to investigate differences in skill at estimation between the two groups that you have chosen.

If you and your learners are to use the 11 summary values calculated by the **1-Var Statistics** command of the calculator, it is important to understand how these are arrived at. For some summary statistics, the calculation is unambiguous, but for others it is not. For example, statistics textbooks vary in the method used for the calculation of the quartiles. How do you think the calculator does it for data sets of, say, five or eight or 12 data items?

Task 10.2.8 Investigating Quartiles   **C**

(a) By experimenting with various small data sets, investigate how the calculator calculates the quartile values.

(b) How might you use investigations of this sort in your teaching?

10.3 STATISTICAL PLOTS WITH A GRAPHICS CALCULATOR

As you saw in Section 10.2, once data have been entered into the list editor of a graphics calculator, creating summaries is a quick and painless process. The same is true about producing graphical displays of the data. In this section, you will see how to create box plots from the data currently stored in lists L1 and L2 and use them to draw conclusions about girls' and boys' heights.

Before plotting list L1 as a box plot, you should set the Window. Press $\boxed{\text{WINDOW}}$ and choose window settings that you think appropriate. Note that **Xmin** and **Xmax** define the minimum and maximum values on the x-axis and **Xscl** defines the gap between adjacent tick marks on the x-axis.

The Y settings work on a similar principle. However, since a box plot is a one-dimensional plot, the Y settings are largely irrelevant (the only condition being that the **Ymax** setting must exceed the **Ymin** value, otherwise an error message is displayed). The seventh item in the Window menu, **Xres**, merely determines the resolution of the plot and, correspondingly, affects how quickly the graph is plotted. You are recommended to leave this setting unchanged at **Xres** = 1.

Task 10.3.1 Creating a Box Plot

Follow the instructions below for creating a box plot of list L1.

- Press $\boxed{\text{2nd}}$ **[STAT PLOT]** to select the Statplot menu and set it as follows.
- Press **1** to select Plot1.

The cursor is flashing on **On**. Press $\boxed{\text{ENTER}}$ to switch it on (notice that the On is now highlighted).

- Press $\triangledown$ to select plot Type.
- Using the $\triangleright$ key, place the cursor on the fifth of these six icons (standard box plot) and press $\boxed{\text{ENTER}}$ to confirm.

- Press $\triangledown$ $\boxed{\text{2nd}}$ **[L1]** to select the Xlist as list L1.
- Ensure that Freq is set to 1.
- Press $\boxed{\text{TRACE}}$ to display the box plot.

- Use the $\triangleright$ and $\triangleleft$ cursor keys to get more information about each part of the box plot.

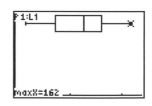

Task 10.3.2 Creating a Second Box Plot   C

Use Plot 2 to create a second box plot, one showing the heights of the boys in list L2. You may find that this second plot will not fit entirely onto the screen, in which case the Window settings will need some adjustment. As before, pressing TRACE will enable you to see both plots together. The up or down cursor keys will allow you to move between the two plots, while the left and right cursor keys let you move within a plot.

Do the box plots confirm the conclusions that you made in Task 10.2.5?

Task 10.3.3 Exploring Other Graphs

As you may have noticed, the STATPLOT menu provides six different types of statistical plot, of which you have used the fifth one, standard box plot. Now would be a good time to explore some of these other plots and see what they do.

Task 10.3.4 More Comparing

Choose suitable data sets from Table 10.2 at the end of the chapter, enter them into the lists of the graphics calculator and then use box plots to investigate differences in skill at estimating between the two groups or within one of the groups.

Here is an example of the sort of investigation that can be supported by this data base.

P stage: a possible question is, 'Are people more comfortable in making estimates with metric or imperial units?'

C stage: the data used here (from Table 10.2 at the end of this chapter) are the estimates of a person's height in the two units, imperial and metric.

A stage: Figure 10.1 is a box plot showing the adult estimates of a particular individual's height (the person was accurately measured at 1.70 m). The top plot shows the estimates made in metres. The second plot is based on the same group's imperial estimates, which were subsequently converted to metres for ease of comparison. Finally, a vertical line has been drawn at the correct height of 1.70 m. (This was done using the **Vertical** command, which is in the DRAW menu.)

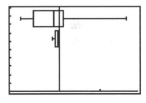

Figure 10.1 **ADULT ESTIMATES**

The corresponding box plots from some Year 7 learners are shown in Figure 10.2. The scale is very much broader here, in order to accommodate their widely varying estimates. For example, the current cursor position (marked opposite with an 'x') shows that the upper quartile estimate (Q3) of a particular person's height was 3 metres!

I stage: it is clear from the adult data that the estimates made in metric units were much more widely spread than those made in imperial units. There are two main elements contributing to successful estimation of someone's height:

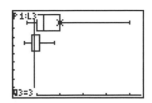

Figure 10.2 **YEAR 7 ESTIMATES**

- knowing your own height in the required units;
- being sufficiently confident with the units of measure to adjust your height to that of the person being estimated.

It seems likely that most adults know their height in feet and inches and can therefore use this as a benchmark on which to base their estimate of someone else's height in these units. Contrast this with the 11-year-olds who had a very shaky grasp of either units of measure.

It should not be too surprising that adult estimation is better than, say, that of 11-year-olds, for the following reasons:

- a child's height is likely to be further away from the height of this individual's height of 1.70 m and so estimation is not supported by personal familiarity;
- a child's height is constantly changing, whereas adult heights are pretty fixed;
- in most schools, children are largely taught metric units, but tend to hear largely imperial units outside school, as a result of which some have a poor grasp of either unit;
- adults may be more likely to know their height, by virtue of having to fill in official documents such as their passport details.

Note: you may wish to know how all the values in an entire list can be converted or rescaled with a single calculator command. To take this example, the imperial data (in inches) are currently stored in list L2. From the home screen, enter the command shown here and all these values will be converted to metres.

```
L2*.0254→L2
```

If you are interested in exploring more fully the potential of graphics calculators in the teaching of statistics, you might like to consider some of the classroom materials produced by Alan Graham and Barrie Galpin of A+B Books. Two that are particularly relevant are: Graham and Galpin (2002) (aimed at learners aged 16+) and Graham and Galpin (2000) (aimed at learners aged 11–16). Details of these and other classroom resources can be found at the A+B Books website (www.AplusB.co.uk).

10.4 RELATIVELY SPEAKING: COMPARING ON A SPREADSHEET

In this section, you are asked to use a spreadsheet to make comparisons. Both of the examples below look at an important distinction when making comparisons – choosing between *relative* and *absolute* differences.

Asylum Seekers

An issue of particular concern affecting countries in the EU during this millennium has been how to deal with the large number of people from around the globe who are seeking asylum. The data in Figure 10.3, which were adapted from the UK government publication *Social Trends*, could be the basis of a worthwhile investigation about asylum seeking.

Task 10.4.1 Raising Questions

On the face of it, the United Kingdom appeared to have most asylum seekers in the EU in 2002. However, these data do not tell the whole story. What additional data might you want to include in order to make a fairer comparison between countries?

Although the UK is at the top of this list, the figures do not take account of the relative sizes of each country. For example, it would not be sensible to expect a tiny country like Luxembourg to accommodate as many asylum seekers as, say, the UK or France. A more useful comparison (and the one used in *Social Trends*) would be to use a *relative* rather than an *absolute* measure – for example, to compare the number of asylum seekers per 1 000 of the population. In order to make this calculation, you need to find the populations of these countries. (Alternatively, you may take the view that the area of *land mass* of a country is a more relevant basis for relative comparisons than its population and compare countries by the number of asylum seekers per million hectares.)

	A	B
1	Number of asylum seekers 2002	
2		
3	COUNTRY	NUMBER
4	United Kingdom	103100
5	Germany	71100
6	Austria	39400
7	Sweden	33000
8	Belgium	21400
9	Netherlands	18700
10	Ireland	11600
11	Italy	7300
12	Spain	6200
13	Denmark	5900
14	France	5900
15	Greece	5700
16	Finland	3400
17	Luxembourg	1000
18	Portugal	200
19	All apps to EU	386100
20		
21	(Source: Social Trends 34, Table 1.14)	

Figure 10.3 **ASYLUM SEEKERS (2002)**
Source: *Social Trends*, 34, Table 1.14

Task 10.4.2 Calculating Relative Figures   C

(a) Create the spreadsheet for the data shown in Table 10.2.

(b) On your browser, use a search engine such as Google to find the approximate populations of these countries and enter them into Column C of the spreadsheet. A possible web address would be the 'Internet World Stats' site, which provides data on internet usage in different countries, but also gives population estimates for each country (www.internetworldstats.com/ stats4.htm#eu).

(c) Create, in column D, the number of asylum seekers in each country per 1 000 of the population (round these answers to a suitable number of decimal places).

(d) Select the data in cells A4:D18 and sort them in descending order by column D. (The **Sort**... command is in the DATA menu.) This has the effect of re-ordering the data in relative rather than in absolute terms.

(e) On the basis of this revised spreadsheet, come to a conclusion about which countries have the greatest relative number of asylum seekers in the EU.

Comparing Spreads

Have another look at the appendix to this chapter (Table 10.2), which lists the 'adult' estimates of the seven measures contained in the spreadsheet file 'Estimates-all.xls'. In Section 10.3 (Task 10.3.5), you have already compared these respondents' skill at estimation using imperial and metric units of measure. The next three tasks ask you to compare their comparable skill when applied to two very dissimilar variables: estimating the price of a Mars bar (pence) and estimating the population of the UK (millions). At the time of writing, an informal survey of 'local shops' showed that the price of a standard Mars bar varied from one shop to another, but fell within the 35–43p range. This gives a 'true' mean value of 39p. From official government sources, the 'true' population of the UK in 2005 was very close to 60 million.

Task 10.4.3 Comparing across Different Units

For which of these two variables do you think these 23 people provided the best estimates? How would you measure this? What problems do you anticipate in making these comparisons?

The quality of these estimates can be judged by two criteria – how closely the estimates are centred on the 'true' value and how widely spread the estimates are. These two criteria correspond to the measures of location and spread mentioned in Chapter 1. It would be possible, for each variable, to find the average absolute error and to calculate the IQR. (Calculation of the average absolute error involves treating each error as a positive number – otherwise the positive and negative errors would add to zero. Why?) However, when it comes to comparing these summaries between each variable, you hit a problem. Because these measures are in different units, it is impossible to compare them directly. To take an extreme example, if height estimates were made in cm rather than m, the average error and hence the value of the IQR would be a hundred times as big.

Task 10.4.4 Standardising the Measures

Can you think of a way of standardising the average absolute error (and the IQR) for each variable to make them comparable with each other?

These measures can be standardised by dividing them by the 'true' values and finding the corresponding relative measures, which can then be compared from one variable to another. So:

- relative average absolute error = average absolute error/'true' value;
- relative IQR = IQR/'true' value.

Task 10.4.5 Spreadsheet Calculation

On a spreadsheet, find the relative IQR for the two variables, 'estimated price of a Mars bar' and 'estimate of the population of the UK' and come to a conclusion as to which set of estimates is better.

The screenshot in Figure 10.4 shows a possible solution, based on the following commands.

Cell	Enter
B26	= AVERAGE(B3:B25) (*Then fill right to cell C26.*)
B27	= MEDIAN (B3:B25) (*Then fill right to cell C27.*)
B28	= QUARTILE(B3:B25,3)-QUARTILE(B3:B25,1) (*Then fill right to cell C28.*)
B29	= B28/39
C29	= C28/60

In both cases, the means and medians match closely the true mean values of 39p and 60 million, respectively, so in terms of location these estimates are good. As you can see, the relative spread of the Mars bar data was greater than for the population estimates, suggesting that these adults were, overall, closer in their estimates of the population of the UK than those of the price of a Mars bar. However, a word of caution should be given here regarding which measure of spread is used – the IQR or some other measure. A feature of the IQR is that it disregards the top and bottom quarters of the data, so in this example, all of the highly inaccurate population estimates such as 2, 3 and 250 million are automatically filtered out.

◇	A	B	C
1		Mars Bar	Population
2		(pence)	(millions)
3		35	60
4		50	5
5		38	2
6		30	55
7		35	52
8		30	70
9		40	52
10		38	60
11		40	60
12		32	50
13		30	27
14		33	53
15		35	65
16		28	250
17		50	30
18		46	58
19		35	55
20		40	70
21		45	60
22		75	56
23		40	56
24		28	56
25		35	62
26	Mean	38.6087	59.30435
27	Median	35	56
28	IQR	7.5	8
29	Relative IQR	0.192308	0.133333

Figure 10.4 **MARS BAR AND POPULATION DATA**

10.5 PEDAGOGY

This section looks at some of the PTT teaching and learning themes in relation to ICT.

Language Patterns

Task 10.5.1 Calculator Summaries   **C**

When applied to a data list, the calculator command **1-Var Stats** provides 11 summary statistics.

(a) Do you think that these are the most important or most useful summary statistics for you and your learners?

(b) Is the order in which the statistics are presented the most sensible for your needs and those of your learners?

(c) What are the implications for this collection of statistics in terms of the language used in teaching summary statistics?

Different Contexts

Task 10.5.2 Choosing the Right Tool for the Job   **C**

(a) As a relatively experienced mathematician carrying out your own statistical investigation, how would you decide which item of ICT to use for the analysis? What factors might contribute to your decision?

(b) Now consider your (potential) role as a mathematics teacher, asking learners to do an investigation for themselves. How could you help them to choose which item of ICT to use for their analysis?

Root Questions

A key question in statistical work, and one that was explored with the aid of a spreadsheet in Section 10.4, is whether certain comparisons should be based on absolute or relative measures. A difficulty in the past, before the easy availability of calculating devices, was that converting absolute measures into relative measures was a slow and error-prone calculation. However, these are just the sorts of procedures that spreadsheets (and graphics calculators) do best – the same basic calculation is applied to one value, the formula is 'filled down' and, in an instant, the corresponding calculations are applied to a long list of values. Not only does this sort of exercise help learners, quickly and easily, to experience the benefit of making relative comparisons, but they can also be impressed by the ease of use and processing power of a spreadsheet or graphics calculator and, perhaps, be more enthusiastic about using ICT in other situations.

Techniques and Methods

Most teachers would acknowledge the value of providing variety in the teaching and learning approaches offered to learners. Not only does it give different learners choices in terms of preferred learning styles but, for all learners, variety usually reduces boredom. A learning style that most learners enjoy is to experiment and explore within a structured environment (explorations within an unstructured environment can lead to frustration due to a lack of direction or clear purpose).

Task 10.5.3 Creating a Box Plot **C**

(a) Look back to Task 10.3.2, where you were encouraged to define your own window settings. The wording was deliberately open-ended. Was there enough information provided here for you/for your learners or would you prefer to have been given more explicit or more detailed instructions?

(b) What might learners learn through experimenting with window settings? How could you exploit the Window feature of a calculator (or equivalent feature on a computer) to extend learner understanding?

Making the Most of the Graphics Calculator

The examples of calculator use in Sections 10.2 and 10.3 illustrated the calculator's potential as a teaching and learning tool. To end this section on teaching and learning issues, you might like to reflect for a few minutes on whether/why you might make use of the graphics calculator in your teaching of statistics.

Task 10.5.4 Calculator Benefits **C**

Thinking particularly about statistics teaching, write down at least two advantages and two disadvantages of using graphics calculators rather than a computer spreadsheet or statistical package.

Here are some of the issues you might have identified.

Personal technology: the chief advantage of a graphics calculator is that it is a personal tool that each learner can use in his or her own way, which can easily be incorporated into the teacher's preferred teaching styles. With computer-based applications, on the other hand, the lessons tend to be either based on a single computer, which usually requires a highly teacher-led approach, or involve learners working in groups of one to three per computer, which creates other problems (such as the need to book a school computer room and issues about handling learner attention).

Public examinations: there are many examinations where graphics calculators are permitted, whereas this is not the case with computers.

Cost: a classroom can be equipped with a full class set of calculators for roughly the cost of three personal computers. Of course, the cost argument can be turned against graphics calculators, if they are seen as additional to the costs of equipping schools with computers.

The right tool for the job: it is difficult to establish an objective view on this aspect – calculator enthusiasts point to the calculator's versatility, reliability, ease of use and accessibility (the 'handy in the kitchen drawer' factor), whereas computer enthusiasts may see calculators as 'fiddly', with small, difficult-to-read screens.

Personal confidence: perhaps the main factor is about whether the teacher, personally, is a confident user of a graphics calculator – if this is not the case, he or she is unlikely to see the calculator's potential or use it enthusiastically in the classroom.

APPENDIX: ESTIMATION DATA

Your gender (M/F)
Your age (yrs)
Cost of a standard Mars bar bought in a corner shop (p)
Number of years ago that TV was invented (yrs)
Height of your teacher (m)
Height of your teacher (feet/inches★)
Age at which a person first becomes 'middle aged' (yrs)
The population of the UK (millions)
How long, on average, an elephant lives (yrs)

Note: ★later converted to inches for convenience.

TABLE 10.2 Estimates

Gender	Age (years)	Mars (pence)	TV (years)	Height (metres)	Height (inches)	Middle (years)	Population (millions)	Elephant (years)
M	57	35	70	1.6	67	50	60	60
F	56	50	52	1.75	66	60	5	60
F	54	38	70	2.2	65	48	2	88
M	69	30	80	1.67	66.5	35	55	100
F	32	35	60	1.7	67	40	52	40
F	54	30	78	1.4	66	40	70	90
M	52	40	70	1.4	67	40	52	50
F	30	38	80	1.65	65	45	60	70
F	22	40	70	1.7	66	40	60	45
F	42	32	80	1.8	66	45	50	40
F	57	30	75	1.6	70	50	27	60
F	61	33	60	1.7	66	60	53	70
M	56	35	80	1.6	64	40	65	30
M	24	28	60	1.58	68	35	250	150
F	29	50	60	1.5	67	35	30	80
M	24	46	70	1.8	68	45	58	30
F	22	35	70	1.8	69	55	55	70
M	23	40	65	1.8	66	40	70	40
F	21	45	100	1.75	67	40	60	50
F	58	75	65	1.7	66	50	56	35
M	60	40	55	1.65	66	40	56	60
F	34	28	50	1.7	68	42	56	65
M	42	35	49	1.8	68	45	62	75

11 Interrelating with ICT

This chapter starts with a brief description of the origins and uses of spreadsheets. Section 11.2 picks up the statistical theme of interrelating and links it to the use of the graphics calculator. Similar ideas are explored in the next section but applied to spreadsheets. Section 11.4 examines a data-handling package called *Tinkerplots*, designed from the bottom up, for younger learners. As usual, the final section of the chapter deals with pedagogy, here applied to ICT issues in general.

11.1 THE STORY OF SPREADSHEETS

This section looks at how spreadsheets first came into being and some general issues to do with how they are used in statistics. Several of the ideas are drawn from an article 'Spreadsheets in education – the first 25 years', which was published electronically in the first issue of a free Australian journal *Spreadsheets in Education*. To read this and other articles from the journal in full, visit the website: www.sie.bond.edu.au

A Brief History of Spreadsheets

Spreadsheets made their first appearance on a personal computer in 1979, but not in the form that they are known today. The application, called *Visicalc*, was created for the Apple II computer and was designed mainly for record-keeping and accounting tasks. The spreadsheet idea was conceived by Dan Bricklin, while the programming was carried out by Bob Frankston. Bricklin's conceptual metaphor was 'an electronic blackboard and electronic chalk in a classroom'. It is claimed that *Visicalc* was the 'killer application' that was largely responsible for the high volume sales of the Apple II. According to R.S. Houghton (2004):

> The invention of the spreadsheet made personal computers have real value in the marketplace and legitimated the personal computer industry. Without the invention of this software category, spreadsheets, the impact of the personal computer might have been delayed for years. (p. 1)

In the early 1980s the rights of *Visicalc* were sold to the Lotus Development Corporation and by 1982 it took the form of *Lotus 1–2–3*, which was a central feature of the new IBM PC.

The next milestone was the Microsoft *Excel* spreadsheet, originally written for the 512K Apple Macintosh in 1984–85. *Excel* was one of the first spreadsheets to use a graphical interface, with pull-down menus and the point and click capability of a mouse. Not surprisingly, the *Excel* spreadsheet with a graphical user interface proved to be easier for most people to use than the command-line interface of PC-DOS spreadsheet products. Since the mid 1990s, *Excel* has become unquestionably the dominant spreadsheet application and currently commands over 90% of the relevant market. When Microsoft launched its Windows operating system in 1987, *Excel* was one of its first software applications and quickly became Microsoft's flagship product. (Microsoft did not release *Word for Windows* until 1989. Word's first general release for MS-DOS computers was in late 1983.)

Why Are Spreadsheets Useful in Statistics?

The basic idea of a spreadsheet is a very large rectangular screen that stores information in cells, organised by columns and rows. The data can then be manipulated by use of formulas to give sums, averages, percentages, and so on.

These features are still central to a spreadsheet's capabilities but, as spreadsheets have developed, they have been greatly extended to include libraries of statistical and mathematical functions and the capability of displaying charts.

In *Excel*, a function can be accessed as follows:

- place the cursor in the cell where you want the function to go;
- click the INSERT menu and choose Function;
- select your preferred Function category – for example, 'Statistical';
- select the required Function name and follow the on-screen instructions.

Note: when a particular Function name, such as AVERAGE, is selected, the syntax of this command is indicated at the bottom of the dialog box (Figure 11.1).

As well as providing an array of statistical commands, spreadsheets are also useful for plotting data in the form of statistical graphs. The easiest way of doing this is via the *Chart Wizard*, which is displayed as an icon at the top of the screen. The three main charts on offer that are relevant at school level are bar charts (both horizontal and vertical bars are available), pie charts and scatter plots. It is possible to draw histograms, but unfortunately this is a bit cumbersome. Other educationally orientated graphs such as dot plots, stem plots and box plots are not currently available in *Excel's Chart Wizard*. However, with a little effort they can be constructed. Baker (2004) explains how *Excel* can be encouraged to draw histograms, as well as a number of Exploratory Data Analysis displays such as stem plots, back-to-back charts and box plots. (These graphical techniques, based on the work of EDA pioneer John Tukey, were introduced in Section 6.2.)

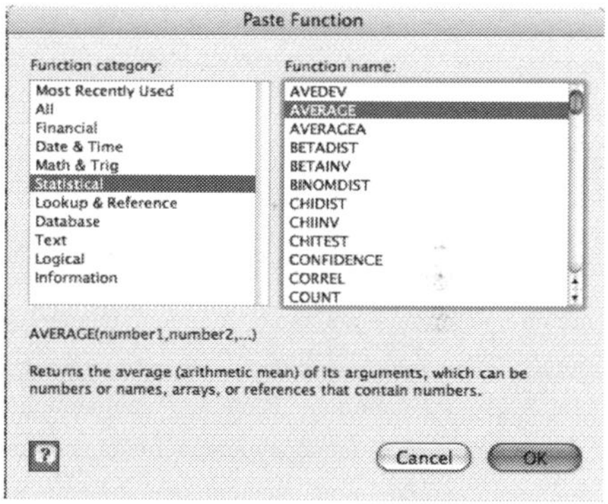

Figure 11.1 **EXAMPLES OF ACCESSING A FUNCTION**

What Are the Main Strengths of *Excel*?

Most mathematics classrooms are not well served when it comes to specifically educational mathematical software on the computer. The main strength of a spreadsheet package is that it is available in every school.

Task 11.1.1 Spreadsheet Benefits

Note down five or six benefits that you think can arise from learners using spreadsheets.

Here is what Richard Beare (1993) has to say about the benefits of using *Excel* in a lesson.

> Spreadsheets ... facilitate a variety of learning styles which can be characterised by the terms: open-ended, problem-oriented, constructivist, investigative, discovery oriented, active and learner-centred. In addition, they offer the following additional benefits: they are interactive; they give immediate feedback to changing data or formulae; they enable data, formulae and graphical output to be available on the screen at once; they give learners a large measure of control and ownership over their learning; and they can solve complex problems and handle large amounts of data without any need for programming. (p. 123)

On a more practical note, another important feature of spreadsheet use is that it can save time. As one teacher observed (quoted in Ruthven and Hennessy, 2002):

> We've used spreadsheets in Year 7 and 8, to enable them to look at handling data, because they can quickly get tables and produce charts that are much better quality than those that they can produce themselves. I've got the bottom set in Year 7 and it can take them the whole lesson to draw a bar chart. So it's particularly successful from that point of view because they don't have to draw all the axes so much, and it doesn't take them so long to develop the ideas because they're not having to spend a whole lesson drawing something. They can draw twenty graphs in a lesson and actually see connections, rather than spend twenty minutes drawing the axes and then twenty minutes talking and then twenty minutes drawing all the graph. (p. 64)

The DISCUS Project

Although spreadsheets were designed for and are predominately used in the commercial world, there are several important initiatives where their potential is explored in statistics education. One of these is the DISCUS project at Coventry University, spearheaded by Neville Hunt and Sydney Tyrell. DISCUS is an acronym for 'Discovering Important Statistical Concepts Using Spreadsheets' (www.mis.coventry.ac.uk/research/discus/discus_home.html).

The DISCUS website above provides a set of freely-available interactive spreadsheets, written in Microsoft *Excel*, which are aimed at teaching statistics at sixth-form and first-year undergraduate level. The materials are designed to be used off the shelf by learners working on their own and little preparation by teaching staff is required. The first of the eight packages, *Descriptive Statistics*, has relevance at KS4. There is also a sequel to this site, run by Hunt and Tyrell, called DISCUSS, located at: www.mis.coventry.ac.uk/~nhunt/home/

As explained on the website:

> The DISCUSS project is a modified and supplemented web-based implementation of the widely used DISCUS materials for teaching elementary Statistics. It

aims to integrate the powerful interactive capabilities of Microsoft *Excel* with the convenience of web-based resource materials using Microsoft *Internet Explorer*.

Task 11.1.2 DISCUS website

Visit the DISCUS website and look at the *Descriptive Statistics* package, noting particularly how the spreadsheet's transparency has been exploited by 'laying bare' a statistical calculation.

11.2 INTERRELATING WITH A GRAPHICS CALCULATOR

Interrelating Relationships

Most people are interested in the nature of human relationships – for example, when two people fall in love, it is interesting to speculate on the possible basis for their mutual attraction. Although there are exceptions, it seems that, in general, people tend to pair up with those of roughly similar age.

Task 11.2.1 *Amor Vincit Omnia*

Try to think up an investigation based on people's age preferences in relationships. Think particularly what sort of information you would require to answer your question and how you might collect the data.

Your investigation and proposed data source are likely to be different from the one considered here. Here is a possible version:

'Do people prefer to pair up with those of their same age?'

As worded, this question is not very clear – for example, there are four possible areas for investigation here: women seeking men, men seeking women, men seeking men and women seeking women. A more precisely worded version could be:

'Is there a difference between men's and women's preferences in terms of the preferred age of partner?'

There are many possible sources of data for investigating this question. One is to look at a newspaper lonely-hearts column, such as the *Observer*'s 'Soulmates' page. To simplify things, the investigation below focuses just on the 'women seeking men' and 'men seeking women' data. Here is a typical entry under the heading 'women seeking men' (Table 11.1).

★**Cuddly** F, 45, confident, outgoing & sociable WLTM M, 30-40, …

(*Observer* (Review section), 30 January 2005, p. 19)

Not all correspondents in these two categories provided both their own age and the ideal age range of partner. Those who did were the following 22 'women seeking men' and 15 'men seeking women' (Table 11.1).

TABLE 11.1 Soulmates data

Women seeking men		Men seeking women	
Women	Men	Men	Women
33	30–40	50	40–50
38	34–45	mid-40s	35–45
50	48–56	50	30–50
52	49–56	35	30–40
33	33–43	45	35–50
31	32–47	31	23–35
31	30–40	25	25–35
30	30–40	43	25–48
36	32–45	59	40–60
30	20–45	32	25–40
46	40–55	50	40–50
25	25–35	42	32–42
22	20–35	50	35–40ish
43	25–45	47	33–43
32	30s	58	45–55
45	30–40		
48	37–55		
25	20–40		
42	35–45		
43	40–50		
31	30s–40s		
31	40–47		

Source: *Observer* (Review section), 30 January 2005, p. 19.

There are number of important issues that arise from this investigation.

First, one possibility for accessing relevant data would be to look at the ages of a sample of the parents of learners in the class. However, this may provide a very restricted age range of couples and some may consider this intrusive: you never know what personal details such questions may uncover that could create embarrassment for learners.

Second, this data set can give rise to a number of possible investigations – for example, do men tend to specify age as a criterion more or less frequently than women, do men tend to specify a wider or narrower age range, and so on.

Finally, where an age is specified as a range, it is not directly usable as an item of data for this investigation. In the particular investigation below, range mid-points have been used.

Task 11.2.2 Entering the 'Women Seeking Men' Data

As was explained in Task 10.2.1, reset the calculator's RAM or clear all lists.

Enter the first two columns of data into lists L1 and L2.

L1	L2	L3	3
33	35		
38	39.5		
50	52		
52	52.5		
33	38		
31	39.5		
31	35		
L3(1)=			

Task 11.2.3 Drawing the Scatter Plot

In Tasks 10.3.1 and 10.3.2, you saw how to set the Window menu and use the STATPLOT menu for drawing a box plot. The procedure is similar for a scatter plot, except this time you need to choose the scatter plot option and enter *two* lists under **Xlist** and **Ylist**. You also need to choose a 'Mark' to indicate the location of the points.

The relevant screenshots are shown here – use them to create a scatter plot for the 'women seeking men' data. Press [TRACE] and use the left and right cursor keys to see the co-ordinates of each point displayed at the bottom of the screen.

On the basis of this scatter plot, there does seem to be a fairly close connection between the ages of these women and the preferred age of their ideal partners – in general, the older the woman, the older her preferred choice of male partner. However, what is, perhaps, more interesting is whether or not women tend to choose men who are older than themselves.

This can be demonstrated by pressing [Y=] and entering **Y1=X**.

Now press [GRAPH] in order to see the $y = x$ line drawn on the scatter plot.

Task 11.2.4 Interpreting the $y = x$ Line   C

There are only four points below the line. What do these points represent?

An alternative to drawing in the $y = x$ line on the scatter plot is to create a new list (L3), one containing the difference between the women's ages and the preferred ages of their potential partners. This is done as follows:

Return to the home screen by pressing:
[2nd] [QUIT].

Enter the command opposite by pressing:
[2nd] [L2] [−] [2nd] [L1] [STO >] [2nd] [L3] [ENTER]

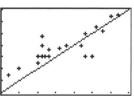

Now plot the values in L3 against the women's ages to produce a scatter plot like the one here (note that this required adjustment of some of the window settings). Note also that there are two 'minus' keys, one for subtraction, marked on the calculator keyboard as '−', and one for entering negative numbers, marked '(−)'.

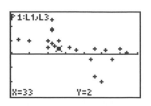

Task 11.2.5 Interpreting the New Scatter Plot   C

How would you interpret this second scatter plot?

Before leaving the 'women seeking men' data, it might be revealing to find the mean of the age differences between these women and that of their ideal partner.

To do this, return to the home screen (that is, the original clear screen).

Press 2nd [LIST] ◁ to enter the List MATH menu.
Press 3 to select the **Mean** command.
Press 2nd [L3]) ENTER to complete the command.

```
mean(L3)
            2.545454545
```

In the next task, you are asked to investigate whether the patterns of women's age preferences are mirrored in the preferences of the 'men seeking women'.

Task 11.2.6 The Preferences of the 'Men Seeking Women'   C

Using a similar approach to that taken in Tasks 11.2.2 to 11.2.5, investigate the age preferences of the 15 men given in Table 11.1.

This section has just given an example of how the graphics calculator can support thinking about statistical relationships. There are other possibilities. For example, ideas of regression have not been mentioned and there is a powerful range of commands available covering a wide range of regression models. This will be addressed in Chapter 13, 'Models and Modelling'.

This chapter has guided you through an investigation linking age and love, in order to illustrate some of the useful and powerful 'interrelating' facilities available on a graphics calculator. Before moving on to the next section, Task 11.2.7 asks you to reflect on some of the calculator's strengths in this area and to consider how they might be exploited in statistics teaching.

Task 11.2.7 Handling Paired Data on a Calculator   C

(a) What unique features has the calculator contributed to this investigation that might not have been so easily available using, say, a spreadsheet or statistical package?

(b) Try to think up two more 'interrelating type' investigations that might be tackled in a similar way to the 'age and love' investigation.

11.3 INTERRELATING WITH A SPREADSHEET

Investigating Estimation Skills

If you were asked to make an estimate of the date of an historical event, what sort of information would you draw on? The example considered here is the number of years ago that television was invented.

Task 11.3.1 Make a Guess

(a) Make a guess at the number of years ago that television was invented.

(b) What information did you draw on in order to make this guess?

(c) How do you think children make these sorts of judgements? What additional difficulties might they have in making estimates such as these accurately?

There is no clear consensus as to when television was invented, but most people would agree that a significant milestone occurred on the 26 January 1926 when John Logie Baird demonstrated his system to the Royal Institute and a reporter from *The Times* newspaper by transmitting moving pictures of moving human faces over short distances.

If the event in question occurred within your own lifetime, you may try to link it to experiences that happened to you ('Which school was I attending when the event happened?', for example). Alternatively, you may base your judgement on the conversations of older generations such as your parents or grandparents. You could draw on information gained from the media. And, of course, you might even have learned about it in school!

Children are not good at making these sorts of estimates, for a number of reasons. First, they are further away in time from the historical event than are adults and are therefore less likely to have direct personal links to it. Second, they have a less well-developed web of interconnecting facts and understandings about the world, which is an essential backdrop against which estimates such as these can be made.

Task 11.3.2 Posing a Question on Interrelating   **C**

Open the application *Excel* (or another spreadsheet of your choice) and then open the file 'Estimation.xls', which contains the data from Table 10.2. As you can see, column D contains data of people's estimates for the number of years ago that television was invented.

(a) Form a question that can be investigated from these data on the theme of interrelating that includes some or all of the data in Column D.

(b) Interrelating requires data from two variables. Which of the two variables you have chosen to investigate is to be designated the 'explanatory' and which the 'response' variable? (These terms were explained in Chapter 3.)

(c) Decide, with reasons, whether you will use all of the data in the two selected spreadsheet columns or just a subset of them.

Copy the relevant data into columns A and B of a new worksheet where they can be analysed. But before making the analysis, it is usually a good idea to check the data to ensure that there are no missing or 'dodgy' data.

Task 11.3.3 Checking the Data   C

Inspect the 23 paired data items visually. You could sort them into ascending order of estimates in order to check the extreme values. However, do make sure to *select both columns* before doing this, otherwise the correspondence between the data pairs will be lost.

Decide whether any of these data pairs should be rejected because they are 'dodgy data' or extreme outliers.

Task 11.3.4 Plotting the Data

Using the *Chart Wizard*, plot these data as a scatter plot. Make sure that the appropriate (explanatory) variable is allocated to the horizontal axis. Note that, where data are recorded in two adjacent columns, Excel chooses the first column to be plotted as the *x*-variable.

When the scatter plot is complete (Figure 11.2), select the chart by clicking on it and then some new menu options will appear at the top of the screen. Choose the option Add 'Trendline' from the CHART menu. In the 'Type' dialog box, select 'Linear' to display a *linear* regression line. To display its equation and the value of the *coefficient of determination*, R^2, select the 'Options' tab and check these two buttons.

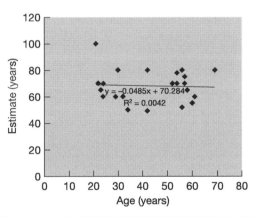

Note that this displayed information is contained within a text box, which can be moved to a more convenient position on the screen simply by clicking and dragging on

Figure 11.2 **SCATTER PLOT SHOWING ESTIMATES WITH AGE**

its perimeter. Note also that in *Excel*, the coefficient of variation value (R^2) is given with a capital R, but it is more usually written in lower case, as r^2.

Task 11.3.5 How Strong is the Relationship?   C

Is there evidence to suggest that people's estimates vary with age?

The comments to Task 11.3.5 suggested the following more interesting question that could be investigated with these data:

'Are older people *better* at making this estimate than younger people?'

If Baird is deemed to have invented the television in 1926, then a correct estimate in 2005 (when this survey was conducted) is 79 years. It follows that an estimate of 90 years is as good as one of 68 years – they both have errors of 11 years. Using the spreadsheet, it is easy to convert from estimates to absolute errors. (An absolute error is the difference between the estimate and the 'true' value, treating all such differences as positive. The idea of 'absolute error' cropped up in Section 10.4, in the discussion on relative average error.)

Task 11.3.6 Plotting Errors

(a) Enter an appropriate formula in Column C of your spreadsheet to convert estimates to absolute errors.

(b) Draw a scatter plot of absolute errors against ages and display a linear regression line and a corresponding R^2 value.

(c) Is there now evidence that older people's estimates are better than those of younger people?

You can use the built-in function $=ABS()$, which calculates absolute values. If the 'Estimate' data are placed in column B, the errors can be calculated in column C as follows:

- enter into cell C2 the formula $=ABS(B2-79)$;
- fill down as far as cell C24.

In order to plot 'absolute error' against 'age of respondent', you need to select two non-adjacent columns (columns A and C). This can be achieved by holding down the Control (Ctrl) key while selecting both data sets in cells A2:A24 and C2:C24. (If you are working on a Mac computer, this is the Command key, marked with an apple, .)

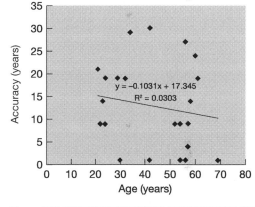

Figure 11.3 **SCATTER PLOT SHOWING ACCURACY WITH AGE**

As you can see (Figure 11.3), the regression line now slopes downwards, suggesting that perhaps older people have smaller errors. However, the scatter of points is so wide that there is no clear evidence from this sample that older people's estimates really are better than those of younger people. This is confirmed by the fact that, once again, the value of R^2 is almost zero.

Investigating Correlation

To end this section, you are asked to use the spreadsheet to 'lay bare' the calculation of two measures of linear correlation – the coefficient of determination, r^2 and its square root, the correlation coefficient, r. By now, you should have a reasonably good working knowledge of how a spreadsheet operates, so Bruner's scaffolding in terms of textual support will be less in evidence.

Calculating the strength of correlation can be a messy business. In order to get to grips with these two measures of correlation, you need to start with the building bricks of the calculation – the means of x and y (written $\bar{x}$ and $\bar{y}$), the deviation of each individual x-value from its mean and the deviation of each y-value from its mean. These last two items can be written, respectively, as $(x_i - \bar{x})$ and $(y_i - \bar{y})$.

The correlation coefficient, r, is defined in terms of the following three components.

$\Sigma(x_i - \bar{x})^2$: this is calculated by taking the deviation of each x-value from $\bar{x}$, the mean value of all the x_i, squaring them one by one and then adding all the results together. It is called the 'sum of squares of the x-deviations' and can be written as S_{xx}.

$\Sigma(y_i - \bar{y})^2$: this is calculated by taking the deviation of each y-value from $\bar{y}$, the mean value of all the y_i, squaring them one by one and then adding all the results together. It is called the 'sum of squares of the y-deviations' and can be written as S_{yy}.

$\Sigma(x_i - \bar{x})(y_i - \bar{y})$: this is calculated by taking the products of each pair of deviations from their respective means one by one and then adding all these products together. This can be written as S_{xy}.

Combining these three components in the following way gives the following formula for the coefficient of correlation, r.

$$r = S_{xy}/\sqrt{(S_{xx} \cdot S_{yy})}$$

Note that, unlike the values of S_{xx} and S_{yy} (which will always be positive no matter what the data – can you see why this must be so?), the value of S_{xy} can be positive or negative depending on the data, and so therefore can be the resulting value of r. Negative (linear) correlation is associated with a trend line that slopes downwards to the right. The coefficient of determination, r^2, is the square of this value, and hence is always positive. In the next task, you are asked to lay bare this calculation using a spreadsheet based on the 'Women seeking men' data, used in Task 11.2.2.

Task 11.3.7 Calculating r and r^2

The aim of this task is for you to use a spreadsheet to work through the main steps in these calculations, thereby getting a better understanding of the overall structure of the underlying formulas. Using the spreadsheet extract in Figure 11.4 as a guide, have a go at laying bare the calculation of these two measures of correlation. The final results are displayed in cells H4 and I4. To check your result, apply directly the appropriate commands from the function menu (displayed in cells H6 and I6).

Here are a few pointers:

- you will need to use the $ symbol in cells C7 and D7 before using 'fill down';

- the correlation coefficient formula, **=CORREL**, was entered directly into cell H6 and the coefficient of determination was calculated as the square of this value in I6;

- the coefficient of correlation formula was entered directly into cell H4 (based on the formula given in the text above) and the coefficient of determination was calculated from it in cell I4.

Note that if you get stuck, you can check the formulae on the completed spreadsheet at the following website www.paulchapmanpublishing.co.uk/resource/statistics.pdf

◇	A	B	C	D	E	F	G	H	I
1	**Correlation**								
2									
3	*Mean x*	*Mean y*			*Sum Xdev^2*	*Sum Ydev^2*	*Sum Xdev.Ydev*	*r*	*r^2*
4	36.227273	38.72727			1557.86	963.364	996.36364	**0.8133**	**0.6615**
5								**Check**	
6	*x*	*y*	*Xdev*	*Ydev*	*Xdev^2*	*Ydev^2*	*Xdev.Ydev*	**0.8133**	**0.6615**
7	33	35	-3.22727	-3.7273	10.415289	13.892562	12.0289256		
8	38	39.5	1.772727	0.77273	3.142562	0.5971074	1.36983471		
9	50	52	13.77273	13.2727	189.68802	176.16529	182.801653		
10	52	52.5	15.77273	13.7727	248.77893	189.68802	217.233471		
11	33	38	-3.22727	-0.7273	10.415289	0.5289256	2.34710744		
12	31	39.5	-5.22727	0.77273	27.32438	0.5971074	-4.0392562		

Figure 11.4 **SPREADSHEET DATA**

11.4 *TINKERPLOTS*

In this section, you are asked to look at the data-handling package *Tinkerplots*. Even if you are unable to gain access to a copy of the software, you should find it worthwhile to read through the section and visit the *Tinkerplots* website.

It has already been observed in Section 11.1 that applications such as spreadsheets were designed primarily for commercial rather than educational needs. *Tinkerplots*, in contrast, has been designed from the bottom up as an educational tool for younger children. As has been suggested by Clifford Konold (2002), one of *Tinkerplots'* designers, from the Scientific Reasoning Research Institute at the University of Massachusetts: 'data analysis instruction … should be structured according to how statistical reasoning develops in young learners and should, for the time being, not target specific graphical representations as objectives of instruction' (p. 1). This point is endorsed by Rolf Biehler (1995, p. 3), who argues that most of the existing statistical tools for young children have been developed from the top down and many classroom packages consist merely of subsets of the tools contained in adult packages.

Tinkerplots is designed around the idea of a database of 'cases', each case consisting of a number of different measures (both nominal and numerical in nature). For example, as you will see shortly when you view the helpful five-minute introductory movie, the database may consist of various measures of a group of cats, listing such information as their name, gender, weight, body length, colouring, and so on.

When a data batch such as **cats.tp** is first opened in *Tinkerplots*, the data items are displayed as a haphazard collection of small 'spots' (or other icons, such as the cats shown in Figure 11.5), each one corresponding to a case (in this example, a particular cat). The underlying point of this choice of haphazard representation is that these are raw data that have not yet been processed, so placing them in any particular order would be premature. Click on any one 'spot' and its case details are displayed

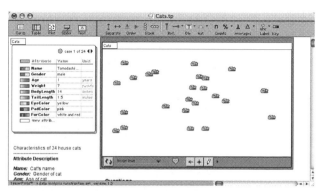

Figure 11.5 **THE INITIAL SCREEN OF A *TINKERPLOTS* FILE**

on the left of the screen on its data card. As you will see from the movie, investigations of the data base are very 'hands on' and intuitive. To start off, simply click on a particular attribute on the left and the data immediately change in colour, coded according to their value.

Task 11.4.1 Making a Start with *Tinkerplots*

(a) Visit the website below and view the *Tinkerplots Basics* introductory movie, which has a playing time of 5 minutes 24 seconds (www.umass.edu/srri/serg/projects/tp/tpmovie.html).

(b) If you are able to gain access to the *Tinkerplots* application, open it up, then open the file **cats.tp** and spend at least 15 minutes exploring different ways of viewing the cats database. Make sure you see the effect of moving an object, once an attribute has been assigned to an axis.

(c) Open some of the other data files supplied with the application, pose different questions about each one for investigation and then analyse the data in as many different ways as possible. Spend as long as you can on this task.

In Chapter 1, you were introduced to the distinction between nominal and numerical measures. If necessary, revisit this chapter now to remind yourself of these terms.

Task 11.4.2 *Tinkerplots* Terminology

How does *Tinkerplots* distinguish between nominal and numerical measures?

At the top of the data-card window on the left of the *Tinkerplots* screen is the word 'Attributes'. This term is used to describe *all* of the measures in the data cards, whether they are simply names or numerical variables. This is a somewhat non-standard use of the term 'attribute', which is normally reserved for names only. However, you may have noticed another way of making this distinction in the data cards, based on the use of colour. As you can see in Figure 11.6, the colour key for the numerical variable 'Age of cat' is indicated by a single colour gradient (from light to dark), whereas attribute 'EyeColour' is depicted using different colours.

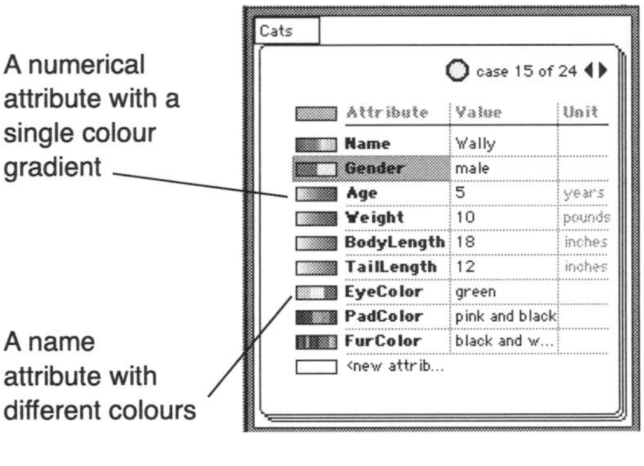

A numerical attribute with a single colour gradient

A name attribute with different colours

Figure 11.6 **A *TINKERPLOTS* DATA CARD**

An important point emphasised by Konold is that, when faced with a scatter plot to represent a co-variant relationship, many children (as well as many adults) fail to grasp fully what the graph is showing. Yet, as you saw from the example in Chapter 3, where a 3-year-old child observed, 'The more the long time, the littler my balloon grows', the problem is not a failure to grasp a bi-variate relationship, but rather a failure to understand this particular form of its depiction. Whereas an abstract display such as a scatter plot is both convincing and useful to experienced and confident users, it seems to be hard for beginning learners to use with understanding. There is increasing evidence (quoted in Konold, 2002) that, even where considerable use is made of scatter plots in teaching, relatively few learners subsequently choose to use one to represent a two-variable relationship.

So what might be a viable alternative to a scatter plot for depicting two-variable relationships? Here is one possible approach that, according to Konold, learners seem to find intuitively easier; it is based on grouping one of the variables (in this case, the 'BodyWeight' variable) into several categories.

Figure 11.7 was created in *Tinkerplots* using one of the supplied data sets, **Backpack.tp**. It shows the backpack (that is, school-bag) weights carried by 79 learners, grouped in various body-weight categories. (To turn this into a full-blown scatter plot, you need to drag any one of the spots off the screen to the right. The four small triangles to the left of each body-weight grouping show the location of its mean.)

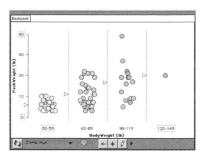

Figure 11.7 **A** *TINKERPLOTS* **DATA FILE ARRANGED INTO GROUPS**

Task 11.4.3 Easier than a Scatter Plot

Why do you think learners might find this form of representation intuitively easier to grasp than a scatter plot?

Here is what Konold (2002) had to say about why learners might prefer this form of representation.

> It is striking how facile learners are in making judgments about covariation using a superimposed color gradient. We do not yet fully understand why this is, but suspect that part of the advantage comes from separating the task into two discrete steps: learners first anticipate what they will see and then afterwards look at the new display. Also, the fact that the icons do not change their positions when the new color gradient is added probably helps learners keep in mind that the cases are still ordered according to the original variable, which then allows them to systematically scan the cases in search of a pattern. (p. 8)

Task 11.4.4 Exploring Relationships

Return to the *Tinkerplots* website and view the movie *Exploring Relationships*.

If you have access to the software, open the data file **Ozone levels.tp** in the 'Science and Nature' folder in Tinkerplots and repeat some aspects of data analyses covered in the movie.

Try to identify which particular aspects of data analysis *Tinkerplots* seem to facilitate when investigating statistical relationships.

Finally, here are some of the pedagogic suggestions and comments extracted from the companion booklet (Konold, 2005) provided with the *Tinkerplots* application.

- Whenever possible, encourage learners to discuss among themselves the 'story' of the data: what the data are, how they were collected, how particular attributes were probably measured, what questions they have about the data and what they think they will find.

- Learners are encouraged to learn about the context of the data, make a hypothesis about what the data might show, then investigate their hypothesis and finally write up their conclusions .... This helps learners understand what they are looking at, engages them in the data, builds their reasoning, writing and critical thinking skills and gives them a common experience that can serve as a basis for a class discussion.

- Learners new to the study of data tend not to see overall patterns in the data.

- We believe that by allowing learners to use methods that make sense to them, and having them discuss what they do with other learners and with teachers, they will come to see the limitations in their approaches and develop more powerful methods.

- Often when learners (or experts) get confused looking at a graph, it is because they lose the connection between a point on the graph and the data card to which it refers.

(pp. 9–18)

Task 11.4.5 Exploring Relationships   **C**

Choose one of Konold's five points above (preferably one that you agree with) and write down how you might approach this issue in your teaching.

11.5 PEDAGOGY

This section looks at teaching and learning issues, based on four of the six PTT themes.

Techniques and Methods

One of the issues raised in Chapter 7 (Task 7.2.5) was that the speed, power and convenience of a well-designed ICT tool can be both a strength and a weakness in teaching. A confident learner with clearly understood learning goals who can exploit the tool wisely is likely to have a good grasp of what the results mean. However, a less confident learner may simply see the tool as a magical 'black box' that performs calculations and displays graphs, but have little understanding of what these signify.

As a teacher, you need to think carefully about how to handle this issue, particularly when faced with a class of learners of varying abilities and levels of mastery of the technology.

Task 11.5.1 Thinking Out of the Box

How can you help learners to make the best use of ICT tools at their own level and prevent them from adopting a 'black box' mentality about ICT?

One rather extreme view of ICT taken by teachers who have not yet fully embraced its role in teaching might be, 'I don't let learners use ICT tools until they have shown that they understand the topic fully and can first do it in their head or on paper'. The main weakness with this view is that it fails to acknowledge the potential role of ICT as an aid to novel learning. In order for learners to use an ICT tool with understanding, they need to know:

- what keys to press and in what order;
- where the keys are located;
- how the various keys and commands are organised into 'families', as well as that these families correspond to certain 'big ideas' in mathematics.

The third of these abilities is crucial to a learner's intelligent use of ICT and it is not something that is often addressed explicitly in the classroom. It may be possible to help learners in this area by drawing their attention to the mathematical structure that underlies the design of the ICT tool in question – an idea referred to in Section 9.2 (in the sub-section, 'The formatting power of technology') and at the end of Section 10.1 (in the sub-section 'Formatting learner thinking').

Here is a possible task that might help learners to develop this overview of mathematical or statistical structure. Ask the learners to create an imaginary calculator (or other tool) to tackle just one particular statistical task, such as displaying paired data on a scatter plot or summarising a set of data. As their (imaginary) calculator is required to perform only this one task, they can dispense with the vast majority of the other calculator functions and focus just on a particular family of keys and commands that serve the purpose of the task in hand.

A possible way of doing this is to take advantage of the programming commands on the calculator. These provide a suitable microworld within which learners could specify a narrow range of commands for performing a particular task that you might set them. For ideas on helping learners in the 11–16 age range to create their own very short programs, using the programming commands of a graphics calculator, see Graham and Galpin (2003).

Language Patterns

Here you are asked to continue thinking about 'formatting learner thinking', but now in terms of the associated terminology. In Chapter 10, you were asked to be on the lookout for some of the ways in which the screens, menus and organisational structure of statistical packages and graphics calculators can help or hinder learner learning.

Task 11.5.2 Calculator Terms   **C**

(a) Look back at Section 11.2 on the calculator and note any calculator-specific terms that were used when drawing a scatter plot.

(b) How might you use this terminology to help learners with their understanding of two-variable relationships?

Different Contexts

A variety of contexts have been used for the investigations in this chapter, including love, skill at estimating and the formula for calculating the coefficient of correlation.

Additionally, if you were able to look at the application *Tinkerplots*, you will have seen more than 40 data sets, each of which could spark off several interesting investigations. These data sets have been organised into the following categories:

- health;
- science and nature;
- social studies;
- sports and entertainment.

Task 11.5.3 Contexts   **C**

If you had access to these data sets, how might you adapt and use them effectively with learners? What problems might you envisage?

Root Questions

One danger with using ICT in statistical work is that it is easy to become seduced by the number-crunching and graphing capabilities of the software, at the expense of maintaining a clear overview of why you are doing the investigation at all. On p. 18 of the Key Stage 3 National Strategy document (DfEE, 2001), this overview is maintained by stressing the four-stage model summarised elsewhere in this book by the acronym *PCAI*.

Task 11.5.4 Maintaining an Overview   **C**

(a) How have the designers of *Tinkerplots* chosen to encourage their learners to see the bigger picture?

(b) In science education, learners are encouraged to understand and use the 'investigative cycle' in their experimental work. Have a look at the following Science Standards website (created by the DfES), which provides some background on this term as it is used in science (www.standards.dfes.gov.uk/schemes2/secondary_science/sci09m/?view=list&column=objective).

Write down in your own words what the term 'investigative cycle' means to you. How does it relate to the ideas you jotted down for part (a)?

12

Probability with ICT

This chapter starts by looking at the programming language Java and how it is increasingly being used to create applets and other forms of software that are useful in teaching statistics. Section 12.2 considers ways in which spreadsheet applications such as *Excel* can be used to teach probability. Section 12.3 turns to graphics calculators and their role in helping learners investigate some important questions in probability. The fourth section builds on these ideas, looking at how the calculator can help learners get a handle on more advanced concepts such as probability density functions. Finally, as with previous chapters, this chapter ends with some pedagogic issues.

12.1 JAVA APPLETS

This section is based on the web-based article entitled 'Java™ technology: an early history' (www.comedition.com/Computers/Java/JavaHistory.htm).

What Is Java?

Java is a programming language, enabling users to write powerful programs that run in the browser application that is installed on their own computer, rather than running directly on their machine's native operating system. (A *browser* is an application such as *Netscape, Internet Explorer, Safari*, and so on which is used to surf the world wide web.) This means that any computer system with the Java Virtual Machine (JVM) application installed can run a Java program, regardless of the computer system upon which the application was originally developed. So, most Java applications will run happily on the browser of a PC, Sun or Apple Mac computer. It is the widespread use of Java on the Internet and the world wide web, and the fact that its use is based on widely supported standards, that comprise the keys to its success.

A Brief History of Java

Java technology was created as a programming tool by a secret 'Green Team' of 13 people, chosen by the computer manufacturing company Sun Microsystems, in 1991, to anticipate and plan for the future developments in computing, such as digitally controlled consumer devices and computers. In their search for a mass market for Java, the Green Team (later renamed 'FirstPerson') tried to encourage the US cable companies to apply the new technology to the television set-top box and video-on-demand. In the event, the cable companies were not ready to give their customers that degree of control in the use of their product and the negotiations stalled.

Looking for a new market, they decided to try the fast-growing internet, which seemed to offer the sort of network configuration that the FirstPerson team had envisioned for the cable television industry. At that time, the internet was already being used as a way of moving media (text and graphics, for example), using the programming language HTML (short for 'hypertext mark-up language). They could see that Java technology (in the form of so-called *applets*) offered the capability of moving procedures as well as media content. In other words, Java could provide the environment in which the content could be viewed as well as the content itself.

May, 1995, brought the arrival of Java technology and its incorporation into Netscape Navigator, the world's first internet browser. At that time, the entire Java technology team numbered less than 30 people. Since its introduction in 1995, the Java platform has been adopted rapidly across the industry, with major computing platform vendors signing up to include Java technology as a core component of their products.

Using Java Applets

There are many thousands of Java applets freely available for use across the web. All you need in order to access and use them is a web browser and a suitable version of the freely available application Java.

Task 12.1.1 Exploring Statistics Applets   **C**

(a) Visit the website http://cme.open.ac.uk/ICT/index.htm and explore the following applets designed for teaching purposes by Roger Duke of the University of Queensland:

  (i) Monty Hall;

  (ii) Down the middle.

(b) Note your thoughts about the nature of these applets as environments for learning. What learning might take place when using them?

(c) How might you wish to use them with learners?

Look back at Task 4.2.4 (page 54), where you were asked to think about the Monty Hall dilemma. This is one of a number of examples in probability where one's intuition may fail to clarify the problem and where some sort of simulation would be helpful. In Section 12.2, you will use a spreadsheet to create your own simulation, but for now, explore the applet suggested in the task below.

Task 12.1.2 The Monty Hall Dilemma   **C**

Return to the Roger Duke applets and run 'Monty Hall'. (Monty Hall hosted the television game show *Let's make a deal.*)

(a) Read carefully the text in the file associated with this applet. Spend long enough using the simulation to see a clear pattern emerge in the results that might lead to insights about the problem.

(b) What advantages and disadvantages are there in using this simulation over actually playing the game?

12.2 PROBABILITY WITH A SPREADSHEET

Here is what a KS3 teacher had to say after his class had spent a noisy, chaotic lesson rolling dice and recording the results:

My aim was to let them see (by actually doing it) that all the six faces were equally likely. Disaster! They all came away convinced of the exact opposite! None of the faces of the dice came up the same number of times, so they clearly believed that the outcomes were *not* equally likely.

Actually tossing coins and rolling dice can be a valuable starting point for developing a good intuition about probability in learners. However, the great drawback is that such actions generate data too slowly for learners to be able to see beyond short-term fluctuations and start to become aware of longer-term underlying patterns.

One of the benefits of using ICT in a statistics lesson is to let learners generate a sufficiently large number of trials for the teacher to be confident that the underlying patterns will emerge. However, for the learner, this speed and efficiency brings with it the danger that what is happening on the computer screen can easily become totally divorced from the physical event that the computer is simulating.

One way of trying to avoid this loss of awareness of the context being simulated by the computer is to encourage learners to *state in advance their own intuitions* about the question under investigation and perhaps to roll the die (or toss the coin) enough times in order to confirm the precise nature of the investigation. Only when this is clearly understood can a computer simulation be of benefit.

Generating Random Integers

In order to simulate tossing coins and rolling dice on a spreadsheet, you could use a very convenient command called **=randbetween**. Unfortunately, at the time of writing, this command is not available as standard in Excel – it is provided in an 'analysis toolpack', which needs to be installed as an 'add-in'. Fortunately, there is a 'work-around', based on combining two commands, **=rand()** and **=int**, which is the approach taken here.

The command **=rand()** generates a random number in the range 0 to 1. The command **=int** calculates the integer part of a number. For example, entering **=int(3.71)** will produce the value 3. Combinations of these two commands enable you to generate random integers in a range of your choosing and these can be used to simulate the tosses of dice, coins, and so on. If you have not used these commands before, you will need to spend a few minutes familiarising yourself with them.

Task 12.2.1 Getting to Grips with the rand and int Commands   C

(a) Open a blank spreadsheet and enter into cell A1 the command **=rand()**. Fill down as far as, say, A30. You should see 30 random numbers in the range 0–1. Click in the formula bar and then click the green tick mark to the left of the formula bar. This recalculates all cell entries. You will see the random numbers change value (different random decimals will be displayed each time the screen is recalculated).

Then try changing the command to **=rand()*10** and observe the effect.

(b) Try using the **=int** command with different decimal numbers inside the brackets to see the effect.

(c) To simulate the tossing of a coin on the spreadsheet, one solution is to generate integers in the range 0–1, where the outcome 0 means 'tails' and 1 means 'heads'. Using a combination of the **=int** and **=rand** commands, generate a simulation of 10 coin tosses.

(d) A fair die generates equally likely integer outcomes in the range 1–6. Using a combination of the **=int** and **=rand** commands, generate a simulation of ten die throws.

(e) How could you explain to learners the command you created in part (d) above?

A 'back-of-an-envelope' sketch such as the one in Figure 12.1, which builds the command up in stages, may help learners understand what is going on. It may be worth stressing that the first three commands produce what are effectively continuous ranges of outputs, whereas the final command generates discrete outputs in the range 1 to 6 inclusive.

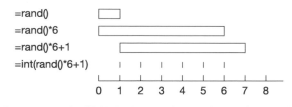

Figure 12.1 **A STAGE-BY-STAGE DEVELOPMENT OF DICE SIMULATION**

A major theme of this book, and indeed the issue that distinguished Block 2, has been the importance of using pictures in expressing and interpreting statistical ideas. Sometimes, 'back-of-an-envelope' sketches (such as the one above) can provide insights that words alone cannot convey. Perhaps a key element of visual approaches to information handling is that in a picture, unlike with text, the eye can wander over the depiction at will, moving from one detail to another in any order or moving from broad overview to small details and back again in a moment.

A Six Is Hard to Get

Task 12.2.2 Fallacious Claims

(a) Evaluate the two statements below, which are sometimes made by younger children when talking about board games involving dice.

   (i) 'A six is hard to get.'

   (ii) 'The other person usually gets a six before I do.'

(b) How could you use the simulation possibilities of a spreadsheet to help learners test these sorts of statements?

These statements may not be quite as fallacious as they first appear. Many dice-based board games require a 'six' to start. Any outcome other than 'six' (that is, a 'non-six') is therefore a *fail* and a 'six' is a *success*. So, when children say that 'a six is hard to get', they may really be saying that 'a six is harder to get than a non-six', which is indeed true.

The second statement above is also true — if there are more than two players, someone else *is* more likely to get a 'six' before you, provided that the claim is not applied to a particular person who is specified in advance, but instead refers to *any* other player.

There is no single correct answer to the second question, but here is a possibility that you might like to try for yourself, which investigates the first of these questions – is a 'six' hard to throw? The approach taken makes use of the =if command.

- Enter into cell A1 the command **=int(rand()*6+1)**.
- Fill down as far as cell A60, to simulate 60 dice rolls.
- Enter into cell B1 the command **=if(A1=6,1,0)**.

The syntax of the **=if** command is **=if(***test, value if true, value if false***)**. In other words, if the statement 'A1=6' is true, display 1, otherwise display 0.

Select cell B1 and fill down as far as cell B60. This column now consists of a series of zeros and ones, where the ones correspond to getting a six in the corresponding cell in column A. The number of sixes in column A can now be displayed in a convenient cell, simply by finding the sum of values in column B.

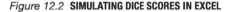

Use the 'recalculate' facility described in the previous sub-section to see the simulation rerun as often as you wish. Learners will see that the results vary, but seem to centre around 10, which is one sixth of the outcomes. Extracts from the relevant screens are displayed in Figure 12.2.

	A	B	C	D
1	6	1		
2	6	1		Sixes
3	1	0		11
4	5	0		
5	1	0		
6	5	0		
7	5	0		
8	6	1		

	A	B	C	D
1	=INT(RAND()*6+1)	=IF(A1=6,1,0)		
2	=INT(RAND()*6+1)	=IF(A2=6,1,0)		Sixes
3	=INT(RAND()*6+1)	=IF(A3=6,1,0)		=SUM(B1:B60)
4	=INT(RAND()*6+1)	=IF(A4=6,1,0)		
5	=INT(RAND()*6+1)	=IF(A5=6,1,0)		
6	=INT(RAND()*6+1)	=IF(A6=6,1,0)		
7	=INT(RAND()*6+1)	=IF(A7=6,1,0)		
8	=INT(RAND()*6+1)	=IF(A8=6,1,0)		
9	=INT(RAND()*6+1)	=IF(A9=6,1,0)		
10	=INT(RAND()*6+1)	=IF(A10=6,1,0)		

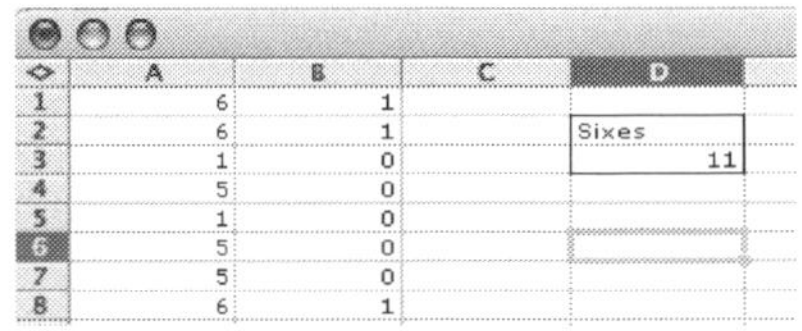

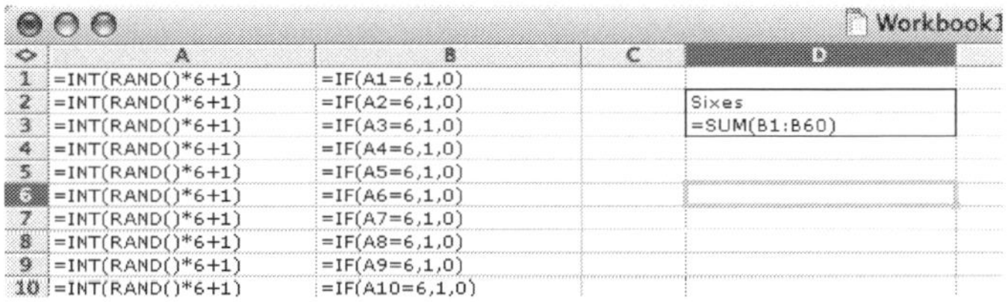

Figure 12.2 **SIMULATING DICE SCORES IN EXCEL**

The Gambler's Fallacy

In Section 4.4, you were introduced to the 'gambler's fallacy'. It described a belief, popular among some punters, that after a run of one particular outcome, a different outcome is more likely on the next trial, just to even things up. Look back at this section now, if you want to refresh your memory.

Task 12.2.3 The Gambler's Fallacy

How could you use the simulation possibilities of a spreadsheet to help learners test the truth or otherwise of the gambler's fallacy?

One possibility would be to consider a long sequence of coin tosses. A 'long run' could be defined as four of the same outcome in a row. If the gambler's fallacy were true, the next outcome would be more likely to be different.

This can be easily simulated using the command **=int(rand()*2)**. Learners can easily identify a run of four consecutive zeros or ones and then check whether the next outcome matches the previous outcomes. Doing this, say, 40 times should indicate that on roughly half of the occasions the next outcome is the same, thereby calling into question the truth of the gambler's fallacy.

Hospital Births

Task 4.2.2 asked you to investigate the births in two hypothetical hospitals, one larger than the other. The question centred on whether one or other of these hospitals was more likely to have over 60% of their births as girls in a single day of deliveries.

Task 12.2.4 Investigating Birth Patterns

How could you use the simulation possibilities of a spreadsheet to help learners test the truth or otherwise of the 'hospital births' question?

The sex ratio, measured as the ratio of male to female births, is considered to be roughly 1.06:1 in most industrialised countries. However, for simplicity, you could assume that the sex ratio is 1:1. The question of sex of a baby can therefore be modelled, whereby each new birth is represented by the toss of a coin, with 'heads' signifying 'girl' and 'tails' signifying 'boy'. On a spreadsheet, create in Column B, 45 coin tosses and in Column C, 15 coin tosses. The extract below shows how summary data can be included at the top of the screen. Try recalculating the screen repeatedly and note the two percentage figures in cells B3 and C3. You should find that, due to the smaller size of data set, a much wider spread of values is displayed in cell C3 than in cell B3. For example, in the example shown in Figure 12.3, the proportion of female births in the small hospital on this particular 'day' was over 70%, something which would be practically unheard of in the larger hospital.

⬦	A	B	C	[
1	Girls	23	11	
2	Boys	22	4	
3	% girls	51.1111111	73.3333333	
4		Large H	Small H	
5		1	0	
6		1	1	
7		0	1	
8		1	1	
9		0	0	
10		1	1	
11		0	1	

⬦	A	B	C
1	Girls	=SUM(B5:B49)	=SUM(C5:C19)
2	Boys	=45-B1	=15-C1
3	% girls	=B1/45*100	=C1/15*100
4		Large H	Small H
5		=INT(RAND()*2)	=INT(RAND()*2)
6		=INT(RAND()*2)	=INT(RAND()*2)
7		=INT(RAND()*2)	=INT(RAND()*2)
8		=INT(RAND()*2)	=INT(RAND()*2)
9		=INT(RAND()*2)	=INT(RAND()*2)
10		=INT(RAND()*2)	=INT(RAND()*2)
11		=INT(RAND()*2)	=INT(RAND()*2)

Figure 12.3 **SIMULATING THE 'HOSPITAL BIRTHS' PROBLEM IN EXCEL**

Task 12.2.5 Adapting Ideas

Which of the tasks that you have tried in this section could you try with learners? How and why would you adapt them for younger or less experienced learners?

12.3 PROBABILITY WITH A GRAPHICS CALCULATOR

The randInt Command

An excellent feature of graphics calculators is the ease with which random integers can be generated using the **randInt** command.

Press MATH ◁ to select the MATH PRB menu and then press **5** to paste the **randInt** command onto the home screen. Complete the command as shown and press ENTER several times to simulate dice scores. Then try simulating several tosses of a coin using the command **randInt(0,1)**.

```
randInt(1,6)
                    3
                    2
randInt(0,1)
                    1
                    1
```

If you wish to generate, say, 30 dice scores and store the results in a list, simply add the third argument, 30, to the command and complete it as shown here, not forgetting to press ENTER .

Now you can investigate some of the questions that you looked at in the previous section, armed with little more than this **randInt** command.

Task 12.3.1 Fallacious Claims Revisited · C

How could you use the simulation possibilities of a graphics calculator to help learners test the statement 'a six is hard to get'?

Hint: As you did with the spreadsheet in Task 12.2.1, you need to generate a number of dice rolls and then see whether the outcome '6' is under-represented.

Some people might claim that the calculator provides a more satisfactory microworld than a spreadsheet for investigations like these. See what you think after trying this task.

A Six Is Hard to Throw

The approach taken in the comments to the previous task has several benefits – the solution can be seen in two or three clearly defined steps and also the final picture gives a clear overview of the relative frequencies of all six outcomes, not just the outcome of interest (the '6'). Here is an alternative approach, one which calculates the number of 6s in list L1 using a single command, without recourse to graphing the data. Note that it makes use of the = command, which can be found in the TEST menu.

Press 2nd [LIST] ◁ to enter the LIST MATH menu and press 5 to paste the sum command onto the home screen.

To complete the command and display the number of 6s in list L1, press 2nd [L1] 2nd [TEST] 1 6) ENTER

In fact, the use of list L1 can be dispensed with entirely with the following command. Each press of ENTER generates a new list and the command sums the number of sixes.

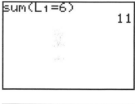

Task 12.3.2 For and Against

What are the arguments for and against using this final approach as compared with the histogram method?

This final approach is extremely efficient. Also, it generates a new data set every time it is used, so the user can quickly see that the results vary widely, but they seem to centre around 10 (which is the point of the exercise). However, for many learners this might be too concise a solution. There is often a decision to be made by the teacher in the trade-off between conciseness and pedagogic clarity. Which decision is taken usually depends on the mathematical and technological sophistication and confidence of the learner.

Two Dice

Many learners are aware that the outcomes on a fair die are equally likely. It is not surprising, perhaps, that they often wrongly apply this assumption of equal likelihood to the situation where two dice are rolled and the combined scores are compared. For example, some learners assume that, if two dice are rolled, combined scores of 12 and 6 are equally likely.

Task 12.3.3 A Two-dice Surprise   **C**

How could you use the simulation possibilities of a graphics calculator to help learners test the statement: 'If two dice are rolled, combined scores of 12 and 6 are equally likely'?

The centrally peaked shape of the 'sums' distribution in the last task may surprise some learners – they may believe that if each die has equally likely outcomes, then any combination of the two dice must produce equally-likely outcomes.

Task 12.3.4 Two-dice Fallacies

How might you convince learners that, when the sum of two dice is found, all of the possible outcomes are not equally likely?

Here are two worthwhile approaches.

Repeat the investigation several times. Provided the sizes of the data sets are not tiny, learners will find that the central peak effect appears each time. Repetition of probability experiments is very important. Not only does it help learners to see that underlying patterns really do exist, but it also enables them to get a feel for the degree of variation each time the experiment is carried out. They should discover that the larger the size of data set, the smaller the degree of variation from one run to the next. The ease of use and rapid processing power of the calculator makes this sort of repetition of experiments based on fairly large data set sizes very simple to carry out. (Note that if too many very large data sets are stored into lists, you may experience calculator memory problems.)

The suggested task above may help to convince learners that the probability distribution for the sum of two dice is centrally peaked. But they also need an explanation of *why*. In Chapter 4, you read about the distinction between empirical and theoretical approaches to probability. Up to now, the learners have investigated these probability questions empirically, by generating simulated dice scores and exploring patterns. At some point, learners need to think more theoretically about how these sums are formed and consider the different ways in which each outcome might have come about. A useful starting point is to create a table, as in Table 12.1, which reveals that there are six different ways of producing the sum '7', but only one way of producing '2' or '12'.

TABLE 12.1 Different ways of creating dice sums using two dice

	1	2	3	4	5	6
1	2					7
2					7	
3				7		
4			7			
5		7				
6	7					12

Creating Programs

There are several alternative names for a graphics calculator (for example, graphing calculator or graphic calculator). What they have in common is the stress on the word 'graph'. While these hand-held boxes of fun certainly do make a useful contribution to the world of graphing, they have many other features that are equally attractive but less well recognised. One of these is their programming capability, which is both powerful and, once a few basic ideas are mastered, delightfully easy to use.

Below is an extract adapted from the calculator classroom resource, *Handling Data*, produced by A+B Books. It describes a calculator program, SETTLE, which simulates 80 coin tosses and then plots the proportion of heads against the number of tosses to see a 'settling down' effect.

Explanation

```
PROGRAM:SETTLE
:0→T:ClrDraw
:For(X,1,80)
:randInt(0,1)+T→
T
:Pt-On(X,T/X)
:End
:Horizontal .5
```

: Set T (the total so far) to 0. Clear any existing drawings.
: For a run of 80 tosses.
: Toss a coin. If it shows 'heads' (that is, scores 1) add 1 to the total.
: Plot the proportion of heads so far (T/X) against the number of tosses so far (X).
: End the **For** loop.
: Draw a horizontal line at .5.

Execute the program. You should see something like this.

Describe the shape of your graph.

Does it seem to settle down to .5 as the number of tosses increases?

Edit the program to increase the number of tosses to, say, 500.

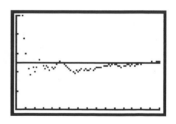

Adjust the setting of **Xmax** accordingly in the Window menu and run the program again.

Is the 'settling down' effect more apparent or less apparent now?

(Adapted from Graham and Galpin, 2000, p. 15)

Task 12.3.5 Creating a Short Program

If you can create this program, SETTLE, do so now. (Note that, if you are unfamiliar with creating programs on a graphics calculator, you should *not* enter each command letter by letter, but rather select it from the list of programming commands that are available once you select the programming editor. Also note that, once a program is complete, you must quit the programming editor by pressing [2nd] [QUIT].)

Choose suitable window settings and then execute the program to see the 'settling down' graph shown in the extract.

How might the use of a short calculator program contribute to your teaching of this topic?

The classroom resource *30 Calculator Programs* (Graham and Galpin, 2003) is designed to help 11–16-year-old learners to create their own short programs on the calculator ('short' means very short – in some cases, only two lines). The book provides a number of statistical programs. For example:

SIX: how many rolls of a die before a six appears?

LOTTERY: choosing and sorting lottery numbers.

DOTTY: an approximation for π using randomly chosen dots.

SOCCER: simulating scores in a football game.

The full range of the A+B calculator books can be found at their website (www.AplusB.co.uk).

12.4 MORE ADVANCED CALCULATOR FEATURES

In this section, you will look at some of the more advanced calculator menus and functions that would not normally be taught to learners in the 11–16 year age band. It should be an opportunity for you to extend your own knowledge about the calculator and apply it to probability.

Probability Density Functions (pdf)

Look back to Section 8.2 where probability distributions were discussed. There you saw that what distinguished, visually, a probability distribution from a frequency distribution was the scale on the vertical axis – in the case of the probability distribution, the vertical scale measured the proportion that each column represented of the entire area of the distribution. This is fairly easy to understand

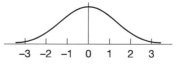

Figure 12.4 **THE STANDARDISED NORMAL PROBABILITY DISTRIBUTION**

when the distribution is grouped into bars of equal width, as was the case with the robin egg weights. But what interpretation can be put on the vertical scale of a probability distribution where there are no intervals at all, such as the one in Figure 12.4? This question is explored below.

A defining property of all probability distributions is that the area contained between the curve and the *x*-axis is equal to 1. A *standardised* normal probability distribution has a mean of zero and a standard deviation of 1 – that is, the variable *X* is distributed normally with mean = 0 and SD = 1. This is usually written as: $X \sim N(0, 1)$

A standardised normal probability distribution will look like Figure 12.4, with most of its area (99.73%) contained within three standard deviations units on either side of the mean.

Task 12.4.1 No Bars

How would you interpret the vertical scale of a probability distribution like the one in Figure 12.4 where there are no intervals at all?

It is possible to do a rough back-of-an-envelope calculation to answer this question, based on the simplifying assumption that the area contained under the curve between −3 and 3 on the *x*-axis is equal to 1. Imagine a rectangle of area equal to 1 placed along the same horizontal length from −3 to 3 (Figure 12.5). Since its length is 6 units, its height must equal 1/6 units, or roughly 0.17. This gives a rough feel for the maximum height of the normal curve – roughly twice the height of this rectangle, or about 0.35.

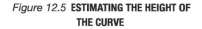

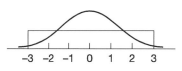

Figure 12.5 **ESTIMATING THE HEIGHT OF THE CURVE**

The *probability density function* of a probability curve is the height of the curve at any given point on the *x*-axis. It is exactly equivalent in meaning to the variable *y* for a function $y = f(x)$.

You can use the calculator command **normalpdf** to calculate the height of the normal curve at any value of *x* of your choosing. For example, the command opposite calculates the pdf for a standardised normal curve (mean = 0, SD = 1) at the value *x* = 2. Note: the **normalpdf** command is in the calculator's DISTR (that is, distribution) menu.

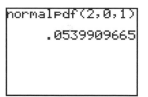

Task 12.4.2 Calculating pdf Values

(a) Guess roughly what value the pdf will have for the following values of *x*:

  $x = 0, x = 1, x = 1.5, x = 3, x = -3$.

(b) Explain these answers. What are likely areas of confusion about the notion of pdf?

Accurate results for these pdf values are shown here. Note that, because of symmetry, the pdf results corresponding to these negative *x*-values match the positive ones.

Learners do find ideas of pdf confusing. Consider the first result from the screenshot, which shows that for a standardised normal curve, the pdf at $x = 0$ is 0.3989. A common learner misunderstanding is to believe that this shows the probability that $x = 0$ to be equal to 0.3989. However, because X is a continuous variable, the probability that it takes any particular (exact) value is zero. For probability to have meaning with a continuous variable, you need to consider the area under the probability curve, corresponding to an *interval* for X. As was stated above, the probability density function of a probability curve is the height of the curve at any given point on the x-axis and is equivalent in meaning to the variable y for a function $y = f(x)$. However, as you will see in the next sub-section, entitled *Cumulative density function*, knowing something about the pdf provides a useful clue about how to set the Window when displaying and calculating areas under the probability curve.

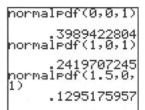

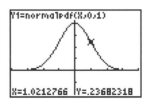

Task 12.4.3 Tracing pdf Values

Press ⬚Y =⬚ and enter the **normalpdf** command as shown in the Y= screenshot (Figure 12.6).

Press ⬚WINDOW⬚ and type in the window settings shown in Figure 12.7.

Press ⬚TRACE⬚ and use the ◁ and ▷ cursor keys to see the cursor trace along the standardised normal curve, displaying pdf values (shown as 'Y') at the bottom of the screen (Figure 12.8).

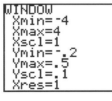

Figure 12.6 **THE Y= SCREEN**

Figure 12.7 **THE WINDOW SETTINGS**

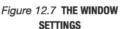

Figure 12.8 **TRACING THE STANDARD NORMAL CURVE**

Areas under the Normal Curve

In most practical situations, it is not particularly useful to know the pdf values of a normal curve. What is more useful is to be able to calculate areas under the curve. On the calculator, this can be done in several ways, the neatest of which is the **ShadeNorm** command, which provides a helpful picture, as well as performing the calculation.

The Window setting that you used in the previous task is ideal for doing this. Note that the choice of **Ymax** = 0.5 has been based on knowing that the pdf at $x = 0$ is 0.3989, which was calculated in Task 12.4.2. Also, the choice of a negative value for **Ymin** is simply to create a space below the graph in order to display text.

- Select the DISTR menu once more and press ▷ to see the DRAW menu.
- Press 1 to select the **ShadeNorm** command. As the name implies, this shades areas under the normal curve.

Complete the command as shown to shade the area under the standard normal curve (indicated by the final two arguments of the command) between $x = 0.5$ and $x = 1.5$ (the first two arguments) and display the value of the shaded area.

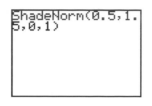 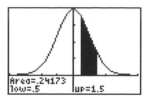

This shaded area corresponds to the probability that a value selected randomly from this probability distribution lies between 0.5 and 1.5. Note that if you wish to use the **ShadeNorm** command more than once, you need to use the **ClrDraw** command (from the DRAW menu) after each use, in order to provide a clear screen for the next time the command is used.

Task 12.4.4 Finding Areas   C

Use the **ShadeNorm** command to answer the following questions.

(a) If a value, *X*, is randomly chosen from N(0, 1), what is the probability of it: lying between 1 and 2; lying between ⁻1 and 2; being greater than 0?

(b) A large number of robin eggs were weighed and found to approximate to N(2.7 g, 0.2 g). If a robin egg is chosen at random, what is the probability that it weighs: between 2.7 g and 3 g; between 2.5 g and 2.8 g; more than 3.1 g?

APPS

Calculator Software Applications (Apps) are programs that can be downloaded to a TI graphics calculator, similar to software programs that can be downloaded to a computer. At the time of writing, the TI-83 Plus and TI-84 Plus calculators provide a number of these special programs at purchase of the machine, with the possibility of further APPs available to be downloaded at the user's discretion.

Task 12.4.5 Probability Simulation APP   C

Press the key marked **APPS**. Scroll down to find and open the probability simulation application, ProbSim.

(a) Run simulation 2, Roll dice, by pressing 2. The commands that are available to you are marked at the bottom of the screen. These five commands are activated by the corresponding row of five keys at the top of the calculator keyboard. Choose the ROLL option by pressing WINDOW several times. Use the on-screen options to increase the number of rolls first by 10 and then by 50. Use the ◁ and ▷ cursor keys at any time to select the bars on the bar chart and read the frequency of each outcome. Note that the vertical scale is automatically rescaled as new data are added.

(b) Can you pick out any features of the graph that change as the number of trials increases?

(c) How might you organise a teaching episode with one or more learners, linked to this calculator simulation?

Task 12.4.6 Two-dice APP   C

(a) Use the APP to investigate the two-dice situation as follows:

   (i) launch the probability simulation APP again and this time, choose the Set option to increase the number of dice to two (keeping all other settings unchanged);

   (ii) run the two-dice simulation roughly 60 times and see the overall shape of the distribution of scores;

   - repeat several times to get a sense of the variation;

   - increase the number of trials to around 300 and run this new simulation several times to see how the change affects the underlying distributional shape.

(b) The investigation that you have just carried out closely parallels what you did in Task 12.3.3. What are the advantages and disadvantages of each approach?

In general, when using ICT in teaching, there are choices to be made between using proprietary packages specially designed for a particular task and generic tools that can be used for creating a wide variety of self-designed tasks. This is an important choice, both in your own learning and as a teacher planning the learning of others. Clearly, there are different goals for different teaching situations. If the aim is to provide a quick demonstration of a particular topic, then the proprietary package such as this calculator APP is very helpful. (For example, it could be used in teacher demonstration mode, with the image projected onto a screen or electronic whiteboard.) However, a teacher also aims to provide learners with generic tools, so that they can control their own learning in unknown situations. This is where mastery of generic ICT tools has great value, not just within statistics/mathematics but also right across the curriculum and beyond school needs into the learner's life outside the classroom. This philosophy reflects the ancient Chinese saying: 'Give a man a fish and you feed him for a day. Teach a man to fish and you feed him for life.'

Task 12.4.7 Calculator Story

As light relief in your study of ICT, take a break to read a very entertaining tale about how the graphing calculator application used in Apple Mac computers came into being. It can be found at: www.pacifict.com/Story/

12.5 PEDAGOGY

This section looks at teaching and learning issues, based on four of the six PTT themes.

Language Patterns

There is clearly a rich vocabulary surrounding ideas of chance and probability. One possible area of investigation with learners is to ask them to list several phrases or sayings linked to likelihood or uncertainty (for example, 'the 'law of averages', or 'some people have all the luck'). After a discussion in which the meanings of their chosen phrases or sayings are clarified, ask them to design an experiment to test whether the saying is true. It is likely that simulation with an ICT application will support such an investigation.

Task 12.5.1 Histogram

In Section 12.3, you used the calculator's histogram option to display the results of a dice-rolling experiment. The name 'histogram' may not be correct in this situation. How would you present this 'terminological difficulty' to learners who might be wishing to use the calculator's 'histogram' plot to display data from simulations of dice or coins.

As was discussed in Chapter 5, the term 'histogram' is normally reserved for depicting continuous data. Discrete data such as these would normally be displayed using a bar chart (where gaps deliberately left between adjacent bars emphasise the discrete nature of the data). It is valuable to discuss these issues with learners. They should be aware that calculator designers have created this graphing facility to be capable of depicting data from both discrete and continuous variables, therefore the calculator user needs to be aware that the term 'histogram' may sometimes be misapplied (as it sometimes is in certain science textbooks).

If you or your learners are offended by the idea that discrete data are being portrayed with touching bars, there is a 'work-around', namely to reduce the **XScl** value to, say, 0.5, as shown here. It should also be pointed out to learners that, for discrete integer values such as these, the range of values contained within a single bar is somewhat arbitrary, since only the integer values are picked up.

Note: what would happen if the value of **Xscl** were reduced to 0.25? Try it and see.

Imagery

Task 12.5.2 Adding Lists

The term 'adding lists' is rather ambiguous.

(a) What two alternative meanings can you think of?

(b) What pictures might help learners to understand the two possible interpretations?

The phrase 'adding lists' could mean one of the following:

- joining two lists, each of, say, 60 items to make a single list of 120 items;
- adding the corresponding values of each list to make a single list of 'sums' containing 60 items.

On the calculator, the first of these is achieved using the **augment** command, from the LIST OPS menu. For example, enter two items of data into L1 and three items of data into L2, apply the command **augment(L1,L2)->L3** and this will result in five items of data in L3. This process is sometimes referred to as *concatenation*.

The second interpretation is, in fact, the correct one and is achieved using the command described in Task 12.3.3, namely, **L1+L2->L3**. Note that addition of lists can only work if the lists are of equal length.

Visually, the distinction between these two procedures can be made with back-of-an-envelope sketches such as those shown in Figures 12.9 and 12.10.

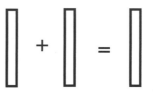

Figure 12.9 **CONCATENATING LISTS (USE THE AUGMENT COMMAND)**
Note: the lists may be of unequal length.

Figure 12.10 **ADDING LISTS (USE THE + COMMAND)**
Note: the lists must be of equal length.

Standard Misconceptions

Task 12.5.3 Many Misconceptions   **C**

(a) At least five misconceptions were mentioned in this chapter. Look back through the text now and see how many of them you can find.

(b) Choose the misconception that seems most important to you and consider how you might use ICT to help learners gain greater clarification and understanding.

Techniques and Methods

In this final sub-section, you are asked to ponder two important issues:

Formatting learner thinking: in Chapters 9, 10 and 11 you read about the ways in which technological tools can bring important benefits in terms of helping to format learner thinking about certain concepts.

Critical thinking: a feature of ICT use in statistics is that it tends to focus learner attention on the *A* stage of the *PCAI* cycle of statistical thinking. Also, it does so in a way that fails to encourage learners to ask important critical questions about the source and meaning of the data and what the implications are for their analysis of the data in the context of questions that may have generated the data in the first place. These two issues are looked at more closely in the next block.

Task 12.5.4 Wider Issues about Using ICT

(a) Look back through the teaching ideas suggested in Chapters 9–12 and identify examples where aspects of the technology could be usefully made explicit to learners in order to help format their thinking about certain statistical ideas.

(b) How might you organise the use of ICT with learners to ensure that their critical thinking skills are not compromised?

Introduction to Block 4

Chapters 13 to 15 form the fourth and final block of the book. They deal with the themes of models and modelling, statistical investigations and, in the final chapter, general teaching and learning issues. Note that in these three chapters there are no final sections on 'preparing to teach' (PTT) as there were in Chapters 1–12.

The terms 'model' and 'modelling' appear regularly in the statistical and mathematical literature, but their usage is often confusing and misleading. In Chapter 13, the various interpretations of these words are teased out in the fields of mathematics, statistics, mathematics education and statistics education.

Statistical investigations have formed a major theme of the book. Chapter 14 sets out how the *PCAI* framework can provide a useful organising tool for teachers and learners of statistics alike. The final chapter looks at a number of important general issues in statistics education including its place in the wider curriculum, where statistics should be taught and alternative forms of assessment. It closes with a review of the main ideas contained in the rest of the book.

13 Models and Modelling

One of the most overworked words in statistics education and mathematics education is 'model'. Appearing in a variety of dissimilar contexts, its usage is at best unclear and at worst, inappropriate. If you were to read a textbook in the area of statistical education, it is likely that the word would crop up often. However, unlike many other technical terms, 'model' may not even be listed in the book's index. Models and modelling are such important ideas in statistics that this chapter is devoted to trying to specify them and to see how they contribute to developing thinking in statistics. In all, four different meanings of the word model are uncovered, so look out for them as you work through the chapter.

The chapter starts with a look at how the word 'model' tends to be used in everyday speech. This is followed by a section on mathematical modelling, in which the *PMAI* modelling cycle is introduced and an important distinction is made between mathematical modelling and modelling in mathematics education. Section 13.3 then looks at some of the important models in statistics, including the uniform, normal and binomial distributions. The chapter ends with a look at how the *PMAI* cycle can be adapted and applied to statistical investigations (the familiar *PCAI* statistical investigation cycle which has been used throughout this book).

13.1 EVERYDAY MEANINGS OF 'MODEL'

> We all depend on models to interpret everyday experiences. We interpret what we see in terms of mental models constructed on past experience and education. They are constructs that we use to understand the pattern of our experiences. (Bartholomew, 1995, p. 6)

Three people, with no background in statistics, were asked what the word 'model' meant to them. Here are their responses.

> Respondent A: To me it means something that's perfect – like saying someone was a model pupil or a 'role model'.
> Respondent B: I think of a fashion model – someone who models clothes.
> Respondent C: When I was a kid I used to love making models – model aircraft and that kind of thing. So I think of a model as some object that's smaller than the thing it represents – like a scale model.

Task 13.1.1 Connecting to Statistics

Note down any aspects of these responses that may connect with your thinking about how the term *model* is used in statistics.

Two aspects emerge from the above observations that may be relevant to statistical modelling – the idea of a model being 'perfect' and of it being a scaled-down version of reality.

Encarta, the resident dictionary on the word-processing computer application Microsoft Word, was consulted as to the range of meanings for the term 'model'. The following ten definitions of the noun 'a model' were provided, along with four of the verb 'to model'. (In the extract below, t = transitive verb and i = intransitive verb.)

model

noun

1. a copy of an object, especially one made on a smaller scale than the original (often used before a noun);
2. a particular version of a manufactured article;
3. something that is copied or used as the basis for a related idea, process, or system;
4. somebody who is paid to wear clothes and demonstrate merchandise as a profession, for example, in fashion shows and photographs for magazines and catalogues;
5. a simplified version of something complex used, for example, to analyze and solve problems or make predictions;
6. an excellent example that deserves to be imitated;
7. somebody who poses for a painter, sculptor, photographer, or other artist;
8. an animal species repellent to predators which another animal mimics for protection;
9. an interpretation of a theory arrived at by assigning referents in such a way as to make the theory true;
10. (UK) the first sewn example of a couturier's or clothing manufacturer's design, from which a new line of garments is produced.

verb

1. to work as a fashion model, wearing clothes, makeup, and other items in order to display them to others (ti)
2. to sit as a model for somebody such as a painter or photographer (i);
3. to base something, especially somebody's appearance or behavior, on somebody or something else (t);
4. to make something by shaping a substance or material, for example, clay or wood (t).

Task 13.1.2 Mix-and-match Meanings   C

Look carefully through these 14 dictionary meanings of 'model'.

(a) Which seems closest to your understanding of how the term is used in statistics?

(b) Note down three aspects that may usefully inform your thinking about how the term model is used in statistics.

Task 13.1.3 Which Is the Model?

Which of these two statements is correct or can they both be correct?

• 'Equal likelihood is modelled by rolling a fair die.'

• 'Equal likelihood is the underlying model for rolling a fair die.'

Unfortunately, and confusingly, both these statements are regularly used in statistics textbooks and learners need to deal with the reality that the word 'model' can be used in two opposite senses. In the first statement, the model is *a physical object* with certain symmetrical properties such that its shape embodies and manifests the properties of equal likelihood. In the second, the model is an *abstract concept* (equal likelihood) that underpins our use of dice and coins.

In the rest of this chapter, you will consider ways in which the word 'model' is used in mathematics and statistics.

13.2 MODELLING IN MATHEMATICS

A useful document for all mathematics teachers in the UK, available on the DfES standards website, is the *National Numeracy Strategy Handbook for Leading Mathematics Teachers* (www.standards.dfes.gov.uk/primary/publications/mathematics/lmt_handbk/handbook_lmt_ss.PDF).

This document uses the term 'model', or 'modelling', 44 times. Here are two examples, taken from the stated aims of Session 2 of the handbook, 'Mathematical modelling and problem solving'.

Example 1

To explore how mathematical *modelling* supports children's development of calculations.

The illustration in Figure 13.1 is offered to help children to add 12 and 39.

Modelling 12 + 39

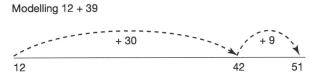

Figure 13.1 **MODELLING ADDITION**

Example 2

To consider how problem-solving strategies might be modelled for children.

Later in the text, this aim is elaborated with the following statement:

The term 'modelling' will be used to mean the process that the teacher uses to teach and demonstrate the skills of problem solving.

Task 13.2.1 Muddling?

In what senses do you think the word 'modelling' has been used in these two examples?

The first example uses 'modelling' *within the world of mathematics*. It refers to situations where a learner is helped to tackle a mathematical question by adapting it into a form that makes it easier to handle with known mathematical methods (in this case, using the number line for addition). The second example is largely for the teacher and relates to *the world of mathematics education*. It refers to pedagogic principles or steps to help organise the teacher's thoughts about presenting ideas to learners. This distinction between 'mathematical modelling' and 'models in mathematics education' is not well understood or clearly drawn in the copious literature about modelling in mathematics. These two aspects will be explored further in this section.

Mathematical Modelling

Questions that arise in the real world are not usually in a form that can be instantly solved mathematically. They usually require a number of steps such as:

- making a clear statement of the question;
- 'modelling' the problem into a form that can be tackled with known mathematical methods;
- tackling the (modified) problem within the mathematical world;
- interpreting the solution back in the real-world context and answering it in the terms in which the problem was posed.

A popular picture for representing mathematical modelling shows how the problem-solver tackles a real-world problem mathematically by moving between the two domains, the 'real world' and the 'mathematical world'. These two domains are shown in Figure 13.2 and in the next task you are asked to fill in the details.

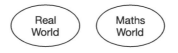

Figure 13.2 **AN INCOMPLETE MODELLING DIAGRAM**

Task 13.2.2 Fleshing Out the Diagram   C

In the text above, the following four stages of problem-solving were identified:

- pose the problem (*P*);
- model the problem mathematically (*M*);
- analyse the problem mathematically (*A*);
- interpret the solution (*I*).

Using the four letters *P*, *M*, *A* and *I*, and any additional artwork that you feel appropriate, complete the diagram in Figure 13.2, by showing where these four stages fit with the 'real' and 'mathematical' worlds.

In the next task, you are asked to think through the solution of a simple real-world problem that requires mathematical thinking and then to relate your solution to the diagram you created in Task 13.2.2.

Task 13.2.3 First-class Stamps   **C**

(a) Imagine that you walk into a post office with £5. What is the greatest number of first-class stamps you can buy and how much change would you expect?

(b) Identify all the stages you went through in your answer to part (a) and relate them to the *PMAI* diagram.

In the 'First-class stamps' example, 'modelling' referred to the stage of problem solving where the problem is translated into terms that can be tackled using known mathematical techniques. You are now asked to think about a second meaning of the term 'model', this time within mathematics education. This refers to a set of guidelines or diagram that helps teachers to think about presenting ideas to learners.

Models in Mathematics Education

In the *PMAI* framework, the *M* stage referred to the modelling stage of problem solving. However, confusingly, the diagram itself is often referred to as a 'model' for problem-solving. Solving the problem by following through the stages set out in the diagram is often known as completing the 'modelling cycle'. Indeed, the diagram is often referred to as a mathematical modelling diagram, which further complicates things, as it is unclear to which type of model this is referring.

There are many such problem-solving models in mathematics education. Figure 13.3 is the five-stage modelling diagram that is used in the Open University course, *Using Mathematics*, MST121.

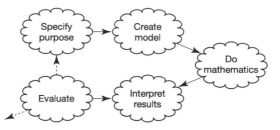

Figure 13.3 **A FIVE-STAGE MODELLING DIAGRAM**
Source: *Using Mathematics* (MST121), chapter B1, Modelling with Sequences, p. 7

Task 13.2.4 Same and Different

Compare the five-stage MST121 modelling cycle with the *PMAI* cycle given earlier. What features do they share and which ones are different?

Table 13.1 shows the match between the two models.

TABLE 13.1 Match between the PMAI cycle and the MST121 cycle

PMAI cycle	MST121 cycle
Pose	Specify purpose
Model	Create model
Analyse	Do mathematics
Interpret	Interpret results
	Evaluate

The first four stages are almost identical, but the MST121 model contains the extra step of evaluating the interpretation. At this point, the two dotted lines (in Figure 13.3) suggest that the problem-solver has a choice of either leaving the model (presumably because the problem has been satisfactorily resolved) or of returning to the original purpose and rethinking the problem, with a view to completing the modelling cycle again. A feature of the *PMAI* cycle that is not shared by the MST121 model is the placing of the steps on the page, so as to emphasise the 'real world'/'mathematical world' distinction.

Here is another 'problem-solving model' that looks very different from the previous two.

Problem-solving model

What are my key words?

Do I need a diagram? List? Table?

Is there a formula or equation that I'll need? Which one?

Will I use a calculator? Is there a pattern I can use and or follow?

('About Mathematics' website: math.about.com)

Task 13.2.5 Model or Checklist   **C**

(a) How is this 'About Mathematics' model distinguishable from the previous examples?

(b) Is this 'problem-solving model' above a model or more of a checklist?

The Centre for Mathematics Education at the Open University creates books and distance-learning materials and courses for teachers (and others) wishing to work on their professional development. Their materials are largely *task-based* – that is, learners are expected to do some mathematics themselves, reflect on what they have done and then consider the implications for their teaching. The members of the Centre believe that much of their writing is based on this *APC* model, where the letters refer, respectively, to 'Adult', 'Process' and 'Classroom'. Their model is usually written as:

$$A \rightarrow P \rightarrow C$$

Task 13.2.6 APC

(a) Explain in your own words your understanding of the thinking behind the *APC* model.

(b) Having now read a large proportion of this book, to what extent has the *APC* model worked for you? Try to identify particular examples where you found this approach helpful.

It should be borne in mind that learners taking courses created by the Centre for Mathematics Education are mostly either teachers or aspiring teachers. The idea behind *APC* is that, in working on the course materials, learners should experience the following three stages.

A: They tackle tasks and questions at the *adult* level.

P: They are then invited to reflect on the tasks they have just undertaken and try to identify conceptual *processes* (mathematical or pedagogic) that underlie them.

C: Having clarified their thinking about the related mathematical processes, and experienced personally some of the corresponding learning issues, they are asked to consider the implications for the *classroom*.

13.3 MODELS IN STATISTICS

Section 13.2 looked at modelling in mathematics and in mathematics education. Attention now turns to how the word 'modelling' is used in statistics (Section 13.3) and in statistics education (Section 13.4).

Real-world data tend to be messy. First, they may contain errors of measurement, recording and transcription. But there is a second form of messiness. Particularly when the data sets under consideration are small, there may be messiness due to sample variability, so that underlying patterns are hidden by randomness.

It is usually the case that, where underlying patterns do exist, this is only clearly apparent when a fairly large number of items are chosen for consideration. At an elementary level of statistics teaching, the term 'underlying pattern' is sufficiently explicit for most learners. However, at a more advanced level, the term 'model' is a more appropriate description of the nature of this pattern. Depending on the nature of the data and the patterns that you wish to investigate with them, there is a choice of possible statistical models available to extract or explain the underlying structure. In general, probability theory is a way of modelling uncertainty. Shortly, you will look at the uniform (equally likely) model, which can be used to model random selection.

Below are four examples of statistical models: the *uniform, normal* and *binomial* models provide ways of thinking about single-variable data sets, while *regression* models provide different ways of describing possible relationships between two variables.

The Uniform Model

As has been evident from previous tasks, roll a die, say, 30 times and you are unlikely to achieve anything approaching equal frequencies in the six outcomes. Increase the number of trials to, say, 300 and the idea of underlying equal likelihood of the outcomes becomes more plausible, as evidenced by a more uniform shape shown by a bar chart of the results. As was set out in Chapter 4, there are two ways of thinking about the underlying probabilities of the six outcomes: the *empirical* approach, based on actually rolling dice, and the *theoretical* approach, based on what outcomes you might expect, given that the die is symmetrical with six identical faces.

Assuming that the die is fair, there is a clear correspondence between the symmetry of its shape and the idea of equal likelihood.

Equal likelihood is a perfect or ideal underlying 'state of grace', that exists in one's mind, whereas an actual physical die, however carefully engineered, can never achieve perfect symmetry. The uniform distribution in Figure 13.4(a) is the picture that represents this uniform model, based on equal likelihood. When a die is rolled repeatedly, the vagaries of natural variation (that is, chance) will mean that exact equality of outcomes is most unlikely to occur in practice. This unevenness is illustrated in Figure 13.4(b). In the long run, with an unbiased die, the relative frequencies would settle down to be almost equal – hence the uniform model for the distribution is a sensible one.

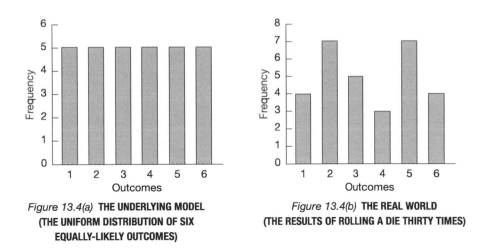

Figure 13.4(a) **THE UNDERLYING MODEL**
(THE UNIFORM DISTRIBUTION OF SIX
EQUALLY-LIKELY OUTCOMES)

Figure 13.4(b) **THE REAL WORLD**
(THE RESULTS OF ROLLING A DIE THIRTY TIMES)

The Normal Model

Most measurements taken of natural phenomena (birth weights, leaf lengths, duration of pregnancies, and so on) have a shared characteristic – that, when plotted, the values are bunched in the middle with diminishing tails on either side. At a more advanced level in statistics, it is possible to be more precise about the shape of the distribution of these variables. Many of them closely approximate to a normal distribution with certain parametric values. Only two parametric values are required to define, uniquely, a particular normal distribution – the mean, μ, and the standard deviation, σ. As with the other examples of statistical models covered here (uniform, binomial and regression), the normal distribution is a convenient, easy-to-manage simplification of data that enables further statistical calculations and inferences to be made.

The normal distribution is not just *any* centrally peaked curve that tails off to either side. In fact, it has a very precise shape (Figure 13.5). For example, its points of inflection (the two points on the curve where its curvature switches from convex to concave) each lie exactly one standard deviation from the mean.

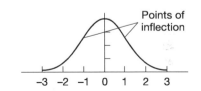

Figure 13.5 **THE PRECISE SHAPE OF THE NORMAL CURVE**

The Binomial Model

How likely do you think it is that, in a family of four children, all of them are girls (or all are boys)? As was shown in Block 3, tree diagrams are useful for helping to answer these sorts of question. (At a more advanced level, the binomial theorem can be used to calculate the probabilities for each outcome.) If you were to draw the tree diagram, you would find that there are basically five separate outcomes (0, 1, 2, 3 and 4 girls) and these have underlying probabilities (sometimes referred to as the *relative frequencies*) of 1/16, 4/16, 6/16, 4/16 and 1/16, respectively. It is the word 'underlying' in the previous sentence that reveals the model contained within this question.

Assuming that the birth of a boy and girl are equally likely, then the probability of getting a girl, $p = 0.5$. Note that, in this context, the choice of $p = 0.5$ is an *approximation* to make the model easier (and may be good enough for most practical purposes). However, in a larger, more sophisticated survey of births, a more accurate value for p may be used. This interplay between simplicity (that is, 'near-enough approximation') and tweaking for better modelling with more complexity is an important part of modelling.

If you were to conduct a survey of 16 randomly chosen families, each with four children, you should find that there are more with two boys and two girls than with all girls or all boys, but you are unlikely to get the exact proportions predicted above by the binomial model. When data do not exactly match the model, there are two things to be considered. First, is the model correct? In this case, you may wish to question certain assumptions such as whether there is *independence* (if the first child is a girl, then is the family more likely to have a girl next time, which is a question for biology). Second, due to natural variation, you would not expect there to be an exact match between the data and the model. However, provided you have not made unwarranted assumptions, the model should provide a useful simplification of the data.

As was the case with the uniform bar charts, the symmetrical distribution of the relative frequencies in Figure 13.6(a) is the picture that represents this theoretical binomial model. However, in practice in the real world, natural variation will mean that sampled data will not exactly match the theoretical model, as illustrated by the actual frequencies of a particular data set in Figure 13.6(b).

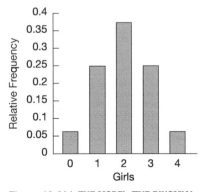

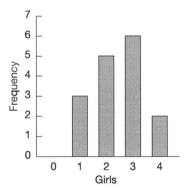

Figure 13.6(a) **THE MODEL (THE BINOMIAL DISTRIBUTION OF THE SEX COMPOSITION OF A FOUR-CHILD FAMILY)**

Figure 13.6(b) **THE REAL WORLD (THE RESULTS OF SURVEY OF 16 FOUR-CHILD FAMILIES)**

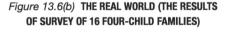

Task 13.3.1 Bicycles, Biscuits and Binomial   **C**

All of the words in the title to this task have the prefix 'bi-', indicating *two* of something. For the first two words, these are, respectively, two wheels and bread that is cooked twice, but wherein lies the two-ness of 'binomial'?

Before leaving the binomial model, it is worth applying it to *hospital births*, one of the problems introduced in Chapter 4 (Task 4.2.2), which was discussed again in Chapter 12. This task described two hospitals, one with an average of 45 births per day and a smaller one that averaged 15 births per day. Each hospital counts the number of days that the proportion of girl births exceeds 60%. You were asked whether you would expect each hospital to have roughly the same number of such days? For the larger hospital, 60% of the 45 daily births corresponds to 27 or more girl births, while the corresponding figure for the smaller hospital is 9 or more girl births.

In Chapter 12, the sex of the baby was 'modelled' by the toss of a coin. The statistical model underlying this situation is the binomial distribution, where p, the probability of getting a girl, equals (roughly) 0.5 and n corresponds to the number of births. If you have a TI graphics calculator to hand, you can explore one of the more advanced commands which makes calculations based on the binomial distribution – the **binomcdf** command, from the Distr submenu of the DISTR menu. This calculates the sum of the probabilities of a specified range of outcomes.

```
binomcdf(45,.5,2
6)
          .8836534043
1-Ans
          .1163465957
```

For example, the first command calculates the cumulative probability of getting 0, 1, 2, 3, …, 26 'successes' (that is, girls) out of 45 births, for $p = 0.5$. Therefore, the probability of getting 27 or more girl births is 0.116.

The corresponding calculations for the smaller hospital are shown in the second screenshot. So, based on binomial models, getting 60% or more girl births is nearly three times as likely in the smaller hospital as in the larger hospital.

```
binomcdf(15,.5,8
)
          .6963806163
1-Ans
          .3036193837
```

Regression Models

When you display paired data in a scatter plot, whether using a spreadsheet such as Excel or on a graphics calculator, a likely next step is to fit a trend line. As can be seen from Figures 13.7 and 13.8, there are many possibilities here apart from the standard linear option – for example, polynomial (quadratic, cubic, quartic), power, exponential, and so on. Whichever choice of regression option you choose, the line (or curve) of best fit represents a simplified *model* of the data. The term 'model' can be used here in the sense that the variation exhibited by the data is stripped away and only the underlying mathematical relationship is left. The mismatch between data and a model that has been fitted to the data is often referred to as the 'residuals' (as discussed in Section 7.2). The relationship can be expressed more formally as:

DATA = FIT + RESIDUALS.

A model that shows a 'good' fit is one where there is no discernible pattern to the residuals. If a pattern can be discerned in the residuals, it should, theoretically, be possible to build this element into the model and so improve its predictive power.

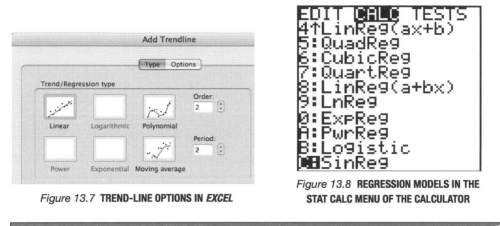

Figure 13.7 **TREND-LINE OPTIONS IN *EXCEL***

Figure 13.8 **REGRESSION MODELS IN THE STAT CALC MENU OF THE CALCULATOR**

Task 13.3.2 Regression Models   C

What are some of the assumptions and dangers with choosing a regression model?

Statistics and Modelling

It is the job of statisticians to represent the data taken from the real world with theoretical models. For single-variable data, these may take the form of probability distributions (such as the uniform, normal and binomial distributions); for paired data, bi-variate models (such as the regression model) are used.

When statisticians engage in sampling, they have a choice of whether to access their data from the real world or from a model of the real world. For example, think back to the robin egg example given in Chapter 8. The data provided in the histogram below Task 8.2.4 was not based on weighing and recording 100 actual robin eggs. Instead, they were actually simulated from a known model of robin egg weights, namely that they approximate to the following normal distribution: N(2.7 g, 0.2 g).

Task 13.3.3 Modelling Eggs   C

How might you use the model N(2.7 g, 0.2 g) to simulate a sample of the weights of 100 robin eggs?

To end this section, you are asked to think back to one of the 'lay' ideas about models and see whether it connects with your understanding of a statistical model.

Task 13.3.4 Are Models 'Perfect'?   C

One of the aspects of models mentioned at the start of this chapter was that they were, in some sense, perfect. On the basis of what you know and have read about statistical models, would you say that a statistical model could be described as a 'perfect' version of real-world data?

Clearly, there is a degree of elegance and perfection about some of the models that you have looked at here (such as the normal, uniform and binomial models). These 'ideal' distributions are mathematical constructs that exist only in the imagination, unsullied by all the inherent problems of inaccuracy and variability that are associated with real data. However, it would be dangerous and indeed wrong to suggest that these models are *better* than the data they represent. They are merely *simplified* and *idealised* models of the real world and are useful only because they are often convenient approximations to data. Sometimes these models are oversimplifications of the data, failing to pick up subtle features or patterns that exist in the real world but that have not been identified.

13.4 MODELS IN STATISTICS EDUCATION

Section 13.3 looked at how the word 'modelling' is used in statistics. This section turns to consider its meaning in statistics education.

In Section 13.2, you saw a number of models for thinking about problem solving in mathematics education. The first of these, referred to as the *PMAI* cycle, is easily adapted for statistical investigations, with the second *M* stage replaced by *C*, collecting data (Figure 13.9).

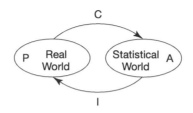

Figure 13.9 **THE *PMAI* MODELLING CYCLE**

The *PCAI* Model of a Statistical Investigation

In this book, and indeed in many of the research papers and books in statistics education, a great deal of attention has been given to the so-called 'statistical investigation' model. This is such a big idea in statistics education that the next chapter is devoted to looking at it more closely.

Task 13.4.1 Using the *PCAI* Model

How might it be useful to use a model such as the *PCAI* framework in statistics teaching?

A model such as *PCAI* can be useful for both teacher and learners in a statistical investigation for the following reasons.

- It provides a sense of purpose and direction in statistical work. Specifically, it sets out a clear requirement that the statistical work of a statistical investigation needs to return to the original question that started it off and learners must check that there has been a resolution to their problem. (If not, they may need to go around the cycle again or maybe change the question should it prove not to be satisfactorily answerable.)
- It helps teachers to think about useful strategies to support each of the four stages, as well as the interface between successive stages.

- More generally, it helps teachers consider questions of the balance of their teaching and whether the stages really should (always) be in that order. (For example, there may be situations where they would prefer to start at the *C* stage with some data.)

These issues are explored more fully in Chapter 14.

There are a number of variants of the basic four-stage model, of which two are considered here. The first comes from the UK National Strategy document and the second is due to Chris Wild and Maxine Pfannkuch. The UK Key Stage 3 National Strategy document (DfEE, 2001, p. 18) suggests the data-handling cycle shown in Figure 13.10.

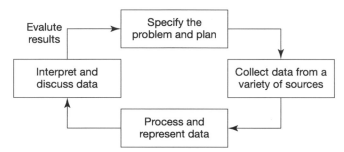

Figure 13.10 **THE NATIONAL STRATEGY 'DATA-HANDLING CYCLE'**

New Zealand researchers Chris Wild and Maxine Pfannkuch (1999) prefer to use a five-stage model, one which they refer to as *PPDAC*. These letters correspond to the following stages:

Problem → Plan → Data → Analysis → Conclusion.

The National Strategy model is almost identical to *PCAI*. The *PPDAC* model is essentially the same, but with the addition of the 'Plan' stage between stages 1 and 2. This marks a useful additional step, in that it draws attention to the fact that the collection of data often requires considerable thought and advanced planning before it is carried out.

Wild and Pfannkuch (1999) set out a number of different models that relate to different aspects of statistical thinking, one of which addresses the important idea of *variation* in statistical thinking. They point out that 'no two manufactured items are identical, no two organisms are identical or react in identical ways' (p. 235). This phenomenon corresponds to what they refer to as 'real' variation that is characteristic of the system. However, this variation is supplemented by the observer at the measurement and data-collection stage: this they refer to as 'induced' variation. Their model is shown in Figure 13.11.

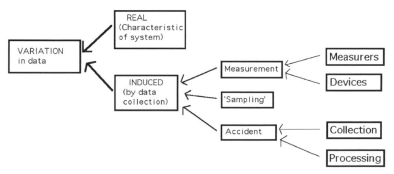

Figure 13.11 **WILD AND PFANNKUCH'S 'SOURCES OF VARIATION IN DATA' MODEL**

Task 13.4.2 Reading the Picture

(a) Spend a few minutes working out what you think the 'variation' model is claiming.

(b) Why do you think the model has been drawn so that the arrows go from right to left?

Wild and Pfannkuch (1999) refer to the fact of 'real variation inherent in the system' (p. 235). However, they go on to say that, 'when we collect data from a system, [this] real variation is supplemented by variation added in various ways by the data collection process' (p. 235).

In the western world, people tend to read from left to right, so where there is a development in a diagram, it is normally set out in this way. In the Wild and Pfannkuch example, the model is easiest to understand by starting with the big picture (the idea of variation) and then breaking it down into its component sources. So, these ideas are presented from left to right. However, in terms of the causal chain being described, the movement is in the opposite direction. In other words, these two key elements of the model are in opposition to one another. This is an example where the ease of understanding of the overall diagram (in terms of the conceptual framework) has been given priority over the causal mechanism it describes.

Task 13.4.3 Reviewing the Models

Here are the four meanings of 'modelling' set out in this chapter.

(a) An object (for example, a die) used to embody an abstract concept such as equal likelihood.

(b) The reverse of the above – that is, the abstract concept (equal likelihood) underlying random number generators such as dice and coins.

(c) The *M* stage of the *PMAI* problem-solving cycle.

(d) Schematic frameworks (often presented in pictorial form) that set out the main stages or steps involved in solving problems. For example, the *PMAI* and *PCAI* frameworks are themselves models.

Work through the chapter, starting in Section 13.2 and, armed with a highlighter pen, mark each use of the words 'model' or 'modelling'. For each one, decide which of the four meanings above is implied.

14

Statistical Investigation

In Chapter 13, several models for statistical thinking were presented. In this chapter, you are asked to concentrate on the central one used throughout this book, which is the *PCAI* modelling cycle (Figure 14.1). These four stages – pose the question, collect the data, analyse the data and interpret the results – comprise the four sections of this chapter.

It is worth making a general remark about models such as the one in Figure 14.1. When you have become familiar with it, such a diagram can provide a useful summary of a set of ideas. However, many people may find this sort of visual model off-putting when seen for the first time.

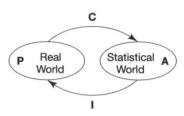

Figure 14.1 **THE *PCAI* MODELLING CYCLE**

There are two main problems here. First, these diagrams are often much easier to grasp if you see them being built up stage by stage. This can be done face to face over time (for example, drawing the model from scratch on paper, on a whiteboard or seeing it 'grow' using a suitable computer application such as PowerPoint), but this is virtually impossible to achieve on the printed page. Second, the first-time viewer may fail to identify clearly the entry and departure points of a diagram. This is particularly confusing when the diagram is cyclical, as is the case with the *PCAI* framework.

14.1 POSING QUESTIONS

Some History of Problem-Posing

Teaching mathematics and statistics by means of tackling problems and investigations is not a new idea. There have been many successful initiatives, of which two are described below.

Unified Science and Mathematics in Elementary Schools (USMES) was a project started in 1970. It was based on the idea that learners could carry out investigations of real and practical problems based in their local environment: examples included 'Soft drink design' and 'Weather predictions'. The solutions to these problems were strongly cross-curricular, particularly in the areas of science, social science and mathematics. The problems could be tackled at different levels of sophistication, depending on the age and experience of the learners. The challenges were deliberately complex, often requiring division into several sub-activities and a high degree of learner collaboration. For a more detailed description of this US-based project, use the following URL: www.coe.ufl.edu/esh/Projects/usmes.htm

Project on Statistical Education (POSE) was a UK Schools Council-funded project that began in 1976, with a brief to assess the state of statistical education in schools, to survey the needs of teachers, to plan for the implementation of teaching ideas and to produce good-quality teaching materials in statistics. During 1981–82, POSE published a wealth of classroom materials on statistics and probability, aimed at the 11–16-year-age range, under the general title *Statistics in Your World* (Schools Council, 1981). These materials are now freely available at: www.rsscse.org.uk/pose/index.htm

The project's materials were designed to link together the statistics used and taught in different disciplines (geography, science, social science, the humanities and mathematics) and to help pupils develop an insight into the statistical problems of everyday life. This approach emphasises the practical background of statistical investigations and the inferences that can be drawn from them, as well as introducing pupils to basic statistical techniques.

Both of these projects were based on the view that the learning of statistical technique could be at least partly motivated by learners doing investigations. Clearly there is a close relationship between tackling investigations and acquiring skill: problem solving motivates skill acquisition, while skill acquisition facilitates problem solving.

Task 14.1.1 Skill First or Problems First?

Do you feel that problem solving should precede (and therefore provide the motivation for) skill acquisition, or should the skill development precede (and therefore facilitate) problem solving?

There are two main schools of thought on this question, which are not mutually exclusive. Hugh Burkhardt (1981) has suggested that investigations should be delayed until after the techniques are known and well established. He argues that this requires something like a year's gap before techniques can be used fluently in an investigation. The POSE project took the view that, for a problem-solving curriculum to be successful, early investigations need to be geared to using elementary techniques where not too many are introduced at once. Practice to develop and establish skill can result from learners doing several investigations requiring the use of similar techniques. However, there may need to be some additional practice beyond the context of the investigations.

Starting with a Question

In Section 6.4, there was a discussion about handling the *P* stage of a statistical investigation. Before reading further, look back at the five suggestions made there to help learners form a good question for investigation. For many decades, there has been a great deal of enthusiasm expressed in statistics education books and journal articles about the benefits of statistical investigations.

Task 14.1.2 The Benefits of Statistical Investigations   C

What do you think are some of the benefits to learners of tackling statistical investigations?

Despite the many positive benefits of using statistical investigations, they are still used by only a minority of teachers. It is likely that the thought of a whole class of learners doing the same or different investigations may be rather daunting. If this is not a way of working with which you have had much experience, it is best to start modestly and gradually build up to something more challenging over time. This may mean starting with a teacher-led investigation with the whole class working together.

In this section, you are asked to consider possible starting points to an investigation. Questions for investigation need to be interesting and motivating, but they also need to be answerable. So, before setting off on an overly ambitious investigation, it is a good idea to ask learners, to move mentally through the complete modelling cycle and try to anticipate the tasks and challenges ahead.

Task 14.1.3 Planning Checklist   C

Bearing in mind the four *PCAI* stages (pose, collect, analyse and interpret), write down a list of possible questions that might help learners to clarify their investigation and think through what approach they might take.

The ideas suggested in the comments to the last task are useful general questions for any piece of investigative work, not just in a mathematics lesson. The transcript below describes how a science teacher adapted such questions when helping learners with an investigation into the factors that might influence the speed of a chemical reaction.

Teacher:	What is it that you are looking for here?
Learner A:	Well, when reactions are fast and when they are slow.
Teacher:	What sort of factors, then?
Learner B:	Would temperature affect it?
Learner C:	And it usually speeds things up if you give it a stir.
Learner D:	How concentrated the solution is would matter.
Teacher:	Anything else?
Learner A:	How big the particles are?
Teacher:	Yes, those all seem reasonable – now, how would you measure them?
Learner C:	Well, temperature's easy!
Teacher:	How would you measure stirring, then?
All:	Um.
Teacher:	Let's think about the sorts of experiments you might do …

Graham, (1987, p. 24)

Sources of Ideas

Millie comes from a gardening family and wanted to do her statistical investigation on some aspect of gardening. Eventually she chose the question: 'Are people more interested in gardening than they used to be?' Her teacher used the questions from the last task to encourage Millie to think through the details of her investigation and to anticipate some of the problems before they occurred.

Teacher:	What data will you need?
Millie:	I'll have to pick a time, say a hundred years ago, to compare with today. I need to look at people's lifestyles then and now, like whether they had allotments and gardens.
Teacher:	Where will you get that information?
Millic:	I don't know – the census?
Teacher:	How will you actually measure how interested people are in gardening?
Millie:	Um!

It did not take too long for Millie to abandon this project in favour of something more easily measurable. Her mother grew roses and Millie had remembered her mother saying that the natural pink roses had more scent than the cultured red ones. She decided to test whether this was true, by picking five red and five pink roses and doing a blindfold test to see if she could differentiate the scents from each colour of rose.

While you might like to ask learners to come up with their own ideas for investigations, it is always possible that they are bereft of ideas, or that the ideas they suggest are not do-able. For this reason, it is useful to have some ideas of your own in the background. There are two main sources of ideas for statistical investigations – questions that arise naturally in other school subjects and questions that arise from the learners' out-of-school experience. In the next task, you are asked to give some thought to these two contexts.

Task 14.1.4 Thinking Up Ideas for Investigations   C

(a) If possible, talk to teaching colleagues from other disciplines and try to identify some of the investigations and experiments that they do. You might like to explore the possibility of collaborating with them on a cross-curricular investigation.

(b) Bearing in mind the interests that young people have, list some suitable questions that they could investigate.

14.2 COLLECTING THE DATA

Data for a statistical investigation usually come from one of two possible sources – these are commonly referred to as *primary* sources (where you collect your own data) and *secondary* sources (where you use data already collected by someone else). Where primary data are collected, this may involve conducting an experiment or perhaps the design and administration of a *questionnaire* and the selection of a suitable *sample*. For secondary data, you need to know where to look, so *statistical sources* are an important consideration. These three aspects form the basis of this section.

Questionnaires

Just as there is no point in reinventing the wheel, it is a waste of everyone's time to collect primary data when a perfectly good source of suitable information is already available (unless the aim of the lesson is simply to practise data gathering). However, there are two problems here. The first is knowing that suitable data do actually exist (and here a web search engine like Google is a valuable resource). Secondly, it is often the case that 'perfect' secondary data turn out not to be quite so perfect for your needs as they first appeared.

Primary data can be generated from an experiment, study or survey. In the case of the survey, this may require that learners design and administer a questionnaire (Figure 14.2).

Figure 14.2 **SURVEYS IN THEORY AND PRACTICE**

Where the survey is conducted in a school or community setting, learners should be mindful of the frustrations that a badly worded questionnaire can cause. To avoid this, they should give considerable thought to its purpose, content and wording before unleashing it on other learners or the general public. Carrying out a pilot survey (which may involve a quick preliminary tour around the *PCAI* cycle using a small data set) can help them eliminate errors in advance and anticipate what may be involved in processing and analysing the results.

Task 14.2.1 A Checklist on Conducting a Questionnaire   C

Assuming that learners have checked that there are no suitable secondary sources available and they need to carry out a survey, write down a checklist of five or six general guidelines to help them plan their survey.

Learners may find it difficult to see that their questions are ambiguous or poorly worded and this is an area where they will need to develop skills. A useful training exercise is to take a poorly constructed questionnaire and try to improve it.

Task 14.2.2 A Duff Questionnaire   C

Imagine that you are conducting a survey on health. Jot down four or five questions that are ambiguous or poorly worded for learners to improve upon.

Selecting a Sample

Harry and Jed were carrying out a survey to find the most popular sports. They concluded that soccer was the only sport that people were interested in. Their teacher was slightly surprised at this and asked them who had filled in their questionnaire. It turned out that they had restricted the survey to just their friends, all of whom happened to be soccer-mad boys.

The whole point of taking a sample is that it reveals something about the wider population from which it was taken. For a sample to be a 'good' one, it must therefore be representative of that population, otherwise, generalisations will not be valid. As well as being sufficiently large, a 'good' sample should be randomly (or otherwise fairly) selected.

Sampling is said to be random if every item in the population from which the sample is selected has an equal chance of selection. A random sample can be chosen using tables of random numbers or, more conveniently, random numbers generated by a computer or calculator.

Task 14.2.3 Random Sampling with a Calculator

Suppose you wanted to choose, randomly, a sample of five learners from a class of 30 learners. How could you do this using a calculator?

You could go through the following steps. Allocate to each learner a number from 1 to 30. Using the **randInt** command, generate a random number in the range 1–30. Repeat this procedure four more times. Note: it is possible that a number will be generated that has already appeared. How should learners respond to this situation?

One possibility would be to disregard it and apply the command again – effectively, this is the basis of sampling without replacement. In this example, learners numbered 8, 15, 21, 24 and 26 are to form the sample.

It is worth spending a few minutes thinking about the connection between a *representative* and a *random* sample. *Randomness* is a technique for selecting a sample which, if large, is more likely to be *representative* than if the sample were small. When items are selected randomly, they are then equally likely to be selected. Also, the selection of each one is independent of any other one – in other words, knowing that one item has been selected does not change the chances that another (say, nearby) item will be selected. These properties are crucial for population estimates to have validity, hence the importance of randomness in sampling.

Although random methods have many advantages, this is not always the most convenient way of taking a sample. Alternative approaches include *systematic*, *cluster* and *stratified* sampling. Space does not permit further discussion of these approaches here, but further details can be found in Chapter 7 of Graham (2004).

Secondary Sources

Several useful sources of secondary data have already been mentioned in earlier chapters. Increasingly, learners are accessing the vast amounts of interesting data through a web browser. Below are just a few of the useful UK-based sources.

Text-based sources

1. *Social Trends*, an annual UK government publication that provides information on a variety of topics including population, education, health, leisure and crime. Every UK school library should have this publication. Note that the latest issue of *Social Trends* can be freely downloaded from the following web address: www.statistics.gov.uk/statbase/.
2. The *Family Expenditure Survey (FES)*, which provides data on the income and spending patterns of a sample of about 7 000 UK households.
3. The *British Attitudes Survey*, which reveals attitudes and opinions from a sample of roughly 4 000 adults.
4. The UK census of population, which takes place every ten years (1981, 1991, 2001, and so on).
5. The *Guinness Book of World Records* (published annually).

Web-based sources

There are literally thousands of interesting websites containing data that would be useful for a school statistical investigation, most of which are easily accessed via a search engine such as Google. Here are just two sources which will provide instant data, data that will be useful for getting started on an investigation.

Censusatschool: this is an international children's census that has collected and disseminated real data for use by teachers and pupils in data handling, ICT and across the curriculum for learning and teaching (www.censusatschool.ntu.ac.uk/).

Estimates data: a set of estimates made by roughly 100 children and adults on such things as the cost of a Mars bar, the age of the onset of middle age, the height of someone in metric and imperial units, and so on. Currently this file can be accessed at: students.open.ac.uk/desktop/me626-06d/

Task 14.2.4 Exploring the Web

Increasingly, learners are using the web rather than textbooks as sources of data for their investigations. As a teacher, you will need to be confident and competent in this area. Spend as much time as you can spare now exploring a range of web-based data sources and consider how they might be used in your teaching of statistics, either as part of an investigation or in directed teaching of particular topics.

14.3 ANALYSING THE DATA

The statistical ideas that comprise the *A* stage of an investigation represent a collection of statistical knowledge and techniques that have traditionally defined statistics for most learners. A virtue of the *PCAI* framework is that it helps to place these analytical skills within a wider context, emphasising the idea that purposeful statistical work starts from somewhere (with a question and relevant data) and is also going somewhere (to a resolution of the initial question).

Having collected their data, the key issue for learners at the *A* stage of an investigation is deciding what statistical elements (data summaries, graphs, and so on) would be most helpful to use. There are two major constraints in making these choices: the *nature of the data* and the *purpose of the enquiry*. These are looked at below.

The Nature of the Data

A number of ways of classifying data have been explored in earlier chapters. For the purpose of making good choices at the *A* stage, the following distinctions are particularly useful. Are the data:

- single or paired;
- discrete or continuous?

Combining these distinctions creates four possible data formats:

- single/discrete;
- single/continuous;
- paired/discrete;
- paired/continuous.

Task 14.3.1 Matching Graphs to Data Types   **C**

Here is a blank table showing a variety of graphical representations listed against these four data formats. Look at each graph in turn and tick the boxes corresponding to the sort of data it normally depicts.

	Single		Paired	
Graphs	Discrete	Continuous	Discrete	Continuous
Bar chart				
Box plot				
Histogram				
Line of fit				
Pie chart				
Scatter plot				
Stem plot				

The Purpose of the Enquiry

The second obvious factor affecting the choice of statistical tool at the A stage of an investigation relates to the sort of question(s) being asked of the data. A useful set of categories to use here is the structure used for (most of) the chapter headings of the first three blocks of this book – describing, comparing and interrelating.

Task 14.3.2 Matching Graphs to Purposes · C

Here is a blank table showing a variety of graphical representations listed against these three purposes; describing, comparing and interrelating. Look at each graph in turn and tick the boxes corresponding to the sort of enquiry that it normally informs.

Purposes

Graphs	Describing	Comparing	Interrelating
Bar chart			
Box plot			
Histogram			
Line of fit			
Pie chart			
Scatter plot			
Stem plot			

Reading the Graphs

It is one thing for learners to be able to draw graphs and calculate summary values (with or without the aid of ICT), but what really matters is that they know what insights graphs and summaries can provide about the data and how these can be used to inform their enquiry. A teacher needs to encourage learners to be active in their reading of summaries and graphs and to take every opportunity to draw sensible inferences from them.

Task 14.3.3 Matching Graphs to Purposes · C

Consider the four representations listed in this table. For each one, note down three or four questions that you might pose to learners to encourage them to think more deeply about what it might reveal. Two examples have been provided to get you started.

Representation	Possible teacher questions
Bar chart or pie chart	
Box plot	
Table	How do the rows compare?
Scatter plot	Is there an underlying pattern to the points?

The Role of ICT

In parallel with the question of, 'What statistical technique should learners use at the *A* stage of an investigation?', is the corresponding question about appropriate technology – 'What ICT tool(s), if any, should learners use in order to apply this technique?' In Block 3, a number of issues were raised about ICT use in statistics teaching, including the match between the various ICT tools on offer and the four *PCAI* stages of a statistical investigation.

Of course, there are many statistics lessons that are not based on conducting an investigation and many of these may benefit from ICT use. For example, you may wish learners to learn about box plots by entering a set of simple data into a graphics calculator, choosing the box–plot option and then asking them to make sense of what is displayed.

14.4 INTERPRETING THE RESULTS

It is remarkable how many learner investigations run out of steam by the time they get to the *I* stage. Perhaps this is because, traditionally, doing calculations and drawing graphs have been presented as the real point of statistics, and so many learners have also absorbed this view. It often takes a considerable amount of energy from the teacher to encourage learners to take that final step of relating their analysis to the initial question, to take seriously the issue of whether or not their question has been resolved and to consider how to proceed if it has not.

In order to encourage learners to complete their investigation, it is often a good idea to ask them to present their findings to other learners and invite constructive comments and criticism. This may be an occasion when sound methodology and good statistical practice are rewarded by positive peer feedback. It could also be an uncomfortable experience for some learners, should their confidence and enthusiasm be undermined.

Task 14.4.1 Peer-review Sessions   **C**

How could you try to ensure that learner presentation sessions are valuable but not too demoralising?

Linking the Stages of the *PCAI* Model

The *PCAI* model has been proposed as a useful structuring device for helping learners to organise their work on a statistical investigation. It would be valuable for this structure to be made explicit to learners, so that they are aware of which stage they are currently operating in and therefore how it relates to the rest of their project. However, as they move from one stage to the next, there are still choices to be made – for example, what data to collect, what analytical tool to use, and so on. In Figure 14.3 below, the arrows provide opportunities for helpful teacher questions that would encourage learners to think carefully about the links between the successive stages.

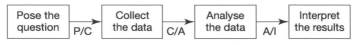

Figure 14.3 **OPPORTUNITIES FOR HELPFUL TEACHER QUESTIONS**

Task 14.4.2 Taking an Overview   **C**

What general questions might be useful for the teacher to ask learners at the three links indicated by the arrows in Figure 14.3 – these correspond to links *P/C, C/A* and *A/I* respectively.

Writing Up

Although oral presentations are valuable, learners are likely to be required to submit a written account of what they did and what they discovered. Experience has shown that the *PCAI* framework has proved a very useful template for such a write-up. Using this sort of structure provides a number of direct benefits. For example:

- it helps learners organise their thinking and planning of the tasks that they need to carry out;
- it encourages learners to write up stage by stage, as they are going along, rather than creating for themselves a long and perhaps boring writing chore at the end of their investigation;
- it provides a clear statement of their thinking, so that the teacher and other learners can grasp the main features of their investigation and be constructively critical of it;
- it emphasises the notion of statistical modelling and reminds learners of the importance of thinking statistically, as opposed to merely practising statistical skills;
- it prompts learners to create a useful summary at the beginning (so that readers know what is coming);
- it can provide a useful structure on which to hang assessment criteria. (A discussion of some assessment issues is included in Section 15.3 of Chapter 15.)

Summary of *PCAI*

In this chapter, a case was made for the benefits of using the *PCAI* (or similar) model explicitly with learners to support their statistical thinking skills. An important additional benefit for the teacher is that it provides a template within which learner work can be discussed and assessed.

Task 14.4.3 The Case for Using *PCAI*   **C**

Look back through the chapter and jot down four or five positive benefits *for learners* of using a framework such as *PCAI* explicitly with them.

15

Teaching and Learning Statistics

In this the final chapter, there will be a round-up of the main ideas of the first 14 chapters and an attempt to provide an overview of some key issues in statistical education. Section 15.1 looks at the relationship between statistics and mathematics, outlining some of the arguments for and against teaching statistics as a topic within mathematics. In Section 15.2, you will examine some of the 'big ideas' within statistics education, such as the *PCAI* framework for carrying out a statistical investigation and the three main types of inquiry in statistics: describing, comparing and interrelating. Section 15.3 turns to the question of how statistical thinking might be assessed, beyond the superficial testing of basic facts and skills. Ideas from Joan Garfield and Peter Holmes are considered here. The final section looks back over the entire book and identifies some of the main ideas that might contribute to helping learners develop their thinking with statistics.

15.1 THE IMPORTANCE OF STATISTICAL EDUCATION

On the question of why it might be worthwhile to teach statistics in schools, mathematics educator Paul Cobb (1999) had this to say:

> It is already apparent that debates about public policy issues tend to involve reasoning with data. In this discourse, policy decisions are justified by presenting arguments based on the analysis of data. In many respects, this discourse is increasingly becoming the language of power in the public policy area. Inability to participate in this discourse results in *de facto* disenfranchisement that spawns alienation from, and cynicism about, the political process. (p. 37)

In other words, Cobb suggests that if you want people to be able to understand and actively shape their world, they need to be competent at both using and reasoning with data. Cobb argues that our goals for statistical education should not merely aim to teach a set of ideas and techniques, but that learners should be helped to develop the capacity for thinking critically about the world in which they live.

Task 15.1.1 Critical Thinking

Spend a few minutes thinking about your own statistical education, both at school and beyond. What opportunities were taken for supporting and developing your thinking critically about wider social issues? How could useful statistical techniques be turned into usable tools for critical thinking?

This section looks at the nature of mathematics and statistics and explores fundamental questions about the importance of statistical education, including why, how and where it should be taught.

Mathematics and Statistics

It is clear that mathematics and statistics share certain features, including the use of measurement, numbers, calculations and the drawing of graphs. However, there are certain important philosophical differences between the ways that mathematicians and statisticians see the world, the sort of questions they ask and what, for them, constitutes an answer to such questions.

Task 15.1.2 Two Ways of Seeing

Sort the following words into two categories – those that seem to refer to statistical thinking and those that are more mathematical in character:

uncertainty, deduction, inference, precise, proof, approximation, opinion, fact, logic.

Bearing in mind the classification that you made, how might you characterise statistics and mathematics?

A reasonable classification (though 'approximation' might well feature in both lists) could look as follows:

- *statistical* words: uncertainty, inference, approximation, opinion;
- *mathematical* words: deduction, precise, proof, fact, logic.

Your classification of these terms may have pointed to certain fundamental differences in the ways that statisticians and mathematicians see the world. The context for pursuing (pure) mathematics tends to be thought of as an idealised world that is the creation of the mind. Mathematicians often make logical deductions of the form, 'if ..., then ...'. The 'if' part of the statement is unquestioningly true – this is a given within the rules of mathematics. *From this starting point*, the challenge for the mathematician is, by a process of deduction, to reach certain conclusions that they can prove to be unambiguously true (or not). Pure mathematics is a closed world governed by known rules and facts that enable absolute truths to be reached, even if such truths can only apply strictly within that world of axioms and ideas.

Contrast this with the life of the statistician, where questions are posed out in the messy, unpredictable real world, where facts are never secure and where there is a great deal of uncertainty about a variety of relevant influences, some of which you know about and some you do not. Measurements are of limited accuracy and indeed these may represent opinions rather than something that can be placed alongside a ruler. Decisions tend to be inferred (rather than deduced) on the basis of the most likely explanation or outcome. As E.W. Howe is quoted as saying, in statistics, 'a reasonable probability is the only certainty'.

Below are four quotations, all of which come from Moore and Cobb (2000). They capture certain perceptions of how statistics is commonly viewed and how it may differ from mathematics.

All models are wrong, but some are useful. (George Box)

In mathematics, context obscures structure. In data analysis, context provides meaning. (George Cobb)

Mathematical theorems are true; statistical methods are sometimes effective, when used with skill. (David Moore)

It is mainly cultural differences that prevent closer relations [between statistics and mathematics]. We might say that mathematics is French, while statistics is resolutely Anglo-Saxon. The French, proud of a long history and high culture, are wary of aggressive Anglo-Saxon pragmatism. In the words attributed to a French diplomat, 'It works in practice, but does it work in theory?' (David Moore and George Cobb)

Teaching Statistics within Mathematics

In most parts of the world, the teaching of school statistics is located within the mathematics curriculum. There are, no doubt, good historical and practical reasons for this. However, at the time of writing, in the UK, this choice of location for statistics teaching is being questioned. One controversial recommendation of the UK's Smith Report (Smith, 2004) runs as follows.

Recommendation 4.4

The Inquiry recommends that there should be an immediate review by the QCA [Qualifications and Curriculum Authority] and its regulatory partners of the future role and positioning of Statistics and Data Handling within the overall 14–19 curriculum. This should be informed by: (i) a recognition of the need to restore more time to the mathematics curriculum for the reinforcement of core skills, such as fluency in algebra and reasoning about geometrical properties and (ii) a recognition of the key importance of Statistics and Data Handling as a topic in its own right and the desirability of its integration with other subject areas. (p. 154)

Task 15.1.3 Where Statistics Should be Taught

What are your views (with reasons) on where statistics should be taught at school level?

Clearly there is no single correct answer to the question of where statistics should be taught. The two main arguments of the Smith Report for removing statistics teaching from mathematics and relocating it in other subject areas were:

- it would ease the strain on an overcrowded mathematics timetable, thereby making space for important 'core' topics, such as developing geometric reasoning and algebraic skill and fluency;
- it would be beneficial for the teaching of statistics to place it within meaningful contexts in other subject areas.

This second argument suggests that the present location of statistics within mathematics teaching has tended to create a very technique-based topic, with little emphasis on either context or problem solving. Teachers of geography, biology and history may well be better placed than mathematics teachers to find situations within their discipline where statistical investigation has a natural and comfortable place.

However, here are several arguments to counterbalance these, in favour of keeping statistics teaching mainly within mathematics.

- It is likely that most mathematics teachers have a better grasp of statistical ideas than teachers of other subjects and are therefore better equipped to provide a firm and coherent foundation of statistics.

- There is a strong synergy between much of the remainder of the mathematics curriculum and statistics, particularly in the areas of problem solving, measurement and arithmetic.
- Teachers of mathematics may be better disposed to promoting the cause of statistics teaching, by virtue of their training and interest in quantitative matters. It is not just teachers of mathematics who feel that their timetable is overloaded. If the future of statistics teaching is left to other subject specialists, who have their own subject agenda, it may simply not happen.
- Finally, there is the problem of the overall balance of what would be the received curriculum, wherever it is taught. It is possible that certain important topics would be overlooked (for example, the use of statistics in the pharmaceutical industry in the development of new drugs would not fall under any of the standard school subjects).

15.2 WHAT ARE THE 'BIG IDEAS' IN STATISTICS?

It is relatively easy to list the techniques and methods of data handling – for example, the calculation of the mean or median, drawing a box plot or a stem-and-leaf diagram, and so on. However, such a list on its own fails to capture the nature of what it means to 'think statistically'.

Solving Problems

The website of the influential US-based National Council of Teachers of Mathematics (NCTM) is: standards.nctm.org
Visit this site and you will find their statement of the sort of data handling and probability 'key skills' expected for learners up to the age of 18. These topics are grouped into the following four headings for which:

school instructional programs from pre-kindergarten through grade 12 should enable all learners to:
- formulate questions that can be addressed with data and collect, organize, and display relevant data to answer them;
- select and use appropriate statistical methods to analyze data;
- develop and evaluate inferences and predictions that are based on data;
- understand and apply basic concepts of probability.

(p. 1)

Task 15.2.1 What Are the Key Skills?

Try to relate the NCTM list of 'key skills' to any similar model(s) of statistical thinking that you have come across in this book. How close is the correspondence between the two lists?

You may have spotted that the first three items in the NCTM list match closely the stages of the *PCAI* modelling cycle. These three items have been reorganised in Table 15.1, so that the close correspondence is spelt out more clearly.

TABLE 15.1 NCTM list correspondence with the PCAI modelling cycle

PCAI cycle	NCTM list
Pose the question	Formulate questions that can be addressed with data;
Collect the data	and collect, organize, and display relevant data to answer them;
Analyse the data	Select and use appropriate statistical methods to analyse data;
Interpret the results	Develop and evaluate inferences and predictions that are based on data.

Breaking Up the *PCAI* Model

Not all statistical learning can or should necessarily take place within the context of a statistical investigation. Nevertheless, the *PCAI* framework can still provide a useful tool for helping the teacher plan a variety of different types of learning experience. For example, a lesson might start at the *C* stage, with an interesting data set, such as data that learners may uncover when exploring at the CensusatSchool website.

Task 15.2.2 Starting at the *C* Stage

How might the *PCAI* framework help teacher and learners to use the CensusatSchool data effectively to support their statistical thinking?

Here are some useful questions that can quickly be drawn from the *PCAI* model:

- the *C* stage: how were these data collected (issues about the design of the question-naire and the use of ICT as a data collection tool)?
- the *P–C* link: for what questions/investigations might these data help to provide answers?
- the *C–A* link: what analytical tools (calculations and graphs) would be appropriate for these types of data?

Describing, Comparing, Interrelating

Another set of 'big ideas' used throughout Chapters 1 to 12 of this book are the three main types of statistical enquiry, referred to as describing, comparing and interrelating. As a reminder, Table 15.2 lists three investigations to exemplify each type.

TABLE 15.2 Three main types of statistical enquiry

Type	Example
Describing	How good are people at estimating height?
Comparing	Are people better at estimating height in metric or imperial units?
Interrelating	Are people's estimating skills linked to their age?

Investigations of the 'describing' type typically involve collecting a single data set and summarising it in some way (in words, numbers or graphically), in order to discover its main features. 'Comparing' investigations usually involve collecting two data sets of the same type and then comparing them, either graphically or by means of summary statistics. With an 'interrelating' type of investigation, learners are looking at the relationship between two variables that measure different things. The data are therefore 'paired' (and it follows that the two lists of numbers contain the same number of values). Typically, the analytical tools required fall into the general statistical areas of regression and correlation.

It is useful for learners to be aware of these three forms of enquiry. Not only is it an important generalisation about what they are doing, but knowing the form of enquiry should help them to select suitable analytical tools at the *A* stage of their investigation.

Task 15.2.3 Helping Learners Focus on the Type of their Enquiry

In order to help learners think in more abstract terms about these three types of enquiry, it would be a useful exercise to present a list of possible investigations for them to classify into the relevant enquiry type and also to anticipate what analytical tools they are likely to need. Put together such a list now.

Table 15.3 lists some possible investigations – for your convenience, they have already been classified by type of enquiry.

TABLE 15.3 Possible investigations

Describing	How good are people at estimating the number of peas in a jar?
	How are the ages of teachers in a secondary school distributed?
Comparing	Are people better at estimating height in metric or imperial units?
	Are girls' names longer than boys' names?
	Do men or women live longer?
	Are adults or children better at using metric units?
	Are large conkers tougher than small ones?
Interrelating	Does people's skill at estimating link to age?
	Can people with longer legs run faster?
	Can you use a person's index finger length to estimate their height?

Other Big Ideas Not Covered in this Book

Clearly, there are some important ideas of statistics and statistics education for which there has not been space in this book. For example, in the field of statistics, ideas of inference and probability theory have only been touched on. As a teacher of statistics, you will regularly come across terms and ideas that are unfamiliar and which you might like to read about in more detail. As well as using reference books in the library, a good web-based resource is often the quickest and easiest way to satisfy your curiosity. A useful such source is the 'Statistics explained' glossary, which can be found at: www.animatedsoftware.com/statglos/statglos.htm Select the *flash-based option without the tutorial* and spend a few minutes exploring the meanings of some of the ideas listed.

Finally, note that, at the time or writing, the American Statistical Association is about to produce a detailed report following up the NCTM Standards, specifically on the teaching of statistics. The project is currently known as GAISE (Guidance in Assessment and Instruction in Statistics Education) and preliminary versions of the reports can be found at: it.stlawu.edu/~rlock/gaise/

Task 15.2.4 Confounding Factors

An important idea in statistics is the notion of 'confounding factors'. This is a term with which you may not be familiar.

(a) Think about this phrase and note down what you think it refers to.

(b) Look up *confounding factors* in the 'Statistics explained' glossary and then summarise its meaning in your own words in a couple of sentences.

15.3 ASSESSMENT

This section on the assessment of statistics draws on the following two articles: Garfield (1994) and Holmes (2002, pp. 87–9).

The Purpose of Assessment

According to Joan Garfield, the main purpose of assessment is to improve learner learning.

Task 15.3.1 The Purpose of Assessment

Do you agree with the view presented above?

What other useful purposes do you think can be served by gathering assessment information?

As well as the justification given above, Joan Garfield lists the following six 'secondary purposes' for assessment.

(a) To provide individual information to learners about how well they have learned a particular topic and where they are having difficulty.

(b) To provide information to the instructor about how well the class seems to understand a particular topic and what additional activities might need to be introduced, or whether it is time to move on to another topic.

(c) To provide diagnostic information to instructors about individual learners' understanding or difficulties in understanding new material.

(d) To provide information to teachers about learners' perceptions and reactions to the class, the material, the subject matter, or particular activities.

(e) To provide an overall indicator of learners' success in achieving course goals.

(f) To help learners determine their overall strengths and weaknesses in learning the course material.

(Section 2)

As you read through her list given above, try to keep the following three questions in mind.

- To what extent could these six secondary benefits fulfil Joan Garfield's overall goal of 'improving learner learning'?
- Have you had direct experience of these potential benefits, either as a teacher or a learner?
- How, in practice, could you envisage organising teaching so that these benefits actually materialised?

Assessing Deeper Levels of Understanding

A concern expressed by both Joan Garfield and Peter Holmes is the need to devise questions and tasks that assess deeper levels of understanding. Garfield remarks:

> As goals for statistics education change to broader and more ambitious objectives, such as developing statistical thinkers who can apply their knowledge to solving real problems, a mismatch is revealed between traditional assessment and the desired learner outcomes. It is no longer appropriate to assess learner knowledge by having learners compute answers and apply formulas, because these methods do not reveal the current goals of solving real problems and using statistical reasoning. (Section 1)

In order to facilitate a more thoughtful approach to assessment that taps into deeper concepts and skills, Garfield suggests the following five-stage framework for ensuring that the assessment is both appropriate and effective.

- *Which* aspects to assess? These may be broken down into concepts, skills, applications, attitudes and beliefs.
- What is the *purpose* of the assessment? For example, is it for the benefit of the learner(s) or the teacher?
- What is the *method* of assessment to be used? Examples include a test, a report, an individual or group project, piece of writing or portfolio.
- *Who* will do the assessment?
- What will be the *action(s)* taken as a result of the assessment and the *feedback* to learners?

Garfield provides four examples of her framework in action, of which one is shown in Table 15.4 (in shortened form).

TABLE 15.4 Garfield's framework: an example

What to assess?	Learners' ability to apply basic techniques of exploratory data analysis.
Purpose	To determine whether learners are able to apply their skills to the collection, analysis and interpretation of data.
Method	A learner project, where instructions are given as to the sample size, format of report, and so on.
Who is to assess?	First, the learner completes a self-assessment using a copy of the rating sheet the instructor will use, which has been distributed prior to completing the project. Then, the instructor evaluates the project according to each of the following six categories: communication, visual representation, statistical calculations, decision-making, interpretation of results and drawing conclusions.
Actions/feedback	Scores are assigned to each category and given back to learners early enough in the course, along with written comments, so that they may learn from this feedback in working on their next project.

Task 15.3.2 Using the Garfield Framework

Choose a topic that you might wish to assess with one or more learner and apply the Garfield framework in order to plan a possible assessment strategy.

Assessment Using Real Data

In his article, Peter Holmes (2002) provides examples of how the deeper statistical skills and concepts specified in the UK National Curriculum could be assessed using a large data set such as the CensusatSchool data. For example, consider the following objective:

> Specify the problem and plan: identify questions that can be addressed by statistical methods.

Holmes offers two suggestions for assessing this objective, of which one is given below. Note that in this extract, he refers to two types of assessment: *summative* and *formative*. As the name suggests, *summative* assessment is used to check the level of learning at the end of the programme of study. *Formative* assessment is usually carried out during the learning process, to help *form* the subsequent teaching and learning. Classroom assessment is one of the most common formative assessment techniques and the main aim is to improve quality of learner learning – it is not intended to be evaluative or involve grading learners.

> Celia wants to compare the heights of pupils in her class with heights of pupils of the same age in the UK as a whole. Write down an outline plan for her project. You should show:
>
> - how she will get data from her own class and appropriate data from the CensusatSchool site;
> - how she will represent the data;
> - what calculations she will make with the data;
> - the sort of final conclusion that she might make.
>
> *Class activity*: Carry out the plan you have devised for Celia. How well did your plan work – what changes did you have to make? What had you forgotten? (This is more suitable for formative than for summative evaluation, because pupils would not like to show weaknesses to an examiner. The ideas could, however, be incorporated into the project work and its assessment.)

Task 15.3.3 Create your own Assessment Question

(a) Read through the assessment question (and follow-up class task) above and try to judge their strengths and weaknesses.

(b) Choose another of the deeper global objectives such as:

'Process and represent the data: turn the raw data into usable information that gives insight into the problem.'

By exploiting the CensusatSchool data set, create your own set of questions and devise a suitable class task that you feel will assess the skill you have chosen.

15.4 A ROUND-UP OF STATISTICAL THINKING

In this, the final section of the book, you are asked to revisit its main theoretical and pedagogic ideas.

Scales of Measure

The Stevens taxonomy (explained in Section 1.2) provides a helpful way of thinking about the nature of measuring scales. These are:

- nominal (or naming) scale;
- ordinal (or ordered) scale;
- interval scale;
- ratio scale.

Only the final ratio scale supports the full range of properties of measurement.

A related important distinction is that between 'discrete' and 'continuous' scales of measure.

The Six PTT Themes

As you may recall, the final sections of each of the first 12 chapters were mostly organised around the following six 'Preparing to Teach' themes:

- *language patterns*;
- *imagery* that will help learners to create a richer inner sense of the topic, from which further connections can be made;
- *different contexts* that can be used to enhance learner understanding and motivate learners;
- *root questions*;
- *standard misconceptions* (or different or incomplete conceptions);
- *techniques and methods*.

These six themes were offered as a way of helping you to think through a topic prior to teaching it, so that you understand it more fully yourself, and were prepared to present it from different points of view, with a rich variety of ideas and examples.

Telling Tales

This was an approach to statistics teaching used in Block 1, based on the idea that everyone likes a good story and that many of the big ideas of statistics can be shared and enlivened by using interesting and entertaining anecdotes. The word 'telling' has a dual meaning – not only do these stories require a narrator to do the telling, but also, to be effective, they need to be 'telling', in the sense of having resonance with the hearer while at the same time conveying an important idea in statistics.

Relative and Absolute Differences

Comparisons are invariably misleading unless you are comparing 'like with like'. For example, the fact that there are more telephones in China than in Ireland is a misleading measure of the relative affluence of the two countries, since the population of China is so much larger than the population of Ireland. A *relative* measure (such as the number of telephones per million of the population) would be a more useful calculation.

Constructivism

Section 3.5 contains a discussion of an important set of pedagogic ideas, loosely referred to in the literature as *constructivism*. Included here are the main features of what von Glasersfeld (1984), Moore (1997) and others have referred to as 'naïve constructivism':

- learners learn by actively building or constructing their own knowledge and making sense out of this knowledge;
- individuals construct new knowledge internally by transforming, organising and reorganising previous knowledge, as well as externally, through environmental and social factors that are influenced by culture, language and interactions with others;
- regardless of how clearly a teacher explains a concept, learners will understand the material only after they have constructed their own meaning, which may require restructuring and reorganising new knowledge and linking it to prior or previous knowledge;
- learning should be facilitated by teachers and that interaction and discussion are critical components during the learning process.

The crunch question for this book is how these ideas might impact on the learning and teaching of statistics.

Explanatory and Response Variables

When investigating the relationship between two variables, it is dangerous to assume a *cause-and-effect* connection. Even where there *is* cause and effect, it is not always clear which is the cause and which the effect. However, often this causal link can be demonstrated, in which case, the 'explanatory' and 'response' labels are useful ways of distinguishing the role of each variable in establishing the relationship in question.

Useful Contributors to Data Visualisation

Six of *A.S.C. Ehrenberg's* guiding principles were set out for presenting information clearly in a table.

Edward R. Tufte is an important chronicler of the historical development of graph design and a number of interesting examples of his work were included in Chapter 5.

As well as being the 'lady with the lamp', *Florence Nightingale* made a useful contribution to statistical ideas, including some innovative methods of data representation, such as the coxcomb diagram.

John Tukey introduced a number of important ways of graphing data during the 1970s, many of which are now in common currency in the classroom (for example, the box plot and stem plot).

Jerome Bruner and EIS

In Chapter 8, you read about Bruner's three modes of classifying thought processes – enactive, iconic and symbolic. An awareness of these alternative ways of thinking can help the teacher to consider using a wider range of approaches when working with learners.

ICT Options

In Block 3, you looked at a number of ICT options for teaching and learning statistics, including:

- graphics calculators;
- spreadsheets;
- statistics packages;
- Java applets.

Models and Modelling

You looked at alternative meanings of two overused and misunderstood terms, *model* and *modelling* (Chapter 13). An important model that lies at the heart of statistical work is the *PCAI* framework, which can be useful for both the teacher and the learners in planning their work and being constructively critical of what is done at each stage (Chapter 14).

APC

It is appropriate to end with a pedagogic idea that has provided the overall design for this book. Throughout, you have been asked to engage in tasks yourself, in order to accumulate experience that can then be used as the basis of thoughtful reflection about pedagogy. Such a task-based approach to professional development can be summarised by the triple Adult–Process–Classroom or *APC* for short. It is recommended for working with colleagues or learners. The idea is that you:

> *A*: start with your own *adult* recent experience (such as your work on a task from this book);
> *P*: use that experience to make sense of past experience by reflecting on *processes*, re-entering significant or salient moments and recalling details;
> *C*: imagine yourself working with learners (perhaps in a *classroom*) or with colleagues, using or adapting the task, informed by your personal reflections on the relevant processes.

The *APC* triple is the most powerful potential aid to your professional development, as it draws on an outstanding and under-utilised teaching resource that is both richly varied and easily accessible – yourself.

Comments on Tasks

0.1 Attitudes

While there are no uniquely 'correct' explanations, here are some possibilities:

(a) This person may believe that reducing information to mere numbers is dehumanising and fails to address (indeed, may mask) those aspects of the human condition that really matter. It may suggest that the two are somehow 'oppositional' types of people. Alternatively, this may be an avoidance strategy by someone who lacks numerical skill.

(b) This may be a case of someone's heart ruling his or her head: it also may signify not discriminating among those numbers. Good decisions are usually made when the heart and the head are working closely together!

(c) This appears to suggest a (misplaced) pride in a lack of numerical skill. Many people who should know better (including Sir Winston Churchill) have boasted that they are not good with figures, thereby providing a negative role model for young people.

(d) This person seems to have a very utilitarian view of learning statistics – there is nothing intrinsically valuable to learn here, only the piece of paper to say that they studied it.

(e) This implies that all statistics are bogus and all statisticians are snake-oil salesmen. Alternatively, this may be an avoidance strategy by someone who lacks numerical skill or does not wish to engage. People often say, 'You can prove anything with statistics'. This is only true if they are misused.

1.0.3 The Big Ideas of Statistics

Your solution may look something like Table C1.1 (below).

1.1.1 Thinking it Through

Questions should include:

- Whom should you sample? What does being 'representative' mean here?
- How many people should be in your sample?

- How will you contact them?
- What if someone refuses to take part?

1.1.3 Eliminating Questionnaire Bias

Best practice is to conduct pilot interviews where the questions are tried out and improved on the basis of the outcome. It is also important that the interviewers be well briefed, so that they understand clearly the nature and purpose of the questions they are asking and are therefore in a position to know if respondents have gone off on a wrong or unhelpful track.

1.2.1 Words or Numbers

Words are excellent for describing hard-to-measure qualities and for conveying subtle shades of meaning; for example, describing human characteristics such as mood, confidence, beauty, and so on. The weakness of words is that they cannot easily be compared from one situation to another (is 'pleasant' a better or worse characteristic than 'nice'?). Also, as anyone who has taken part in an interview selection panel will affirm, it can be hard to agree on meaningful word descriptions between one person and another.

1.2.2 Only Words?

Here are some possibilities – there may well be others.

(a) This list can be interpreted in terms of the developmental stages that a baby goes through. For most children, they can be ordered chronologically as: roll, sit, crawl, walk, run. Another might be in terms of speed of locomotion.

(b) One way of thinking about these words is in terms of traditional gifts for wedding anniversaries. Again, ordering them chronologically, they are:

paper (1 year), wood (5 years), silver (25 years), ruby (40 years) and gold (50 years).

(c) These fabrics can be ordered in terms of maximum temperatures for ironing. From coolest to hottest, this gives: rayon, silk, wool, cotton, linen.

TABLE C1.1 Big ideas and statistical tools and techniques

Tools and techniques	Summarising	Measure of location	Spread	Variation	Interrelating
Range	√		√	√	
Median	√	√			
Bar chart	√				
Scatter plot	√		√	√	√
Quartile	√	√	√		

Note that in all three of these examples, the ordering has been from least to most (that is, in *ascending order*). These lists could also have been given in *descending order*, from most to least of some quality.

1.2.3 Twice

Items (a) and (c) are correct in their use of 'twice', but (b), (d) and (e) are not. The problem is revealed when the values are converted to a different scale of measure. So, with example (b), 6 p.m. and 3 p.m., when converted to the 24-hour clock give 18.00 hours and 15.00 hours respectively. Clearly, 18 is not twice 15. Similarly, with example (d), convert the temperatures to degrees Fahrenheit and the 'twice' property no longer holds (15 °C ≈ 59 °F and 30 °C ≈ 86 °F). The problem here is that these scales of measure (time and temperature) possess an arbitrary zero which affects any comparisons based on calculating ratios. Contrast this with examples (a) and (c), where the quantities being compared do not possess any arbitrary zero and for which ratio properties hold true.

The earthquake example (e) is incorrect because the Richter scale is logarithmic, rather than linear. So, an increase of one unit on the Richter scale actually means an increase of intensity by a factor of 10^1, that is, 10. An increase from 2 to 4 on the Richter scale means that the second shock is 10^2, or 100 times more powerful. The biggest earthquake in the last hundred years happened in Chile in 1960, with a force of 9.5 on the Richter scale. The Indonesian tsunami that struck on December 26 2004 was caused by an earthquake measured at 9.0 on the Richter scale, a force of roughly one third that of the Chilean disaster. This factor of three can be calculated as follows: $10^{9.5}/10^{9.0} = 10^{0.5} \approx 3.2$.

1.2.4 Testing Your Take on the Taxonomy

(a) (i) ordinal; (ii) ratio; (iii) ratio; (iv) nominal; (v) ordinal.

(b) Using the conventional scales of Fahrenheit and Celsius, temperature is an interval scale because the zero is arbitrary. However, using the Absolute scale of measure, zero degrees Absolute (roughly −273°C) really means zero heat – it represents the lowest possible temperature allowed by the laws of thermodynamics.

(c) Time of day is measured on an interval scale (because the zero is arbitrary, midnight does not mean 'no time'), whereas time elapsed is measured on a ratio scale (because zero time elapsed really means no time has elapsed).

1.2.5 Grammar, Timothy!

(a) To be grammatically correct, Timothy should have used 'how many', rather than 'how much'. 'How many' should be used where the items under consideration are discrete and countable. 'How much' should be used where there is a continuous scale of measure. This convention appears to be contravened with 'How much' being used to ask about the price of something – at least in terms of ready change, prices cannot be measured by less than 1p and are therefore discrete. However, exchange rates and, occasionally, petrol prices do operate with amounts that are subdivided into units smaller than 1p.

(b) You might talk of a book having *fewer* pages than another, but a given jug has *less* water than the other.

1.2.6 Distinguishing Discrete and Continuous Measures

The discrete measures are: (b), (e), (g), (i), (k). Note that in the case of example (b), a discrete variable need not be restricted to whole numbers (shoes in the UK can be in half sizes).

The continuous measures are: (a), (c), (d), (f), (h), (j).

Item (l) is rather ambiguous – strictly speaking, it is a discrete variable, given that there is a basic unit of 1p below which measurements cannot be taken. However, 1p is so small in relation to an annual salary (even the annual salary of a teacher) that in practice it is treated like a continuous variable.

1.2.7 Wales Has Been Moved!

Although the sentences contain the same number of characters, their grouping into words determines the placing of the line breaks. In the first sentence, the second, third and fourth lines all start with a long word, which means that the lines that precede them are shorter than they might otherwise be. It is the *discrete* nature of word lengths that introduces an element of unpredictability into where the line breaks occur.

1.3.1 Rough Estimates

(a) Dividing 1 million seconds by 60 (convert to minutes), then by 60 again (minutes to hours) and then by 24 (hours to days) gives an answer of about 11.5 days.

(b) Dividing 1 billion seconds by 60, then by 60, then by 24 and then by 365 (days to years) gives an answer of about 32 years. (Has your first billion already ticked by? If so, do try to use the next billion more productively!)

(c) Assume that the average lifespan is 60 years. (This is a very rough estimate, as lifespans vary widely in different parts of the world.) So, each year, roughly 1/60th of the world's population dies. Each day, the fraction who die on average is 1/(60 × 365). The world's population is roughly 6.5 billion, so the number of deaths is 6 500 000 000/(60 × 365) or roughly 300 000 people. (Note: this estimate assumes a uniform population distribution by age, which is not the case. A more sophisticated estimate would take into account the fact there are higher proportions of younger people.)

(d) Roughly 30% of adults (above, say, 15 years) are smokers. Assume that the average level of smoking is 15 cigarettes per day. Assume that the population in the UK above the age of 15 is 40 million. So, number of smokers = 0.3 × 40 000 000. Number of cigarettes per annum = 0.3 × 40 000 000 × 365 × 15 = 66 billion roughly.

(e) From personal experience, hair seems to grow at a rate of roughly 1cm per month, which is 0.00001km per month. Allowing 30 days per month, this is 0.00002/(30 × 24) = 0.000000014 km per hour.

1.3.2 Adapting Tasks

The first two statements could be extended as follows:

- Roughly how many seconds has writing been around? (Answer, roughly 150 billion seconds.)
- Roughly how many seconds has rock music been around? (Answer, over 1 billion seconds.)
- Roughly how many seconds have elapsed since the time of Jesus (about 60 billion), the time of Mohammed (about 40 billion), the first human on earth (15 000 000 000 000 or 15 thousand billion), the creation of the earth (15 000 000 000 000 000 000, or 15 billion billion), ...

1.3.3 Visualising Facts

It may be helpful to think of audiences in square blocks of ten rows and ten seats per row – that is, 100 at a time. Increase the number of rows and seats to 32 and you have accommodated roughly 1 000 people. It is harder to get a grip on numbers in the millions and billions, but Bryson's examples are helpful.

Here is a metaphor for the final one, provided by John McPhee (1990) in his book *Basin and Range* (quoted in Bryson, 2004, pp. 409–10).

> Stand with your arms held out to each side and let the extent of the earth's history be represented by the distance from the tips of your fingers on your left hand to the tips of the fingers on your right. Now, if someone were to run a file across the fingernail of your right middle finger, then the time that humans have been on the earth would be erased.

1.3.4 Converting Numbers into Standard Form

(a) The answers are: 1.5E19, 1.4E11, 1.4E⁻8, 8E⁻8.

(b) Here are two of the numbers displayed on a calculator.

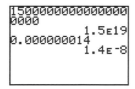

(c) As was suggested earlier, it is difficult to grasp the magnitudes of very small or very large numbers when displayed using conventional notation, for the reason that it is not easy to see at a glance how many zeros there are. Scientific notation provides this information explicitly, thereby making it easier for such numbers to be compared.

1.3.5 Calculating with Standard Form

You should have got the answer 2.4E36. At first sight, this seems to be a surprising result. However, when you think about it, you will realise that the calculation is actually calculating 2400000000000000000000000000000000000000 – 2400000000000. The second number is relatively insignificant compared with the first one and the subtraction has little impact on the value of the starting number (certainly the impact is not registered in terms of the accuracy of the calculator display).

1.4.1 Learner Definitions

These definitions were provided for, respectively the median, mean and mode.

This definition for the mean (number 2) is quite satisfactory, but the median (number 1) and mode (number 3) definitions require a bit more work! Could you have more than one mean for a single set of data?

Median: there are several important gaps here. First, the data must be placed in order of size. Secondly, this definition implies that for these data the value of the median is 10. This is a common mistake – this learner has only calculated the *position* of the median (wrongly, as it happens), not its *value*. Finally, if there are 20 items, it is not the tenth but the midway point between the tenth and the eleventh item *when placed in order of size* that is the median. What would it be if there were 21 items? Could you have more than one median?

Mode: Again this is a common error. The 'largest frequency' is what identifies the mode, but the mode is the *item* that has this (largest) frequency, not the *value* of that frequency. It is possible to have more than one mode. Why?

1.4.2 Create Your Own Task

The range is the difference between the highest and lowest value of a set of numerical data and gives some sense of how far apart the two extreme values are. Another measure of spread is the 'interquartile range', which is the difference between the 75% quartile and the 25% quartile (this is discussed further in Section 2.2). You could help learners to think a bit more deeply about measures of spread by asking a question such as, 'Which would you expect to be greater, the range or the interquartile range? Why? Could you create a data set where the two measures of spread are equal?'

1.4.3 When Averaging is Appropriate

Four suitable data sets might be:

> Nominal scale: Country of birth (Scotland, England, USA, India, France, ...)
>
> Ordinal scale: Rating on a 1–5 scale (3, 4, 3, 1, 2, 5, 3, ...)
>
> Interval scale: Daily air temperature (12 °C, 16 °C, 15 °C, 12 °C, ...)
>
> Ratio scale: Height of class (1.67 m, 1.54 m, 1.28 m, ...)

It is worth spending a few minutes thinking about how meaningful it would be to calculate the mean, mode and median for these data sets. For example, it would be impossible to calculate the mean of the various countries of birth, but finding the mode (which country had the greatest number of choices) is straightforward and meaningful. An overview in the form of a table is given in table C1.2.

TABLE C1.2 Stevens's taxonomy and measures of location

	Mean	Mode	Median
Nominal	N	Y	N
Ordinal	N	Y	Y
Interval	Y	Y	Y
Ratio	Y	*	Y

Note: * Ratio data are normally continuous variables, so, unless rounding takes place, it is unlikely that any two values will be exactly the same. This makes calculation of the mode meaningless. A way around this problem is to arrange the data into equal *intervals* and then choose, as the mode, the interval with the greatest frequency. This could be called the modal interval, or modal group, rather than the mode.

1.5.2 Using PTT

Here are a few notes on preparing to teach the mode.

Language patterns: stress the 'most likely value' or 'the value that occurs most often'.

Imagery: the tallest bar in the bar chart represents the mode.

Different contexts: the mode is particularly useful for nominal and ordinal data – find examples of these.

Root questions: what single value is most representative of these data?

Standard misconceptions: learners may believe that the mode is the *frequency* of the most commonly occurring item, rather than the item that occurs most frequently.

Techniques and methods: with interval and ratio data, it is usual to group the data into intervals. The modal group is the one with the largest frequency.

2.1.1 Taller, Better, Lighter

These investigations raise a number of important statistical ideas, of which three ('variation', 'comparing like with like' and 'looking for other explanations') are discussed in the text.

2.1.2 Four Times as Dangerous

This is fallacious because there are roughly four times as many cars on the road at that time. Therefore, the proportion of vehicles involved in accidents is roughly the same at these two times. Note, however, that if you tend to drive more often at 7 p.m. than at 7 a.m., then your chances of being involved in an accident in the evening may be greater. However, this information is not supplied as part of the 'if' statement in the question.

2.2.1 The Range as a Measure of Spread

Two groups of children, aged 11 and 16 years, gave estimates of how long they thought one minute lasted. Here are their estimates, in seconds (sorted in order, for convenience).

11-year-olds: 40, 42, 43, 47, 49, 50, 58, 60, 65.
16-year-olds: 21, 55, 57, 57, 58, 61, 65, 65.

There are several points of discussion that could emerge from these data. First, what does it mean for a class of pupils to give

good estimates? Once this has been agreed, how can the figures be usefully summarised to reflect this – is it the average or the spread that is the better measure of their skill at estimation?

In fact, both are relevant, since the skill at estimation of a group of people is judged both by their accuracy (where the values are centred) and by their consistency (how widely spread the values are). Next, if the range is used as a measure of spread, the 16-year-olds show a much wider spread than the 11-year-olds. Is this a fair comparison, given that this large spread is largely caused by the extreme outlier value of 21 seconds? Most learners will agree that this one value is highly unrepresentative and therefore the range of 16-year-old estimates gives a misleading impression. They should be able to deduce that this is an unsatisfactory feature of using the range and could be invited to say how they might deal with this problem. This sows the seeds for introducing other measures of spread, such as the interquartile range, which is discussed in the next sub-section.

2.2.3 Calculating Quartiles with a Calculator

The calculator algorithm is identical to Tukey's, except that the median is *always* excluded from each subset involved in calculating the quartiles. Thus, for the 11-year-olds, the value of Q1 is the median of 40, 42, 43 and 47 (that is, 42.5 seconds), while the value of Q3 is the median of the values 50, 58, 60 and 65 (that is, 59 seconds). In the case of the 16-year-olds, the values from either algorithm are identical. Can you see why?

2.2.4 The Five-figure Summary

(a) The five-figure summary enables you to see at a glance the five key numbers that summarise the data set in question. Also, as you will see in Chapter 6, it is a useful way in for learners to learn about box plots.

(b) Here is a five-figure summary of the 16-year-olds' data from Task 2.2.2.

45	59	69
23		73

2.2.5 Turning to Location

The mean uses all the values, while the median uses just one (or, more precisely, at most two). The mode draws on all the values in the set, but does not use them directly in its calculation, simply in terms of ascertaining their relative frequency. As with the measures of spread, using all the values makes for a very representative summary measure, but it can be easily affected by extreme outliers, which is not true of the median or mode.

2.3.1 First Impressions

The notion of how 'sporty' a country might be is hard to define. This measure (of the number of Olympic gold medals) measures achievement at the highest level, but perhaps a better measure might be to look at the overall rates of participation in sport by all the citizens. A first impression of the 'gold medal' data might be that the USA is the most sporty nation because it won the most medals. However, this conclusion fails to take account of the fact that the populations of the four countries are very different.

2.3.2 Second Impressions

A fairer comparison would be to calculate the rate of gold medals per, say, 10 million population. This gives the following results:

Gold medals per 10 million population

USA	35/28.9	= 1.21 gold medals
China	32/130.8	= 0.24 gold medals
Russia	2/14.3	= 1.89 gold medals
Australia	17/2	= 8.50 gold medals

This second impression calculation suggests that Australia is roughly seven times as 'sporty' as the USA and 35 times as sporty as China.

2.3.3 Big Dipper

A first response might be that the comparison is not fair – people spend much more time cycling, on average, than on a fairground ride. To make the comparison fairer, assume an equal amount of time spent on each. In fact, based on this assumption of equal time spent, according to the British Health and Safety Committee data, you are roughly 40 times more likely to be killed cycling for an hour on a main road than spending an hour on 'Nemesis' or 'Oblivion'. The reason this seems hard to believe is that fairground accidents tend to make front-page news, while roughly 10 people die on our roads every day with scarcely a mention. Fairground rides are also roughly seven times safer than car travel.

2.3.4 Relative and Absolute, Revisited

(a) This is an absolute figure.

(b) Roughly 6.5 deaths per 100 000 per annum. This is a relative figure (expressed as a rate per 100 000 and also per year, though the graph does not say that explicitly).

(c) The population of the UK is roughly 60 million, so using the rate of 6.5 deaths per 100 000, this gives 3 900 deaths per year or roughly 10.7 deaths per day. This confirms the previous claim, approximately, though 11 would be a more accurate figure.

2.4.1 Thinking Up a Question

Traffic survey: A suitable 'describing' question could be: 'How fast are the vehicles travelling?' A suitable 'comparing' question could be: 'How much faster do cars travel than lorries?

Getting to school: A suitable 'describing' question could be: 'What are the most popular ways of getting to school?' A suitable 'comparing' question could be: 'Do people who walk to school live closer than people who come by bus or car?'

2.4.4 Doing a Calculation

The obvious calculation is to find the mean score for men and for women. In the event, the men in the survey scored 72%, while the women scored slightly less with 71%. Another approach is to investigate whether people are better at reading the genuineness of the smiles of their own or of the opposite sex. In this experiment, the men were accurate in their judgement of 76% of the female faces, whereas the women were accurate in judging only 67% of the male faces.

2.4.5 What Are They Really Saying?

(a) Richard Wiseman appears to be making the fair point that the scores are based on the conflation of two skills – the ability of those being photographed to create a convincingly false smile and the ability of people to read these smiles. He suggests that, if the five photographed men were better at forming a false smile, the insincerity of the five male photographs would be actually more difficult to read than the five female ones. Quite whether this 'skill' can be attributed to their 'more limited emotional system' is another matter.

Susan Quilliam wants us to believe that it is women's more optimistic life view that has resulted in their less well-developed skills in reading faces. Well, um, er ... it is difficult to know how to respond to this suggestion.

Gladeana McMahon's comment calls into question what is meant by intuition and whether the ability to read faces is a useful or valid way of measuring it. This is a good point and one that was raised in the discussion following Task 2.4.2. However, it is not obvious how this characteristic could be usefully measured so a distinction is made between the *amount* of talk that people engage in about feelings and the *quality* of insights they have when they talk about feelings.

2.4.6 Deducing the Missing Data

You should have found that the missing data were 6, 6 and 6. Clearly, these scores are higher than the data in the first column in the table. The point of this exercise is to show that if the mean of a subset of a data set is greater than the overall average, it follows that the mean of the remaining values must be less than the overall average. This is a point not picked up in the *Daily Telegraph* article and one that could have led to a very different headline such as, 'Women better at reading their own sex than men!'

2.5.1 Aunt Betty

The 'point' of the Aunt Betty story was to illustrate how statistical data can sometimes contain a very powerful message that can greatly affect our personal lives and decisions.

2.5.2 Statistical Words and Phrases

Some of the terms listed in this chapter were: size, in general, in order of size, interval, uncertainty, seeking out patterns, representative, spread, relative differences.

Two of these, 'size' and 'in general' are looked at below in more detail.

Size: invite learners to list some contexts where word descriptions of size (large, tiny, huge, ...) are meaningful and reasonably unambiguous and other cases where they are not. In the latter case, what sort of numerical scale would they suggest as an alternative. Are there any disadvantages in moving to a numerical scale?

In general: the phrase 'in general' seems to mean something different in mathematics from the way it is used in everyday situations. For example, the term is often used with a negative connotation ('You are making a generalisation there!'), as if all generalisations were false or unjustified. Can learner(s) find other words whose meaning in mathematics are not exactly shared outside the mathematics classroom (for example, mean, volume, scales, ...).

2.5.3 Visualising

To take the 'gold medals' example (Tasks 2.3.1 and 2.3.2), a relative comparison between any two countries means, in effect, considering the density of gold medals spread through the entire population of each country. Figure C2.1 shows Australia's 17 gold medals spread through their population of 20 million people, alongside Great Britain's 9 gold medals spread through their population of 58 million.

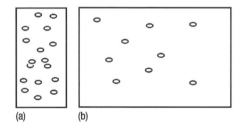

(a)   (b)

Figure C2.1 **THE RELATIVE DENSITY OF GOLD MEDALS (a) AUSTRALIA AND (b) GREAT BRITAIN**

Australia, with a population of roughly one-third that of Great Britain, won almost twice as many gold medals – giving them a gold medal 'density' of roughly six times that of GB.

2.5.4 Contexts

Here are some suggestions on the theme of comparison:

Investigating differences – compared to, say, the world of Victorian children. This may include comparison of heights at different ages, health and disease, household sizes, and so on.

Relative comparison – when young journalists are using relative comparisons, they are taught to avoid percentages (because many readers do not understand them) and to 'bring numbers down to size'. For example, talk about '1 in 4' rather than '25%'.

2.5.5 Root Questions

Standard deviation – 'What would be a fair way of measuring the spread of these figures, so that all the values were included in the calculation?'

Five-figure summary – 'How can I see at a glance the key summary values of this data set and know which is which?'

Standard form – 'How can I re-present this very large/small number in order to understand its size and compare it with other numbers of similar size?'

2.5.6 Misconceptions

Another problem with the median occurs when it is used with discrete data. For example, you might ask learners what is wrong with the following statement: 'The median mark gained by a large number of learners in a spelling test was 7 (out of a possible 10), so half of the learners scored more than 7'. The point here is that many of these learners will almost certainly have a score of 7, so there will be a number of learners in the upper half of the data set who scored exactly 7. Learners can confront this possible misunderstanding by creating a suitable data set of their own and showing that the statement is wrong. How might you rephrase it to be more accurate?

2.5.7 Techniques

As was indicated earlier in the text, it is more important that learners are aware that the quartiles lie one quarter and three quarters of the way through the data when placed in order than that they are able to calculate them accurately. This awareness can be fostered by taking an active approach to finding the quartiles. For example, draw a number line on the floor, showing a range of heights between, say, 1 metre and 2 metres. Ask each learner to place a tiny square of card marked with their initials beside the number line in a position corresponding to their height. They can then identify the three people whose cards correspond to Q1, Q2 and Q3 and these three heights can be revealed.

3.1.1 Direct and Inverse Relationships

(a) Two possible examples are: 'The more I practise the fiddle, the better I play' and 'The more I eat, the fatter I get'.

(b) Two possible examples are: 'The more I fly, the less nervous I get of flying' and 'The more Christmas cards I make myself, the fewer I'll have to buy'.

(c) 'Too many cooks spoil the broth'; 'Money doesn't buy happiness'; 'Opposites attract'; 'Lucky in cards, unlucky in love'; 'Many hands make light work'; 'When the cat's away, the mice will play'; 'A stitch in time saves nine'.

3.1.2 Independent and Dependent Variables

The mass is the independent variable and the extension of spring the dependent variable.

3.1.3 Choosing the Explanatory Variable

A reasonable choice for the explanatory variables in the first five examples would be: (a) height; (b) time spent jogging; (c) child's age; (d) distance from home to school; (e) time of day. Note that, in most cases involving time, it is normally accorded the status of the explanatory variable on the grounds that the passing of time has a habit of continuing to tick by, regardless of what other factors are doing. As you will see in Chapter 7, this is particularly apparent with time series graphs, where time is always placed on the horizontal axis, indicating its explanatory status. However, there are exceptions to the general rule that time is always the explanatory variable and you need to distinguish time of day or month or year (which is always independent) from time measured in an experiment (which may not be independent). An illustration of the latter case is example (d) above.

Option (f) is one where there is no clear cause and effect relationship one way or the other. In cases like this, where there is no designation of dependency in the relationship, it does not matter which variable is drawn on the vertical or horizontal scale.

3.2.1 Clarifying the Measures

(a) The measure is mobile phone ownership.

(b) Both sex and mobile phone ownership are nominal measures.

(c) Both these measures are attributes. The distinction between an attribute and a variable is that the term 'variable' is normally reserved for scales with numerical data. Attributes refer to nominal data. Note: do not be put off by the fact that there are numerical data in the table, even though these variables are classified as 'non-numerical'. With any category, the number of occurrences of a particular value can be counted and so these numbers in the table cells are merely counts, rather than measures. Contrast this with numerical measures, where each item of data is itself a number. With non-numerical variables, the numbers only appear as a summary of the entire data set, as a result of finding the frequencies of each category.

3.2.2 Good Table Layout

Most of Ehrenberg's principles are in evidence here.

1. The row and column averages have been included. The column average refers to the mean per quarter and the row average is the mean population of all the cities. (Note: Q1, Q2, Q3 do *not* refer to the quartiles, merely the first three quarters of the year.)

2. The rows have been ordered by population size. Note how this feature provides additional information to the well-trained eye. As you can see, the ordering by population correlates well with the output data of the table, with the exception of Sheffield, and Luton, which have slightly lower outputs than their position in the table would suggest. In other words, in these cities, sales of product X are slightly lower than might be predicted given the size of their populations.

3. There is no clear indication as to whether the rows or the columns are to be compared, so this aspect has not been changed. At present, the data have been organised to facilitate the comparison of the quarters. If you need to compare the cities, then interchange the rows and columns.

4. The data have been rounded to two significant figures.

5. The layout has been improved with the use of spaces and lines.

6. No verbal summary has been included here, other than the heading which draws attention to a different criterion for ordering than the arbitrary alphabetical order of the first table.

3.3.1 Fire the Firefighters?

(a) You are likely to find that the number of fires has grown steadily with the number of fire engines over the period.

(b) One possible response would be to conclude that the increase in the number of fire engines has caused the increase in fires. However, this would be a foolish conclusion. A more likely explanation is to point to the fact that Birmingham's population has more than trebled over that period; since 1950, Birmingham's population has grown from about 325 000 to over 1 million today. A larger city can expect more fires and also will require a larger fire service with more fire engines. There may indeed be a cause and effect relationship here, but it is likely to be the increase in the number of fires (due to the increase in the size of Birmingham) that has caused the growth in the number of fire engines, rather than the other way around.

3.3.2 The Four-card Problem

Many people's first response is to choose A and 3. Was that your initial response? Well, you are half right (this is trickier than it may first appear!).

Consider each card in turn and evaluate the wisdom of turning it over.

A: It *would* be sensible to turn this card over, in order to test the rule. If there is not a 3 on the opposite face, the rule is contravened.

D: There would be no advantage in turning this card over as it does not test the rule.

3: If you thought that you were testing the rule by checking whether there was an 'A' on the reverse side, think again! This would be attempting to test the rule in reverse, namely that 'any card with a '3' on one face has an 'A' on the other'. Note that it does not contravene the rule to have a card with, say, 'B' on one face and '3' on the other. It is only required by the rule that cards with 'A' on one face that must have a '3' on the other'. So turning over this card does not test the rule – if there is an A on the other side it confirms the rule, but if you should get some different letter on the other side it tells you nothing about the rule.

7: Surprisingly for many people, you *should* turn this card over in order to test the rule. Should it turn out that there was an 'A' on the other side of this card, the rule would be contravened.

3.3.3 On the Mend

Here are a number of alternative explanations for a patient's return to rude health.

- Many patients simply get better anyway (time is a great healer).
- Some patients may be taking other forms of treatment and these may be what are really helping them.
- Sometimes patients are embarrassed to report to the doctor that their treatment did not work and report improvement where none has occurred.

3.3.4 Down with Milk

The experts failed to note that people in England in the 1930s were economically much better off than people in Japan and so tended to live much longer (at that time, the average English woman had 12 years greater life expectation than her female counterpart in Japan). Old age brings with it a much greater incidence of certain diseases such as cancer. So, to put it in stark terms, many of the Japanese women were dead of other causes before cancer could kill them.

3.3.5 Blaming the Parents

An alternative explanation might be that once a young person embarks on a life of drug dependency, the parents get very emotionally upset. It would not be surprising if this created strains in their relationship with their child, which would be in evidence by the time they visited the psychoanalyst. As with the fire engine example in Task 3.3.1, there may well be a cause and effect relationship here, but which is cause and which effect is not so clear.

3.3.6 Israeli Pilots

An alternative accounting for these findings can be explained by the notion of 'regression to the mean', which is addressed in Section 3.4.

3.4.1 Meanings of Regression

One way of thinking about this question is to consider each point on the scatter plot as representing all the variety and richness of the variation of individuals. Now imagine the trend line drawn in as a straight line passing among the points. This line represents a primitive underlying relationship between height and weight in general. Now, imagine moving each point vertically up or down until it meets this underlying regression line – this can be thought of as returning each point to its primitive state, which is akin to the lay definition of the word.

3.4.2 Reasons for Claiming Spurious Correlation

Alternative stories for cause and effect relationships include the following:

- The nature of the cause and effect may be the reverse of what is claimed (for example, the number of fires and the number of fire engines).
- Often there is a third controlling variable – such as general economic well-being *over time* – that affects both variables in a similar way. For example, it is easy to show that,

over the past 40 years, there is a strong statistical correlation between national spending on armaments and the average levels of pocket money given to 10-year-old girls.

- In situations where there is a strong random element, apparent patterns appear when short-term successes are followed by a decline in performance. While this may be due to a cause and effect relationship, it could simply be explained by a 'regression to the mean'.

3.5.1 Words

Here are some of the key terms used in the chapter: bi-variate, double comparative, response and explanatory variables, dependent and independent variables, attributes and variables, two-way tables, cause and effect, regression, regression to the mean, correlation, spurious correlation.

One task to help two or more learners become more confident with the use of some of these terms is to ask them to write each one on a card and then try to form a definition of the word on the other side. The cards are then shuffled and placed on the table, definition side up. Learners try to deduce what words are being defined from the definitions on display. This could lead into a discussion of how the definitions might be improved.

3.5.3 Contexts

Spurious correlation

This anecdote may help learners get to grips with this important idea.

In parts of Europe, there is a strong positive correlation between the number of nesting storks in a particular conurbation and the size of the conurbation (hamlet, village, town, and so on). One possible explanation for this statistical association is that the storks are bringing the babies – well, that is possible, but you should look for other explanations. A more likely one is that the bigger the conurbation, the more people, the more babies, the more houses (with chimneys) and hence the more nesting storks (which like nesting in chimneys). So, in a sense, it is the babies who are bringing the storks, rather than the other way around.

3.5.4 Misconceptions

In Task 3.3.2, an easy mistake was to interpret the rule as applying in both directions (this misconception leads to the answer that turning over the 3 tested the rule). It may help learners to deal with this sort of problem if they were to separate out the 'if' and the 'then' parts of the statement. Below are two fallacious examples to help them see the difference.

(a) Here the 'if' and 'then' parts have been reversed.
   If I am a goat, then I am a hoofed creature.
   I am a hoofed creature.
   Therefore, I am a goat.
(b) Here the (false) deduction is a result of a failure to accept the 'if' part as being true.
   If I am in Rome, then I am in Italy.
   I am not in Rome.
   Therefore, I am not in Italy.

3.5.5 Techniques

Task 3.2.2 provided some guiding principles of good table layout and you were then shown 'before' and 'after' versions of a table of data based on the application of these principles. An alternative approach would have been to provide the two versions of the table and let you try to deduce the principles for yourself. Either of these approaches could be used or adapted for your learners when teaching a topic that includes a set of general principles.

3.5.6 Ownership

- Encourage statistical investigations. These should be organised around genuine concerns and questions posed by the learners. Encourage them to follow such investigations through to the I stage, so that they can test out their solutions against reality and also experience for themselves the power of statistical ideas to solve problems

- Encourage them to offer critiques of the statistical work of others (classmates as well as in wider society, such as politicians, advertisers and the media), so that they develop critical awareness and statistical survival skills in the real world. This will involve an expectation that, in classroom situations, they should provide regular feedback sessions in which learners are able to state opinions and findings confidently in a friendly but sceptical collegial atmosphere, one where every statement is seen as a conjecture.

- Encourage learners to think about and discuss the big ideas of statistics, rather than an overemphasis on developing skill and technique for their own sake.

4.1.1 Words of Chance

(a) Most people would agree that the order is: improbable, fifty-fifty, likely, certain.

(b) Here are some additional terms used to describe likelihood (they have been sorted in order by one reader, but there is no unambiguously correct answer to this question).

Never in a million years, in your dreams, once in a blue moon, not in a month of Sundays, highly improbable, a long shot, very unlikely, unlikely, possible, an even chance, on the balance of probabilities, probable, highly likely, beyond all reasonable doubt, a dead cert.

(c) Terms for which there is broad agreement are 'impossible', 'fifty-fifty' and 'certain', but the 'correct' ordering for the other terms is a subject for debate. One word that causes particular problems is 'possible'.

(d) Because these words or phrases can (in theory) be ordered, they represent an ordinal scale of measure.

(e) 'A long shot': from the lack of success to be expected when firing at a distant target. 'Once in a blue moon': here are two plausible derivations for this phrase. One has to do with the rare occurrence of dust particles and certain atmospheric conditions that make the moon appear blue. The other has to do with the appearance of two full moons in the same month, which also occurs infrequently. What

both explanations share is a description of events that are rare, namely with a low probability of occurrence.

4.1.2 From Words to Numbers

(c) Most people find a clustering around the three points, 0, 0.5 and 1. The reason is, possibly, that these levels of uncertainty (impossible, equally likely and certain) represent interesting or important states in our lives that people like to talk about and therefore for which a range of vocabulary has evolved.

(d) Another pattern that you may have noticed is the effect of the words 'very' or highly', which is to push the adjectives to which they are attached to a more extreme position on the probability line. For example, while 'likely' is to the right of centre on the probability line, 'highly likely' is further to the right. Similarly, while 'doubtful' is to the left of centre on the probability line, 'very doubtful' is further to the left.

4.1.3 An 'Odds' Way of Thinking

(a) The sum of these eight 'probabilities' is:

$$11/19 + 1/6 + 1/6 + 1/11 + 1/51 + 1/101 + 1/251 + 1/251 = 1.041.$$

However, each individual probability does not represent the probability of that player winning the competition, for the following reason. Since eight probabilities are mutually exclusive (that is, non-overlapping) and represent the only possible outcomes, they should actually add to 1. To adjust for this factor, each probability should be divided by 1.041, thereby ensuring that they add to 1.

(b) An advantage of using odds in teaching about probability is that these are measures of likelihood used in the real world that learners are likely to have heard of. The downside is that, particularly with younger learners, the association with gambling may not be considered appropriate by some teachers and parents.

4.1.4 Odds and Probability

No; this is an unfortunate difference in terminologies. High probabilities are associated with short (or small) odds and low probabilities with long or (high) odds.

4.2.1 Jannie and Peter

(a) This brief description of Jannie slightly favours an interest in Classical Studies compared with English. However, in the UK, there are roughly 400 teachers of Classical Studies whereas there are about 40 000 teachers of English. Given, therefore, that there are roughly 100 English teachers for every Classical Studies teacher in the UK, Jannie is much more likely to be one of the former, even if she has particular interests in classicism.

(b) Comparing the first two options, more people play tennis than play in a successful rock band, so option 2 is more likely than option 1. Option 3 is the least likely since it is a subset of the other two options.

(c) This question is similar in type to part (b). All the words ending in '-ing' are a subset of words with 'n' as the penultimate letter. If you are not convinced, think of some examples (ant, doing, fine, sing, …). Therefore the second option must be the more common.

4.2.2 Red Star Births

Although it is tempting to think that both are the same (because the proportions of female births are the equal), the answer is actually the smaller hospital. In Chapter 12, you will be guided in how to investigate these sorts of questions.

4.2.3 Shared Birthdays

(a) If there were 366 people, allowing for a leap year birth on the 29 February, there is the (albeit unlikely) possibility that everyone had a different birthday. So, to be certain that at least two people share a birthday, the answer is 367.

(b) It turns out that the probability of getting at least one shared birthday is roughly 0.71 (assuming uniformity of shared birthdays across the year). For most people, this is a surprising result. In fact, the break-even group size at which there is roughly a 50% chance of getting at least one shared birthday is 23 (with a probability of 0.507). The complication here is that there are many possible pairings of people in the room, so there are lots of opportunities to score a shared day. These ideas are explored in more detail in Chapters 8 and 12.

4.2.4 The Monty Hall Dilemma

Intuition might suggest that it makes no difference whether to 'stick' or 'switch', since all three doors were equally likely at the outset and this has not changed. However, this logic is invalid. You will revisit this problem in Chapter 12, with the aid of computer simulations. Note that the setting of the problem is similar to the routine on the television game show *Let's Make a Deal*, hosted by Canadian Monty Hall – hence the choice of name. This problem is also discussed in the striking book *The Curious Incident of the Dog in the Night-Time* by Mark Haddon (2002, pp. 62–5).

4.3.1 Give Me Credit!

(a) Other examples include spiritual intervention, the force of karma, and so on.

(b) Terry is a successful software designer and a big fan of Arsenal football club. He now refuses to let his girlfriend Anna come with him to a game because he says that she is a jinx – he claims that they always lose when she comes to a game. Throughout history, women have been blamed (and in many cases put to death) for natural disasters such as drought, earthquakes, illness, and so on.

Many golfers change their putter more often than seems necessary because they 'just didn't get on with it'.

4.3.3 Virtuous Superstitions

Here is a superstition for thrift: 'See a pin (or penny) and pick it up, all the day you'll have good luck'.

This one possibly promotes good hygiene: 'Never put new shoes on the table'.

These superstitions vary in different parts of the country. For example, in parts of Shropshire 'shoes on the table' are thought to bring about a quarrel in the household. In other regions, shoes on the table are considered to be a harbinger of death.

There is still a great deal of superstition in the theatre. Whistling in the theatre is taboo for the good reason that, traditionally, the job of operating the theatre's flying system backstage was given to sailors who used whistles to convey instructions to each other. A whistle in the wrong place and you could end up with a lighting gantry on your head. Another theatrical example is that it is considered bad luck to refer to Shakespeare's 'Scottish play' by its real name, *Macbeth*. To wish a performer 'Good luck', one says, 'Break a leg'. (It was once common for people to believe in sprites who enjoyed wreaking havoc. If the sprites heard you ask for something, they would try to make the opposite happen. Telling someone to 'break a leg' is a sort of reverse psychology in an attempt to outsmart the sprites.)

4.3.4 Patterns of Belief

Overall, there is not much difference between male and female beliefs among the top four listed supernatural phenomena, but there are substantial differences among the less widespread beliefs, with females being more sceptical than males. There is not much difference between the two age groups, with the exception of 'witchcraft' and 'clairvoyance', where the older respondents showed greater levels of belief. The high degree of belief in angels may be linked to the fact that levels of religious belief were high in 1988 among young people in the USA. Note that the results of this survey are specific to a particular time, place and age group. It is likely that different findings would result if such a survey were carried out in the UK today.

4.4.1 Is it True?

(a) The obvious approach in each case is to choose a fair die and roll it many times (in other words, taking an empirical approach). For example, with the second claim, roll it gently and then hard to see if the manner of rolling makes a difference. In the third case, define a 'desired outcome' (say, getting 'four') and roll it many times, blown and unblown.

When the data have been collected, a decision must be made as to whether one outcome has come up more that the other(s). Of course, this decision is complicated by the fact that, due to natural variation, some differences are inevitable. Another issue here is how many times should dice be rolled and coins tossed in order to convince someone that any underlying patterns are real and not simply a result of random variation. This question is touched upon again in Chapters 12 and 14.

(b) It may be that some of these beliefs are not as surprising as you might think. For example, the belief that a 'six' is hard to get may result from the fact that many board games require a 'six' to start. A player, therefore, is not attending to the fact of six separate outcomes (1, 2, 3, 4, 5 and 6) but just to two relevant outcomes, 'six' and 'not six'. In the context of the game, a 'six' is clearly harder to get than a 'not six' (in fact, a 'not six' is five times as likely an outcome).

4.4.2 The Lottery *is* Biased

It is true that this cannot be proved – to some extent, one must take on faith that the random number generator used to produce lottery numbers is free from bias. However, the key question to ask is whether this would be a surprising result if there were no bias in the selection of the balls. To take a simpler example, the six faces of a fair die are equally likely to crop up, but roll it 30 times and you will observe a great unevenness in the frequency of each outcome. The effects of random variation are often larger than most people expect. This issue comes up again in Chapter 12, which describes how these sorts of experiments can be simulated quickly and visually using a computer or a graphics calculator.

4.5.1 Words

A group of 28 teachers attending an Open University summer school carried out this task, based on quantifying meaning for the words 'possible' and 'probable'. For this particular group of teachers, the means for these words were 0.35 and 0.8 respectively, while the ranges were 0.7 and 0.25 respectively. It is clear from the large differences in the ranges that the word 'possible' is rather loosely defined compared to the word 'probable'.

4.5.2 Visualising

In Task 4.2.1(c), you were asked whether there were more English words ending in '-ing' or words with 'n' as the penultimate letter. A possible exercise designed to exploit imagery would be to place a smaller ring (representing English words ending in '-ing') inside a larger one (representing words with 'n' as the penultimate letter). Each learner could then write suitable words on a card and place them appropriately, as in Figure C4.1.

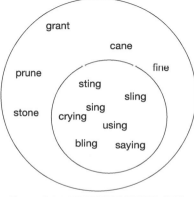

Figure C4.1 **VISUALISING NESTED SETS**

4.5.5 Techniques

Another investigation where the outcomes are not all equally likely and may not be easily predictable in advance is for learners to roll a pair of dice and record the frequencies of the sums of the possible dice scores (2, 3, 4, ..., 12).

5.1.1 Interrogating the Map

(a) The six variables are:

- the size of the army, which is written in various places at an angle alongside the flow of troops;

- the army's location – this counts as *two* variables, as the troop flow is shown in two dimensions;

- the direction of the movement of soldiers;

- temperature, which is shown at the bottom of the chart, linked to the return journey;

- date, which is written at key points on the temperature chart. For example, the final date entry, $^-26^\circ$ le 7 X^{bre}, is shown on the extreme left of the temperature chart. It means that on December 7, the temperature was $^-26^\circ$ F.

(b) For most people, the main impact of this chart is that 422 000 men set out and only 10 000 returned – a loss of over 400 000 lives.

(c) It would be misleading to suggest that his army froze to death. In fact, the bulk of the losses (over 300 000 men) were incurred on the outward journey – temperatures are not recorded for the outward journey, but since this was during the summer months, it is clear that these men did not freeze to death.

5.1.2 Cholera Patterns

John Snow could see a clustering around the Broad Street pump (located on the map just to the right of the letter 'D' in the word 'BROAD'), showing that this pump was almost certainly a major source of contamination. He immediately ordered the handle of this pump to be removed, thereby ending an epidemic that had cost more than 500 lives.

5.2.2 Crusty Pie

(c) A better graphic to use here would be a bar chart. Alternatively, the data could be plotted as a scatter plot – in this instance, with 'time' as the 'x' variable, adjacent points could be justifiably joined to form a line graph.

5.2.3 Bar Chart to the Rescue

An important feature of any bar chart is that there should be gaps separating the bars (as is the case in Figure C5.1). This emphasises that the data are discrete in nature; this might be because they are either categorical data, which are always discrete, or discrete numerical data, as is the case here.

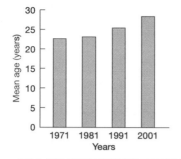

Figure C5.1 **BAR CHART SHOWING FEMALE AGE OF FIRST MARRIAGE (1971–2001)**

Source: *Social Trends* 34 (2004 Edition, Table 2.12)

5.3.3 Marking the Intervals

An assumption needs to be made about what it means to be, say, 24 years of age. From the context, this can be assumed to refer to the interval 24 – 24.999… years. In other words, a person is 24 from the first moment of their twenty-fourth birthday until the last moment before their twenty-fifth birthday. Based on this definition of age, the boundaries of the intervals are at 16, 25, 35, 45, and so on.

A second assumption concerns where the final interval ends. Although people do live beyond the age of 100, not very many live beyond the age of 95. A choice needs to be made, therefore, about where to place the upper boundary and 95 seems to be a reasonable stopping point (but whether you will feel the same when you reach this age is another matter!).

Based on these assumptions, the interval boundaries will look like this:

```
0     16  25   35   45   55   65   75        95
|     |   |    |    |    |    |    |         |
0    10  20   30   40   50   60   70   80   90
```

5.3.5 Corrected Histogram

Column	Width	%age	Adjusted height
0–15	16	27	$(10/16) \times 27 \approx 17$
16–24	9	14	$(10/9 \times 14) \approx 16$
25–34	10	13	13
35–44	10	12	12
45–54	10	12	12
55–64	10	11	11
65–74	10	7	7
75–95	15	3	$(10/20) \times 3 = 1.5$

Figure C5.2 **CORRECTED HISTOGRAM BASED ON THE POPULATION DATA**

5.4.2 Summarising the Coxcomb

(a) It starts in April 1854, shown at the '9 o'clock' position. For the first three months, levels of mortality are small. From July, they started to rise (formal hostilities broke out in September 1854), reaching a peak in January 1855. Deaths due to battle (shown at the centre of the diagram) represent a relatively small proportion of all deaths during this period, the bulk being due to 'non-battle' causes – that is, infections.

5.4.3 Investigating the Coxcomb

The larger (January) wedge has a radius roughly 2.5 times greater than that for the previous October. However, since area is a two-dimensional measure, this factor must be squared in order to compare the areas of the wedges. (If you are not convinced about this, compare the area of a circle of radius 1 cm with a circle of radius twice as large.) Squaring 2.5 gives an area factor of just over six, thereby confirming the claim.

5.5.1 Words

(a) Here are some of the key terms used in the chapter: coxcomb (or polar-area diagram), dot map, time series, categorical data, numerical data, pie chart, bar chart, histogram, interval, boundary, proportional.

(b) It may be appropriate to point out where the names for these different graphics came from. For example, some young children may have a limited experience of pies that are circular in shape. They may not all have realised that a pie chart is so named because it looks like a pie with the various slices corresponding to the different categories.

Similarly, a time series graph plots a *series* of points over *time*.

The term *histogram* is derived from the Greek word *histos* meaning a web.

5.5.2 People Graphs

To create a pie chart, the four rows can be joined together into a long line and then formed into a circle. At the points where different hair colours meet, these learners are given a piece of string which they hold at one end, the other end being connected to a common point at the centre of the circle. Hey presto – a people pie chart.

If you can get hold of a digital camera, these 'people graphs' can be photographed from above (the teacher may need to stand on the desk) and then displayed on a television or computer monitor. Not only will the personal nature of these graphs be motivating, but they should provide a useful focus of discussion about the nature of the graphs (for example, 'the reason for maintaining gaps between adjacent bars in a bar chart').

5.5.3 A Passion for Pie Charts

(a) The sectors could depict *albums* or *amount of recorded time*. This choice of category could make a difference for a learner who liked classical music with fewer but longer tracks on each album.

(b) Motivating contexts will often arise from children's personal interests or hobbies. They might be asked to collect their own data and use a graphic to represent it clearly for others.

(c) There are, of course, many examples of pie charts and bar charts in newspapers and on television and these can often provide interesting contexts for older learners. It is well worth making your own collection of such 'recent and relevant' examples. You could also ask learners to bring in their own examples and ask individuals to summarise what main points the various graphics are conveying.

5.5.5 Getting it Wrong

An example of a common mistake is to use an inappropriate form of representation for the data type. For example, learners will sometimes attempt to use a pie chart with interval or ratio data or, perhaps, to use a pie chart when the sum of the categories does not amount to a meaningful or coherent whole. It is easy (too easy, perhaps) to create inappropriate graphs on a computer. The teacher could provide a range of inappropriate graphs and ask learners to spot the deliberate mistakes.

Another common mistake is to use pie charts in situations where the data are not mutually exclusive. For example, some people may have more than one pet (say, a cat and a dog) and in this situation it is unclear whether or not the complete pie represents the total number of pets *owned*.

5.5.6 Made by Hand

To draw a *pie chart* by hand, a learner must be able to:

- calculate the angles of each 'slice';
- use a pair of compasses to draw the circle;
- use a protractor to construct the angles at the centre of the circle.

Issues of gains and losses with using computers and calculators are discussed in Chapters 9–12.

6.1.1 Creating a Bad Impression

(a) Many people think that roughly half of the boxes have been marked with an 'X'. In fact, the actual proportion is 37%.

(b) The most socially unacceptable crimes have been placed at the top and bottom of the chart, which is where most people will look. Crimes buried in the middle, such as 'tax evasion' will go largely unnoticed.

(c) Notice the large thick font used to create each 'X' – they really dominate the graphic and appear to shout, 'These are bad men!' In the event, the jury seemed to think so and Gotti and his co-defendants stood to applaud the jury as they left the courtroom after delivering their 'Not guilty' verdicts.

6.1.2 Don't Blame the Drink

You may be surprised to learn that this glass is actually half full.

6.2.1 Creating a Box with Whiskers

Here is a possible set of instructions.

The number line below covers the range of possible marks, from 0 to 100. As you can see, above the line are two short vertical lines corresponding to the positions of the Min and Max values.

(a) Draw two further vertical lines corresponding to the positions of Q1 and Q3. Draw these lines slightly longer than the Min and Max lines, but centred on the same vertical position as them.

(b) By drawing two horizontal lines joining the Q1 and Q3 lines, create a horizontal box. This is the *box* part of the box-and-whisker diagram.

(c) Draw a horizontal line joining the mid-point of the Min line to the mid-point of the Q1 line. Draw another horizontal line joining the mid-point of the Max line to the mid point of the Q3 line. These are the two *whiskers*.

(d) Draw inside the 'box' a vertical line corresponding to the position of the median, Med.

(e) Finally, write on the diagram immediately below the five vertical lines their numerical values.

You have now completed the box-and-whisker diagram, which should look like this.

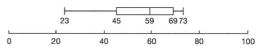

6.2.2 The Long and the Short of a Box Plot

The second statement is the valid one, not the first. Bear in mind that the box plot breaks the data into quarters with (roughly) the same number of data items in each quarter interval. Shorter intervals will therefore be more densely packed with data items than longer intervals.

6.2.3 Box Plots Compared

(a) A problem with this measure is that it considers only speed and not accuracy. With traditional tests of typing speed, a limit is normally set on the number of typing mistakes allowed. Should a similar condition apply here? Learners might like to explore the advantages and disadvantages of doing this and come up with a sensible suggestion.

There may be problems ensuring accurate measurement of the times. One solution might be to start a stopwatch at the word, 'Go', and stop the watch when the phone receiving the message starts to signal, 'Message received'. (Note: this assumes that the processing time for receiving messages is the same for all mobile phones. This is something that learners may need to check.)

(b) Your sketches should look something like this:

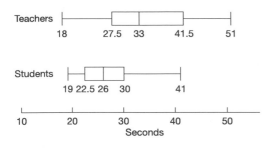

6.3.1 Creating a Stem-and-leaf Diagram

Additional comments are included in the text following the task.

Your summary may have looked something like this.

Here are the stages involved in creating a stem-and-leaf diagram (based on the learner times above).

(a) Sort the data by size into ascending order – this has already been done here. Note that data sorting is easy to do using a graphics calculator or computer.

(b) You will now arrange all the items in a way that will look like leaves attached to a plant. The 'tens' part of these numbers will form the stem of the plant and so these are arranged in a vertical line from 0 to, say, 5. Place the 0 at the top and the 5 at the bottom. In order to separate the tens from the units, draw vertical lines to the right of each stem value.

(c) Go through each data value in turn, select its 'units' part and place this alongside its corresponding 'tens' digit. For example, the first value, 19, is represented as shown here, with the 9 set alongside the 1 on the stem.

(d) To complete the stem plot, write a 'key' that explains what the stem and the leaves refer to. For example, you could write 'stem = tens, leaves = units' or '1|9 means 19'.

```
0|
1|9
2|
3|
4|
5|
```

Now, complete the stem plot.

6.3.2 Deeper Questions about a Stem Plot

(a) The main advantage is that you can point to particular values in the data set and see their place in relation to the other values. The disadvantage of a stem plot is that it is not suitable for very large data sets of, say, 500 or more.

(b) Like these other two representations, a stem plot gives a quick visual picture of the shape of the distribution – a very important feature of a stem plot that learners will need to be encouraged to explore.

(c) It is important that the values on each branch are ordered, because this ensures that all the values are in order, thereby making it possible to pick out key values such as the median, minimum and maximum values (see Task 6.3.3).

(d) One drawback of using this ordering is that it contradicts the convention that values on a vertical axis increase going upwards. One benefit is that, if a stem plot were rotated 90° anti-clockwise, it would look very like a conventional block graph or histogram.

6.3.3 Interpreting the Stem Plot

You can see at a glance that the two extreme values are 19 (Min) and 41 (Max). As there are 12 values, the median is half way between the sixth and seventh values. These are easily identified (by counting from either extreme) as 25 and 27, so the median is 26.

6.4.1 Choosing the Right Question

Two possible questions are:

'Which of these authors makes greatest use of direct speech?'

'Which of these authors writes the simplest sentences?'

6.4.2 Selecting the Sentences

One possibility would be to choose the first 30 sentences from each book. However, this has the disadvantage that they may be untypical. Learners need to be alert to the possibility of confounding factors such as the proportion of text that is direct speech. In general, sentences based on direct speech tend to be shorter than general narrative and the opening sentences may contain less direct speech than the rest of the book. For comparison among authors, it might be fairer to concentrate either on direct speech or on narrative or a similar mix of both in the samples chosen.

Another choice would be to select the sentences at random. For example, you could close your eyes, open a page at random and then stick in a pin. Whichever sentence the pin marked would be the sentence to measure. There is, however, a problem with this approach. Long sentences will take up more space on the page than short sentences, so the pin approach is biased in favour of selecting longer sentences.

A third possibility is to use the second method above, but rather than using a pin to choose a particular sentence on the page, take instead, say, the third sentence on that page. You could, of course, randomise the sentence number more formally by using a random number generator, but this adds to the time and effort involved.

6.4.3 Visualising the Data

An obvious tool here would be to use box plots. Below are the relevant box plots for these data (rounded to the nearest whole number).

Although a box plot is a good choice here, learners should be aware that the value of 136 in the Austen data set is an *outlier*. Tukey's criterion for an outlier is that the maximum length of a whisker should be 1.5 times the interquartile range. Values outside these limits (which this value certainly is)

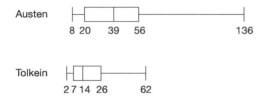

Austen

8 20 39 56   136

Tolkein

2 7 14 26   62

should be treated as outliers. (As an aside, you may be wondering why Tukey chose 1.5 here. When asked by Paul Velleman why he chose 1.5, Tukey replied, 'Because 1 is too small and 2 is too large'.)

6.4.4 Interpreting the Box Plots

(a) The box plots show that Jane Austen's sentences, as measured by the number of syllables, are considerably longer than Tolkien's. This is true for all of the five summary measures. However, the Max value of Austen of 136 has quite a strong influence on one's overall impression. In fact, her second longest sentence had only 79 syllables and, had that been the Max value on the Austen box plot, you might not have come away with the same sense that her sentences were so very much longer than Tolkien's.

(b) There are many possible alternative measures – for example, number of letters per sentence, degree of difficulty of language used, and so on.

(c) The relevant summaries for Rowling are:

Mean = 36.6, Range = 70, IQR = 17.5, Min = 10, Q1 = 26, Median = 32.5, Q3 = 43.5, Max = 80.

6.5.1 The Long and the Short of it

The terms 'box-and-whisker diagram' and 'stem-and-leaf diagram' are longer but more descriptive titles than their shorter counterparts, 'box plot' and 'stem plot' respectively. When learners are first exposed to these types of representation, the longer terms may help them to clarify in their minds the component parts (box, whiskers, stem, leaves, and so on.). As they become more familiar and confident with using them, learners may find the shorter terms to be neater and quicker to use.

6.5.2 People Plots

Start the exercise by drawing a very long number scale the full length of the floor (this can be done using tape).

To enact the box plot, learners stand in line on one side of the number scale in positions corresponding to their times, from smallest to largest. Then the five summary measures are calculated and those learners corresponding to Min, Q1, Med, Q3 and Max are asked to step to the other side of the number scale. (Note that, depending on the number of learners, it may be the mean of two learners' times that correspond to a particular summary value, in which case, both learners step out.) The box and whiskers are then created around these learners, using white tape.

To enact the stem plot, each person writes the units digit of their time (they must also remember the tens digit of their time) on a blank playing card. A stem, corresponding to the tens digits, is created on the floor and each learner is asked to lay their card alongside the appropriate branch of the stem. The cards should all be of equal size and equally spaced (a discussion point for later). They have now formed an 'unsorted' stem plot. Each branch can then be sorted in order of size to create the final 'sorted' stem plot.

6.5.3 Sporty Plots

Here are some examples where either back-to-back stem plots or a pair of box plots could be used:

- the runs scored by the batsmen in the England and Australian cricket teams in a one-day series;
- the number of supporters present at Manchester United home matches in the 1994–95 and the 2004–05 seasons;
- the US and European golf scores in the Ryder cup competition;
- two athletes' times over their previous 20 races.

6.5.4 Root Question

One example could be: 'Might a difference of this magnitude have been caused by chance alone?'

6.5.5 Symmetrical Box Plots

(a) Here, it is likely that the learner has a misconception concerning the median. Perhaps they believe that the median, being the 'middle value', is halfway between the minimum and maximum. So in this case, since the minimum is 23 and the maximum is 73, half-way between them is 48. Based on a similar misconception, the lower quartile has been marked a quarter of the way along at 35.5 and the upper quartile three quarters of the way along at 60.5.

6.5.6 Comparing Charts of Comparison

Below are some factors: you may well have thought of others:

- some are much easier than others to draw using a computer/calculator;
- some are much easier than others for the reader to interpret;
- a box plot is very good for showing bunching of the data;
- a back-to-back stem plot can only be used to compare two data sets: with box plots, you could compare many;
- stem plots, box plots and histograms can only be used with numerical data;
- pie charts are not good for showing numerical data;
- histograms are good for displaying and comparing grouped data;
- a stem plot retains all the detail of the original data set (unless you use rounding as in Task 6.3.5), whereas with a box plot the actual values are lost.

When learners are engaged in statistical activity that involves the use of graphs, it is easy for them to get so caught up in the mechanics of drawing or interpreting a chart that they fail to see the bigger picture. Once they have acquired a basic competence with creating a range of charts, deciding for themselves which representation to use in a particular circumstance is a considerably higher-order skill. A task such as this may be a good way of helping them to stand back and see the bigger picture.

7.1.1 Which Variables?

The graphing labels are as shown in Table C7.1.

TABLE C7.1 Graphing labels

(a) Foot length/height
(b) Gender/height
(c) Head circumference/height
(d) Vertical reach/height

7.1.2 Outliers

These two points stand out from the rest in graph (a) (showing foot length against height). These foot lengths of 15 cm and 18 cm seem much too low. In particular, the foot length of 15 cm is of a boy whose height is 155 cm (you can check this from the original table) and it is possible that this was a transcription error, where the 'correct' measurement was 25 cm.

Remove these two points (cover them with your hand) and look at the pattern in the remaining 18 points. They now show a clear pattern suggesting a strong relationship between foot length and height.

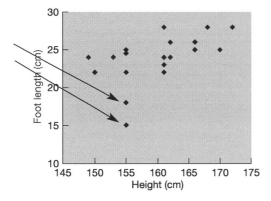

Other possible outliers are the reading of 45 cm for the head circumference of the tenth learner in the table and 189 cm for the vertical reach of this same learner (whose height is 170 cm).

7.2.6 Deviations from the Mean

An important and unique property of the mean is that it is the one point for which the sum of the deviations is zero. Put another way, the sum of (the absolute values of) all the deviations below the mean equals the sum of the deviations above the mean.

7.2.7 From 2D Back to 1

This is an example of a useful mathematical strategy known as 'stressing and ignoring'. By ignoring the information on the graph about vertical height and placing them on the same horizontal line, you create a dot plot showing rainfall. Now, ignore the information on the graph about horizontal position and place the points on the same vertical line, you have a dot plot showing hours of sunshine.

7.4.1 Spot the Cheat

(a) Here are the five 'cheats'.
  A: Break in vertical axis not shown. Note: there is an additional possibility for misleading the reader in this example – the viewing figures were taken from a particular evening in November 2004, which may or may not have been representative of other evenings' viewing figures (for example, if there is a pre-announced big event where, say, a main character is to be 'killed off', viewing figures tend to be much greater.)
  B: Selecting a small subset of the data only.
  C: Comparison graphics based on area distortion (drawn in proportion to height but the eye actually compared areas).
  D: Uneven scale on the vertical axis where the variable is continuous.
  E: Stretching and squashing axes and the effects on the steepness of the graph (simply changing from 'landscape' to 'portrait' has this effect).
(b) A sixth possible form of distortion is where the labels are absent or misleading. You may have thought of others of your own.

7.5.1 Simplifying

Here are some of the ideas that you might have included: (linear and non-linear) regression, linear model, prediction, a statistical relationship, a causal relationship, regression coefficients, coefficient of determination, coefficient of regression, confounding variables.

7.5.2 People Plots

Two measurements can be taken from each member of the class – for example, 'distance they live from school' and 'time taken to get to school'. Giant axes are set up for these two variables (out of doors is best for this) and marked and labelled. Each learner then stands in the correct (x, y) location corresponding to their score on these two variables. As with the previous examples of people graphs, a photograph taken from a top floor in an adjacent building will ensure that a clear record is made for later discussion.

7.5.3 Across the Curriculum

In a biology lesson, learners were investigating whether there was a link between an animal's gestation period and its expected longevity. From the internet, they managed to find suitable data, a small extract of which is given in Table C7.2.

TABLE C7.2 Animals' gestation period and longevity

Animal	Gestation or incubation in days (average)	Longevity, in years (record exceptions)
Bear	180–240	15–30 (47)
Cat	52–69 (63)	10–12 (26+)
Cow	280	9–12 (39)
Dog	53–71 (63)	10–12 (24)
Etc.		

Source: www.infoplease.com/ipa/A0005140.html

Learners needed to choose a particular representative value from each cell in the table. These values were plotted as a scatter plot and the learners concluded that there was a strong positive correlation between the two variables, gestation and longevity.

7.5.4 Correlation for a Younger Audience

It should be possible to explore ideas of the *strength* of a relationship without having to use the language of correlation or its measurement. For example, the notion of strong and weak relationships can be explored from everyday examples and by interpreting the patterns shown in scatter plots. Another useful topic for discussion would be whether changes in one of the variables *causes* the changes in the other. What other explanations might there be for this statistical connection?

7.5.5 Dot-to-dot

(a) It would be appropriate to join adjacent points on a scatter plot depicting a child's height over time, but would not be suitable for a scatter plot showing weight plotted against height for a group of 30 children.

(b) A sensible approach would be to choose some intermediate point between two adjacent points on the scatter plot and ask learners to explain what this point represented. In the 'child's height over time' example, it would be a reasonable estimate of how tall the child might be between the two known heights, but, in the second example, it would represent weight/height data from some unknown child who did not exist.

7.5.6 Preparation for Scatter Plots

In order to grasp what a relationship is, learners may find it helpful to be exposed to the idea of a double comparative statement (see Chapter 3). Then, in order to understand a scatter plot, they will need to have a secure grasp of plotting and interpreting co-ordinates and a general appreciation that a graph (line or curve) is a visual summary of the underlying relationship between the two variables recorded on the axes.

8.1.1 Trials and Events

As was mentioned in the text, in the context of probability, a *trial* (or experiment) refers to the carrying out of a task or

activity, the outcome of which cannot be predicted in advance. As you should see more clearly later in this section, an *event* refers to the outcome or combination of outcomes that result from an experiment or trial. For example, Table C8.1 lists some of the possible events that might result from five different trials.

TABLE C8.1 Trials and possible events

Trial	Possible event
Rolling a die	Getting an even score
Tossing two coins	Getting exactly one head
Selecting a Scrabble letter from a bag	Getting a 'vowel'
Choosing a playing card	Getting a 'heart'
Rolling two dice	Getting a sum of 3 or 7

8.1.2 Conditional Probability

(a) The proportions are: 31/100, 23/29, 69/100, 63/71.

(b) The two errors are the drunk person who tests negative (proportion = 6/29) and the sober person who tests positive (proportion = 8/71). These two types of errors are important in the field of statistical inference and are often referred to, respectively, as a Type 1 error (the probability of getting a false negative, or, in other words the probability of rejecting an initial hypothesis when it is true) and a Type 2 error (the probability of getting a false positive, or, in other words the probability of accepting an initial hypothesis when it is false).

8.1.3 Tree Diagrams

A typical solution will look something like this.

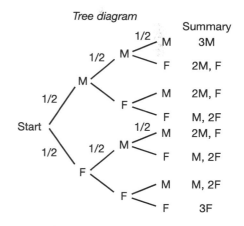

Tree diagram

Sample space

The eight outcomes in the sample space are: summarised in the diagram.

The probability of each outcome is

$1/2 \times 1/2 \times 1/2 = 1/8$.

The probabilities of getting MMM or FFF are each equal to 1/8. So the probability that all three children are not of the same sex = 1 − 2/8 = 6/8, or 3/4.

When determining a sample space, it is important for learners to consider *all* possible outcomes. They therefore need to be systematic and this is supported by using a visual representation such as a tree diagram. In particular, the tree diagram helps by:

- creating a systematic structure that emphasises the importance of considering, in turn, the first child, second child, third child, and so on;

- laying out the probabilities on the branches, thereby prompting learners to multiply these together in order to calculate the probability of each combined outcome;

- making it easy for the learner to group similar combined outcomes – for example, learners can see at a glance that there are three outcomes with exactly one boy and therefore the probability of getting exactly one boy is 3 × 1/8 = 3/8.

Note that it is not a requirement of a tree diagram to include the probabilities, but their inclusion can be very useful in helping learners to 'discover' the multiplication law by taking particular examples and following the calculations through. The multiplication law can be justified on the basis of what proportion of trials can be expected to go down each route at each node (this approach is the basis of the statements in Key Stage 4 of the English National Curriculum).

The limitations of the tree diagram occur when more than, say, three stages are involved, as the branching can then become complicated and confusing.

8.1.4 Venn Diagrams

You can think of the probability of A occurring as the ratio of the area of set A to the area of the complete sample space, S. The picture stresses this view. So, if you think of the entire sample space (inside the rectangle) as having an area of 1, the probability of A, P(A), corresponds to the area contained within circle A, the probability of B, P(B), corresponds to the area contained within circle B, and so on. The probability of A *and* B, P(A∩B) is the area of the intersection of A and B and the probability of A *or* B, P(A∪B) is the area of the union of A and B.

8.1.5 Picturing Mutual Exclusivity and Independence

A Venn diagram is useful for illustrating ideas of mutual exclusivity, because it shows, pictorially, the various events and outcomes that result *from a single trial or experiment*. A tree diagram is better suited to illustrating ideas of independence, because it is a good way of representing *two or more trials or experiments*.

8.2.4 Whose Egg?

This is certainly heavier than a typical robin's egg, but without information on the degree of variation that robins' eggs

exhibit, you cannot say whether this falls outside the typical range or not.

8.3.1 Two Spinners

(a) The correct answer is B: No.

Since the two spinners are independent, the combined probability of getting (Black, Black) is the product of the separate probabilities, which is 0.5 × 0.5 = 0.25. The problem could also be tackled pictorially using a tree diagram, as shown here. The diagram sets out the sample space in the form of the four equally likely outcomes, BB, BW, WB, and WW.

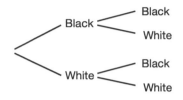

8.4.2 Applying Bruner's Modes to Other Problems

Peter – Rock band or tennis?

Exactly the same thinking that applied to Jannie can be applied to Peter's situation. The three categories are 'Interest in sport and guitar' (S&G), 'plays in a successful rock band' (RB) and 'is a member of a tennis club' (TC). These could be created using physical hoops (E mode) or diagrammatically (I mode).

As before, the key to the argument is the fact that there are many more people who are members of tennis clubs than people who play in a successful rock band and this factor outweighs anything else.

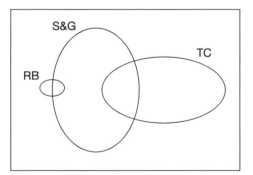

'-ing' words

Whereas the first two examples were supported by iconic forms of representation, learners struggling with the '-ing words' problem may find it helpful to use a visual approach initially. As with the previous example, pictures could be created using physical hoops (E mode) or diagrammatically (I mode).

As was shown in Task 4.5.2, a possible task is for learners to write down on separate pieces of paper a number of words ending either '-n-' or '-ing' and find a suitable way of classifying them using circles. Shown below is a likely representation that they will reach, once they become aware that '-ing' words are a subset of words ending '-n-'.

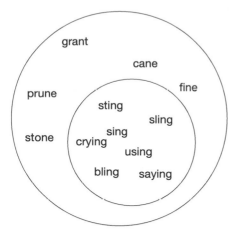

Hospital births

A useful mathematics education principle is, if the problem is too hard, then simplify it. In this case, the numbers 15 and 45 are too big to manage comfortably without the use of ICT, but the spirit of the question is about comparing a larger batch with a smaller one. The problem can be simplified to two hospitals whose average daily number of births are 5 and 20 respectively. The data can now be simulated using coins ('heads' for a girl and 'tails' for a boy). The 'E' and 'I' modes would be used here.

The Monty Hall dilemma

As with many conundrums of this type, you never fully understand the problem until you actually do it or, at the very least, 'walk through it' several times. Here is a possible scenario for setting up repeated 'plays' of the Monty Hall dilemma.

First, the class is divided into two groups, called the 'stickers' and the 'switchers'. The teacher then inverts three cups on a tray and marks them A, B and C, respectively and, out of sight of the learners, places a token underneath one of them. The cups are then shown and one learner is invited to select the cup for the whole class (that is, A, B or C). The teacher then lifts a (different) cup that does not contain the token. The 'stickers' then stick to the chosen cup while the 'switchers' switch their choice to the other cup. The token is then revealed and the participants score success or failure. This game is repeated, say, 20 times and the results compared between the 'stickers' and the 'switchers'.

An ensuing discussion will centre on questions such as 'under what circumstances will the 'stickers' win?' and 'under what circumstances will the 'switchers' win?'. Eventually, the penny may drop that stickers will only win if they chose the correct cup in the first place (a 1 in 3 chance) whereas the 'switchers' win if they chose an incorrect cup in the first place (a 2 in 3 chance).

9.1.1 Pros and Cons

Some potential benefits of ICT:

- technology can greatly ease the technical burden of calculation and graph-creation, so as to free up learners' attention for more important statistical questions, such as analysing data, drawing sensible conclusions, developing their problem-solving strategies or gaining insights into the big ideas of statistical thinking;

- as Peter Johnson-Wilder argues, learners can be shown how to interact with data in a dynamic way, so that general principles are revealed;

- as is reported by Biehler (2002), software tools encourage an exploratory approach to data analysis;

- sensible use of ICT can emphasise visual approaches to data handling, which often provide learners with particular insights;

- the majority of learners enjoy ICT-supported learning;

- making explicit the structure of well-designed software can help format learners' thinking about important concepts (see the sub-section in Section 9.2, entitled 'The formatting power of technology');

- ICT is widely used outside the classroom and learners will be expected to have some mastery of these tools when they leave school.

- it is a clear government requirement on schools to use ICT in the teaching of mathematics. Note that a major DfES study on the impact of ICT on educational attainment in England reported that 'ICT has been found to be positively associated with improvement in subject-based learning in several areas' (www.curriculumonline.gov.uk/WhyUseICTs/WhyteachwithICT.htm).

Some potential drawbacks of ICT:

- using a machine with which to manage data handling introduces a further step from the context. Learners may lose sight of what the problem was and where the data came from;

- where learners are interacting with a machine, this may (or may not) diminish the quality of learner–learner and learner–teacher human relationships;

- not everyone enjoys using technology and for some software packages (especially statistics packages and spreadsheets), there is a steep learning curve which may result in slow progress, particularly in the early stages;

- technology (especially computer-based technology) sometimes goes wrong through either machine or user error. When working with a class of learners, this can be disastrous if the problem cannot easily be resolved;

- there may be political or commercial vested interests behind the promotion of technology in education that cloud the issue of its positive benefits to learners.

9.1.2 Tools and Goals

Task

Tool	Carrying out a statistical investigation	Learning statistical concepts
Statistical packages	HD	DS
Spreadsheets	HD	DS
Web browsers	AD	
Java applets		HD and DS
Graphics calculators	HD	HD and DS

9.1.3 Educational or Professional Tools?

There is clearly no one correct answer to this question, but as a counter to Biehler's comment, here are three points questioning the wisdom of starting learners off with 'educational' tools:

- learners need mastery of tools that are currently in general use outside education and the sooner they start to learn to use these the better;
- commercial/professional tools are designed to help users solve problems, whereas sometimes educational tools can disempower learners, requiring them to do tasks that the software designer wants them to do rather than those that *they* want to do;
- educational tools are not always designed in a form that can be developed into a full professional tool.

9.2.1 Which Software?

(a) Here are some of the common applications, classified according to these three headings.

- specialist: Minitab (database);
- general: spreadsheets (e.g. Excel), graphics calculators;
- specifically geared to education: Tinkerplots, Fathom, Autograph.

(b) The strengths of specialist applications tend to be the weaknesses in general ones, and vice versa. For example, a specialist database such as Minitab will be very efficient at doing a relatively small number of very specific statistical tasks (particularly where data sets are huge), but will not be a tool that you would want to use for a wide range of purposes. A spreadsheet, on the other hand, may not be as effective as Minitab in certain situations, but it has a much wider applicability in statistics, in mathematics and right across and beyond the school curriculum. As a teacher, you need to weigh up the pros and cons of these factors, not just for the subject(s) that you teach, but also for the learners in terms of the potential benefits for their overall education and the relevance of the skills they will acquire outside the narrow confines of the mathematics classroom.

(c) It is hoped that the ICT skills that a learner learns in mathematics will be of benefit to him or her in other curricular areas, and vice versa. This raises the question of who should teach the basic skills of these computer applications and, indeed, who teaches the more specific ICT skills required for the statistics? Another issue here concerns the balance between choosing educational tools such as Autograph or a graphics calculator that might be of great benefit in the classroom, but which are little used outside school settings. Learners need to be equipped with ICT skills for life, not just for the mathematics classroom.

9.2.3 ICT Tools and the *PCAI* Framework

Table C9.1 below shows how four ICT tools (web browser, graphics calculator, spreadsheet and word processor) might be used at the various stages of a statistical investigation.

TABLE C9.1 Use of ICT tools

	ICT tool			
Stage	Web browser	Graphics calculator	Spreadsheet	Word processor
P				
C	Surfing the web for relevant data	Generating simulated data	Generating simulated data	
A		Summarising and graphing data	Summarising and graphing data	
I				Writing up the final report

9.3.1 Next-day Mail

(a) The spreadsheet below shows the data entered into cells A1:B20. Select cell B21, click the sigma icon, Σ, at the top of the screen and the sum of all letters arriving on time, 56, is displayed. Since there were 100 letters in all, this means that only 56% of the letters arrived the next day, a figure considerably less than the target figure of 92.5%.

	A	B
1	Glasgow to Plymouth	3
2	Plymouth to Glasgow	5
3	Cardiff to London	0
4	London to Cardiff	4
5	Belfast to Manchester	0
6	Manchester to Belfast	0
7	County Durham to Warwickshire	5
8	Warwickshire to County Durham	1
9	London to Buckinghamshire	4
10	Buckinghamshire to London	5
11	Cambridge to Southampton	5
12	Southampton to Cambridge	3
13	Tunbridge Wells to Orkney	5
14	Orkney to Tunbridge Wells	0
15	Jersey to Dumfries	0
16	Dumfries to Jersey	0
17	Stoke to Bristol	1
18	Bristol to Stoke	5
19	Cheltenham to Carlisle	5
20	Carlisle to Cheltenham	5
21	TOTAL	56

Figure C9.1 NEXT-DAY MAIL SPREADSHEET

(b) It seems likely that the speed of delivery is linked to the distance that the letter has to travel. Therefore, an interesting 'interrelating' question might be to explore the relationship between success rates and distance between the towns.

(c) One possible explanation could be that the particular journeys chosen in this survey were not typical of the sort of journeys that letters actually make. For example, 10% of these journeys were between Dumfries and Jersey, two regions of the UK that are very far apart and two locations between which relatively few letters are ever exchanged. In the real world of typical postal deliveries, a very large proportion has a local destination and indeed much of the UK mail never leaves London! This is an example where the sample used was not very representative of the wider population about which the generalisation has been made.

9.3.2 Laying Bare the Standard Deviation Calculation

There are two ways of calculating the standard deviation of a set of data, based on the following formulas:

$\sqrt{(\Sigma d^2/n)}$, where d stands for the deviations of each value (denoted as X) from the batch mean

and

$\sqrt{((\Sigma X)^2/n - (\Sigma X/n)^2)}$

Note that, algebraically, these two formulas are the same, but the choice of which to use will depend on context.

Computationally, the first form is more susceptible to rounding errors, because the subtraction step to calculate each difference takes place before squaring the differences between each value and the mean. Educationally, the first form is more attractive as it shows more clearly the standard deviation as root, mean, squared deviation. The attraction of the second form is that the component parts of the formula are familiar summaries that can easily be calculated from the raw data.

The spreadsheets in Figures C9.2(a) and C9.2(b) show the calculation based on the first of these formulas. Note that the second spreadsheet has been set to display formulas rather than values (this is one of the 'Windows' options in 'Preferences ...'.

	A	B	C	D
1	Calculating the mean and standard deviation			
2				
3		X (mm)	d	d^2
4		44	-12.15	147.6225
5		37	-19.15	366.7225
6		86	29.85	891.0225
7		74	17.85	318.6225
8		54	-2.15	4.6225
9		24	-32.15	1033.6225
10		37	-19.15	366.7225
11		69	12.85	165.1225
12		60	3.85	14.8225
13		47	-9.15	83.7225
14		51	-5.15	26.5225
15		82	25.85	668.2225
16		43	-13.15	172.9225
17		55	-1.15	1.3225
18		93	36.85	1357.9225
19		42	-14.15	200.2225
20		54	-2.15	4.6225
21		62	5.85	34.2225
22		38	-18.15	329.4225
23		71	14.85	220.5225
24				
25	Mean	56.15		
26	Variance	320.4275		
27	SD	17.9004888		
28				
29	Excel SD (pop)	17.9004888		
30				

Figure C9.2(a) SPREADSHEET WITH VALUES DISPLAYED

	A	B	C
1			
2			
3		X (mm)	d	d^2
4		44	=B4-B25	=C4^2
5		37	=B5-B25	=C5^2
6		86	=B6-B25	=C6^2
7		74	=B7-B25	=C7^2
8		54	=B8-B25	=C8^2
9		24	=B9-B25	=C9^2
10		37	=B10-B25	=C10^2
11		69	=B11-B25	=C11^2
12		60	=B12-B25	=C12^2
13		47	=B13-B25	=C13^2
14		51	=B14-B25	=C14^2
15		82	=B15-B25	=C15^2
16		43	=B16-B25	=C16^2
17		55	=B17-B25	=C17^2
18		93	=B18-B25	=C18^2
19		42	=B19-B25	=C19^2
20		54	=B20-B25	=C20^2
21		62	=B21-B25	=C21^2
22		38	=B22-B25	=C22^2
23		71	=B23-B25	=C23^2
24				
25	Mean	=AVERAGE(B4:B23)	
26	Variance	=AVERAGE(D4:D23)	
27	SD	=SQRT(B26)	
28			
29	Excel SD (pop)	=STDEVP(B4:B23)	

Figure C9.2(b) SPREADSHEET WITH FORMULAS DISPLAYED

Here are the steps required to create this spreadsheet:

- type the data into cells B4:B23;
- into cell B25, type the formula for the mean, **=average (B4:B23)**;
- into cell C4, enter the first 'd' value, with the formula **=B4–B25**. Note the use of dollar signs here to ensure that the value in B25 remains fixed when the formula is filled down. Reselect cell C4 and fill down as far as cell C23;
- into cell D4, enter the first 'd[2]' value, with the formula **=C4^2**. Select cell D4 and fill down as far as cell D23;
- into cell B26, enter the formula for the variance (which is the mean of the d^2 values);
- into cell B27, enter the formula for the standard deviation (which is the square root of the variance);
- into cell B29, enter the Excel function that calculates population standard deviation, **=stdevp(B4:B23)** (as you can see, this gives the same result as that displayed in cell B27).

There are several ways in which this approach can be used with learners, depending on their mathematical experience and their confidence with using spreadsheet commands. Here are three possibilities:

- ask them to follow through the stages outlined above;
- create a template spreadsheet with all the formulas in place (learners are asked to type in the data, watch the results and try to work out what is happening);
- carry out a teacher-led demonstration using an electronic whiteboard.

Whichever approach is used, it would be instructive to let learners alter particular data values and try to predict the effect on other displayed values. For example, could they alter the data so that the mean is reduced to 40 and the standard deviation increased to, say, 25?

9.3.3 Entering the Data

To produce the final row, enter the formula **=B2+B3** into cell B4 and fill right as far as cell M4.

9.3.4 Graphing the Data

There are several choices here, of which two are shown in Figures C9.3(a) and C9.3(b).

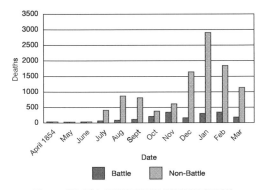

Figure C9.3(a) **'CLUSTERED' COLUMN GRAPH**

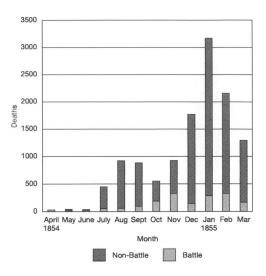

Figure C9.3(b) **'STACKED' COLUMN GRAPH**

In the first (a 'clustered' column graph), the battle and non-battle deaths are shown side by side; in the second (a 'stacked' column graph), they are stacked vertically.

In the first column graph, the battle deaths and non-battle deaths can be read off for each month but not the totals, whereas the reverse is true for the second graph, where the height of each combined column corresponds to total deaths. As a quick check that Excel has handled the addition correctly on the right-hand graph, read off the aggregate total for one or two of the columns and confirm that they give the same answer as the final row of Table 9.2. For example, the January 1855 figure should be 3 168, which looks roughly correct.

9.3.5 Other Formats

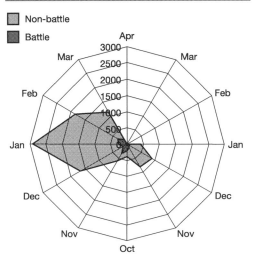

Figure C9.4 **RADAR DIAGRAM**

The radar diagram as drawn in Excel is shown in Figure C9.4. It has produced something a bit like Nightingale's first coxcomb, where values are drawn proportional to the radius rather than area. Note that for the chart below, the order of the rows of data has had to be changed, because the area representing the second row of data is superimposed on that of the first row. In other words, you need the smaller values superimposed on the larger. Is the coxcomb the same – that is, is the Battle area superimposed on the non-Battle, or are they 'stacked' like stacked columns in the bar chart that you drew in Task 9.3.4?

9.4.1 Understanding the data

(a) There are a number of interesting points to observe here. First, the blanks occur either because there was no post that day (for example, every Sunday) or the mum in question forgot to make a record that day. Second, there is one interesting anomaly, namely the (only) afternoon delivery that took place on the second Wednesday. This figure is clearly an outlier and should probably be excluded from any further investigation. (Note: the comments to Task 6.4.3 included a discussion of outliers, including how they were defined by John Tukey.)

(b) Two possible investigations would be to check whether Saturday deliveries are earlier than weekday deliveries and also if they are less (or more) widely spread.

9.4.2 Exploring the Data in Excel

It is quite easy to set up a number of cells to display appropriate summary values that will help to answer these questions. As can be seen in the screen shots below, a useful set of summaries include the mean, along with the five key summaries outlined in Chapter 4 (the minimum value, lower quartile, median, upper quartile and maximum value). Once these measures of location are made available, two measures of spread can easily be calculated – the range and the interquartile range.

A complication when calculating with data that are formatted to times (these data are currently formatted as time in hours:minutes) is that further values calculated from them may not automatically be displayed with the correct formatting. For example, when you display the quartile values, you will find that they are automatically reformatted to fractions of a day. To illustrate the point, using this formatting, 6:00 (6 a.m.) would be displayed as 0.25, because it is one quarter of the way through the day. Inappropriate formatting can be corrected by selecting the cell in question and completing the following steps:

- click the *Format* menu and choose *Cells...*;
- choose the *Number* tab at the top of the dialog box;
- under the *Category* headings on the left, select *Time*;
- select the first example of *Type* offered, 13:30, and click *OK*.

(Alternatively, the same effect can be achieved very quickly using the *Format Painter*, which you may wish to explore for yourself.) The completed spreadsheet is shown in Figure (9.5(a)), together with the relevant commands required for creating the summary values (shown in Figure (9.5(b)).

◇	A	B	C	D	E	F	G
1	July and August						
2	Sunday	Monday	Tuesday	Wednesday	Thursday	Friday	Saturday
3		9:37	9:19	9:59			8:51
4		9:13				9:52	8:48
5		10:28	9:06	9:18	8:18	10:01	8:23
6		9:47	9:09	9:50			8:38
7			9:28	9:37			
8		9:41	10:06	9:44	9:46	9:49	8:21
9		9:35	8:47	10:07	10:21		8:35
10				8:52	9:54	10:50	
11							
12		Weekday	Saturday				
13	Mean	9:39	8:36				
14	Min	8:18	8:21				
15	Q1	9:18	8:26				
16	Median	9:44	8:36				
17	Q3	9:56	8:45				
18	Max	10:50	8:51				
19	Range	2:32	0:30				
20	IQR	0:38	0:19				
21							

Figure C9.5 (a) **SPREADSHEET WITH VALUES DISPLAYED**

		Weekday	Saturday
12		Weekday	Saturday
13	Mean	=AVERAGE(B3:F10)	=AVERAGE(G3:G10)
14	Min	=MIN(B3:F10)	=MIN(G3:G10)
15	Q1	=QUARTILE(B3:F10,1)	=QUARTILE(G3:G10,1)
16	Median	=MEDIAN(B3:F10)	=MEDIAN(G3:G10)
17	Q3	=QUARTILE(B3:F10,3)	=QUARTILE(G3:G10,3)
18	Max	=MAX(B3:F10)	=MAX(G3:G10)
19	Range	=B18-B14	=C18-C14
20	IQR	=B17-B15	=C17-C15

Figure C9.5(b) **SPREADSHEET WITH FORMULAS DISPLAYED**

9.4.3 Interpreting the Results

On the basis of these data, the weekday delivery times (mean = 9:39 a.m.) are later than the Saturday delivery times (mean = 8:38 a.m.) and also much more variable (the two IQRs were 38 minutes and 19 minutes, respectively).

9.4.4 Entering and Summarising the Data

(a) The underlying question here is whether it is the scores with the higher location (in this case, English) or the higher spread (Mathematics) that have the greater effect on the average score.

(b) and (c) Your spreadsheet should look something like those in Figures C9.6(a) and C9.6(b). As before, two versions are provided, so that you can see how they were created.

	A	B	C	D
1	Conflating marks			
2	Student	Maths	English	Mean
3	A	21	85	53
4	B	29	83	56
5	C	35	82	58.5
6	D	42	81	61.5
7	E	55	80	67.5
8	F	61	79	70
9	G	70	78	74
10	H	82	77	79.5
11	I	88	76	82
12	J	91	75	83
13	Mean	57.4	79.6	
14	Range	70	10	

Figure C9.6(a) **SPREADSHEET WITH VALUES DISPLAYED**

Workbook3

	A	B	C	D
1	Conflating marks			
2	Student	Maths	English	Mean
3	A	21	85	=(B3+C3)/2
4	B	29	83	=(B4+C4)/2
5	C	35	82	=(B5+C5)/2
6	D	42	81	=(B6+C6)/2
7	E	55	80	=(B7+C7)/2
8	F	61	79	=(B8+C8)/2
9	G	70	78	=(B9+C9)/2
10	H	82	77	=(B10+C10)/2
11	I	88	76	=(B11+C11)/2
12	J	91	75	=(B12+C12)/2
13	Mean	=AVERAGE(B3:B12)	=AVERAGE(C3:C12)	
14	Range	=MAX(B3:B12)-MIN(B3:B12)	=MAX(C3:C12)-MIN(C3:C12)	

Figure C9.6(b) **SPREADSHEET WITH FORMULAS DISPLAYED**

(d) Look at the order of the values in Column D. As you can see, reading down this column, the values are in strictly ascending order, which is the same as the order for the Mathematics scores. So, the influence of the English scores on the averaged scores is minimal. It affects their absolute values, of course, but their narrowness of spread ensures that they barely affect the class order when combined with the widely spread Mathematics scores. You can conclude from this that it is the *spread* of the values, not their *location* that matters when combining scores.

9.5.1 Scaffolding and Fading

When teaching ICT skills, teachers may start off by providing fairly detailed and prescriptive instructions but, over time, will want to 'back off' and encourage learners to take greater initiative for themselves. For example, when learners first use a software application, they may require very explicit *scaffolding* in the form of detailed keying-in instructions (for example, 'Click this cell, enter that command, press this button, and so on.'). However, over time, the teacher will want them to develop a deeper understanding, so that they can respond to more generic instructions (for example, 'Sort these values into ascending order, and so on.'). This is where the *fading* stage applies. Helping learners to make this transition from specific to generic instructions is a subtle process that requires a learning style in which learner attention is regularly directed from the particular to the general.

9.5.3 Laying Bare a Calculation

(a) Most statistical calculations can be explored in this way. For example, this was the approach used in Section 9.2, subsection 'Standard misconceptions', where the median was calculated in a 'laying bare' manner.

(b) The median example also used the built-in **=median()** function as a check. There are several benefits of doing this, of which here are three:

● it confirms that the 'laying bare' approach resulted in the correct answer;

● it reinforces the point of the lesson which was that the learners are finding the *median*, rather than some other summary value;

● the 'laying bare' approach is a useful pedagogic device for improving understanding about what a median is, but it is certainly not the quickest way of finding the median. At other times, learners will want to find the median quickly and they need to know how to use the **=median()** command directly.

Finally, a word of caution when planning a 'laying bare a calculation' style of lesson and then comparing the result with the single function. Do check in advance that the answers really do match up. For example, in Excel, you are offered two possible formulas for standard deviation, **stdevp()** and **stdev()**. As will be explained shortly in this section, the first of these, the so-called 'population standard deviation' calculates the standard deviation of the data batch in question and so mirrors the calculation demonstrated in the text. The second formula is used when the data represent a sample from a wider population and you wish to use this sample to estimate the *population* standard deviation. Another example of this possible mismatch could be in the calculation of quartiles, for which there is no single agreed method (see Tasks 10.2.7 and 10.2.8).

9.5.4 Sample Standard Deviation and Population Standard Deviation

(a) As you can see from the TI-84 Plus calculator screenshot, the formula for Sx gives the bigger answer. This is because it has $n-1$ rather than n in the denominator.

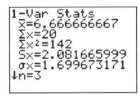

```
1-Var Stats
x̄=6.666666667
Σx=20
Σx²=142
Sx=2.081665999
σx=1.699673171
↓n=3
```

(b) You would choose the Sx formula if the data set under consideration is a random sample taken from some wider population, and your intent is to make an estimate of the standard deviation of the wider population.

(c) This is tricky stuff and there is much scope for confusion amongst learners. One obvious problem of terminology is the use of the terms 'sample' and 'population' to describe σx and Sx. For example, a learner might be forgiven for thinking that, since estimation is all about coming to a conclusion about the wider population, then Sx should be referred to as the 'population' standard deviation. To clarify the terminology, learners really need to focus on what the words 'sample' and 'population' mean and how they are being used here. They should be aware that:

- when you simply want to find the standard deviation of a set of data and have no agenda about making estimates of a wider population, you are treating that data set as a population – hence, σx is the 'population' standard deviation;
- the key aim of taking a sample is to make estimates of the underlying population, so the 'sample' standard deviation is the adjusted measure, Sx.

10.2.1 Making a Fresh Start

Two data sets of unequal size can be compared – for example, by comparing their medians or means. For paired data, the two data lists must always be the same length.

10.2.3 Notation in the List Editor

To take the example of the second screen shot in Task 10.2.2, L2(15) refers to the fifteenth value of list L2. This is an interesting choice of notation from three points of view.

- There is a parallel with spreadsheet notation where a cell reference might be given as B15 (that is, the fifteenth row of column B).
- There are also close connections with subscript notation set out in Section 10.1, where x^{15} referred to the fifteenth value of x. Note that, because of the display restrictions on a calculator screen, the number does not appear as a subscript, being instead placed inside brackets.
- The use of brackets rather than subscripts brings other complications. Note that the notation L2(15) does *not*

match function notation in mathematics, where f(15) refers to the value of f(x) when the value $x = 15$ is substituted into it. In other words, with function notation, 15 is the value of x, not its position in a sequence. This is a subtle but important and potentially confusing distinction.

10.2.4 Summarising the Data in Lists

The six summaries (in cm) are:

L1 (female): mean = 151.8, minimum = 141, Q1 = 147, median = 152.5, Q3 = 156, maximum = 162.

L2 (male): mean = 151.5, minimum = 137, Q1 = 142, median = 151, Q3 = 156, maximum = 173.

10.2.5 Interpreting the Summaries

The girls' and boys' summaries are shown below.

L1 (girls, cm)   L2 (boys, cm)

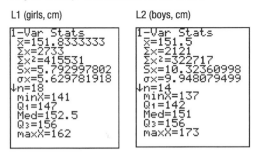

In terms of *location*, the girls are slightly taller than the boys (the means differ by only 0.3 cm and the medians differ by 1.5 cm). However, as you can see in Table C10.1, the boys' heights are much more widely *spread* than those of the girls. It is likely that, due to their earlier onset of puberty, the majority of these girls have already had their adolescent growth spurt, whereas some of the boys have and some have not. This would explain why the girls are slightly taller and also why the boys' heights are more widely spread. Note that there is a choice of two standard deviations, Sx and σx. Their meanings were explained in Section 9.5.

TABLE C10.1 Spreads

	Girls	Boys
Range	162 cm – 141 cm = 21 cm	173 cm – 137 cm = 36 cm
IQR	156 cm – 147 cm = 9 cm	156 cm – 142 cm = 14 cm
Standard deviation, Sx	5.8 cm	10.3 cm

10.2.8 Investigating Quartiles

(a) Try entering the values 1, 2, 3, 4, 5 into a calculator data list and apply the 1-Vars Statistics command to the list. This gives a value for Q1 of 1.5. Experiment with other data lists of different sizes and you should discover how the calculator finds the lower quartile, which is to consider the bottom half of the values, when placed in ascending order, *excluding the median*, and then finds the median of this subset. Check this with a data set where the batch size is an even number (say, $n = 4$ or 6) and you will find that the same principle of excluding the median from the calculation holds.

Now compare this procedure with how quartiles are calculated on a spreadsheet or statistical package. For example, in Excel, the same list {1,2,3,4,5} produces a value for Q1 of 2, which would suggest that, in Excel, the median is *included* in the calculation of quartiles. However, what happens in Excel when the batch size is an even number? Enter the values {1,2,3,4,5,6} into Excel and it calculates the lower quartile as 2.25. A full explanation of how Excel calculates quartiles is not given in the application, but it is explained on the Microsoft website: support.microsoft.com/?kbid=214072.

(b) Possible learners' questions such as, 'What does this button do?' and 'How does this command work?' would seem to display a healthy curiosity about mathematics and technology and are to be encouraged. There is a wide scope for conducting investigations along these lines. For example:

- Enter three easy numbers into a list and apply the 1-Var Statistics command to the list. Use your skill and judgement to work out what the following summaries mean: Σx, Σx^2, and so on.

10.3.2 Creating a Second Box Plot

These screenshots in Figures C10.1(a)–(d) summarise one person's solution to this question. Her first attempt at plotting the two box plots was unsatisfactory, because the original Window setting was not wide enough to accommodate both box plots – part of the lower box plot disappeared off the screen. In order to accommodate both plots on the same screen, the **Xmin** and **Xmax** values needed to lie outside the more extreme values of the two lists. A revised Window setting was made and both plots were displayed correctly. These box plots confirm visually the earlier conclusions, namely, that, in terms of location, the girls are slightly taller than the boys but the boys' heights are more widely spread.

Figure C10.1(a)
SETTINGS FOR PLOT 2

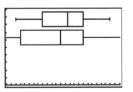

Figure C10.1(b)
A FIRST ATTEMPT AT PLOTTING THE TWO BOX PLOTS BASED ON THE ORIGINAL WINDOW SETTINGS

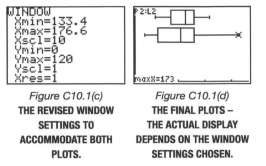

Figure C10.1(c)
THE REVISED WINDOW SETTINGS TO ACCOMMODATE BOTH PLOTS.

Figure C10.1(d)
THE FINAL PLOTS – THE ACTUAL DISPLAY DEPENDS ON THE WINDOW SETTINGS CHOSEN.

10.4.2 Calculating Relative Figures

Your final spreadsheet should look like the version in Figure C10.2. Note that the formula entered into cell D4 (and then filled down) was: **=B4/(C4*1000)**.

Note that the figures in the final column differ slightly from those given in Table 1.14 of *Social Trends*, 34, because of slight differences in the population estimates used. These relative figures give a rather different picture to that suggested by considering only the absolute number of asylum seekers. When measured relative to population size, the UK falls from top of the list to sixth, with rates far lower than Austria, Sweden and Ireland.

	A	B	C	D
1	Number of asylum seekers 2002			
2				
3	COUNTRY	NUMBER	POPULATION (M)	NUMBER/'000
4	Austria	39400	8.2	4.8
5	Sweden	33000	9.0	3.7
6	Ireland	11600	4.0	2.9
7	Belgium	21400	10.4	2.1
8	Luxembourg	1000	0.5	2.0
9	United Kingdom	103100	60.0	1.7
10	Netherlands	18700	16.3	1.1
11	Denmark	5900	5.4	1.1
12	Germany	71100	82.7	0.9
13	Finland	3400	5.2	0.7
14	Greece	5700	11.2	0.5
15	Spain	6200	43.4	0.1
16	Italy	7300	58.6	0.1
17	France	5900	60.3	0.1
18	Portugal	200	10.5	0.0
19	All apps to EU	386100		
20				
21	(Source: Social Trends 34, Table 1.14)			
22				

Figure C10.2 **RELATIVE FIGURES**
Source: *Social Trends*, 34, Table 1.14

10.5.1 Calculator Summaries

(a) These 11 summary statistics (given in the comments to Task 10.2.5) provide a very comprehensive list and it is hard to imagine what might be missing.

(b) The order chosen seems to reflect the historical development of summary statistics rather than educational needs. For example, the five summary values that represent the five key points on a box plot are currently placed at the end of the list and are, initially, 'off the screen'. Since younger learners are more likely to use these, a case could be made for having them be the *first* five items on the list, leaving the more advanced summaries to be located lower down.

(c) To save space on the display, the summaries are listed symbolically rather than in words. It is likely that teachers and learners will therefore tend to talk about 'X bar' rather than the mean, '*n*' rather than 'sample size', 'Q1' rather than the lower quartile, and so on. This may be beneficial in terms of giving learners greater facility with abstract notation. However, at least initially, it may be confusing for learners if they are not familiar with these symbols.

10.5.2 Choosing the Right Tool for the Job

(a) This is a difficult question to answer in the abstract. Choice of tool depends on three main factors:

(i) how easily available it is;
(ii) how confident you are with using it;
(iii) how suitable it is for the task in hand.

In practice, the third of these is often subsidiary to the first two. In fact, all of the popular ICT tools (calculators, spreadsheets and statistical packages) will very effectively tackle most statistical tasks at the level under consideration. You may also be influenced by factors to do with ease of use of the tool – how straightforward is it to enter, change and manipulate data?

(b) Again, practical factors often determine the choice of tool in a classroom – access to the computer lab, availability of the relevant software on the network, availability of a class set of calculators, and so on. Another important factor in determining whether and how a particular item of ICT is used, is the level of learner confidence and competence in using the tools. However, acquiring ICT skills takes time and effort. It is an example of what sociologists call 'deferred gratification' – making a sacrifice in the short term in exchange for an anticipated longer-term benefit. At the initial stages of acquiring mastery of technology, progress is often slow and the benefits are hard to see. Providing opportunities to practise using ICT devices in as wide a variety of contexts as possible will help learners to develop their skill and will improve their own sense of what tools are most suitable for which tasks.

10.5.3 Creating a Box Plot

(a) Note that from the Zoom menu, Command 9, **ZoomStat**, will automatically choose, for Window, settings suitable for the particular statistics plot currently selected. This is a convenient feature, but it can also lead learners into an unthinking approach to graph plotting. Another problem with **ZoomStat** is that it does not always choose sensibly. For example, if you were to enter dice scores into a list, and then select histogram as graph type and press **ZoomStat**, the resulting Window will include a non-integer value for **Xscl**, which is plainly silly. The message here for the teacher is that it may be wise to use the **ZoomStat** command sparingly until learners have a reasonable understanding of what window settings are all about.

(b) The first six of the seven settings in the Window menu control all of the information needed to set the axes of a graph. It may be useful for learners to be aware of this fact and to see structure in the way the information is presented. This is an example of how ICT menus can usefully 'format learner thinking' about a topic.

11.2.4 Interpreting the $y = x$ Line

These are points for which the *y*-value is less than the *x*-value – in other words, where a woman has expressed a preference for a *younger* man. Apart from these four exceptions, clearly in this sample at least, women generally opt for older men.

11.2.5 Interpreting the New Scatter Plot

It should not be surprising that there are still four points below the zero line – these represent the same four women identified in Task 11.2.4 who were looking for a younger man. What may not have been so obvious before is that these four women are all in the 40+ age bracket – in other words, preference for a man younger than themselves seems to be more common in older women.

11.2.6 The Preferences of the 'Men Seeking Women'

The screenshots in Figures C11.1(a)–(h) set out the main steps in this investigation.

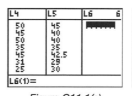

Figure C11.1(a)
ENTER THE DATA INTO LISTS L4 AND L5.

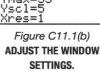

Figure C11.1(b)
ADJUST THE WINDOW SETTINGS.

Figure C11.1(c)
RESET THE STATPLOT MENU.

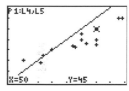

Figure C11.1(d)
PLOT THE DATA AS A SCATTER PLOT AND INCLUDE THE $Y = X$ LINE.

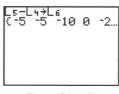

Figure C11.1(e)
CALCULATE THE PREFERRED AGE DIFFERENCES AND STORE THEM IN LIST L6.

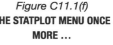

Figure C11.1(f)
THE STATPLOT MENU ONCE MORE ...

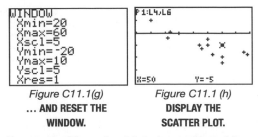

Figure C11.1(g)
... **AND RESET THE WINDOW.**

Figure C11.1 (h)
DISPLAY THE SCATTER PLOT.

The message of the scatter plots is clear – only one of these 15 men seeking women – the 25-year-old – was looking for a woman older than himself. There also seems to be a clear downward gradient in the final scatter plot, suggesting that as men get older they are seeking women who are increasingly younger than them.

Finally, as with the previous investigation, it is interesting to find the mean of the age differences, which this time produces a value of –5. In other words, on average, these men were seeking women who were 5 years younger than them, whereas the women, on average, were seeking men who were 2.5 years older than themselves.

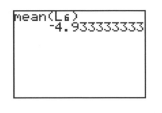

11.2.7 Handling Paired Data on a Calculator

(a) The calculator's Statplot menu offers a small number of standard statistical plots that are very easy to identify and select using the calculator's menu-based selection system. Also, the close link between displaying statistics plots and function graphs from the Y= screen makes it easy to create helpful displays such as the ones below Task 11.2.3.

However, it is clear that these calculator features are only 'convenient' if the user has a reasonable level of mastery of these facilities.

(b) Two other investigations of this type might be:

- Do people with good eyesight also tend to have good hearing?
- Do animals with long gestation periods tend to have long lifespans?

11.3.2 Posing a Question on Interrelating

(a) The initial question chosen for investigation in this section is: 'Are people's estimates for how many years ago television was invented linked to their age?' This requires data from Columns B and D of the spreadsheet.

(b) A person's *age* cannot be a response variable, so this will be taken as the explanatory variable, with their *estimates* as the response variable.

(c) It would not be appropriate to use all of the data because of the way that their ages are bunched – too many of the respondents have the same age and this restriction makes it problematic to explore a bi-variate relationship. Instead, what will be done here is to focus just on the 'adult' data (respondents aged 21 to 69 years).

11.3.3 Checking the Data

If you had chosen to use the data from the 11- and 12-year-olds, you may have felt that the two estimates of 1001 and 2000 years could be treated as extreme outliers and should therefore be rejected. However, all of the data from the 23 adults seem reasonable and worth including.

11.3.5 How Strong is the Relationship?

The R^2 value is extremely close to zero, indicating no significant correlation. However, there is another factor to consider. What have been plotted here are the actual estimates, so the graph does not provide any insight into the *quality* of the estimates in terms of how close they are to the 'true' value. All this graph reveals is that there is no correlation between the values of the estimates and the respondents' ages.

11.4.5 Exploring Relationships

Taking Konold's third bullet point, this can be tackled by encouraging learners to work with data that they feel are meaningful to them and which they might really care to analyse. For example, if they have chosen to collect data about an attribute of class members (for example, journey time to school), when it comes to graphing their data they will be more likely to see patterns if they can identify individual learners from their graph.

11.5.2 Calculator Terms

(a) Here are some of the key terms used in Section 11.2:

Window settings: **Xmax, Xmin, Xscl, Ymax, Ymin, Yscl**

Statplot settings: (Plot) **Type, Xlist, Ylist, Mark**

(b) These terms, as well as the way in which they are organised and presented within their respective menus, provide useful opportunities for learners to consider the following issues.

Window settings: they may find it helpful to know that (these) *six facts* are required to define the two axes fully. This is as true for graphs drawn on paper as on the calculator screen, but the calculator allows you to bring the point to learners' attention.

Statplot settings: these settings represent a neat summary of the characteristics that define a scatter plot. Learners should be made aware that the calculator is cleverly programmed, so that, once the scatter plot option is selected in 'Type', the menu immediately displays a choice of *two* lists. They could investigate this further by selecting each of the six available plot types in turn and observing the number of lists offered for each. What does this say about each of these various representations?

11.5.3 Contexts

There are two chief drawbacks with these data sets. First, they are drawn from US schools and therefore may not be so attractive to learners from other parts of the world. For example, they are based on the weights of 'backpacks' (rather than school-bags), measures are made in imperial rather than metric units, there are data on US cities and the sports data tend to be about basketball. Second, these data sets were (presumably) collected by learners who were actually engaged in these statistical investigations so, for them, there was a strong sense of purpose and identification with the outcome of their findings. Using other people's data is never so much fun. One remedy is to use these data sets for ideas and inspiration, but encourage learners to pose their own related questions. Having collected their own data, many of the Tinkerplots data sets can then be used as a basis of comparison, in a similar way to which the CensusatSchool data are sometimes used.

11.5.4 Maintaining an Overview

(a) In the Tinkerplots guidelines, learners are encouraged to become familiar with the context of the data, make a hypothesis about what the data might show, investigate their hypothesis and finally write up their conclusions. These stages roughly mirror the *A* and *I* stages of the *PCAI* cycle.

(b) Below is an example taken from the Science Standards site. It lists a number of components of thinking to be encouraged when 'using secondary sources to develop and test hypotheses about factors that might affect the pH of rainwater'.

Children should learn:

- to decide which factors may be relevant to an enquiry;
- when it is appropriate to use data from secondary sources;
- how to search for information;
- how to decide which sources of information are appropriate;
- to select appropriate data from secondary sources;
- to identify and describe patterns in data;
- to present information appropriately;
- to look critically at sources of secondary data;
- to look critically at results to decide how strongly they show a trend;
- to interpret results using scientific knowledge and understanding.

These various components represent a more detailed description of the *C*, *A* and *I* stages of an investigation, along with some useful additional remarks about the importance of 'critical thinking'.

12.1.1 Exploring Statistics Applets

A special feature of these and similar statistics applets is that the teaching is not explicit – they simply offer well-defined environments for exploration. The hope is that the user will engage with some important statistical ideas in the process. For example, with the regression applet, they may learn that the regression line is more affected by points that are far away from the underlying line of fit (hence a concern for outliers).

(c) By their nature, these applets offer a very open environment for exploration and would therefore tend to encourage an open learning style, in which the learner was free to 'play' and see what results. Some teachers may prefer to use the applets in association with prepared worksheets, in order to give the lesson greater structure. Another possibility is for the teacher to use these applets in demonstration mode to encourage questions and class discussion.

12.1.2 The Monty Hall Dilemma

(a) In one simulation of 40 trials, where the 'switch' strategy was used each time, 30 were successful. In a second simulation of 40 trials, where the 'stick' strategy was used each time, 16 were successful. Although these could just be fluke results, it is more likely that the 'switch' strategy is fundamentally more successful than 'sticking'.

(b) The simulation greatly speeds up the playing of the game. This means that, in a relatively short time, a sufficiently large sample of results is generated so as to establish a clear settling-down of the underlying probabilities. The downside is that simulations take the learners a further remove from the basic problem and the resulting 'clicking frenzy' with the mouse may cause them to lose sight of what the problem is about (as well as failing to realise this is a simulation and not the actual event: simulations are mathematical models). A sensible compromise is to encourage learners to start off playing the game in some realistic form before moving over to a simulation when they seem ready.

12.2.1 Getting to Grips with the rand and int Commands

(c) The commands =int(rand()*2) and =int(rand()+0.5) will both generate random integers in the range 0 to 1 and either of these commands is suitable for simulating the tossing of a fair coin (where the outcome 0 can represent 'heads' and 1 can represent 'tails').

(d) The six outcomes of a fair die can be simulated by the command: =int(rand()*6+1).

12.3.1 Fallacious Claims Revisited

Clear all lists using the **ClrAllLists** command from the MEM menu.

Use the **randInt** command to generate 60 dice scores and store them in list L1.

A convenient way of counting the frequencies of each outcome (0, 1, 2, ...) is to plot the data using the histogram option. Press TRACE and use the ▷ cursor key to select each column in turn and to see the frequency of each outcome displayed at the bottom of the screen.

In this particular example, the frequency of the outcome '6' was 11 – slightly more than one sixth of the total number of dice rolls. If the simulation is repeated often, learners should be able to come to the same conclusion, as suggested in the comments to Task 12.2.1, namely that 'the results vary but seem to centre around 10, which is one sixth of the outcomes'.

12.3.3 A Two-dice Surprise

This statement can be investigated as follows:

- generate two sets of sixty dice scores and store them into lists L1 and L2, respectively;

- add the corresponding pairs of dice scores in these two lists and store the 60 sums in list L3;

- plot the values in L3 using the histogram plot type and use TRACE and the ▷ cursor key to see the frequencies of each of the eleven outcomes from 2 to 12;

- repeat the investigation several times to see the degree of variation of these outcomes;

- increase the sizes of the data sets to, say, three hundred and repeat several times; this time the degree of variation is much less in evidence.

These steps are summarised in Figures C12.1(a)–(f).

Figure C12.1(a)
GENERATE THE TWO SETS OF DICE SCORES.

Figure C12.1(b)
STORE THE SUMS IN L3.

Figure C12.1(c)
SET STATPLOT TO PLOT A HISTOGRAM OF THE SUMS.

Figure C12.1(d)
SET THE WINDOW.

Figure C12.1(e)
SEE THE GRAPH'S CENTRAL PEAK.

Figure C12.1(f)
TRY LARGER DATA SET SIZES.

12.4.4 Finding Areas

(a) The answers are: 0.1359, 0.8186, 0.5.

Note the use of the value 9EE99 to define the upper limit of the third example. In fact, this probability distribution can, theoretically, take x-values between negative infinity and infinity, but the value 9EE99 should be large enough for practical purposes to represent infinity.

(b) In order to accommodate, on the graphing screen, the probability distribution of the robin egg weights, the Window settings must be altered. Suitable values would be: **Xmin** = 1.9, **Xmax** = 3.5, **Xstep** = 0.1, **Ymin** = ⁻0.5, **Ymax** = 2, **Yscl** = 0.2.

These steps are summarised by the screens here.

(a)

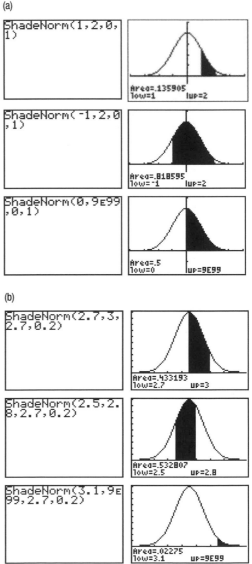

(b)

12.4.5 Probability Simulation APP

(b) As was mentioned in the text, the vertical axis automatically re-scales as the number of trials increases (although, as there is no scale marked on the axis, this is not immediately obvious). The relative heights of the bars may vary widely at first but, as the number of trials increases, the overall pattern should settle down to a fairly uniformly-shaped distribution, where the relative proportions of each outcome are roughly equal.

(c) One possibility is to attach the calculator to a view-screen or other presentational device and conduct this lesson in 'demonstration mode' from the front. Learners can be asked to predict in advance what they would expect to happen. Then the simulation is run and they can see if their guesses were correct. This experience can make for a useful follow-up discussion.

12.4.6 Two-dice APP

The main feature of the investigation as described in Task 12.3.3, was that most of the experimental design was left to the user, whereas this ProbSim APP was ready to go. It is a bit like the difference between preparing a meal from scratch using raw ingredients and heating up an oven-ready meal. The former requires a good deal of technical skill and confidence, but brings with it considerable advantages in terms of retaining an overview of the problem, promoting problem-solving skill, and encouraging mastery of the technology (and a sense of satisfaction when it works). Having said all that, there are times in teaching when all you want (or have time for) is a 'quick bite'!

12.5.3 Many Misconceptions

(a) The following potential or actual misconceptions were mentioned:

- 'a six' is hard to get' (though note, however, that what may at first appear to be a learner misunderstanding may simply be a failure of communication between learner and teacher);
- 'the gambler's fallacy';
- 'the hospital births paradox';
- 'the two-dice surprise';
- at a more advanced level, confusion over the meaning of the term 'probability density function'.

(b) Since many examples have already been provided in this chapter, no further examples are included here. The value of ICT in challenging and remedying misconceptions rests on the machine's processing power, allowing learners to generate large data sets very quickly. However, it should be stressed that simulations appear to work best *after learners have previously committed themselves to making some judgement about what they expect to happen*, rather than them simply pressing buttons or clicking a mouse.

13.1.2 Mix-and-match Meanings

(a) The fifth dictionary definition of the noun is closest to the statistical meaning of 'model'. Here it is again: 'a simplified version of something complex used, for example, to analyze and solve problems or make predictions'.

(b) There are common features with these definitions and the points that emerged from Task 13.1.1. Models are:

(i) 'excellent' or even 'perfect';
(ii) 'scaled-down' versions of reality;
(iii) 'simplified' versions of reality.

While statistical models neither look like fashion models nor miniature aircraft, these aspects are useful starting points for explaining the use of the term in statistics.

13.2.2 Fleshing Out the Diagram

The posing of the problem (*P* stage) starts in the real world, while the analysis (*A* stage) is contained within the mathematical world. The 'modelling' of the problem into a mathematical form (*M* stage) and the interpretation of the mathematical 'solution' into the terms of the real problem (*I* stage) both involve movements between the two worlds, as shown on the diagram here.

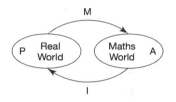

13.2.3 First-class Stamps

(a) A feature of real-world problems that distinguishes them from textbook questions is that sometimes you are not provided with all the information you need to answer the question (and, indeed, you may be awash with irrelevant information that needs to be screened out). A great strength of asking learners to engage in real problem solving is that they get the opportunity to improve at being able to find or isolate the relevant information and disregard the rest. A relevant fact that has not been mentioned here, for example, is the cost of a first-class stamp, which, at the time of writing, is 30p.

Your solution might have looked something like this:

500/30=16.66666667.

Number of stamps = 16.

Change from £5 = 500 − 16 × 30 = 20p.

(b) As with many 'simple' everyday calculations, there is a lot going on here that an experienced problem solver may do quickly, but which is worth making explicit to the learner.

The P stage

The question has already been posed.

The M stage

- knowing the cost of a first class stamp (30p);
- recognising that the £5 needs to be expressed in the same units as the cost of the stamp, hence writing it as 500p;
- knowing that the question is most efficiently done using division, and knowing which way round the calculation should be done (that is, 500/30, rather than 30/500).

The A *stage*

Using a calculator to find the result of 500/30.

The I *stage*

- recognising that the answer refers to 'number of stamps';
- being able to distinguish the integer part of the answer (which gives the number of stamps) from the decimal part of the answer;
- knowing how to use calculator answer to work out the amount of change, in pence.

13.2.5 Model or Checklist

(a) There are two important differences between this model and the previous examples. First, it is entirely text-based, with no helpful graphics. Second, there is no sense of movement or progression here, as these ideas can be used in any order.

(b) It does not seem that this is really a model – more a checklist of useful things to try.

13.3.1 Bicycles, Biscuits and Binomial

A *binomial* expression means, literally, 'two names'. In mathematics, it refers to a situation where there are two terms in a mathematical expression – for example, the terms p and q in the expression $(p + q)^2$ or the terms a and b in the expression $(a + b)^4$.

In statistics, the *binomial* distribution relates to a trial where there are exactly two possible outcomes (for example, heads/tails, girl/boy, success/failure). To take the success/failure example, it is usual to let p stand for the probability of success and q for the probability of failure of a particular trial. (Since there are only two possible outcomes, it follows that, for any binomial model, $p + q = 1$.)

In advanced mathematics, learners are often amazed and delighted to discover that when they expand out the terms of binomial expressions such as $(p + q)^4$, not only does it identify all of the possible outcomes, but also enables them to find their corresponding probabilities.

13.3.2 Regression Models

Sometimes (when the scatter of points is wide), there is no obvious regression model you could choose to fit the data well, in which case any chosen regression model is of limited use in making accurate predictions. The decision to choose a regression model is done for reasons of convenience, to ease the job of making predictions by creating a neat formula. But, remember that the regression is essentially a line (or curve) that represents an *averaged* description of the relationship, one with all the variation removed, and is therefore a simplified model of the relationship.

Note: simple linear regression models such as this should not be seen as deterministic. but can be expressed in a form that indicates their variability, namely as: $y = ax + b + \varepsilon$, where ε, the variability component, usually follows a normal distribution.

13.3.3 Modelling Eggs

The MATH PRB menu of the graphics calculator contains the **randNorm** command, which generates random values from a normal distribution of known mean and standard deviation. The command **randNorm(2.7,0.2,100)->L1** generates 100 values from N(2.7g, 0.2g) and stores them into list L1. Once stored, the values can then be summarised or displayed as a histogram, as shown in Figures C13.1(a)–(c)).

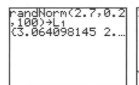
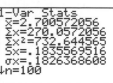

Figure C13.1(a)
GENERATING SIMULATED DATA USING THE RANDNORM COMMAND.

Figure C13.1(b)
USING THE 1-VAR STATS COMMAND (FROM THE STAT CALC MENU) TO SUMMARISE THE DATA.

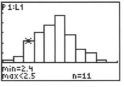

Figure C13.1(c)
DISPLAYING THE DATA AS A HISTOGRAM.

14.1.2 The Benefits of Statistical Investigations

There are many possibilities, of which four are listed below:

- They help learners to see the relevance of statistical ideas beyond the mathematics classroom and indeed beyond school life.
- They enable learners to practise using their developing statistical knowledge skilfully and to good effect, which helps turn it from useful to usable.
- They help learners to appreciate that statistical thinking is wider than the application of a set of narrow tools to arbitrary data sets, but, rather, represents a useful way of seeing the world.
- They encourage critical thinking in learners, so that they are not merely passive receivers of knowledge, but are encouraged to ask 'why?' and 'what if?' questions.

14.1.3 Planning Checklist

Here are some possible questions.

P stage: What are you trying to find out? Is the wording of your question clear?

C stage: What data will you need? What will you need to measure? What units of measure will you use? How/where will you get your data?

A stage: What will you do with the data? Is this relevant to the initial question?

I stage: How will you use your results? Do you think this will answer your initial question?

14.1.4 Thinking Up Ideas for Investigations

(a) *Investigations from other school subjects*

Biology: Do women or men live longer? Does exposure to the elements stunt the growth of algae? What makes a person good at throwing?

Music: At what age do children's musical tastes change most? Does a child's singing range change over time?

Science: How much oxygen is there in copper oxide?

PE: How important is training in improving your running speed?

CDT: Are cars, furniture, kitchen units, etc. designed for the average person?

Also, there is a supplement of examples linked to the UK Key Stage 3 National Strategy website, which suggests a number of possible projects, many of which connect with questions likely to arise in other school subjects.

(b) *General investigations*

Are children whose parents smoke more likely to smoke themselves?

Are large conkers tougher than small ones?

Do people with fast reactions tend to be faster readers?

Does ICT help or hinder learning?

Do boys have more pocket money than girls?

There is also a large number of interesting and mathematically beneficial investigations that can be undertaken under the heading of learners developing skill at estimating and exploring whether they improve with practice. For example estimation of: the number of peas in a jar, dots on a page, size of an angle, pitch of a note, length of a line, height of a person, mass of an object, an interval of time (such as one minute), and so on.

14.2.1 A Checklist on Conducting a Questionnaire

Here are six ideas.

- Can your survey be incorporated into another group's survey?
- Will it provide useful, usable or interesting data?
- Are the questions clearly and sensibly worded and logically ordered?
- Can the responses be recorded quickly and accurately?
- Have you checked that it works by means of a small pilot survey?
- Has your teacher given you the OK?

14.2.2 A Duff Questionnaire

Here is an extract from a 'questionable questionnaire' from Graham (2004, pp. 144-6).

A survey on health

1   How healthy are you?

2   Are the health practices in your household conducted on matriarchal or patriarchal lines?

3   How often do your parents visit the doctor?

4   Do you oppose or support cutting health spending, even if cuts threaten the health of children and pensioners?

The author then identifies a number of general principles concerning questionnaire design, of which four are given here. For example, do not ask questions that are:

Q1 *unanswerable*, without a clear indication of a scale of measure;

Q2 *incomprehensible* to most people;

Q3 *double-barrelled* (in this case, the question asks about two people whose behaviours may be different);

Q4 *biased*.

14.3.1 Matching Graphs to Data Types

TABLE C14.1 Graphs and Data Types

	Single		Paired	
Graphs	*Discrete*	*Continuous*	*Discrete*	*Continuous*
Bar chart	√		(b)	
Box plot	√			
Histogram		√		
Line of fit			√	√
Pie chart	√ (a)			
Scatter plot			√	√
Stem plot	√			

(a) Normally used only with categorical data (that is, not with discrete numerical data).

(b) This might be possible in certain circumstances (it can be done using Excel).

14.3.2 Matching Graphs to Purposes

The completed table below shows the correspondence between graphs and purposes. Complications occur in the 'comparing' column because visual comparisons require graphs that compare two data sets.

Purposes

Graphs	Describing	Comparing	Interrelating
Bar chart	√	√ Compound bar chart	
Box plot	√	√ Two box plots plotted on the same scale	
Histogram	√	? It is difficult to draw two histograms on the same axes	
Line of fit			√
Pie chart	√	√ Two pie charts	
Scatter plot			√
Stem plot	√	√ A back-to-back stem plot	

14.3.3 Matching Graphs to Purposes

Representation	Possible teacher questions
Bar chart or pie chart	What is the largest/smallest bar (or sector)?
	How do the bars (or sectors) compare?
	Taking all the sectors together, what does the complete pie represent?
	What is measured on the vertical scale of the bar chart?
Box plot	What is the largest/smallest value?
	How widely spread are the values?
	Are the values mostly bunched in the middle?
	What does this box plot's shape tell you?
Table	How do the rows compare?
	How do the columns compare?
	What are the row and column totals?
	Would it be helpful to include percentages?
Scatter plot	Is there an underlying pattern to the points?
	Is the pattern a straight line (linear) or something else?
	Is the trend increasing or decreasing?
	How closely do the points lie to the line of fit and what does that tell you?

14.4.1 Peer-review Sessions

Here are a few general guidelines for running successful peer review sessions:

- Promote the view that all utterances are conjectures, subject to subsequent modification. A good start here is to encourage the use of more open phrases such as, '*It seems to me that …*' or '*It appears to be the case that …*';
- Try to develop a healthy tradition of self-criticism in the classroom, where learners are sceptical about their own and each other's conclusions.

14.4.2 Taking an Overview

Useful general questions are:

P/C: Are the data appropriate to the question?

C/A: Is the analysis appropriate to reveal patterns in the data?

A/I: What other possible interpretations might there be?

14.4.3 The Case for Using *PCAI*

Here are four possible benefits for learners.

- They will find their statistical work more interesting and purposeful when they are deploying statistical knowledge and techniques in a meaningful context in order to answer a question, rather that simply to practise developing skill in isolation. The *PCAI* framework requires that the investigation starts and ends with a question, which drives everything else they do within the project.
- The *PCAI* framework helps to offer learners greater independence in their learning, by enabling them to decide what tasks need to be done and in which order.
- *PCAI* provides them with an easy-to-grasp structure for making oral presentations and writing up their work.
- The *PCAI* modelling cycle helps learners to understand the nature of statistical modelling and to see that the application of statistical know-how comprises part of a wider picture.

References

Aczel, A. (2005) 'How to win at love: do your sums', *The Times Review*, 16 April, p. 6.

Baker, J. (2004) 'The charts *Excel* cannot do', *Spreadsheets in Education* 1(3). (www.sie.bond.edu.au/, accessed September 2005.)

Barnett, S. (1989) 'Polls: the loaded question', *Guardian*, 2 January. (Reprinted by the Social Research Association www.the-sra.org.uk/index.htm page 5, accessed September 2005.)

Bartholomew, D. (1995) 'What is statistics?', *Journal of the Royal Statistical Society*, A 158, Part 1: 1–20.

Beare, R. (1993) 'How spreadsheets can aid a variety of mathematical learning activities from primary to tertiary level', in B. Jaworski (ed.), *Technology in Mathematics Teaching: A Bridge Between Teaching and Learning*. Birmingham: University of Birmingham. pp. 117–24, quoted on page 22 of Baker, J. E. & Sugden, S. J. (2003). 'Spreadsheets in Education –The first 25 Years', *Spreadsheets in Education*, 1(1): 18–43. Available online: http://www.sie.bond.edu.au/articles/bakersugden.pdf (accessed October 05).

Biehler, R. (1995) 'Towards requirements for more adequate software tools that support both learning and doing statistics', Occasional paper no 157, Bielefeld, Germany, Institut für Didaktik der Mathematik, Universität Bielefeld. (Revised paper that was presented at ICOTS 4.)

Biehler, R. (2002) 'Students – statistical software – statistical tasks: a study of problems at the interfaces', in B. Phillips (ed.), *Proceedings of the Sixth International Conference on Teaching Statistics: Developing a Statistically Literate Society, Cape Town, South Africa* [CD-ROM]. Voorburg, the Netherlands: International Statistical Institute.

Bryson, B. (2004) *A Short History of Nearly Everything*. Perth, WA: Black Swan Press.

Burkhardt, H. (1981) *The Real World and Mathematics*. Glasgow: Blackie

Carlyle, T. (1855) *Critical and Miscellaneous Essays 1855*. Reprinted 2003. Whitefish, MT: Kessinger.

Cobb, P. (1999) 'Individual and collective mathematical development: the case of statistical data analysis', *Mathematical Thinking and Learning*, 1: 5–44.

Cohen, B. (1984) 'Florence Nightingale', *Scientific American*, March: 98–105.

Department for Education and Employment (DfEE) (2001) *Key Stage 3 National Strategy, Framework for Teaching Mathematics: Years 7, 8 and 9*. London: DfEE. (Also available from: www.standards.dfes.gov.uk/keystage3, accessed September 2005.)

Descartes, R. (1637) *A Discourse on the Method of Rightly Conducting the Reason and Seeking Truth in the Sciences*. Reprinted 2004. Whitefish, MT: Kessinger.

Doll, R. and Hill, B. (1954) 'The mortality of doctors in relation to their smoking habits', *British Medical Journal*, 228:1451–55.

Ehrenberg, A. (1981) 'The problem of numeracy', *American Statistician*, 35(2): 67–71.

Fisher, R. (1925) *Statistical Methods for Research Workers*. 13th edn 1958. Edinburgh: Oliver and Boyd.

Fleming, N. (2005) 'Smiles that destroy the myth of female intuition', *Daily Telegraph*, 12 April, p. 9.

Franklin, B. Letter to Jean-Baptiste Le Roy [Nov. 13, 1789] Sourced from http://www.ushistory.org/franklin/quotable/quote73.htm Franklin's Writings, Bigelow edition, Vol. X Benjamin Franklin, The Writings of Benjamin Franklin, Jared Sparks, editior (Boston: Tappan, Whittemore and Mason, 1840), Vol. X.

Garfield, J. (1994) 'Beyond testing and grading: using assessment to improve student learning', *Journal of Statistics Education* [on line], 1(2). (Available from: www.amstat.org/publications/jse/v2n1/garfield.html, accessed September 2005.)

Graham, A. (1987) *Statistical Investigations in the Secondary School*. Cambridge: Cambridge University Press.

Graham, A. (2004) *Teach Yourself Statistics*. London: Hodder and Stoughton.

Graham, A. and Galpin, B. (2000) *Calculator Maths: Handling Data*. Corby: A+B Books.

Graham, A. and Galpin, B. (2002) *Calculator Statistics*. Corby: A+B Books.

Graham, A. and Galpin, B. (2003) *30 Calculator Programs*. Corby: A+B Books.

Haddon, M. (2002) *The Curious Incident of the Dog in the Night-Time*. London: Random House.

Hanson, W. (2001) 'Sherlock Holmes and the Hawaiian treasure', *American Philatelist Magazine*, 115(7): 636–40.

Holmes, P. (2002) 'Assessment: new ways of pupil evaluation using real data', *Teaching Statistics*, 24(3): 87–9.

Hooper, J. (2004) 'Curse of 53: Italy's unlucky number', *Guardian*, 4 December, p. 18.

Houghton, R. (2004) 'Spreadsheets' (www.ceap.wcu.edu/Houghton/EDELCompEduc/Themes/spreadsheets/spreadsheets.html, accessed September 2005).

Hunt, N. (2005) 'Using Microsoft Office to generate individualized tasks for students', *Teaching Statistics*, 27(2): 45–8.

Johnston-Wilder, P. (2005) 'Thinking statistically: interactive statistics', in S. Johnston-Wilder and D. Pimm (eds), *Teaching Secondary Mathematics with ICT*. Maidenhead: Open University Press. pp. 101–22.

Johnston-Wilder, S. and Pimm, D. (eds) (2005) *Teaching Secondary Mathematics with ICT*. Maidenhead: Open University Press.

Keillor, G. (1985) *Lake Wobegon Days*. London: Faber and Faber.

Konold, C. (2002) 'Teaching concepts rather than conventions', *New England Journal of Mathematics*, 34(2): 69–81. (Also available from: www.umass.edu/srri/serg/papers/KonoldNEJM.pdf, accessed September 2005.)

Konold, C. (2005) *Exploring Data with Tinkerplots*. Emeryville, CA: Key Curriculum Press.

Matthews, R. (1994) 'Improving the odds on justice?', *New Scientist*, 16 April, pp. 12–13.

McPhee, J. (1990) *Basin and Range*. New York: Farrar Straus Giroux.

Moore, D. (1990) 'Uncertainty', in L. Steen (ed.), *On the Shoulders of Giants: New Approaches to Numeracy*, Washington, DC, National Academy Press, pp. 95–137.

Moore, D. (1997) 'New pedagogy and new content: the case of statistics', *International Statistical Review*, 65(2): 123–65.

Moore, D. and Cobb, G. (2000) 'Statistics and mathematics: tension and cooperation' (www.stat.purdue.edu/~dsmoore/articles/Statmath.pdf, accessed September 2005)

Munro, H. (1993) 'The lumber room', in *The Collected Short Stories of Saki*. First published in 1914. London: Wordsworth Editions. pp. 325–9.

Mvududu, N. (2005) 'Constructivism in the statistics classroom: from theory to practice', *Teaching Statistics*, 27(2): 49–54.

Oldknow, A. and Taylor, R. (2000) *Teaching Mathematics with ICT*. London, Continuum.

Open University Discrete Modelling, Modelling with Sequences, Chapter BI, p. 7, Milton Keynes. Open University.

Opie, I. and Opie, P. (1959) *The Lore and Language of Schoolchildren*. Oxford: Clarendon Press.

Pascal, B. (webref) PENSEES 1660 by Blaise Pascal, translated by W. F. Trotter, translation available at: http://oregonstate.edu/instruct/phl302/texts/pascal/pensees-a.html#SECTION%201

Piaget, J. (1970) *Genetic Epistemology*. New York: Norton.

Playfair, W. (1786). *Commercial and Political Atlas: Representing, by Copper-Plate Charts, the Progress of the Commerce, Revenues, Expenditure, and Debts of England, during the Whole of the Eighteenth Century*. London: Corry.

Ruthven, K. and Hennessy, S. (2002) 'A practitioner model of the use of computer-based tools and resources to support mathematics teaching and learning', *Educational Studies in Mathematics*, 49(1): 47–88.

Schools Council (1981) *Statistics in Your World*. Reading: Foulsham Educational.

Shaughnessy, J.M. and Ciancetta, M. (2002) 'Students' understanding of variability in a probability environment', in B. Phillips (ed.), *Proceedings of the Sixth International Conference on Teaching Statistics: Developing a statistically literate society, Cape Town, South Africa* [CD-ROM]. Voorburg, the Netherlands: International Statistical Institute.

Skovsmose, O. (webref) 'Aporism and the problem of democracy in mathematics education', in P. Gates (ed.) *Mathematics and Society, an International Conference, September 1998, University of Nottingham, Conference Proceedings*. Nottingham: University of Nottingham, Centre for the Study of Mathematics Education. (available from www.nottingham.ac.uk/csme/meas/measproc.html, accessed September 2005.)

Smith, A. (2004) *Making Mathematics Count: an Inquiry into Post-14 Mathematics Education*. (Smith report.) London: DfES. (Also available from www.dfes.gov.uk/mathsinquiry/Maths_Final.pdf, accessed September 2005.)

Social Trends, 34 (2004 edition) Table 2.12 Office for National Statistics, The Stationery Office, March 2005.

Stevens, S. (1946) 'On the theory of scales of measurement', *Science*, 161: 677–80.

Sutherland, S. (1992) *Irrationality: The Enemy Within*. Cambridge: Cambridge University Press.

Tatem, A.J., Guerra, C.A., Atkinson, P.M. and Hay, S.I. (2004) 'Athletics: momentous sprint at the 2156 Olympics?', *Nature*, 431: 525–26.

Tierney, J. (1991) 'Behind Monty Hall's doors: puzzle, debate and answer', *New York Times* (21 July), p. 1.

Treffert, D. and Wallace, G. (2002) 'Islands of genius', *Scientific American*, June: 21.

Tufte, E. (1990) *Envisioning Information*. Cheshire, CT: Graphics Press.

Tufte, E. (2001) *The Visual Display of Quantitative Information*. Cheshire, CT: Graphics Press.

Tukey, J. (1977) *Exploratory Data Analysis*. Reading, MA: Addison-Wesley.

Von Glasersfeld, E. (1984) 'An introduction to radical constructivism', in P. Watzlawick (ed.), *The Invented Reality*. London: Norton. pp. 17–40.

Von Glasersfeld, E. (1996) 'Learning and adaptation in constructivism', in L. Smith (ed.), *Critical Readings on Piaget*. London: Routledge. pp. 22–7.

Wason, P. (1966) 'Reasoning', in B. Foss (ed.), *New Horizons in Psychology*. London: Penguin Books. pp. 135–51.

Weaver, W. (1952) 'Statistics', *Scientific American*, January.

Wild, C. and Pfannkuch, M. (1999) 'Statistical thinking in empirical enquiry', *International Statistical Review*, 67(3): 223–65.

Index

Added to a page number 'f', denotes a figure.
Entries in italic refer to tasks and titles of documents and journals